A VOLATILE PICTURE

GLOBAL
SOUTH
ASIA

Padma Kaimal
K. Sivaramakrishnan
Anand A. Yang

SERIES EDITORS

A VOLATILE PICTURE

War and the Political Work of Photography in Sri Lanka

VINDHYA BUTHPITIYA

UNIVERSITY OF WASHINGTON PRESS
Seattle

A Volatile Picture was supported by a grant from the McLellan Endowment, established through the generosity of Martha McCleary McLellan and Mary McLellan Williams.

Design by Katrina Noble   Composed in Minion Pro

Photographs by the author unless otherwise noted.

UNIVERSITY OF WASHINGTON PRESS
uwapress.uw.edu

LIBRARY OF CONGRESS CATALOGING-IN-PUBLICATION DATA
Names: Buthpitiya, Vindhya author
Title: A volatile picture : war and the political work of photography in Sri Lanka / Vindhya Buthpitiya.
Description: Seattle : University of Washington Press, [2026] | Series: Global South Asia | Includes bibliographical references and index.
Identifiers: LCCN 2025047014 | ISBN 9780295754437 hardcover | ISBN 9780295754444 paperback | ISBN 9780295754451 ebook
Subjects: LCSH: Photography—Political aspects—Sri Lanka | Photography—Social aspects—Sri Lanka | War photography—Sri Lanka | Sri Lanka—History—Civil War, 1983–2009—Photography | Tamil (Indic people)—Sri Lanka—Politics and government | Sri Lanka—Politics and government
Classification: LCC TR184 .B88 2026
LC record available at https://lccn.loc.gov/2025047014

For EU product safety concerns please contact Mare Nostrum Group B.V. at Mauritskade 21D, 1091 GC Amsterdam, The Netherlands, or gpsr@mare-nostrum.co.uk.

∞ This paper meets the requirements of ANSI/NISO Z39.48-1992 (Permanence of Paper).

CONTENTS

PREFACE

"WHY ARE YOU USING THIS OLD-FASHIONED WORD *PUGAIPPADAM*?" Mr. Jesurasa, a sprightly septuagenarian film aficionado and writer, whom I had come to know in my time in Jaffna, asked jokingly upon reading a poster I had prepared. We were at an exhibition of photography from Jaffna, "The Jaffna Lens," that I had organized, featuring the work of various photographers whom I had encountered during the time I lived there.

"First there was *pugaippadam* [smoke picture], then there was *nilatrpadam* [shadow picture], and now there is *olippadam* [light picture]!" He laughed and wrote down the three Tamil words on a scrap of paper. I snapped a photograph of it on my phone so that I would not forget. Truth was that it was only very rarely that the formal Tamil word for photography, *pugaippadakkalai* (smoke picture art), was used by the various people I had interacted with over many years of research. Nearly everyone, me included, used the English-language "photo" and "photography," or the simpler *padam* (picture) and *padangal pidikirada* (catching pictures) or *padangal eduppadu* (picture taking). I remain captivated by these words I heard from Mr. Jesurasa on my penultimate day of fieldwork in Jaffna.

These words and their fluid transformations point to the remarkable way in which the Tamil language has kept pace with the technics of photography over the course of nearly two centuries, transmuting from *pugaippadam* (smoke picture) to *nilatrpadam* (shadow picture) and *olippadam* (light picture). This play of புகை, நிழல், ஒளி (*smoke, shadow, light*) evokes the overarching questions of visibility, concealment, invention, and erasure that permeate the Sri Lankan post/war and the volatility of its photographies, making up the ethnographic and theoretical substance of this book.

ACKNOWLEDGMENTS

THIS BOOK IS A LOVE LETTER TO A PLACE AND PEOPLE WHO HAVE endured more than can ever be adequately written down, but who have persisted despite it all with bravery, hope, and generosity. This past and present determined the shape, possibility, and course of my words. I wish for you with all my heart the swift delivery of justice, and futures as grand and happy as the ones imagined in Jaffna's photography studios.

In truth, *A Volatile Picture* is also the work of those who sustained me over the years with lavish gifts of time, trust, encouragement, affirmations, and care. I owe a world of gratitude to my interlocutors in Jaffna, the Vanni, Colombo, London, and elsewhere, whose enthusiasm and incredible benevolence made this undertaking conceivable. My deepest appreciation is for N. Rajaratnam of Baby Photo and N. Kugan of Kugan Studio for sharing their life's work and memories with me and patiently answering my many questions. Athanas Jesurasa, thank you for graciously sparing hours of your time to talk to me about Mark, film, and politics and, importantly, the gift of "smoke, shadow, light." I am so grateful for the thoughtful advice of the inimitable Christopher Pinney. Chris, thank you for your wisdom and generosity in helping me imagine, interpret, and make sense of the unruliness and possibilities of both photography and this work. Sabes Sugunasabesan, I am enormously grateful for our many conversations over many years about home and what it means to be born in and of Ilankai and carry side by side the weight of its devastation and hope with us every day. A special note of thanks to the Manel Fonseka, whose warmth and support has meant so much. Without your foundational scholarship on Wendt, there would be little to be said on twentieth-century Ceylonese/Lankan photography. This book would not have been possible without the willingness with which all of you passed on your knowledge and learning.

My love and appreciation are spilled out across an atlas of people that make up my dispersed home; those who have shared in sundry adventures and endlessly enriching conversations that have healed and sustained me through many a real and imagined calamity. Thank you for cheering me on at my best and worst, and steadying me through this life and these words, which have become so deeply entangled.

I was bizarrely fortunate to have been raised in a household of defiant women: troublemakers, fortune tellers, firebrands, and interpreters of dreams. I honor the memory of Shivabhagyambal Vedagiri, my late great-grandmother, migrant, enchantress, and healer. My late grandmother, Nita Vedagiri, thank you for sheltering my childhood from great personal and political turmoil with care, nourishment, and a thousand lunchtime stories. My fearless and extraordinary mother, Devika Vedagiri, I am grateful for everything I cannot find words for, but most importantly for our shared irreverence for conformity. Your tenacity paved the way for our ambition and revolt. My unwavering and dazzling sister, Shwetha Srikanthan, thank you for the certainty, for the reassurance, for reading everything I write, and for knowing when exactly to put a ribbon cake order in.

I am deeply grateful for the words, kindness, support, encouragement, mentorship, good advice, and friendship of those who have seen me through life and scholarship: Thomas Harrison, Tariq Jazeel, Naluwembe Binaisa, Mallika Leuzinger, Janahan Sivanathan, Nushelle de Silva, Shamara Wettimuny, Sharika Thiranagama, Mythri Jegathesan, Viviane Saglier, Ben Hildred, Bob Simpson, Nayanika Mookherjee, Lotte Hoek, and importantly the PhotoDemos Collective: Chris, Nalu, Konstantinos Kalantzis, Ileana Selejan, and Sokphea Young. I am so glad to have shared in this journey, so rich with pictures, insight, and exchange, with you. I am a better person and scholar thanks to the community and inspiration you have all extended to me.

Heartfelt thanks to Sasikala Thangavel, Keshini Subasinghe, Anushani Alagarajah, Jegan Ganeshamoorthy, Mr. Fernando, Ramachandran Iyer Bhaskaran Sharma, Benislos Thushan, Sancheyan Nanthakumar, Tilaxan Tharmapalan, Amarathaas, the late Vairamuttu Varadakumar of the Tamil Information Centre in London, the late Joe de Livera, Dominic Sansoni, Anu Weerasuriya, and Menika van der Poorten.

My sincerest appreciation for Caitlin Tyler-Richards and the editors of the Global South Asia Series, Padma Kaimal, Shivi Sivaramakrishnan, and Anand A. Yang, for their enthusiasm and support for this book; the anonymous reviewers whose generous, heartening praise and recommendations enriched my work; Dandi Meng, Joeth Zucco, Teresa Jesionowski, and Mamta Jha for their assistance with the design, editorial, production, and indexing process; Molly Woolbright and the UW Press marketing team, and everyone at the

University of Washington Press whose thought, attention, care, skill, and labor transformed this manuscript into a book.

A portion of chapter 5 was previously published in my article "Absence in Technicolour: Protesting Enforced Disappearances in Northern Sri Lanka," *Journal of the Royal Anthropological Institute* 28, no. S1 (April 2022): 118–34. Some materials featured in this book refer to and rework materials in my chapter "'The Truth Is in the Soil': The Political Work of Photography in Northern Sri Lanka," in *Citizens of Photography: The Camera and the Political Imagination* (Durham, NC: Duke University Press, 2023), republished by permission of the copyright holder, Duke University Press.

Finally, I am grateful to the PhotoDemos project, which received funding from the European Research Council (ERC) under the European Union's Horizon 2020 research and innovation program (Grant Agreement No. 695283).

NOTE ON LANGUAGE, PHOTOGRAPHY, AND PSEUDONYMS

TAMIL AND SINHALESE WORDS AND PHRASES ARE USED IN THIS book, and all translations are my own. Where my interlocutors have responded in English, I have made minor adjustments for clarity but have used quotes verbatim where possible. Direct translations have been included in parentheses. Where these words or phrases require longer explanation, they have been described in the endnotes. I have written all Tamil and Sinhalese words phonetically as they sound in English rather than use a standard system for transliteration.

Names and contextual information of all of those who feature in this book have been changed to protect their identity. This is with the exception of certain individuals and photographers whose photographs, studios, images, and words appear in this study with prior and informed consent or in published form to ensure that their work is properly acknowledged.

ABBREVIATIONS

ARED	Association for Relatives of the Enforced Disappeared, North and Eastern Province
EPDP	Eelam People's Democratic Party
EPRLF	The Eelam People's Revolutionary Liberation Front
EROS	Eelam Revolutionary Organization of Students
HSZ	High Security Zone
ICRC	International Committee of the Red Cross
IDP	internally displaced person
IPKF	Indian Peace Keeping Force
ITAK	Ilankai Tamil Arasu Kachchi
JVP	Janatha Vimukthi Peramuna [National Liberation Front]
LLRC	Lessons Learnt and Reconciliation Commission
LTTE	Liberation Tigers of Tamil Eelam
NFZ	No Fire Zone
NIC	National Identity Card
NPP	National People Power
OMP	Office on Missing Persons
PLOTE	People's Liberation Organization of Tamil Eelam
PTA	Prevention of Terrorism Act
SCSL	Supreme Court of Sri Lanka
SLFP	Sri Lanka Freedom Party
SLRC	Sri Lanka Rupavahini Corporation
TEA	Tamil Eelam Army
TELO	Tamil Eelam Liberation Organization
TIC	Tamil Information Center
TMVP	Tamil Makkal Viduthalai Pulikal [Tamil People's Liberation Tigers]
TULF	Tamil United Liberation Front
UNP	United National Party
UTHR-J	University Teachers for Human Rights (Jaffna)

A VOLATILE PICTURE

INTRODUCTION

WHERE THE WAR STARTED

Baby Photo's second life on Palaly Road, one of the main thoroughfares that fanned out of Jaffna Town to the edges of Sri Lanka's northern peninsula, began a stone's throw away from where the war started. What is now the site of a gleaming silver and blue aluminum-clad bank building was on the night of 23 July 1983 the location of an ambush led by Tamil rebels. Four mines, concealed in a ditch dug out to install telephone cables, detonated beneath the jeep leading the Four Four Bravo Army patrol.

The explosion changed the course of Sri Lanka's history in a matter of hours. The accompanying government soldiers scrambling to assist their wounded were met with an onslaught of machine-gun fire and homemade hand grenades. This attack was claimed to have been planned as reprisal for the death of Charles Lucas Anthony, also known as Seelan, one of the founding members of the Liberation Tigers of Tamil Eelam (LTTE), and the abduction and rape of two Tamil school girls by the Sri Lankan armed forces.[1] Twelve soldiers and an officer, Second Lieutenant A. P. N. C. De S. Vaas Gunawardene, belonging to the first battalion of the Sri Lanka Light Infantry and the Tigers' newly appointed military commander, Sathasivam Selvanayagam (alias Sellakili), were killed that night. Tens of thousands would follow over the next twenty-six years.[2]

In an increasingly militarized north and east, tensions between the Sri Lankan armed forces and burgeoning Tamil armed groups, forming under the banner of self-determination, had been escalating for several years. Following the introduction of the 1956 "Sinhala Only" legislation, state-endorsed violence against the Tamil community had steadily intensified.[3] The events that took place at Tirunelveli Junction are widely pronounced as the beginning of the Sri Lankan civil war. In reaction to this assault, the army went on a retaliatory rampage in Jaffna, shooting fifty-one Tamil civilians dead. Meanwhile, the government's inflammatory decision to hold a mass funeral for the deceased soldiers in the capital, Colombo, some 400 kilometers away, took an extraordinarily violent turn. The transfer of bodies was delayed with no explanation and the plan for the public interment of the soldiers' caskets was eventually abandoned. The restless Sinhalese crowd, allegedly numbering in the thousands, who had been transported to Kanatte in government buses, turned lethal, resulting in one of the most horrifying episodes of ethnic violence in recent memory.

Karuppu Yulai, or Black July as it was subsequently referred to, was described by Stanley Tambiah as an "orgy of violence" (1986, 21). The government's silence and lack of action, including the delay in declaring a curfew, coupled with the alleged involvement of politicians and the police assisting the hostile Sinhalese assailants amounted to the events being described as a riot and a pogrom. Armed with official electoral lists enabling the identification of Tamil households and businesses, perpetrators burned, looted, raped, and killed their way unchecked across the island. In Colombo and elsewhere, this ghastly spell lasted for over a week, resulting in Tamils of Sri Lankan and Indian origin being beaten, murdered, or burned alive.[4] Thousands of Tamil-owned properties were destroyed. Official reports recorded 371 deaths, although estimates range from 400 to 3,000.[5] A further 100,000 Tamils were made homeless, creating approximately 130,000 internally displaced persons, 78,000 of whom were either sheltered in twelve temporary camps in the capital or put on cargo ships to be transported to Jaffna (Pavey 2008). Hundreds of thousands of Tamils fled the country in its aftermath, marking the first of many major waves of conflict-induced dispersals to Europe, North America, and Australia.[6]

During the violence of Karuppu Yulai, at least fifty-three Tamil political prisoners in the Welikade Prison in Colombo who were held under suspicion or convicted of terror charges by the state were also murdered in two massacres. Among them were Selvarajah Yogachandran (alias Kuttimani) and Nadarajah Thangavelu (alias Thangathurai), the founding leaders of the Tamil Eelam Liberation Organization (TELO), one of several Tamil armed groups that had formed in the north and east of Sri Lanka. In 1981, Kuttimani famously declared upon being sentenced to death: "I request that I should be hanged in Tamil Eelam. . . . I request that my eyes be donated to some blind person, so that Kuttimani will be able to see through those eyes the reality of Tamil Eelam" (*Tamil Times* 1982, 3). Kuttimani's attackers were said to have gouged his eyes out with iron bars. The slaughter of Tamil political prisoners reinforced the widely held belief of government collusion in the instigation and unconfined spread of violence. A grainy photograph of unknown provenance composed around a pool of blood spilling out of a man's crushed head shows a row of mangled sarong-clad corpses lined up against a prison wall. The image persists in online circulations accompanying annual calls for justice. It was twenty-one years before an apology was extended by a Sri Lankan president.[7]

Chandragupta Amarasinghe, a Sinhalese photographer who worked for a communist newspaper named *Aththa* (Truth), took nine photographs of the devastation caused by the jubilant rioters. Amarasinghe wandered the streets with his camera to document what appeared to be gleeful brutality and looting. Most recognizable among these images, captured at the Borella bus stand, is of a bespectacled man, one of a group of attackers, who grinned at the camera as he extended his leg out in a kick.[8] Sitting on a step, the aggressor's prey clutched his downturned, bleeding head in a position of surrender and helplessness. His face is hidden by his hands. The victim's naked body smeared in dirt is in plain view, reminiscent of the many trophy images that emerged during the final weeks of the civil war in 2009. Press censorship was in strict operation. The Emergency Regulations of the Gazette No. 245/8 issued on 18 May 1983, two months before the pogrom, banned the publication of "incendiary photographs" that could "ferment communal instability" resulting in Amarasinghe being unable to publish the images in Sri Lanka (Weerasooria 2012). However, not long after the events of Black July, the image of assault described above appeared in diasporic Tamil news publications, including the November 1983 issue of the London-based *Tamil Times*, and LTTE propaganda booklets with no mention of the photographer.

Later, the photographs officially appeared in a 1997 supplement of *Ravaya*, a left-wing Sinhalese newspaper, commemorating the fourteenth anniversary of Black July.[9] Amarasinghe's photographs, among many hundreds generated during three decades of war, continue to circulate in an intractable circuit of visual-material horror, despair, remembrance, and outrage. They took the form of accompaniments to newspaper lamentations, angry bold-lettered posters papered onto the walls of village bus depots, commemorative social media posts hashtagged #tamilgenocide #revolution #weremember, and amateur YouTube documentaries stitching together newsreels of a burning cityscape and tearful survivor accounts. These images are part of a sprawling, transnational corpus of visual remains evidencing state atrocities against Tamil bodies over several decades. They variously endorse, condemn, encourage retribution, and illustrate claims of both witness and forgery.

WENT TO NOTHINGS

Baby Photo's first life was nearly at the epicenter of where the war started. A partial glimpse remains in a black-and-white photograph taken by Nadarajah Rajaratnam, its elderly proprietor. It is one of a hundred or so images left of the six decades he had spent as a studio photographer in Jaffna. At the center of the frame, a mustached man in a striped shirt and sarong bears on his head a tall jumble of plastic and aluminum pots and pans placed precariously on a woven palmyra basket clasped with his right hand. The vendor obscures what appears to be a young boy casually leaning against Baby's old shopfront. The specter of a poster of a smiling girl and part of its painted signboard is faintly visible in the background.

"All the things that you are asking me about, I would have had before 1995," Rajaratnam *mama* reflected.[10] In 1995, Baby Photo's archive, a day-to-day catalog of the studio's business of clients' portraits and *mama*'s snaps of daily life in Jaffna as it unfolded outside the studio during moments of respite, was destroyed in almost its entirety. By that time, Jaffna was a stronghold of the LTTE and the site of intense and regular hostilities between the Sri Lankan forces and the Tamil militancy. The government had settled into pursuing a relentless routine of aerial bombardment, paying no heed to resident civilians. Meanwhile, the LTTE struck at Muslim and Sinhalese "border villages" in the peripheries of the territory they occupied and orchestrated a campaign of terror attacks targeting public spaces and infrastructure, including notable Buddhist temples and mosques. The LTTE also carried out politically motivated assassinations elsewhere on the island and abroad. Among the targets were Ranasinghe Premadasa, the former president of Sri Lanka; Rajiv Gandhi, the prime minister of India; various Sinhalese and Tamil government ministers and members of parliament; senior military and police officials; clergy, activists, and journalists, including Tamil moderates critical of separatism, militarism, and the authoritarian violence of the *Iyakkam* (movement).[11]

Rajaratnam *mama* was the oldest photographer I encountered in my time in Jaffna, having begun his profession as a studio apprentice in 1958 at the age of thirteen (fig. 1). By 1972, he had established his studio, Baby Photo. In 1995, during what was dubbed the "Battle of Jaffna," he lost everything.

On 17 October 1995, the army launched a brutal campaign of shelling on Jaffna in an (ultimately successful) attempt to reclaim the peninsula in what turned into a fifty-day siege. Despite its persistent slogan expressing a will "to

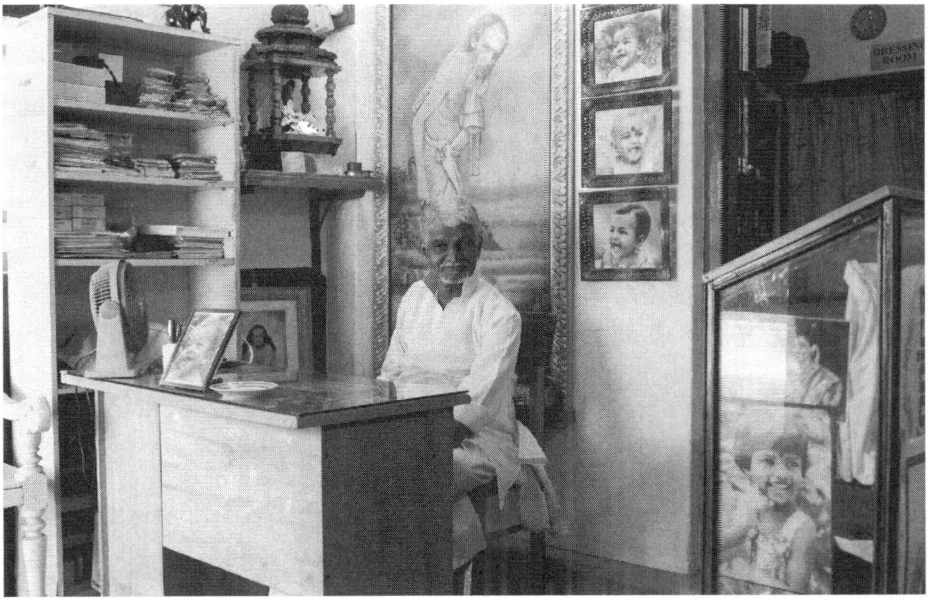

FIGURE 1. Rajaratnam *mama* at Baby Studio (Jaffna, 2018)

liberate the Tamils from the clutches of the LTTE," the Sri Lankan government always insistently and intentionally failed to distinguish between the two.[12] LTTE cadres went from house to house ordering people to leave immediately, and over the next few days, nearly six hundred thousand people were forced to leave the peninsula (UTHR-J 1995). Traveling largely by foot, residents of Jaffna left with only the clothes on their backs and whatever they could carry. This single event, known as the "Jaffna exodus," led to a mass experience of loss and displacement, as people were coerced to leave behind their homes and belongings. Many returned months later to find that there was nothing left except for rubble and the charred remains of what was once there. Rajaratnam *mama* was among those who walked to Mirusuvil near Chavakachcheri, south of the peninsula, where many of those who were uprooted congregated over the next months. Some were sent to government-run camps in Vavuniya, and others were relocated over time to areas like Puttlam in the northwest. Those who could afford it fled to Colombo or left the country behind entirely.

"I could have shown you everything, but they [the military] destroyed the shop, took everything that was inside, threw it out, and burned it all. All the precious things that were collected *went to nothing*."

I imagine the many thousands of photographic portraits carried by Baby's patrons through the agonizing dispersions of war, pasted onto identity documents stamped with the purple ink of government offices, laminated into family albums in Jaffna and Colombo, or framed and garlanded in living room cabinets in Toronto or London. I also imagine the many thousands of photographs and their subjects that were no more.

PATHIVU: WAR AND THE POLITICAL WORK OF PHOTOGRAPHY

This is a book about photography. It is more definingly a book about war. Through this ethnography, I examine how the causes, devastations, and consequences of long-drawn-out ethnonationalist conflict continue to be experienced by the Tamil community, who look to the camera to evidence, articulate, and visualize personal and political possibility.

Photography, like war, is the work of sight. It illuminates the intricate entanglements of visibility, vision, concealment, and crucially, internationalized and localized spectacle transmitted through the visual-material regimes of state, media, and dissidence (see Virilio 1986; Brothers 1997; Phu 2022). The medium simultaneously makes visible and frames encounters to uncover truths and deceptions, as much as to conceal, crop, and distort, heightened by the ideologies, imperatives, and urgencies of political conflict. However, within the bleak and unpredictable cleft of war between the nation and the state, political aspiration and realization, photography also informs everyday imaginings for play, rebellion, artifice, and individual and collective future-making as potently as it evidences the minutiae of violence and the chronologies of terror. It is these diverse and incongruent photographic practices and what their making and moving reveal of Sri Lanka's fraught post/war that inform this undertaking. I use the term *post/war* as an abbreviation to combine *war* and *postwar*. This book also, vitally, constitutes, in the words of Amarathaas, an exiled Tamil photographer, a *pathivu,* or record of a history and tragedy all too often violently erased or silenced.

To write about war is to work with incompleteness, inaccuracy, partial remembering, terror, and the lingering threat and possibility of reprisal. It is a labor of confronting coerced absences and constructing irreparably fragmented accounts with the ashes of burned books, the rubble of unmarked gravestones, and the hearsay and secrets of disrepute and insubordination that endure amid forced forgetting. In solidarity with those whose perseverance and trust are foundational to the existence of this book, I detail uncompromisingly what my interlocutors demanded the world know about what they have seen, what they have experienced, what they have photographed and what they haven't, what they wish to make visible, what they hope for in the shape of justice and accountability, and their visions for personal success and political liberation. I write noting that their lives and worlds remain steeped in the aftershocks of war.

"Conflict photography" has been typically considered through the lens of media and documentary practice. Departing from this convention, I explore a variety of coexisting actors, spaces, types, and pursuits related to everyday photography as social and political practice in post/war Sri Lanka. In this examination of what I have termed the "political work of photography," I define the medium, broadly, as comprising a constellation of images, objects, economies, and representational practices to explore the interweaving of war and image-making (Buthpitiya 2023b, 67). This includes the making, keeping, displaying, losing, concealing, embellishing, altering, sharing, and destroying of photographic images that threaded through the lives of members of the Ilankai Tamil community.[13] It is this multiplicity and the animated everyday visual, material, digital inflections of photography that permit me to bridge the variety of contexts I have encountered during long-term fieldwork undertaken in the Jaffna Peninsula and the Vanni in northern Sri Lanka since 2017.[14] During this time, I followed my interlocutors and oftentimes their images from Point Pedro to Maruthankerny, Kilinochchi, Vavuniya, Mullaitivu, and even Iranaitheevu, a small island off the coast of Mannar. Chance and sustained ethnographic and archival encounters in my hometown of Colombo and in London in the United Kingdom have also significantly determined the matter and trajectory of this work.

My effort is scaffolded by extensive primary research detailing the vibrant but understudied history of photography on the island, and specifically the Jaffna Peninsula. I offer this as a necessary corrective to the sparse documentation and scholarship on the pioneering work and technical prowess of Tamil photographers that have been long overlooked in a partial history of Sri Lankan photography splintered by biases of ethnicity, language, social class, geography, and, indeed, war (Buthpitiya 2019, 2022c). Against this essential backdrop, I show how the particular social, political, and economic conditions and aspirations bound to the Sri Lankan armed conflict gave rise to responsive and mediatory forms of everyday photography. The imponderabilia of photographic practice coupled with the medium's more overt mobilizations during the post/war illuminate its unpredictable and productive capacities.[15] I analyze these manifold expressions that gesture toward anticipation and the possibility of transformation through the idea of volatility.

PHOTOGRAPHIES OF DISORDER

Growing up in Sri Lanka through the war years, I frequently encountered the expression "(a) volatile picture."[16] It refers to a highly mutable status quo of political instability and the ever-present uncertainty and ruptures of conflict. In how it was lived, it signaled changeability. It was a shared recognition and fear of the perpetually unexpected. However, volatility also went hand in hand with chance, buoying what we learned to anticipate. Things could get better just as they could get worse, in elliptic serendipity—a word that incidentally derives from an old Persian name for the island. This charged interaction of volatility and expectation also lends itself to understanding the kinds of photography of Sri Lanka that emerged during this period, invoking the ambivalent and occasionally ominous visual tropes and templates of a "paradise under siege" (Buthpitiya 2019). White sand beaches fringed with windswept palms are patrolled by men with machine guns. The cut-up and burned bodies of murdered insurgents flanked an emerald paddy field as a schoolboy hung his head in distress. The humming market of a small town shattered by a bomb blast is distilled into shots of broken glass, pools of blood, and scattered vegetables and plastic toys. I conjure seen and unseen images with the same ease with which such photographic formulations of the atrocious in step with the Elysian permeated our lives. These came to represent us and our home. The island, cast over a century of British colonialism as an Edenic jewel of empire ripe for extraction, had become routinely bloodied by postcolonial turmoil ranging from state and anti-state terror and deadly ethnic violence to sweeping youth uprisings against the urban political elite.

Drawing on this turn of phrase, my engagement with the entanglement of war and photography in this book is twofold. First, as I have noted above and most directly, *A Volatile Picture* is an ethnographic study of post/war photographic practices in northern Sri Lanka weaving together individual and communal grievances and aspirations. Photography in its everyday social uses and political mobilizations illuminates how the medium is exerted by the Tamil community as a means for personal and collective expression and envisioning. Whether these articulations are cast against the fantastical elsewheres of photography studios, contained within the rigid bureaucratic frames of identity portraits ascribing ethnicity and citizenship, or mapped through the transnational appropriations of atrocity images as objects of public protest, they are inextricable from the Tamil political imagination that is rooted in language, community, and homeland.

Second, my consideration of photography as subject, history, frame, and method is a means to examine the political workings of Sri Lanka's civil war. Within the specific conditions of ethnonationalist conflict characterized by competing and ultimately unreconcilable imaginaries of nation and state, photography informs the making of respective image regimes. War transforms photography. Every image emerging out of a situation of conflict becomes permanently marked with its causes and consequences. To its communities, it cannot be read outside of the language and politics of war. The volatility of such photographs is intensified, where virtually any image might be wielded in its perpetuation, narration, or opposition.

Photographs that transpire out of war are used to demand, improvise, evidence, and necessitate political alternatives and futures that might be achieved through war. Here, photography is an agitant, which brushes against a political status quo. When viewed through the lens of volatility, we might grasp how photography's political efficacy is conceived of and mobilized in response to conflict by its diverse actants. As the Sri Lankan example will illustrate, a single photograph can be used concurrently and contradictorily—deployed all at once toward rousing politically generative violence, realizing aspirational visions for self and community, and underpinning demands for justice and accountability. I argue that this is made possible through the volatility of photography, which enables its makers and movers to place their expectations upon it. Volatility and chance are what empower expectations for what a photographic image can do.

The photographies appearing from the fraught setting of Sri Lanka's conflicts have been wielded not only as reportage, evidence, and mementos but as modes and sites for imagining, improvising, and unsettling. Importantly, they are also foundational to the intimacies of kinship, friendship, and solidarity that keep expectations uplifted by the promise of chance afloat amid anger and desolation. Such images of war elude containment and deftly move between and among uses, typologies, and geographies. The volatility of photographs makes their readings and uses unstable. In the chapters that follow, extending from photography studios, the front lines of combat, sites of protest and remembrance, and the hashtagged, geotagged places and aspirations of Instagram, I show how this volatility permits the medium's simultaneous capacities to order and disorder, to advocate and disquiet, and to be maneuvered to expectant and incendiary effect. The arcs of these volatile pictures are multiple and cannot be fixed to a single or certain outcome, if at all, as they continue to transmit demands and discourses across place and time. Even so, confidence in the political work and the potential of photography were rarely lost. My interlocutors still pin their appeals and expectations to images as they summon and wield the medium's particular potency to a desired effect. Within a context of war characterized by demands for self-determination and violently competing nation-state imaginaries, photography also illuminates the political agency of its actants, not merely in matters of ethno-states but also in commitments to preserving and sharing knowledge and sustaining empathy, community, and solidarity amid violence.

Sri Lanka has been an island of revolutions. These pursuits to confront the political status quo have been tethered to ambitions for state-building as the outcome, resulting in violence between extant and aspirant states, as was the case with the Tamil armed struggle and insurrections led by the Sinhalese Janatha Vimukthi Peramuna (JVP, or National Liberation Front). These instances of potential political reconfiguration through violent anti-state uprising and armed struggle, as well as their forceful suppression, have routinely precipitated episodes of mass atrocity. Even so, these varied and contested nation-state aspirations continue to be demarcated in and by an imperial glossary of a territorially defined ethno-state, bureaucratized socioeconomic ordering, and state-centered sovereignty as resolution rather than one of solidarity or total political reimagining. In such a situation, insurgencies were orchestrated, and wars were fought for, against, and between colonially imposed political denominations rather than for conditions enabling individual and collective freedom.

Similarly, the scholarly language through which we theorize moments, imaginaries, and ambitions for sweeping social and political transformation remains mired in romanticized abstractions of resistance and is ultimately still bound to the state. Comparably, the language of photography's political limits and possibilities remains anchored to the state and power or as hopeful democratic action and expression of solidarity to counter the violence of the sovereign (Tagg 1988; Azoulay 2008, [2012] 2015). Here, too, the inevitability of violence and its visceral nature is rarely accounted for. Writing on decolonization as a "program of complete disorder," Frantz Fanon observes that liberation "must, and can only, be achieved by force"

(1963, 36, 73). Within a context shaped by irreconcilable imaginaries of nation and state, violence is regarded as politically necessary and expedient. Violence, while ambivalent and destructive, is engaged to drive forward political transformation and realize political ambitions. How then does photography illuminate such tense aspirations? To understand the political work of war and photography is also to interrogate the language of nation and state and ideology toward or against which it is wielded. This book is then also a provocation to critically examine the shared, but incomplete, lexicon of the politics of national liberation as it might be grasped through photography as representational, and civil and uncivil practice engaged in the political work of the island's civil war. *A Volatile Picture* inquires, through the Sri Lankan example, whether conceiving of photography and liberation beyond the constraints of the state is possible.

War, as the subject of study, is often characterized as a broad condition or experience of armed conflict and protracted political violence rather than the result of the complex and strategic interplay of incompatible and indeed mismatched ideological objectives actively underpinning the social, political, and economic life of participating or affected communities. This is to say that the anthropological study of war, especially of the postcolonial global south, consistently downplays its decidedly political nature, whose architects, participants, subjects, and victims draw on an existing vocabulary of political theory and practice. It is essential to afford adequate attention to the enactment of this language of political self-determination, where the oppressed "finds freedom in and through violence" (Fanon 1963, 68). Sri Lanka's civil war, framed as a violent and volatile interstitial space-time, was more than a complex social condition, continuum, or transformation, but an explicitly political undertaking intended to realize, by whatever means necessary, aspirations of a nation-state (see Lubkemann 1997; Richards 2005; Thiranagama [2011] 2013). What then of the photographies of disorder that are entwined with ethnonationalism and liberation by way of armed struggle? How might we address an "uncivil" photography, emerging from and produced and mobilized as part of civil war? (Azoulay [2012] 2015). How does photography both disorder and serve as an agitant in a context of ethnonationalist conflict? What are the linkages of community and solidarity through photography that emerge from such a setting? In Sri Lanka, photography has been deployed as both witness to and producer of violence beheld as essential to making freedom conceivable. Yet as a means for political speaking, the medium allows horizontal conversation in the spirit of the demotic, indicating the ways in which photography might elude power (Pinney 2023, 32). What photography reveals to us is the vibrancy of the interstitial as a place and time of personal and collective political imagining where photographs and their inherent volatility and chance are used to politically advantageous effect.

AGITANT IMAGES / UNCIVIL SPECTATORS

To fully comprehend the political work of images and the volatile possibilities afforded by the medium, this book constitutes an attempt to "watch" the photographs that make up the image world of my interlocutors (Azoulay [2012] 2015, 14).[17] This effort extends beyond what is shown in an image or merely the context of photography's explicit political uses, to reconstruct the photographic event and its subsequent alterations and circulations in a manner that accounts for the reinscription of time and movement. Developing the idea of the indexicality of photographs proposed by Peirce (1955), Christopher Pinney notes that a "relationship of physical contiguity between the image and referent" is the basis for complexity and ambivalence as much as for direct truth claims (2003, 6). As mapped against the various ethnographic contexts that make up this book, photography's ambivalence and its modulations in divergent circuits support the rival "truth" claims of war. As Pinney argues, what was there can be much more than what was intended by the photographer's framings, where "a substrate or margin of excess, a subversive code" is present in every photographic image, permitting it to be always "open and available to other readings" (2003, 6). This embeds the photographic image with an enduring potential for unruliness that amplifies its social, and in this instance, political, reproduction and mobilization, and indeed its volatile and "incendiary" nature as well as its capacities for creating agitation and solidarity.

This framing of volatility is grounded in theorizations of the "eventfulness" of images (Strassler 2020, 15). I ask how this relates to ethnonationalist conflict. Ariella Aïsha Azoulay proposes that photographs are part of an ever-unfolding "event of photography" ([2012] 2015, 23). It is made up of an "infinite series of encounters" concerned not merely with the photographer and the photographed but also its diverse spectators ([2012] 2015, 26). This enables multiple potentials for a photographic image to be endlessly (re)-inscribed with new meaning in its social and political uses. Karen Strassler conceptualizes an "image-event" as "a political process set in motion when a specific image or set of images erupts onto and intervenes in a social field, becoming a focal point of discursive and affective engagement across diverse publics" (2020, 9–10). Such endless possibility can be attributed to Walter Benjamin's suggestion of contingency. Benjamin notes that despite the photographer's best efforts to frame a subject's encounter with the camera, "another nature which speaks to the camera rather than to the eye" sears the photograph with actuality ([1931] 2005, 510). A "tiny spark of contingency" linked to the "here and now" of a specific time and place lingers in the photographic image where "the future nests so eloquently that we, looking back, may rediscover it" ([1931] 2005, 510).

As has been examined in-depth by Pinney, it is this "spark of contingency" that enables photographs to disturb and trouble (2012, 150). Azoulay calls for this opportunity to be harnessed by way of the civil contract of photography or a relationship among equals to confront and challenge the violences of sovereign power in an act of civil spectatorship ([2012] 2015, 26). However, where competing national imaginaries and futures are bound to state formation and expansion, the political takes precedence over the civil. The volatile pictures of the Sri Lankan civil war do not abide by demands for responsibility alone. Instead, and often synchronously, the medium's volatile potential and capacity to disorder are deployed as weapons of war, rendering an astoundingly diverse repertoire of photographs politically mutable. The production and circulation of photographic images then fuel forms of *uncivil* spectatorship (Buthpitiya 2023b, 80–81). Where contingency enables the medium's volatility and interlinked potential for politically expedient repurposing, this ethnography centers photography's generative capabilities in a situation of ethnonationalist conflict.

This ethnography is, thus, an empirical investigation of the event(s) of photography in tandem with the event(s) of ethnopolitical self-determination. While Tamil photographic practices of northern Sri Lanka problematize the categories through which we frame calls for civil responsibility and the failures of internationalized regimes for truth and accountability, their expectant everyday uses by communities that engage and interact with their volatility demonstrate that the medium's powers are always recognized and beyond containment. Similarly, how photography's incongruous but nevertheless agitant capabilities continue to be admitted, deployed, and suppressed by state actors reinforce this acknowledgment.

LIVELY TRANSMISSIONS

In Sri Lanka, photography is then a mutable means for invention, incitement, and imagining, embedded with the promise and subversive possibilities of volatility. Images are mobilized to hopeful, reparative, and inflammatory effect among a community navigating a multilayered condition of loss and the slow-burning violence of a state-declared "peace." My interlocutors regarded photography as capable of propelling personal and political transformation forward. Image-making serves as a tool for social and political improvisation, in its perceived capacity to catalyze visions and imaginings of futures and transformations against a backdrop of ethnonationalist civil conflict and unequal citizenship in northern Sri Lanka.

Photography was actively enlisted to not only document and evidence political violence but rationalize and provoke politically generative violence geared toward securing the future of the envisioned nation-state. Such uses do not diminish the medium's spirited uses within communities to imagine aspirational reinventions of the self or express desires for personal mobility and success, and to serve as a cornerstone for friendship and interpersonal connection. The framing of volatility and chance is an acknowledgment that in a situation of conflict, any photograph can become an agitant or a gesture to solidarity and community. It is the complex entanglement of these facets, suspended between the everyday navigation of a volatile context and exploiting the volatile potentials of images, that forms the historical, ethnographic, and visual considerations of this book. Where war and image-making have been deemed inextricable in terms of surveillance, militarization, propaganda, and visual tropes of violence and suffering, *A Volatile Picture* demonstrates how and why these incendiary images take flight.

What follows is an attempt to chart the complex trajectory defined by the coexisting contradictions and possibilities of violent pursuits of nation-state formation of nearly three decades of secessionist armed struggle through the lens of photographic practice. I consider how the politics of national liberation are felt, expressed, and performed in the everyday and, importantly, how this occurs through a photography of disorder and indeed a photography that disorders. *A Volatile Picture* makes a case for the role of photography as an integral component of this often violent enactment against a longue durée of ethnonationalist conflict and civil war. How might we make sense of the entangled accounts of war and photography within the turbulent setting of the Sri Lankan civil war characterized by rival nation-state projects, state violence, anti-state insurgency, and widespread transnational dispersal and displacement? How do we account for the movement of images such as those by Amarasinghe, the unknown Welikada prison photographer or Rajaratnam *mama*? What do war-whittled studio catalogs, artful wedding albums, and passport headshots forging passage through international borders, identity portraits held up in roadside demonstrations, grisly trophy snaps turned into award-winning advocacy documentaries and elaborate commemorative pandals, and the activism and nostalgia of Instagram posts of #homeland have in common? What do these lively transmissions reveal about the visual formation of transnational political claims in an unreconciled and unreconcilable aftermath of ethnonationalist conflict? Ultimately, how can we think through the ways in which photographs emerging out of a site of prolonged conflict concurrently serve as documents and triggers of violence and invocations of solidarity? Might these uses point importantly to whether photography might be freed from the syntax of the state?

WITNESSING

I set out to undertake this research resolving not to ask specific questions about personal experiences of the war, yet the war permeated virtually every conversation I had. The organization of this book mirrors the event(s) of war and photography, beginning from the social history and making of images to their disobedient social and political uses in the face of conflict and political marginalization. Given the pervasive effects of conflict, continued instability, and widespread feelings of unsafety and political repression, vulnerability becomes a difficult category to ascertain or specify within the Sri Lankan context. I only recorded what those I met chose to relate to me and allowed me to photograph, usually with the specific intention of accruing greater visibility to their losses and claims in settings of protest. Where anonymization is standard practice, accommodating such requests became a difficult decision.

Azoulay's call for civil spectatorship might be extended to this ethnography of the political work of photography in solidarity with my interlocutors and their fight for justice ([2012] 2015). It is a commitment to considering what photography, in its volatile forms and chance outcomes, might yield toward understanding solidarity and resistance and if the medium's potentials might be conceived of beyond pursuits for sovereign power. Moreover, as Jeffrey Sluka observes, "The only real leverage anthropologists can hope to exercise lies in public exposure, in breaking the silence that surrounds and nurtures terror" (2000, 35). I use this to think through the ethics, risks, and politics of negotiating precarity and visibility within the space of anthropological knowledge production. Accordingly, *A Volatile Picture* is the work of community, solidarity, and witnessing. The visibility I have attempted to afford is not without caution, thought, and careful adjustment with the greatest respect for the challenges, struggles, and uncertainties faced by those whose sentiments, words, and actions made this work achievable.

CHAPTER OUTLINES

I research and write as a scholar from Sri Lanka perched on the messy cusp of sparring identities, the dividing lines of us and them cutting through body and name just as it has the island and sharing in a status quo of precarity with my interlocutors. This book is located against the vital motivation and quandary of doing anthropology at home, where "homeland" remains disputed and demands for its realization are forbidden. I start by setting out the fraught backdrop of a militarized postwar and the tense negotiations of Tamil citizenship in the wake of a state-declared peace by a military victory that decimated the Tamil liberation struggle (chapter 1).

Following this, *A Volatile Picture* spans the inventive making and moving of images generated by northern Sri Lanka's tenacious photographers and their vivacious political afterlives. Chapters 2, 3, and 4 are connected through the sites and practices of image-making, largely centered on Jaffna's photography studios, which set out the communities and lineage of skills, forms, and aesthetics outlining the types of photographs we see in the second half of the book. I begin with the dedicated photographers who acted as the makers and unexpected keepers of the island's war-ravaged photographic remains, as Tamil photographies are absented from Sri Lanka's broader photographic history (chapter 2). By investigating the potent legacies of the battling image regimes of competing ethno-states amid a fierce civil conflict, I then survey the Liberation Tigers' image world and the transformations to everyday image-making during the war years (chapter 3). These chapters are informed by remembered histories of photography and war to make visible the materialization of the various types of images that are considered in this book, noting also that these images continue to circulate in and inform the photographies of the postwar. Next, I turn to postwar studio practitioners serving as mediators of "cinestyle" fantasies and migrant futures, and preservers of social history alongside "picture palace" framers. Studio photographers sustain a vivid transnational visual economy of matrimony, death, and other photographed life events while exerting subversive skills of compliance in citizen registration and borderwork in the production of identity photography (chapter 4).

The chapters that follow are focused on the explicitly political mobilizations of the images and practices encountered in the preceding chapters speaking to how their volatility and agitant capacities endure after the end of the war. It extends from the haunting display of national identity card and passport headshots at sites of Tamil civilian protest against state-sponsored enforced disappearance to their internationalized ambits as part of transitional justice mechanisms (chapter 5). Exemplified by the public commemoration of the Mullivaikkal massacre that led to the "end" of the war and the making of transient photographic memorials, the following chapter traces the tumultuous transmissions of atrocity images captured by militant and civilian photographers supplementing claims of nation, and postwar demands for truth and accountability (chapter 6). The final chapter explores the future of ethnonationalist self-determination in relation to a dispersed national community by examining practices of social evidencing, social photography, and collective photographic recursions on image-based social media platforms, which make up a digital cartography of hashtags and geotags tethering together the deferred dreams of the Tamil imagination (chapter 7).

The photographies that make up the Sri Lankan post/war featured in this book are remarkably varied. They invoke, collectively, the many complexities, injuries, and imagined possibilities of Tamilness as an ethnopolitical identity and the basis for future sovereignty. I trace their manifold social and political conjugations as a lens through which to illuminate the interstitial time-space of post/war and nation-state yet to be realized. Photography, in responsive and mediatory forms, was integral not only to the consolidation of competing nation-state imaginaries and securitization but the disruptive formation of de-territorialized, transnational political socialities and solidarities that in turn strengthened located claims of multiply conceived belonging and "homeland." For individuals, photography permits remedy, mobility, and means to imagine and improvise for themselves futures that allow them to overcome the enduring political marginalization and the impediments of unequal citizenship. It becomes the foundation for the intimacies and care of family, friendship, and love and remembering. What this book establishes is how the diverse and volatile photographies of the Sri Lankan civil war serve as agitants and intermediaries, urging conflict and political and personal aspiration and community forward.

1 HOME(LAND)

JAFFNA, THOSE DAYS

For as long as I could remember, the island had been imprecisely cleaved as north and south. Northern Sri Lanka had been the epicenter of a cartographically defined political demand rendered "dangerous" and ultimately out of bounds by the long, drawn-out war between the government and the Tamil Tigers. Growing up in Colombo, Sri Lanka's capital city, I was aware of the region grounded in Jaffna, the town and by extension the peninsular district at the northernmost tip of the island. Defined as the cultural, intellectual, and political heartland of Eelam Tamil identity, my impressions of Jaffna and "the north" existed as a series of secondhand evocations and media projections. The endless audio-visual-textual cacophony of my childhood and young adult years, demarcated in its entirety by the war, starkly contrasted with the elicitations of place and people offered by those who belonged to the generations that came before mine.

Elegiac recollections from their once-upon-a-time visits before the war conjured a picturesque landscape clasped by the silvery waters of the Indian Ocean connected to the rest of the island by a thin sliver of land. The Tamils of Jaffna too carried with them a certain cachet—of dignity, discipline, industriousness, and literary, artistic, and scientific accomplishment that spoke of character and mettle. There was a certain renowned *kunam,* or character, associated with this identity rooted in Jaffna as *ur* (home as natal village) (Thiranagama [2011] 2013, 18; Daniel 1984). Jaffna *those days* had been stippled with verdant thickets of fan-leafed palmyra, endless fields of gilded paddy, red shallots, and tobacco, ornate Hindu temples encircled by red and white candy-cane-striped walls and sky-blue and coral pink colonial churches. There were lime-washed courtyard houses with baroque facades crowned with plaster Lakshmis (goddess of wealth) and Saraswatis (goddess of wisdom), and lofty trees weighed down with *karuthakolomban* and *kilimookku* mangos that were no doubt the best on the island. Decorous sari-draped women on bicycles with garlands of jasmine in their hair were said to expertly zip past the palmyra leaf fences lining the region's parched roads. There was legendary Jaffna *kool* and fiery crab curry to be sampled alongside chewy *odiyal* (palmyra tubers) and cardamom-scented *rasavalli kilangu kanji* (purple yam porridge). Jaffna existed, almost fable-like to those beyond the peninsula.

"Did you know they used to grow grapes there? *Grapes*!" was an oft-repeated exclamation. Jaffna's particular magic was so potent that grapes, otherwise "foreign" to the island, grew in its bountiful soil.

The war, of course, had changed everything.

This is a chapter of histories, polities, and imaginaries that set out the trans/national parameters within which the volatile photographies of this book are produced, circulate, push against, and even exceed. "Home(land)" undertakes the vital work of positioning this ethnography in space, geography, time, and community. To situate experiences of post/war, incompatible conceptions of nation and state and arising visual economies, I offer an overview of a complex period of recent history.[1] Confronting the photographies of war is to engage with the social and political life of its assorted spatial, temporal, and visual imaginaries. This chapter considers how a history of conflict wrought the post/war Tamil political imagination and its attendant image-making.

This chapter is also, importantly, an attempt to locate myself as an ethnographer to make clear what made this research essential and conceivable. History, to those who lived in the midst of its violent making, is invariably personal, present and future—not merely a synthesis of events and biographies. I consider my place within it to delve into the complexities of producing anthropological knowledge of "home," where the political imaginary of "homeland" remains embedded in a history and present of violence. Given the complex contemporary context and history and my position as a multilingual "native anthropologist" of mixed ethnicity, I am regarded as native to everywhere and nowhere.[2] I am both of *us* and *them*, but never wholly either. Yet along with my interlocutors, I, too, wrestle with how to distill into words my relationship to that home(land) and community. I must reflect on how I fit into its war, its "peace," and its quicksilver politics, in inevitabilities that have ultimately molded the epistemological, methodological, and ethical implications of this scholarly undertaking where anthropology as a discipline has for so long prioritized a theoretical and procedural lens that I could not see my own thinking and research through. Dilemmas of positionality were equally formative, limiting, and ethnographically fruitful, given the unexpected significance in how my interlocutors understood my presence and relationship to them, about trust and confidences, and indeed what this reveals about the mercurial politics of ethnicity, nation, state, the language of citizenship, and war in Sri Lanka. This chapter is necessary, as what follows would not be possible without this specific arrangement of chance, fate, history, and inheritance.

AN ISLAND OF UNRULY NATIONS

The Sri Lankan civil war (1983–2009) was fought between the majority Sinhalese government and the Tamil militancy dominated by the Liberation Tigers of Tamil Eelam (LTTE). It is embedded in what is frequently described as an ethnic conflict between the Sinhalese and Tamils. The armed conflict arose out of politically irreconcilable imaginaries of nation, state, and citizenship rooted in this ethnic conflict.

Known as Ceylon until it cast off its dominion status in 1972, Sri Lanka's postcolonial period was characterized by the formation of a powerful nation-state building project. It prioritized the country's Sinhalese Buddhist majority through the systemic marginalization of and violence against its ethnolinguistic minorities. This resolute ideological (re)casting of the island as a Buddhist heartland demarcated hierarchies of citizenship and mobility along ethno-religious and geographic lines. The colonially established capital Colombo continues to hold a favored position as the base of the island's postcolonial socioeconomic and political elites.

The unitary character of the modern Sri Lankan state owes its formulation to British colonization. Its indigenous governance was historically fragmented into various regional monarchies and further ruptured following the demise of the Polonnaruwa Kingdom in the thirteenth century as the result of an invasion by the Kingdom of Kalinga in India. This also puts into stark perspective that the island's recorded political insecurity and fragmentation has spanned several centuries. Violently occupied by the Portuguese (1505–1658), the Dutch (1640–1796), and the British (1796–1948), the island had withstood centuries of heated political disorder marked by internal power struggles, invasion, warring colonial interlopers, and ruthlessly suppressed anticolonial rebellions. By the late nineteenth century, non-Sinhalese communities were regularly belittled as "guests," "foreigners," and/or "invaders," implicitly and explicitly othered in popular discourse. Sinhala Buddhist nationalist sentiment, rooted in anticolonial nationalist revival, became rapidly absorbed into majoritarian Sri Lanka's political culture and policy obligations as an electoral tactic. As Jonathan Spencer notes, the process of reconstructing postcolonial Sri Lanka "in the form of an idealized national past" relied on "ideological overproduction" (1990, 10). The island, its history, and its sociopolitical and visual-material landscape continue to be reconfigured with vigor and exceptionalism as a Sinhalese Buddhist nation-state. However, the Sinhalese polity, too, would become fractured by conflict.

Following independence from Britain in 1948, clashes arising out of the widening gap between the island's anglicized political elected officials and increasingly deprived rural Sinhalese population gave way to worsening tensions. The ruthless and systematic quelling of dissent defined the island's transition from Ceylon to Sri Lanka in the shadow of the first (unsuccessful) uprising against the government helmed by Prime Minister Sirimavo Bandaranaike. Many thousands were killed and imprisoned because of this first revolt led by the Janatha Vimukthi Peramuna (JVP) in 1971. Between 1987 and 1989, the group led a second armed insurrection as hostilities between the state and the Tamil militancy committed to national liberation escalated in the northeast of the island. Self-proclaimed Marxist-Leninists, the JVP operated their own guerrilla regime of violence and were ferociously suppressed by the state. This period known as the Bheeshanaya (the terror) resulted in tens of thousands of extrajudicial killings and enforced disappearances. Mass graves from these early decades of mass violence in the north and south continue to be discovered (ITJP 2023). Alex Pillen observes the way in which the Sinhalese hinterland served as "reservoirs of violence" produced out of the wider history of insurgency and counterinsurgency, whereby "the Sinhalese soldiers manning the front lines in the war against the LTTE in the northeast are inevitably a product of this primary regime of violence" (2002, 4–6). These periods of conflict were integral to strengthening militarization, securitization, repressive legislation, carceral practices, torture, and state terror, which deter political expression and activism even today. The complexities of Sri Lanka's conflicts on the grounds of ideology, social class, and ethnicity, coupled with the way "anti-state" dissent was violently quashed, expose an overarching state logic of counterinsurgency weaponized against nonconforming citizens that was championed by successive governments. As relevant to this book, this institutionalization is deeply enmeshed with photography as a means of surveillance, evidencing identity, and producing propaganda. Notably, the swift and extensive expansion of state bureaucratic practices of citizen registration and the issuance of National Identity Cards (NICs) through a systematic project of state-sponsored photography took place as a result of state imperatives to monitor subversion.

The Tamil-speaking community, comprising Eelam Tamils, Indian-origin Tamils, and Muslims, among others, bore the brunt of the forceful consolidation of the unitary Sinhala-Buddhist ethno-state, and its turn to martial governance. This involved the enactment of the Ceylon Citizenship Act (1948) and the Indian and Pakistani Residents (Citizenship) Act (1949) which led to the disenfranchisement and forced repatriation of Malaiyaha Tamils who were brought into the island by the British as indentured labor. Other discriminatory policy interventions—including the 1956 "Sinhala Only" Act, which declared Sinhala as the sole official language of Ceylon, and the 1971 Standardization policy, which curtailed Tamil students' access to university admission—gravely affected the island's Tamil-speaking communities. The period following independence was marred by numerous episodes of communal violence, including most notably in 1956, 1958, 1977, and the heinous act of biblioclasm with the burning of the Jaffna Public Library in 1981 and 1983's "Black July." These compounded the grievous injury and loss of life suffered by Tamils around the country, alongside the daily harassments and humiliations of unequal citizenship. This history of postcolonial violence is essential to understanding Tamil political aspirations for self-determination and self-rule, and the beginnings of the armed struggle.

Up until independence in 1948, the Tamil leadership were largely in favor of a unitary state (Jeyaratnam Wilson 1988, 2000; Uyangoda 1994; Cheran 2009). The "Sinhala Only" movement in the 1950s saw the Tamil polity—which initially sought to unite the Tamil-speaking communities of the island, including the Indian-Origin Tamil and Muslim communities—turn to federalism (Cheran 2009). Rifts of caste, class, ethnicity, religion, and geography hindered the forging of solidarities among the island's Tamil-speakers and by the 1970s, separation was deemed necessary. Advocated for by the Tamil United Liberation Front (TULF) under the leadership of S. J. V. Chelvanayakam, the Vaddukoddai Resolution, adopted on 14 May 1976, called for the creation of an independent Tamil state. The demand is viewed to have received wide democratic endorsement for a "sovereign, secular, socialist state of *Tamil Eelam,*" as the TULF won a resounding mandate in Tamil areas in the 1977 parliamentary election, briefly becoming the main opposition party in Sri Lanka (TULF 1976). This was the only occasion a minority ethnic party has done so. Cheran suggests that the resolution, which was more a token protest against national oppression rather than an articulation of a practical political objective, had a significant impact on the youth who took its demands to heart in embarking on a secessionist struggle (2009, xx–xxi). The emergence of Tamil nationalism has also been considered a response to escalating Sinhala Buddhist nationalism, constituting a form of "defensive nationalism" (Nithiyanandam 1987 cited in Cheran 2009, xiii; Jeyaratnam Wilson 2000). The various strains of Tamil nationalism, from "peaceful" parliamentary processes led principally by the TULF to the emergence of an armed struggle for national liberation, were not solely reactive to the reality that the power of the state resided with the Sinhalese majority. Various local and global historical moments shaped Tamil nationalist demands, from the failed revolts of the JVP to the liberation of Bangladesh (Cheran 2009, xxii). Such efforts to carve out political distinction would shape cultural production and aesthetics that distinguished Sri Lanka's ethnic and geographic communities and their vision for the nation and its image world, informing photographic practices in likely and astonishing ways. These tensions, political and aesthetic, were also invariably reinforced by a broader international milieu of anti-imperialist struggle and decolonization.

During this time, clashes intensified between the Sri Lankan government forces and the burgeoning Tamil groups made up of student activists, whose chances of university admission had been detrimentally affected by standardization. "Black July" and the widespread mass arrests of Tamil youth in the northeast led to greater numbers joining budding armed groups. These, in turn, competed for influence, resulting in severe internecine hostility (Hoole et al. 1992). Significant among these were the previously mentioned LTTE, as well as the Tamil Eelam Liberation Organization (TELO), the People's Liberation Organization of Tamil Eelam (PLOTE), The Eelam Revolutionary Organization of Students (EROS), The Eelam People's Revolutionary Liberation Front (EPRLF), and the Tamil Eelam Army (TEA). These early liberation organizations were also transnational in character, having significant bearing on the production and circulation of related visual materials that were vital to the groups' political activities in Sri Lanka and abroad. Several groups underwent military training in South India with the purported assistance of the central government as well as that of Tamil Nadu. The Marxist-inspired EROS, for instance, was founded by Tamils in London and was less militarily active in Sri Lanka. EROS, PLOTE, and EPRLF are said to have cultivated links with Palestinian counterparts such as the Palestine

Liberation Organization (PLO) and The Popular Front for the Liberation of Palestine (PFLP), resulting in Tamil guerrillas training overseas in Syria and Lebanon (Ragavan 2024).

A former revolutionary, whose allegiances had shifted from the founding days of the LTTE to PLOTE as the armed struggle escalated, remembered his training in Lebanon and Syria. After being threatened by the LTTE, he went into hiding to become a writer of Marxist critiques of the successes and failures of the Tamil nationalist struggle. Now domiciled in North America, he talked passionately about how his friends, doctoral students in London in the 1970s and '80s, had posted treatises by Antonio Gramsci and Louis Althusser, among others, to Jaffna. Benedict Anderson's *Imagined Communities* had compelled him greatly. "We didn't know much English then, so we sat up at night with big dictionaries and read, wondering how to convert these ideas into achieving the independent nation we wanted to build," he mused. "Maybe the mistake was that we dropped the books and picked up guns." The ideals of revolution were imported and experimented with but took on a more ruthless tone with the espousal of martial violence.

The LTTE, founded in 1976 by Velupillai Prabhakaran, would become dominant among the Tamil militant groups. Twenty-year-old Prabhakaran gained notoriety after he shot and killed Jaffna mayor Alfred Duraiappah during a visit to a Hindu temple in Ponnalai in 1975, going on to become the feared and revered leader of the LTTE. The Tigers' success as a "representative" force was enabled by a clever, virtually cinematic confluence of terror, authoritarian coercion, grassroots support, international campaigning, widespread recruitment, the discerning adoption and appropriation of Tamil cultural and religious practices, as well as a powerful image regime that reinvented the visual-material landscape of the northeast of Sri Lanka. The LTTE's potent efforts at cultural production and political propaganda were initially steeped in Marxist liberationist rhetoric and aesthetic. The subsequent formation of a highly visual personality cult around *thalaivar* (leader) Prabhakaran, coupled with the veneration of martyrs, normalized citizenship by devotion to a national cause synonymous with sacrifice. Portraits of Prabhakaran, posed as a valiant fighter, revolutionary, and statesman, were widely displayed and circulated, which firmly established him as brother in arms and deified national leader. The group manufactured an efficacious visual economy of militarism, death, martyrdom, and idolatry that adapted Hindu and Catholic tropes and cinema hero templates. This tenaciously contrived national iconography was cast as visually tantamount to the political aspirations of Eelam Tamil people. Even today, Prabhakaran's image, banned in Sri Lanka, perseveres among the diaspora, personifying the necessity and possibility of Tamil Eelam: framed in living rooms in Canada, on May Day floats in France, and pasted prominently in shop windows in London.

The Tigers mercilessly eliminated rival militant groups, moderate Tamil political leaders and activists, and critics of their increasingly despotic tendencies. They also suppressed dissent and disapproval within the Tamil community. It is important to emphasize that there has always been a diversity of opinion regarding the future of Tamil self-determination and how it might be achieved; this diversity is often damagingly disregarded in accounts of the Sri Lankan conflict. Indeed, such multiplicity that has been effaced in no small part by the LTTE as a part of its claim to be the Tamils' "sole representative," which defines the resultant visual and material cultures of the nation. As Silva notes, the LTTE successfully presented itself as "the only obstacle to the total defeat and destruction of 'the Tamil people' by the Sinhala state and its armed forces" ([1995] 2002, 182). The Tamil community's relationship with the Tigers, even in the face of violent persecution and suppression, was complex on account of its "civilian face" (Thiranagama [2011] 2013, 23). The group's extensive voluntary and forcible recruitment practices resulted in a status quo where "the LTTE occupied an intimate space within the family and the community rather than an external one such as the Sri Lankan state was imagined to inhabit," explicitly blurring boundaries between the family and the nationalist liberation struggle (Thiranagama [2011] 2013, 26). Even members of the LTTE leadership, including Prabhakaran, were referred to in familial terms, such as *thambi* (younger brother) or *anna* (elder brother). The LTTE's vision for Tamil Eelam as ethno-state, thus, cannot easily be undone from a concerted cultural-ideological project of fashioning devoted future citizens. Many Tamils in Sri Lanka and abroad continue to actively champion the group's ideology, and their political agency in this regard should not be dismissed, just as that of those who do not.

Operating alongside yet in conflict with the Sri Lankan state, the LTTE operated as a de facto state and established a judiciary and structures of public administration, including welfare, revenue collection, and departments of economic development and environmental management (Stokke 2006, 1029–30). The LTTE's comprehensive security operation encompassed an army, navy, air force, police, and intelligence wing (Richards

2014). The LTTE had a far-reaching international network, with the early adoption of photography, film, art, print publication, and media technologies such as radio, television, and the World Wide Web. The active control and remaking of the image world of its desired Tamil nation-state were crucial to the Tigers' successful governance effort. The group also espoused numerous terror tactics including suicide bombings carried out by the notorious Karumpulikal (Black Tigers). These were aimed at weakening the Sri Lankan state and economy and crushing internal opposition. Elsewhere in the island, the Tamil enemy "other" was cast as the foremost threat to the sovereignty and territorial integrity of Sri Lanka, just as the predominantly Sinhalese state was transformed into the chief antagonist by the LTTE. The warring photographic regimes of the extant state and the aspirant state were crucial to the political socialization of their constituents, where citizen-making relied significantly on image-making (chapter 3).

As the war progressed, the Tamil community became the variously willing and unwilling "citizens" of the homeland claimed on their behalf by an increasingly tyrannical LTTE, invested in metamorphosing into a legitimate state actor. This vision for an ethno-state and an ideal Eelam Tamil citizenry was no less violent or cogently engineered than that of the Sri Lankan state. In addition to fiercely quashing opposing groups and internal differences, the LTTE engaged in acts of ethnic cleansing targeting the Muslim community. Notable among these was the 1990 expulsion of 75,000 Muslims from the Northern Province and the Eravur and Kattankudy mosque massacres (Thiranagama [2011] 2013, 126). The Muslim community, in turn, was armed by the Sri Lankan state's Special Task Force by way of the Home Guards initiative (Thiranagama [2011] 2013, 126). Cornered between the Sri Lankan military and the LTTE, neither one of whom cared for the safety or well-being of the group, Muslim residents in the northeast were subjected to major violence and displacement during the war. Such an environment led to the aggravation of antagonisms between the Tamil and Muslim communities, its effects lasting in the form of various postwar frictions worsened by anti-Muslim sentiment by Sinhalese and Tamil communities.

Reflecting on the experiences of young people under the rule of the LTTE, Cathrine Brun defines the position of people living in Jaffna as one of "complex citizenship," where there is a lack of "a clear-cut relationship between citizens and the state, but where there are several governing and uncompromising actors that people must relate to" (2008, 401). In what Zachariah Mampilly describes as a "convoluted power-sharing arrangement," the Sri Lankan government continued to provide public goods and services to those living in LTTE-controlled areas throughout the war (2015, 94), though such provisions were never adequate, reliable, or intended altruistically. The Tamil community was ultimately faced with a choice of being killed by their own or the Sinhalese state's other, compelled to pick between vying scripts of violence and oppression. The Tamils were thus united by what was being fought against rather than what was fought for and how, drawing attention to the pitfalls of the incomplete vocabulary of political liberation. This is a sentiment that lingers in postwar Sri Lanka, where a feeling of loss, even among those who did not support the *Iyakkam*, persists. These sentiments are expressed, photographically, from securing desires to migrate elsewhere to the circulation of images of atrocity divulging the continued lack of truth and justice. Such a situation also crucially reveals that the aspiration for self-governance and its applied iterations were not the exclusive purview of the LTTE. How Ilankai Tamils imagine their political present and future has always taken varied forms and modulations in its practical association to and detachment from Sri Lanka, whether through federalism or a separate state. Where the "minority votes" had substantial bearing on national elections, most Tamils were invested in parliamentary and local government politics. "It's about who will build the roads faster," Ronny, a taxi driver from Jaffna, reflected on the tension between the ideal and the practical. "We remember who did what and whose fathers and grandfathers did what. We keep that respect. Yes, [Tamil] national politics is important for our people, and we have suffered a lot and that will not change, but we also understand how to get things done because it has a direct impact on how we get our next meal."

Against the backdrop of the broader geopolitical changes triggered by the September 11 attacks and the interlinked global discourse shift around "terror," a tenuous peace process between the Sri Lankan government and the LTTE, facilitated by the government of Norway, was in effect between 2002 and 2006. This period gave greater credibility to the LTTE's effort at transforming itself into a capable, governance-oriented state actor from a violent non-state actor engaged in guerrilla warfare, despite unremitting low-intensity violence and continued conscription. The LTTE's status was reinforced by acts of diplomacy and engagement with the international media, alongside the institutional and spatial reorganization of the north built around the LTTE's self-declared administrative capital of Kilinochchi.

The dynamics of travel between north and south had been largely disrupted, if not impossible, during the war. The Ceasefire Agreement

(CFA) between the Sri Lankan government and the LTTE motivated the beginnings of "leisure" travel, with the opening of the A9 Kandy-Jaffna highway producing new tourist photographies of the north. Visitors from the south crossed over into LTTE territory through an operational border at the Omanthai checkpoint complex, momentarily replacing imaginaries of fear and violence that were cultivated by the war with prewar romanticization that also glamorized, to an extent, the thrill of facing the "enemy" (Pieris 2014; Fatima 2022).

The ceasefire continued to disintegrate. Cooperation between the warring parties sputtered in the aftermath of the 2004 Indian Ocean Tsunami, in which over 30,000 Sri Lankans were killed. The catastrophe required unprecedented coordination to meet humanitarian needs. This juncture was also marked by the breakaway of what was known as the "K Group" or "Karuna Faction" in eastern Sri Lanka led by Colonel Karuna Amman (Vinayagamoorthy Muralitharan), an LTTE commander, who oversaw 1,200 square miles of territory. He argued that the interests of northern Tamils were being privileged over those from the east, who had suffered disproportionately in the war. Defecting to the government along with 6,000 fighters, Muralitharan, formed a pro-government paramilitary group, Tamil Makkal Viduthalai Pulikal (TMVP, or Tamil People's Liberation Tigers), prior to joining mainstream politics as part of the Sri Lankan government. The subsequent 2005 presidential vote marked a crossroads in the conflict with the election of Mahinda Rajapaksa, who came into power promising to adopt a harsher stance on the LTTE. The group barred Tamils in the north from voting, which is believed to have cemented Rajapaksa's victory. Rumors charging that the former president had paid off the LTTE to promote the boycott linger to this day. By 2006, Sri Lanka had descended back into full-scale war. From 2006 to 2009, fighting between the government forces and the LTTE enflamed dramatically. This period also marked a dramatic shift in the Sri Lankan government's approach to how visual media was deployed as a part of its war effort, mirroring in many ways practices that were long established by the LTTE (chapter 7).

The period from 2006 to 2009 was also beset by the escalation of attacks and atrocities attributed to the Sri Lankan armed forces, police, and intelligence operatives; pro-government paramilitary groups such as the TMVP; the LTTE; and other associated or breakaway factions. As has been extensively documented by human rights organizations, this included widespread factional fighting, targeted killings, massacres, raids, bombings, artillery shelling, suicide attacks, mass and individual abductions (leading to torture, disappearance, or death), extortion and ransom demands, arbitrary detention, attacks on journalists and nongovernmental organization (NGO) personnel, the use of civilians as human shields, and attacks on those fleeing sexual and gender-based violence, forced conscription, child abduction and recruitment, and restrictions on movement as well as the denial of humanitarian assistance (PIAC 2019). The effect of this all-encompassing violence defines the lives of my interlocutors and was inextricable from postwar Tamil political sentiments and claims, but also its photographic practices. In May 2009, the LTTE-led armed struggle to carve out an independent Tamil nation-state was categorically defeated by the Sri Lankan government forces at a devastating cost to civilians. The United Nations (UN) estimates that between 40,000 and 70,000 civilians were killed in the final months (September 2008–May 2009), while advocacy groups claim between 70,000 and 140,000 died (Darusman et al. 2011, 41, 62; Petrie 2012). Through an analysis of various estimates of the 2009 death toll, the International Truth and Justice Project (ITJP) estimates that between 83,000 and 169,796 persons are unaccounted for (2021). This includes those who were "disappeared" after surrendering to the government in 2009. A further 300,000 were internally displaced. Despite this, the Sri Lankan government resolutely maintained a line of "zero civilian casualties" to match its claim of "defeating terrorism" (Human Rights Watch 2011). Statistical inaccuracies and discrepancies related to war and displacement are extremely common. The total fatalities of the conflict are hotly disputed and the focus of various (often politically motivated) expansions and contractions. I have yet to meet anyone in the northeast of Sri Lanka who has not lost one or many more loved ones in the war.

The end of the war was bloodied by credible allegations of war crimes and crimes against humanity leveled at the government and the LTTE by the United Nations and various international advocacy groups (Darusman et al. 2011; PIAC 2019). High-ranking defecting members of the LTTE such as Muralitharan and Sivanesathurai Chandrakanthan (alias Pillayan) who were responsible for child conscription and terrorism were absorbed into the government as ministers and faced no domestic consequences for past involvements (Human Rights Watch 2004). Accusations were routinely and decisively denied by the Sri Lankan government, asserting that it carried out a "humanitarian rescue operation." This was despite the documented shelling of hospitals and "no-fire zones" and the extrajudicial executions of surrendered fighters and mass disappearances (Sooka 2014, 12). Photographic evidence of these events as they circulated in the hands of my interlocutors, many of whom were direct victims, informs this book. The effects of war on the Tamil community also increased movement by lawful and unlawful means. Ilankai Tamils have had a long history of economic migration throughout the twentieth century. This trend accelerated during and after the end of the war because of a perceived lack of opportunity as well as due to persecution by the state security forces, especially of those with past links to the LTTE.

Despite pressures for an impartial international review, no credible, independent domestic investigations or inquiries into these allegations were undertaken. The government's 2010 Lessons Learnt and Reconciliation Commission (LLRC) offered a series of recommendations including "the need for an independent judiciary, a transparent legal process, and strict adherence to the rule of law" that were unfulfilled (Sooka 2014, 67; LLRC 2011). The aftermath of the military victory cemented by the death of Prabhakaran was a burdened, perpetrator's peace. The causes and consequences of conflict bound to countless injustices were overlooked and unaddressed. A shared sense of loss and fear permeated the community as innumerable violences persisted in quiet but insidious ways. Many insisted that the war against Tamils was ongoing, and others vocalized their fears of "cultural genocide." The relationship between the state and its "second-class" minority citizens was characterized by resignation, fear, and the ever-lingering expectation and prospect of violence. However, following its single-minded efforts at machinating a transnational commitment to an Eelam Tamil nation-state and citizenry, specters and echoes of the LTTE's legacy also persist.

I call attention to this past and present to underscore how the Tamil liberation struggle has always been transnational in its articulations, movements, conversations, imaging, and imagining. It is simultaneously located in the place of Tamil Eelam but dispersed in its envisioning and sustenance through conflict-induced migration and global solidarities forged by confronting state violence. Civil wars are rarely civil or domestic in their unfolding, ensnared in global economies of financing, armaments, profiteering, and media, as well as mass displacement, dispersal, and the fragmentation of kin and community. Such manifestations also take place through the visual, which has been vital to political expression. It foregrounds the political work of photography as indispensable to the events and aftermath of war. The postwar has also been defined by the internationalization of calls and mechanisms for truth and accountability, framing Tamil hopes and demands for autonomy and justice. The war that wounded Sri Lanka and its people over decades was visualized, devised, and deeply felt in living rooms in Melbourne and Paris, solidarity marches in London and Toronto, refugee camps in Tamil Nadu, and hotel conference halls turned negotiation tables in Thailand, just as they were in the Jaffna peninsula, the Batticaloa lagoon, or the city of Colombo. This would fundamentally intensify the volatility of the photography that emerged out of and in response to the violence and the anticipated political work through which liberation was necessitated, sought, and fought for, and why it then underpins dreams for future sovereignty and self-determination.

ANTICIPATION NATION: PHOTOGRAPHY AND THE TAMIL IMAGINATION

I use the term *imagination* to frame Tamil political aspirations for self-determination and nation-state-building. It relates to how photography's political potentials have been analyzed (Strassler 2020; Pinney et al. 2023). Here, we must critically engage with nation, state, and citizenship as denominations and categories of analysis when we consider the making of war and the political work and volatility of photography. I turn here to the former revolutionary's invocation of Benedict Anderson who theorizes the nation as an imagined political community, which exists as a "cultural artefact" conceived of as "deep, horizontal comradeship" (1983, 6). Building on this to think through photography, I draw attention to Ariella Aïsha Azoulay's emphasis on the need to consider the term *political imagination* as one that "exceeds the grasp of the individual mind," and as existing between individuals and shared by them, leaving "imprints on history when it breaks boundaries," enabled, she suggests, by way of photography ([2012] 2015, 5–7). The Tamil political imagination is tied to anticipating state formation as the outcome of armed struggle and thus socialized into practices of anticipatory citizen-making. Pradeep Jeganathan's analysis that the 1983 pogrom was pivotal to the construction of Tamil identity in southern Sri Lanka through a set of "signifying practices of Tamilness that are only visible in relation to the presence of violence in the ethnographic landscape of Sri Lanka," which he describes as a "tactics of anticipation," is relevant to this (2000, 111–12). Similarly, Sidharthan Maunaguru considers the significance of "anticipation" as pervading the "the state of being Tamils have regarding movement, violence, social mobility" (2009, 61). This offers an important and necessary opportunity to reframe the category of risk and vulnerability saturating the language of conflict. It evokes the practicalities of mitigation and maneuvering bound to political agency, choice, and possibility, which are often overlooked in contexts where communities are positioned as passive or "resilient" victims (see Nordstrom 1997). Such anticipations might also be viewed as analogous to the expectations placed on the political work of photography.

By drawing together the parallel considerations of nation-state imagining and making, I focus on the photographies that inform this process to consider how the volatility of images is perceived as being capable of realizing political and personal transformation. Photography, here, is also anticipatory. Partha Chatterjee's use of the term *political imagination* draws on Anderson's distinction between nationalism and the politics of ethnicity (1999; 2004). Chatterjee describes unbound serialities, "typically imagined and narrated by means of the classic instruments of print-capitalism," as "potentially liberating" (1999, 128). They allow "opportunities for individuals to imagine themselves as members of larger than face-to-face solidarities, of choosing to act on behalf of solidarities, of transcending by an act of political imagination the limits imposed by traditional practice" (Chatterjee 1999, 128). In photography, this tension between serialities might be extended to how the medium is adopted by "the ruling power" and "the governed" (Azoulay [2012] 2015, 17). Northern Sri Lanka's everyday photography through the post/war period allows us to "see" how these dynamics are visualized by its architects and participants, and how photography exists within and as a part of this fraught political continuum.

The Tamil political present globally is defined by continuing state violence in Sri Lanka, internationalized demands for justice, accountability, and recognition of genocide even as the space for such expressions for Tamils in-country remains limited. To assess its emergent photographies, their volatility and the agitant potentials they contain, we must reconcile binary theorizations of solidarity and authority, where a nation desires transition into a sovereign state. Photography as an act of political expression and realization offers a window into the arc of armed resistance to authoritarian postulant state actor engaged in the organizational, legislative, martial, and visual-material performance of a nation-state. Photography also evidences the aspirant state's subsequent dismantling by a ruthless military defeat and being reverted to a status quo of violent subjection and failed solidarity and civic spectatorship. We are also afforded understanding of how "complex citizens" participate in or refute this nation-state-making (Brun 2008). In postwar Sri Lanka, Tamil liberation as ideal and pursuit coexist, in an interstitial time and space, marked by patent defeat and haunting possibility. Resigned, despairing, but hopeful Tamils envisage and look ahead in this anticipatory in-between of a deferred dream.[3] Photography, even in its volatility suspended between expectation and disappointment, gives shape to this vivid dreaming. The ensuing chapters think through what the medium, in its countless visual and material forms, achieves in practice for realizing personal and political aspirations and solidarities that arise out of war. It thus reframes a different kind of contingency, inquiring into whether photography and liberation can be disentangled from the state through an examination of its state, non-state, and demotic deployments within the Sri Lankan post/war.

Strassler, following Anderson's conception of nation, suggests that "it is through the reflexive production and circulation of images that 'imagined' social entities like nations become visible and graspable, that they come to seem to exist prior to and independent of those images" (2010, 4). The sundry photographic repertoires gathered in this book reveal how the Tamil community is reaching across this unfolding time-space of imagination, anticipation, and dreaming, between extant nation and aspiring state in the wake of war. This anxious cleft between necessary aspiration and realization is one marked by the violent suppression of a long-held demand for political self-determination; death and sacrifice; the fragmentation and dispersal of family, community, and nation; war loss; the impediments of unequal citizenship amid the hostile war; and the "peace" of a perpetrator state.

JAFFNA, THESE DAYS

In 2018, when I first arrived in Jaffna, the town was leaning into the ambit of "postwar development," magnifying rapidly in the years that followed. Luxury hotels built by burgeoning chains advertised bars and swimming pools catering to southern and foreign tourists and returning Tamil expatriates.[4] Investments were poured into ostentatious multi-storied *thirumana mandapams* (wedding halls). Where lavish weddings were a lucrative horizontally integrated enterprise, photography studios, advertising themselves with vinyl printed boards showing the latest Canon cameras and state-of-the-art drones, were thriving. They offered a gamut of services, extending from "cinestyle" engagement shoots and the creation of ostentatious albums, where the couple could be digitally transported anywhere from the temples of Tanjore to the Eiffel Tower, to ushering visa success. In the town's side streets, old homes scarred by bullets and abandoned coral-bricked mansions falling into disrepair leaned against new birthday cake–like houses painted bright pink and orange, paid for with money trickling in from overseas. Backpackers were being beckoned by edgy travelogs inviting them to visit the "time capsule" that had been preserved by war but no longer infected by "the lingering culture of fear" bound to "some of the most horrific carnage in recent history" (Solomon 2016; Hallinan 2017). "Everywhere you look, construction, expansion, new hotels, foreign money. Something that looks a lot like hope," the late Anthony Bourdain famously mused in his postwar foray into the island (2017). Jaffna remained somewhat unprepared as much as it was, in a sense, also reluctant to alter itself like other tourist towns in the rest of the island that were steeped in metaphors of paradise.

A lavish shopping center painted crimson loomed over the busy quarters of Hospital Road, offering hitherto unknown extravagances of a food court and a multiplex that screened Kollywood and Hollywood blockbusters. The peninsula's distinct hand-painted shop signs, adorned with jewel-toned deities from the Hindu pantheon, were slowly giving way to glossy digital reinventions (fig. 2). Residents claimed that the local Pizza Hut and KFC franchises, novelties that were decades behind in opening compared to their southerly counterparts, were among the busiest in Sri Lanka. However, fragments of Jaffna's "prewar" idyll, colorfully bottled and wrapped into "traditional" confections, endured in the market stalls as they did in the Sinhalese imagination. On some days, it was impossible not to be amused (much like the Tamil vendors themselves) by Sinhalese pilgrims dressed in their white temple clothes on pilgrimage bus itineraries frantically scouring the market for *Yaapane rathu loonu* (Jaffna red onions) and *Yaapane midi* (Jaffna grapes) as if these were storied delicacies. It had not occurred to me to go looking for vineries in Jaffna until a Sinhalese taxi driver from Colombo who drove me to the Fort Railway Station asked if I was going to Jaffna to see the *midi kotu* (grape plots). He himself had not been to Jaffna yet but expressed a long-felt wish to see its *midi kotu*. Deep amethyst bunches of Jaffna grapes were sold in the fruit stalls by the central bus depot, and in the town's bazaar. The market had in parts transmuted itself for the benefit of Sinhalese tourists who came looking for luminous green *nelli crush*, sugary Rosetto wine bottled by the Rosarian Sisters in Tholagatty, palmyra jaggery

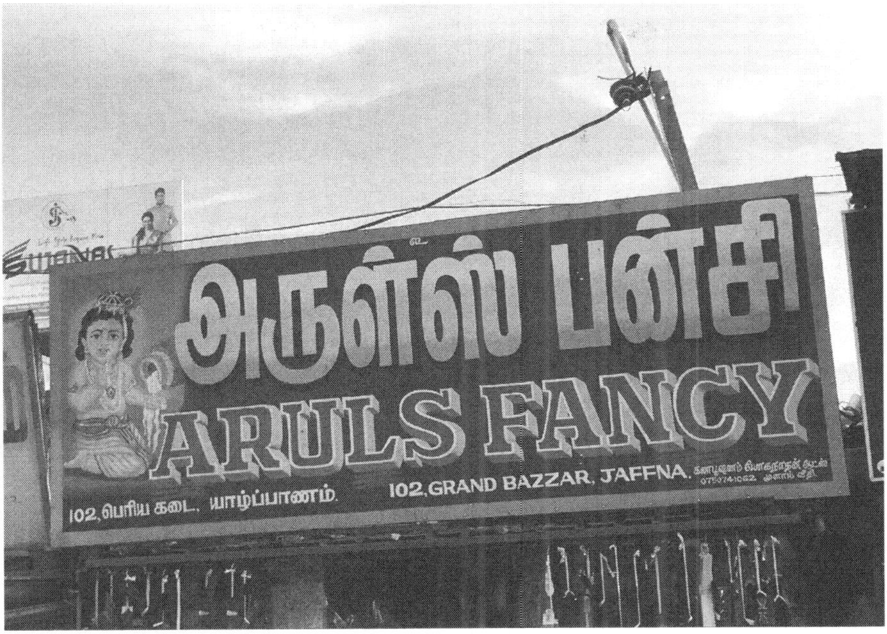

FIGURE 2. Painted shop signs (Jaffna, 2018)

packed in dainty woven leaf pockets, and *Paruthithurai vadai.*[5] I did not happen across a vinery in my time there.

The stately taxicabs once plentiful at hospital junction, Austin Cambridges, Morris Oxfords, and Morris Minors from the 1950s and '60s, which had been tinkered with to have lived many remarkable lives through the war, were no more. Local men driving Tata Nano and Maruti Suzuki surrogates ferried out-of-towners on day trips to a smattering of tourist sites: Cankiliyan Thoppu (Canikiliyan's arch); Mantri Manai (minister's abode), associated with the Jaffna Kingdom (1215–1624 CE); and the Jaffna Library. The seventeenth-century Portuguese-built, Dutch-occupied star-shaped Jaffna Fort, the focus of Dutch and European Union–aided resurrection, hinted at the town's approaching reincarnation under the World Bank's Strategic Cities Development Project and Indian government investment. Various prominent Hindu sites of worship, including the Nallur and Maviddapuram Kandaswamy Temples and the Keerimalai Naguleswaram Temple were rejuvenated with golden accents and brighter hued coats of paint. Kandarodai, modified by the state into a "Buddhist archaeological site," was intentionally inscribed with a Sinhalese name as the Kadurugoda Purana Vihara (Kadurugoda Ancient Temple), along with Jambukolapattinam (Dambakolapatuna) and Nainativu (Nagadeepa) which were incorporated into the military-administered postwar heritage regime. These were central to the tourist whistle-stop tour, as they were to bitter local reproach directed at the insistent government-sponsored "Sinhalization" of the northeast.

An archipelago extends beyond the Jaffna peninsula, including two of the islands famously named and shaped by Dutch colonists—Kayts (Urkavarturai) and Delft (Neduntivu)—and Mandaitivu, Punkudutivu, Nainativu, Analaitivu, Eluvaitivu, and Karainagar, among others. Neduntivu, known for its colonial miscellanies, including a wild pony population, coral-made architectural remains, and a baobab tree, is, like Nainativu, linked to the mainland by a navy-run boat service. The presence of the military, seamless in parts, jarring in others, and no less disconcerting in either iteration, was laced into the landscape of Jaffna and the wider Northern Province. Everyday life on the peninsula and the Vanni was irrevocably shaped by war and ubiquitous militarization, as it has been for many decades by varying occupants, including the Sri Lankan armed forces, the LTTE, and the Indian Peace Keeping Force (IPKF). The military pervaded the northeast in greater concentration than anywhere else on the island, conjuring for most residents dogged feelings of fear and misgiving. The military also occupied extensive swaths of state and private land, aside from its seeping involvement in civilian administration, development, agriculture, school education, religious activities, and profit-oriented tourism and commercial ventures. These included camps, operational bases, checkpoints, and designated High Security Zones (HSZ). The presence of the armed forces, hence, persisted as one of the primary causes of continued internal displacement. This was also the source of significant local political unrest in the form of civilian protests against Army-led land grabs. Relics of the war, too, stubbornly lingered. Crumbling houses, pocked by ball bearings, were long since deserted. The snarl of a tiger stenciled onto the side of a shop had been hastily painted over. The lone elderly with no family left to care for them gathered at temples. Prabhakaran's Vaddukoddai family home was flattened to the ground but still watched by soldiers on field bikes who patrolled residential neighborhoods for illicit acts of loyalty by supporters.

"People were collecting rubble from the site," Deepan, a Jaffna-based photographer recalled. "It wasn't just Tamil people—it was Sinhalese people. Even when the LTTE bunkers were open in the Vanni, I saw people secretly pocketing sand and stones," he remembered. The afterlives of such politically charged material detritus of war was a significant preoccupation in the political mobilization of photography (chapter 6). Immediately after the end of the war, the Sri Lankan state engaged in the strategic preservation of certain LTTE-associated sites to supplement its "official ways of remembering the war" (Hyndman and Amarasingham 2014, 564). Transient "museums" at places like Prabhakaran's bunker that utilized photographic displays of LTTE child soldiers holding weapons captioned as "Fate of Tamil Civilians" juxtaposed against a series of photos of Prabhakaran and his family captioned "LTTE leader's luxurious family life" were subsequently destroyed in a controlled explosion in 2013 (Hyndman and Amarasingham 2014, 564). Northern Sri Lanka became recast and strategically and spectacularly preserved and destroyed to satiate Sinhalese imaginaries of post/war. As Haidy Geismar describes, such instances of state-sponsored "heritage" initiatives demonstrated a "tangle of ideology and expectation," expressing materially "the power dynamics involved in the selective recognition of identity" (2015, 72). For my interlocutors, this amounted to the hostile "Sinhalization" of the Tamil landscape and "cultural genocide."

"We go to Jaffna to see something different, to see the way things used to be. The culture, the people—it's a very special place," I was told by Chathurika, a Sinhalese tourist from Colombo who regularly visited Jaffna "to see the sights and experience the culture" since the A9 highway opened after the war ended. She spoke of Jaffna, rendered unreachable for so long, as if the peninsula emerged from across space and time, not at the end of a six-hour train journey from the capital. "I even heard that there are Chinese restaurants opening now! I pray it won't become spoiled," she remarked wistfully at its many recent transformations, as if the end of the war had marked a return to a time capsule of the past rather than an insecure present (fig. 3). For tourists like Chathurika, who had not known a north before war, the armed forces existed to protect. They enabled the chance of making a "safe" trip by rendering the north less dangerous and a subject of praise and admiration echoing the state-amplified language of *rana viruvo* (war heroes). For resident Tamils, the inescapable presence of the armed forces was a hazard, embodying the ever-present unsafety and threat of violence against them.

But of course, "those days" and the "way things used to be" are for the most part no more these days. They perhaps never were. In a time when personal cameras were a little-known luxury, photos conveying the oft-

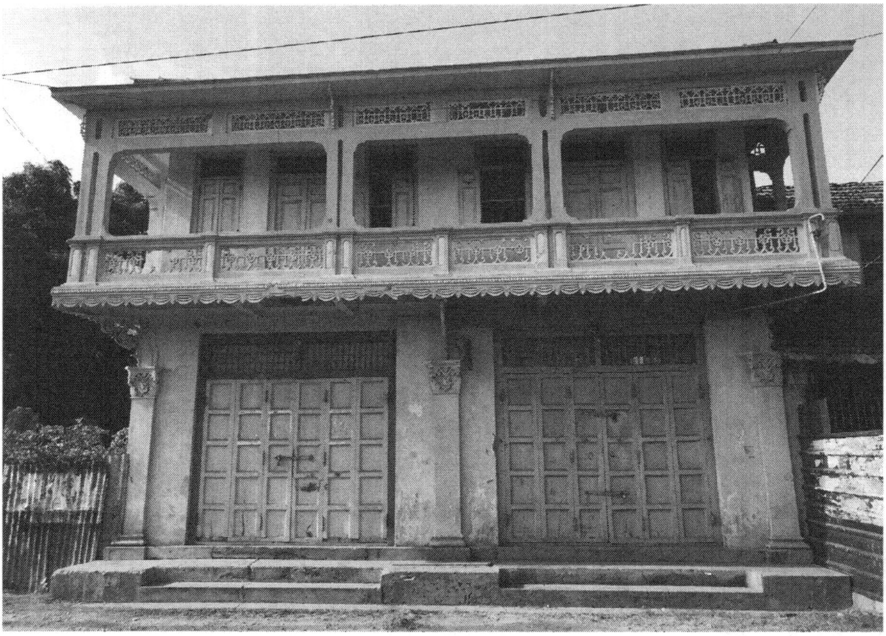

FIGURE 3. A Jaffna shop house (Jaffna, 2018)

extolled splendors of Jaffna were absent from these narratives and interwoven imaginaries. A dreamy 1970s image of a woman emerging out of an arch at the Portuguese-built Hammenhiel Fort in Kayts captured by Colombo-based photographer Nihal Fernando illustrates the mirage-like mood that Jaffna continues to conjure to those outside. As place, people, and entangled aspirations for self-determination and nation, the kaleidoscopic make-believes of Jaffna endured in competing historical, cultural, and political imaginations. Their photographies are equally lively.

In 2018, when the Amparai and Kandy anti-Muslim riots broke out, I was spending the afternoon at Baby Studio. Rajaratnam *mama*'s friends, a little gathering of elderly men from the neighborhood, stopped by daily for chats over cups of tea as the studio wound down for the day. A state of emergency had been declared by the government and even in Jaffna the streets were thicker than usual with soldiers.

"We don't know whether it will spread here as well. We can only hope it won't be us again," someone wondered out loud, and the other murmured agreement. Feelings of precarity bound to ethnic identity remained a constant topic of conversation.

It was a brief window of relative freedom and possibility that opened between 2015 and 2019 that unequivocally made this book possible. The window was subsequently shuttered as an old silence, coerced and self-imposed, befell Sri Lanka through the failed presidency of Gotabaya Rajapaksa, the Covid-19 pandemic, and the 2022 economic crisis (Buthpitiya 2022b, 2022d). As of 2024, the unyielding state is now helmed by the new faces of the National People Power (NPP) Coalition led by the Janatha Vimukthi Peramuna (JVP), which twice failed to seize power (Buthpitiya 2024). The new government continues to sanguinely posture toward "a thriving nation (and) a beautiful life" (NPP 2024).

SO, YOU ARE LIKE MARK?

It was by complete chance that I encountered the name of A. Mark, or Mark Master (1933–2000), as he was known, one of the most prominent Tamil modernist painters. Though well known among the artistic community in Jaffna, the painter's work and legacy were unknown in the largely Colombo-centric canon defined by the vision and oeuvre of the '43 Group. Mr. Jesurasa was the keeper of Mark's remaining works, comprising over a hundred drawings made on and with whatever materials he could find during the war years and his displacement. Portraying the brutality of the war, they ranged from soft pastel sketches on sugar paper to ballpoint pen drawings on cheap Chinese magazine pages. Mr. Jesurasa generously gave of his time to bring out the dusty works from his shed where he had for many years stored them away. The evolution of Mark's work in response to the horrors he had begun to encounter is immediately apparent, transforming from cubist-inspired works that echoed that of the '43 Group's George Keyt to grim depictions of violence that are variously reminiscent of Picasso's *Guernica* or Francis Bacon's writhing anthropomorphic forms. Mr. Jesurasa recalled his own encounter with Mark, a great improviser, during his displacement, when he found him making art in a small hut that he had erected. "There also he was giving free art classes and making some sculptures with *kambi* [wire]."

In an earlier conversation, Mr. Jesurasa, a seventy-something Tamil Catholic, inevitably asked me *what* I was. When conducting fieldwork in Colombo, Jaffna, and London, a question I had habitually encountered during the course of my life in Sri Lanka, became more frequent and insistent. "*What* are you?" I was constantly asked, if not immediately offered imaginative assumptions of my ethnicity and/or nationality predicated on an arcane logic and alignment of appearance, language, dress, and mannerism that eluded me. My Sri Lankan passport was found to be regularly disappointing, as if I had failed as a neither here nor there migrant. I briefly explained my ethnic background as had become practice in all my research encounters in response to perplexed or curious interlocutors.

"So, you are like Mark," he concluded with a characteristic chuckle. "Few people know this, but Mark's father was Sinhalese." One of the most noteworthy Tamil painters in Jaffna was, "like me," half Sinhalese.

"He was about twelve years then and from Matara or somewhere. He had some quarrel with his family, and he came alone to Jaffna. Then he came to our village. Somebody told him—you can stay with us. He was a small boy, no?" Mr. Jesurasa recounted. "From then, he went into fishing. When he grew older, he found his mother and for some time, he had family from Matara visit, but they lost contact. Those days there were a few families like that because of the bakeries. There were no Tamil bakeries. The Sinhalese ran the bakeries. They are efficient people and knew how to make money. They can speak Tamil and brought their families. There was a Sinhala Maha Vidyalam [national school] so that they could study. There is an army camp on Hospital Road? That was the Sinhala Maha Vidyalam. There were some intermarriages—obviously it will happen, no? After '77, less [*sic*] people were there and after '83—fully gone. They refused to go, and they believed no trouble would come to them, but for political purposes the higher-ups and the army forcefully sent them to the south. They made up false stories also, no? That Sinhalese were being cut up into pieces and being put on ice and sent through trains. The Sinhala politicians and media are always vomiting racial issues."

Showing promise in the arts, Mark went on to study at the Technical College in Colombo. Mark's legacy lives on in various students that he has trained and in the drawings that have been preserved by Mr. Jesurasa, an extraordinary keeper of diminishing local histories in a collection spanning art, film, books, and pamphlets that he keeps locked in the front room of the cheerful yellow house he shares with his wife. A writer, poet, and film critic, Mr. Jesurasa channeled his obsession with cinema into founding the Yal Thiraippada Vattam (Jaffna Film Circle) in 1979, arranging for noted films of renowned international auteurs to be shown in Jaffna. With the advent of the war in 1983, the Film Circle's activities ceased. Mr. Jesurasa has since found renewed access to film on the internet and a collection of DVDs, hosting monthly screenings for enthusiasts. He remains a repository of knowledge about Mark Master's life and career—its various remains from art to a smattering of leaflets tucked away in his front room. Mark's work was even noted and celebrated by the Tigers, he revealed. They had once invited him to display his work in a large exhibition to showcase the nation.

Mr. Jesurasa's anecdotes about Mark offer an important insight into the constructions and tangles of ethnicity in Sri Lanka and how their boundaries and political formations transformed during the war. In many ways, I took my own "mixed background" for granted, each identity near-seamlessly stitched to the other within the cosseted space of my household with no demands to identify and enculturate either way. However, the war and heightened securitization magnified the state-determined differences between me and my immediate family members.

The war defined the first twenty-two years of my life. Even within the relative safety of the capital, Colombo, where I was born and raised, the war lurked doggedly. Sometimes, it was no more than a distant rumble in a vague northeast that few in my generation who had grown up in the south had encountered outside the blood and smoke phantasmagoria of words and pictures in the news. At other times, the war revealed itself to us in sudden and malicious ways, often in the guise of LTTE suicide attacks and bombings that plagued the city. In a time before mobile phones, this meant hours of waiting to hear back from loved ones who could not be traced or were stranded in the midst of chaos with no means of contact. Roundups, abductions, enforced disappearances, arbitrary detention, and extrajudicial killings became so routine that new terrors became sutured into the city that evoked Jeganathan's observations on Tamilness and the constant anticipation of violence in southern Sri Lanka (2000). These events, along with many others that came before and after, making up the countless devastations of the civil war, changed, irretrievably, our relationship to Colombo, the island, and to one another in what is variously described as an ethnic conflict, insurgency, armed resistance, liberation struggle, and civil war.

It seems astounding to me now, seventeen years since the armed conflict ended, that we had spent so much of our childhoods preparing for death. In telephone calls, we were taught to expect news of loved ones who had been at the wrong place at the wrong time. There existed continual panic and worry in a family member's unexplained delay or silence, in the "near-miss" stories that were recounted with relish and disquiet at every social gathering. Proximity to almost-certain-death recounted in minutes and sometimes even the distance between traffic lights were animatedly discussed. Children at birthday parties conspiratorially whispered the devious threats of "two-legged Tigers" with bombs strapped to their bellies looking to target Sinhalese schools. The frantic clangor of the school bell announced pretend bombs so that we might rehearse shielding ourselves by swooping under desks with our hands pressed against our ears and noses flattened against the cement. School closed for months; learning was compressed into photocopied "study packs" because the regulation see-through school bags that were diligently checked at a security desk each morning and regularly practiced emergency drills could no longer guarantee safety. These circumstances, however fraught, were still reserved to those of us who count ourselves among the exceptionally fortunate. My family members, friends, and my interlocutors were not.

It is in such a setting that I, broadly Indian-Origin Tamil on my mother's side and Kandyan Sinhalese on my father's side, was socialized, culturally and politically, among my English- and Tamil-speaking maternal family that prayed to a heterodox Hindu-Buddhist-Catholic pantheon in line with various individual spiritual inheritances and choices. This upbringing made me opportunely trilingual and reasonably aware of and practiced in specific cultural and religious pursuits. Within the context of field research, these allowed me to move and be perceived among identity boundaries that after decades of conflict were long hardened, and at least on the surface, separated and sometimes rendered hostile. This background also made me intimately aware of how my last name, written out solely in curlicue Sinhalese on my National Identity Card (NIC), removed my experiences as Sri Lankan from my family and my interlocutors. Their names scribbled bilingually in Sinhalese and Tamil defined their relationship to Sri Lanka and the Sri Lankan state as one of "second-class" citizenship.

I became viscerally aware of the life-or-death optics of ethnic identity as shaped and expected by the state—what it would mean to appear Tamil or Sinhalese in a city (and by extension country) riddled with checkpoints hostile to the other. "Not all Tamils are Tigers, but all Tigers are Tamil," we were constantly reminded, as identity documents were repetitively scrutinized at the dozens of checkpoints that punctuated the island's tangle of roads. Constructed of metal barriers, steel barrels, and sandbags painted yellow and green in approximations of military camouflage, AK-47-carrying army men in olive camouflage inspected faces and identity documents. The bearer of a Tamil face signaled by skin color or wearing *pottu* or *vibhuti*, dress, or identity card was easily and often swiftly subject to longer checks, waiting, and not unusually routine harassment in the form of taunting, threats, or arbitrary detention.[6] During nighttime raids carried out in Tamil neighborhoods in the capital and in the northeast of the island, faces and identity cards of Tamil citizens were matched with compulsory and frequently updated police registration documents listing who was resident in a household at any given time.[7] Verbal and physical harassment and abuse coupled with recurrent roundups of Tamils and torture while in police or military custody became disturbingly frequent. Routine abductions and arbitrary detention by state-sponsored paramilitary groups and intelligence operatives were commonplace. An insidious underbelly of extortion and "ransom rings" targeting Tamils operated with the assumed involvement of state officials and security personnel and complete impunity. Financial "contributions" were strong-armed by state political actors as well as the LTTE.

The relationship of Tamil members of my household and my extended family and friends in Colombo to the state and the wider Sinhalese majority fluctuated between a distinct sense of unbelonging, mistrust, weary resignation, and a desire to conform to expectations of how a "good" minority citizen must speak and act. Most overwhelmingly it was a fear of repercussions for "being Tamil," be it in the ways they announced or silenced themselves in speech or dress, and navigated Sri Lanka's social, cultural, political, and economic landscape. Fluent Sinhalese, class and caste privilege, and their effortless brandishing of the English language, our primary tongue fostered by private education in old colonial Christian missionary schools, smoothed and glossed over the many inconveniences and harassments their ethnic counterparts were subject to. Their Tamilness, however, was never completely overlooked or erased. These were all observations that were explicitly and repeatedly made by my Tamil interlocutors in Colombo and Jaffna.

"Tamil" was an identity that was ascribed to my mother's migrant family by the state, when they acquired citizenship in what was then Ceylon in 1953, after a long association with the island marked by employment, marriage, and children and circular migration between South India and Colombo. This was common practice among Indians who had found their way to Colombo in the twentieth century under the auspices of the Empire. Ceylon's Indian-Origin communities, constituting about

11 percent of the population of the newly independent nation, were collectively disenfranchised. The most susceptible among this diverse group were those brought to the island as indentured labor to build the island's roads and railways and carve out and toil on its tea plantations (see Jegathesan 2019). Following independence from Britain in 1948, they faced forced repatriation to India and protracted statelessness. The details of my family's cosmopolitan Indian heritage, which now only remains in its oral history, was distilled to an identifiable "Tamil," based on the common language that they spoke. Their "Tamilness" acquired various intonations and contradictions in the registration of births and marriages, morphing variously into "Indian Tamil," "Sri Lankan Tamil," and even in one instance "Sinhalese" by inscrutable bureaucratic logic and authority of assimilation. This was a phenomenon that I later learned was surprisingly common among "numerically small" minority communities.

Tamil identity on the island has not been static, and nor can it be confined to or defined by a geographic demarcation centered on a vocal political demand that has for many decades been made to appear universal and homogeneous. I have chosen to use the term *Ilankai Tamil* or "Lankan Tamils/Tamils of Lanka" in this book to emphasize the multifacetedness of Tamil identity on the island, transcending, including, and spanning across language, dialects, region, geographic origin, and convenient categorical markers of ethnicity and political identities that seek to dilute a social, cultural, and political history that is as rich as it is complex. Further, *Ilankai*, referring to a Tamil name for Lanka, respectfully accommodates the diversity of opinions on political identity, belonging, and nationhood among my northern Tamil interlocutors, those who identified with or vehemently opposed various extant categorizations and identifiers (Tamil, Sri Lankan Tamil, Lankan Tamil, Ceylon Tamil, Jaffna Tamil, Indian-Origin Tamil, Eelam Tamil, Malaiyaha or Hill Country Tamil, Colombo Tamil, Batticaloa Tamil, etc.) and others who vehemently opposed one or more of these.[8]

WRITING THE ANTHROPOLOGIST, WRITING HOME

My "multiple subjectivities" as "native anthropologist" were unexpectedly and constantly interrogated by my interlocutors (Mookherjee 2015, 17). Kirin Narayan observes that "to acknowledge particular and personal locations is to admit the limits of one's purview from these positions. It is also to undermine the notion of objectivity, because from particular locations all understanding becomes subjectively based and forged through interactions within fields of power" (1993, 679). My age, race, ethnicity, caste, gender, marital status, social class, citizenship, and other such privileges, identities, inequalities, and hierarchies wholly determined access and informed the formation and sustenance of those relationships as I was viewed as someone who could (and should) be located within a set of preexisting social and political relationships, prior to and indeed above my interlocutors' acknowledgment of my role as anthropologist.

The reality that I too was as shaped by a shared ethnopolitical and social context was surprisingly significant to those I interacted with. While this positionality was occasionally difficult to navigate, particularly as an unmarried young woman subject to the "moral" codes and expectations of Tamil society in a manner that limited my mobility, it also afforded important ethnographic possibilities. Our shared language and my untidy ethnic identity became a surprising mode of connection and solidarity rather than dismissal. Within activist spaces, I bore the sheen of a previous career in policy, expatriation, Western academia, as someone with an audience beyond, who could serve as a sympathetic conduit for what had for so long fallen on disinclined ears. I was told both because I knew and had the capacity to repeat and be "taken seriously." As has been detailed by Sharika Thiranagama in relation to her own fieldwork experience in Jaffna, there was a tacit acknowledgment of "understanding" that "put you in possession of the same secret alongside them," suggesting "that only other Tamils could understand the predicament that all found themselves in" ([2011] 2013, 26–27). This related to criticism of the state and LTTE, given how the group's surveillance and power had operated through a pervasive system of conscription and intelligence networks. Even today, disapproval of the group is often hushed. Support for the government and censure of the militancy were also common, indicating a plurality of views that have too often been subsumed in essentialist narratives bolstering the political claims of the state and proponents of the LTTE. The photographies of this book complicate such dogmatic framings of the conflict, belonging, and the Tamil political imagination.

The scholarship on the Sri Lankan war has also been marked by tensions of stances as it pertained to the LTTE and the wider Tamil nationalist struggle, often irrespective of the scholar's insiderness or outsiderness. Researchers have either explicitly or implicitly felt compelled to "pick sides" in a deeply complex and emotional issue that speaks to a broader moral-political question of the ethics of and right to self-determination.[9] Sri Lankan scholars' engagement with subjects relating to the conflict involves substantial political risk, given aggressive state erasure of the histories of war and tensions of the postwar glossed over with claims of "postwar development" and "reconciliation." Academics and civil society activists who speak out about the grievances of and injustices faced by minorities or state oppression were frequently branded and/or discredited as "Tiger/Terrorist sympathizers," "propaganda agents," "ideological saboteurs," and "traitors," which within a politically repressive environment could easily escalate to a matter of survival or death. Similarly, criticisms of the LTTE remained a challenging subject, given the ardent continued support for the group among a vocal portion of the Tamil diaspora whose own acts of intimidation and silencing opposition and criticism persist. Those critical of the militancy were deemed traitors and viewed as collaborators of the Sinhalese state (Thiranagama 2010). Even in London, far removed from the restrictions on expression one encountered in Sri Lanka, those who spoke reproachfully of the LTTE lowered their voices to a whisper. Offline and online, narratives, histories, and spaces of protest were reliably co-opted by exponents of the group. Navigating these competing ideologies would take a significant toll on my own safety and space for political expression as a citizen and an academic in ways that I could not have foreseen.

So, it is important to emphasize here that condemnation of the Tigers does not and should not detract from the Sri Lankan state's egregious crimes against its citizens. Similarly, recognizing the motivations of armed resistance in the face of decades of violence experienced by Ilankai Tamils does not equate to empathizing with terrorism, endorsing odious acts of violence, or disloyalty to country. Demands for liberation and self-determination must also not be viewed as solely the exertion and purview of the LTTE or resolved by the establishment of a rival ethno-state, just as truth, justice, and accountability should not be contingent on ethnonationalist or statist allegiances.

To write about Sri Lanka is an ongoing process of deciphering my home that has been in seemingly interminable turmoil. It is where I was born in perhaps one of its most turbulent years in recent memory, amid civil war, insurrection, and violent occupation by the IPKF (ITJP 2025). I have spent most of my life against the volatile picture that makes up this book. I am bound to the island by my loved ones, the houses I grew up in, the roads I traveled daily, the schools I went to, the spaces I cut my teeth in as an international development worker long before I found my way back to the academy, and ultimately the sentencing of citizenship. These words also encompass the long labor of tending to an open homewound, just as my interlocutors are.

Undertaking this work has been driven and complicated by a sense of responsibility intertwined with what feels like a perpetual calculation and gamble of risk and danger, in a context where a perpetrator state has for years fattened itself on the violently shortened lives of critics, subversives, and dissidents. I do not presume to be an activist or as courageous as those who have given of their well-being, life, and futures to call attention to the truth. However, I take up this space to underscore the significance of the epistemic bearing and challenges of producing this work—of making sense and being made sense of as the "native anthropologist" subject of a punishing state. There can be no boundaries between my home and field and life and work and scholarship, even though my discipline has been historically built on the frontiers between us and them and home and field. This research emerged out of and was made possible by a community, politics, and engagement that long preceded my incarnation as scholar. Within an ethnicized and gendered context of hotly contested facts, figures, identities, and ethnonationalist allegiances, this ethnographic knowledge is also then inevitably rendered political and partial in its intent, receipt, and/or assimilation and appropriation. This chapter is a critical acknowledgment of this fact, not merely as it relates to me but everyone whose words and sentiments follow. It is an interrogation of treachery where social and moral commitments of solidarity and care stand at perilous odds with the peace proclamations of the state.

Writing on the back of "Black July" to think through what he terms "ethnic fratricide," Tamil anthropologist Stanley J. Tambiah reflects on what it is to be "'phenomenologically' involved" where his examination of the ethnic conflicts is determined by lived experience as much as scholarly pursuit (1986, ix). To be "phenomenologically involved" in the researching, writing, and living of this book enables the necessary clarity with which I state that this work will always be political. Christina Sharpe asks, "How can one presume, still, that there is an 'us' and a 'we' that are in something together? This register assumes that 'we' are all in the world in the same way, that we experience suffering on the same plain, that we can be 'repaired' in the same way, that the structures, the architectures of violence and of affect, reach us in the same ways" (2023, 33). I find resolve in these words. A scholarly "we" cannot and must not exist, if anything, in the service of the integrity of the knowledge we claim to produce. We do not arrive at knowledge in the same way, nor does what we regard as knowledge look the same. Attempting to exist within a discipline that has for so long studied communities like mine categorically reinforcing the hard, fractious boundaries of ethnicity is foundational to this deliberation. Middle-ground affectations of objective social scientific inquiry are not luxuries that I as an anthropologist from and of Sri Lanka or my interlocutors can embrace in a setting of continued threat, urgency, and increasingly precarious facts of recent history in the face of forceful state-led erasure. It is a task of grappling with incompleteness and loss. Faced by the violence of the early 1980s, E. Valentine Daniel, another Tamil anthropologist, asks how we as anthropologists can adequately put into words the kinds of violence we encounter in the places we work, which also happen to be our home countries where violence was not a matter of the past, but the present and ever possible in fickle and relentless ways (1996). With this, I continue to reckon with hope and anticipation just as my interlocutors do.

The work of anthropologists has also been central to documentation and witness in issues pertaining to Sri Lanka's conflicts. For instance, Patricia Lawrence, who carried out her doctoral fieldwork in Batticaloa, was able to provide crucial details of ethnographic depth surrounding the Sathurukondan Massacre (in which 184 unarmed Tamil civilians including 47 children under the age of ten were mass-murdered by army personnel) to the 1994 Commission of Inquiry into the Involuntary Removal or Disappearance of Persons in the Northern and Eastern Provinces (of Sri Lanka) (Jeganathan 2010, 11). Decades later, like Daniel, "In opening up my tape recorder and notebook to my informants, I took upon myself the responsibility of telling a wider world story that they had told me, some at grave risk to their lives, only because they believed there was a wider world that cared about the difference between good and evil" (1996, 5). Where resistance and peace are romanticized and theorization orders abstraction, it is essential to confront the grit and devastation of political violence and colonially designed governance. Within such a context, knowledge is precarious. Those whose narratives and life histories inform this book continue to negotiate the ubiquitous violences of the postwar tethered to their ethnic identity, geography, and interlinked impairments of citizenship. The obligation and accountability I feel toward my interlocutors who have shared so much of their lives with confidence and generosity in hope that this work might afford some "visibility" to their plight is immense. Where I focus on the theoretical, methodological, and ethnographic entanglements of war and photography, "visibility" is invariably a dominant theme. Photography allows precarious citizens to make themselves visible to the state and commit "betrayals" that reveal the political agency of risk-taking centered on a tense relationship of seeing and being seen, surveillance and witnessing.

I hope this book, if anything, is an amplification of the words, hopes, fears, uncertainties, and anticipations of those who have spoken with me over many years from asking about why these minutiae of everyday picture-taking might matter as the subject of academic inquiry as well as those who wish for the world beyond their own to know the cruel injustices and suffering they have endured.

2 THE JAFFNA STUDIO

THE SMILE OF GOD

In 2018, Baby Studio's second incarnation occupied a small, low-ceilinged house that had once been intended as a home.

The front hall had been transformed into an office and reception area, while the large interior studio space was set up with lighting equipment and a rotation of plain-colored cloth backdrops. These were used for making the steady stream of identity portraits that were produced daily by Baby's young apprentices. Two young women attended to the in-house photography, while two young men undertook more elaborate outdoor shoots. The walls were adorned with digitally printed reproductions of what was left of the photographer's archive: various sample images from the studio's portfolio, nearly a hundred images of (eponymous) babies (modeled by Rajaratnam *mama*'s three children), and photographs of various local holy men and temples. A carefully composed display of framed family portraits, including a painting of *mama*'s late parents and photos of his children and grandchildren, welcomes patrons into the studio room. It is scattered with remains from Baby's analog days, including a few boxes of film on an arrangement of wooden shelves and a disused spray-painted backdrop depicting a flowery trellis that has been repurposed as a tablecloth. The dressing room at the back of the studio featured a long mirror and various helpful accoutrements, including plastic combs and talcum powder, along with an assortment of men's clothing, including "tie coats" (suit jackets and ties) that clients might borrow for their shoots.

"I named this Baby Studio because photographing babies is what brings me the most joy. The smile of a baby is like the smile of God. The smile of a baby is a true smile, it can move you," Rajaratnam *mama* explained.[1]

In the front office, a framed government certificate for registration of the studio, which permitted Baby Studio to submit digital passport photographs to the Department of Immigration and Emigration, hangs in a place of prominence. Next to it was a 1973 letter of commendation penned by Nicholas, the proprietor of Sellam's Studio where Rajaratnam *mama* apprenticed for many years. These suggested two kinds of anointments of the studio's photographic trade—as ancillary to the state but also as part of a lineage tethering Baby to Jaffna's photographic history formed through practices of apprenticeship. Flex prints of Rajaratnam *mama*'s black-and-white street photography from the 1970s assembled into digitally saturated montages decorated the outer walls, the old house itself resembling a stationary magic lantern offering glimpses of Jaffna that had long since disappeared. In recent years, his practice had transformed to diligently directing and overseeing the work of his trainees, who wielded the magic of digital cameras and a computer editing suite tucked into a corner of the reception room.

A tall glass cabinet afforded prominence in the middle of the foyer held what little remained of a collection of film cameras and other photographic ephemera (fig. 4). The old Mamiyas and Rolleiflexes and the newer Canon film models were now all obsolete as the last of the color labs processing film in the island had shuttered some years ago. Displayed among these were photographs of Rajaratnam *mama*'s children and grandchildren sent to him from London and Geneva where they lived—he had never been, but they visited when they could. Interspersed were little implements of photographic technologies past: delicate, wispy brushes and glass bottles of translucent paints. Artist-photographers used these for *touching* (re-touching) work to improve the appearance of negatives and photographs, whereby black-and-white images were tinctured into color and sitters' bodies were adorned with painted finery and jewels, reminding of the artisanal skills and labors required of studio practitioners before the arrival of digital photography. Strewn among the antiquated ephemera were religious icons; a little blue and white plaster Virgin Mary standing beneath a glass umbrella; a four-armed Lilliputian Durga (goddess of protection) sitting on a snarling lion encased in a plastic cube holding weapons of destruction and creation in her eight hands.

Rajaratnam *mama* was a devout Hindu, but placed on his cabinet was a vivid, harmonious pantheon of deities evoking a vision of cosmic coexistence. A dapper indigo-faced, hand-on-hip Krishna (god of compassion and love), a golden meditating Buddha, a serene Anthony of Padua (Catholic patron saint for the recovery of lost items) cradling a pink baby Jesus and an open Bible, and a miniature metal elephant-headed Ganesh (god of wisdom and remover of obstacles) sat above the treasures of *mama*'s cabinet of photographic apparatus and curiosities. Saint Anthony, venerated widely across Sri Lanka, spoke perhaps to innumerable losses that stitched together the

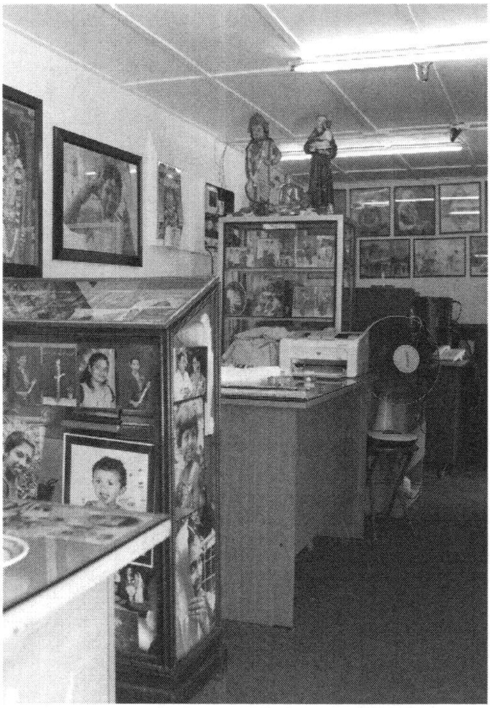

FIGURE 4. The Baby Studio cabinet and resident gods (Jaffna, 2018)

island's communities. Each morning, flowers and incense were placed at the plaster feet of the deities and saints. Even though a decades-long ethnic conflict and fear, suspicion, distaste, and sometimes even outright hatred persisted, the harmonious pantheon remains a striking but common feature of everyday image worlds in places of worship and homes as a talisman of protection and perhaps hope.[2]

Though he no longer took photographs, Rajaratnam *mama* rode his scooter to the studio early each morning to greet his patrons and oversee the work of his young apprentices. He inspected each image printed by the mini-Epson photo printer before they were placed in envelopes for clients, a regular stream of people who were usually seeking out various kinds of identity photographs. Until these were collected, they were housed in a second glass cabinet adorned with portraits the studio has produced in the recent past, alongside sample wedding albums for clients who might be interested in booking their services. At teatime in the morning and afternoon, his friends, older men from the neighborhood, stopped by for a cup of tea and a chat. They talked about the local news, national politics, and on occasion reminisced about the past. Rajaratnam *mama* oversaw the studio from a desk that was flanked by a life-sized painted portrait made with reference to an old photograph of Kodai Sami, an umbrella-carrying Jaffna saint that he worships. Another statue of Kodai Sami was placed on a high shelf next to his desk, along with a blue-and-white statue of the Virgin Mary. Rajaratnam *mama* also kept a box of little photo prints of Kodai Sami within reach of his desk, which he occasionally gifted to patrons as he saw fit. Kodai Sami in these little prints was a hybrid photo-painting: a photo turned into a painting turned into a photo that has been photoshopped into a final composite of Kodai Sami set against a backdrop of a river and some colorful ducks that could not possibly have been native to Jaffna. This layered image evoked aspects of Rajaratnam *mama*'s studio practice, but also the transformations taking place within Jaffna's photography studios in surprisingly resonant ways.

Of Rajaratnam *mama*'s personal archive from a career spanning six decades, all that remained was an assortment of a hundred-odd photographs featuring landscape and street scenes from Jaffna before and during the conflict. These included several black-and-white portraits he had taken from the 1970s onward and a small lot of colored prints from the '90s and the early 2000s documenting the changing surroundings. The studio's surviving catalog was kept in three small plastic bags that studios used to return prints and film negatives to their customers. There was no obvious sequence to these photographs that unevenly narrated erstwhile presences now forgotten by or unknown to most—a landscape, people, way of life and later, glimpses of a war enmeshed in the everyday. Visual residues of Rajaratnam *mama*'s own life history were scattered among these. A handful of black-and-white graduation portraits of young women who had completed university were placed in a bag with other leftovers, including uncollected passport photos, various personal photographs of friends who had stopped by the studio and those who had worked there. Several baby photos documenting the lives of *mama*'s own children who had left to Vavuniya, Switzerland, and the United Kingdom demonstrated the studio's artistry, in exposure techniques as well as presentation—cut with scissors into decorative medallion-like forms (fig. 5).

In a setting where many studios and photographers had become casualties of war, such accounts of photography's vibrant social history and visual-material remains were splintered across threadbare "archives" pared by war and displacement. Fragments remained mostly in individual memories, as

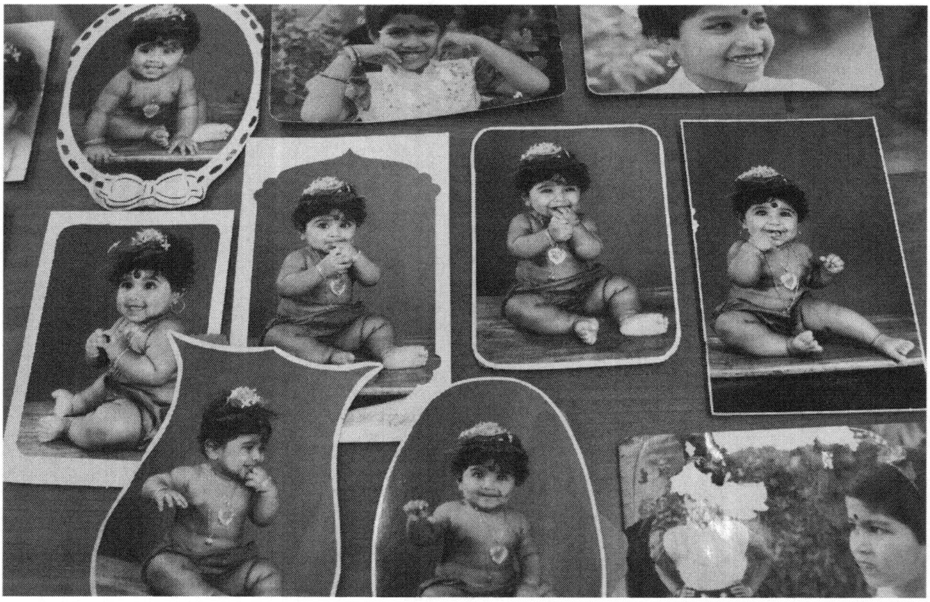

FIGURE 5. Rajaratnam *mama*'s children as the eponymous babies of Baby Studio (Jaffna, 2018)

was the case with N. Rajaratnam, the proprietor of Baby Photo, the focus of this chapter. I outline a concise history of photography in the peninsula as was narrated by a handful of local studio photographers, to establish the lasting importance of photography studios to the social world of Jaffna. This chapter also locates this remembered history in relation to the documented history of Sri Lankan photography and the optimism and dilemma of the "national." It recognizes, importantly, the perceived potency of photography and its long association with northern Sri Lanka where Tamil photographers have served as arbiters of this potency through their immense technical and aesthetic contributions, which are rarely acknowledged.

AN ISLAND PARTLY PHOTOGRAPHED / PHOTOGRAPHY PARTLY STORIED

The sparse chronicle of Ceylonese photography is chiefly focused on colonial practitioners in towns such as Colombo or Kandy, which were forged and consolidated by post/colonial (colonial and postcolonial) governance structures, cultural and religious production, and commerce. Moreover, a postcolonial account of Ceylonese/Sri Lankan photography is effectively non-existent. I seek to cursorily situate this remembered peninsular history within that of the wider Sri Lankan context that largely, if not entirely, privileged urban elite practitioners. This is an essential intervention in remedying the effects of war and Sinhalese ethnonationalism, which has largely overlooked and excluded the history and present of northern Tamil photography.

Plotted along colonially determined hierarchies and traditions of making, the aesthetics and creative pursuits of the island's elites and non-elites remain starkly differentiated. The preservation of these histories and their inclusion in "national" narratives are also sharply ethnicized, with the vast contributions and technical innovations of Tamil photographers absented or overlooked. It is also a historiographic marginalization of the rich empirical promise afforded by the visual in the study of Sri Lanka, where the country has been recurrently framed in the scholarship through the tumultuous political economy of conflict. I also emphasize here the transnational character of the development of photography and the pioneering work undertaken by early local practitioners in Jaffna that complicate views of photography as a colonial burden in a concern that carries through to how conflict photography is theorized. This oral history of photography in Jaffna is rapidly diminishing from living memory, deepened by the effects of war and displacement. The lack of preservation echoes how certain versions and their documentation have been privileged by and in "Sri Lankan" history-writing, archival practices, and nation/state building projects as well as the existing scholarship. Consequently, even historical images become part of a narrative of war. Their volatility sees them mobilized to resist cultural loss, compelled erasure, and the destruction of history. As these move through space and time, they become stripped of the lineages of their making. This chapter is presented as a minor remedy.

For elder studio photographers like Rajaratnam *mama*, Jaffna was irrefutably *Ilankayilaye first!* (First in Lanka!), the birthplace of photography in the island. Their lineage of learning, the skills passed on from one photographer to the next, harked back to the earliest practitioners who acquired their craft from American missionaries in the mid-nineteenth century. It felt necessary to record these stories that were only barely in living memory, as digital photographic technologies expanded studio and commercial practice in extraordinary ways that were no longer necessarily bound to periods of learning and apprenticeship. Karen Strassler observes that "a global technology introduced under colonial conditions and tied to transnational flows of people, capital, industry, and media, photography continues to bring people into contact with imaginings and circuits that necessarily transcend and often undermine the strictly national frame" (2010, 13). Similarly, the histories of Jaffna's photographic practice, though frequently relegated to an imperial imposition, affirmed the transnational quality of not only photographic production, but the development of knowledge and technologies of photography. This keen adoption of and enthusiasm for image-making by studios, amateur practitioners, and the Tamil militancy would significantly inform the imagining and production of Tamil nationhood and was integral to state-building. Such accounts had also survived and were preserved, often by dispersed but committed individuals, despite the war.

PENINSULAR VISIONS

What the sparse remains of Rajaratnam *mama*'s photographic archive revealed was an interest in documenting life around him that I did not encounter among other studio photographers. Jaffna *those days* slowly unfolds into war through this arbitrary assembly of images. Rajaratnam *mama* verbally dated the remaining photos as being taken from 1972 onward when he first set up his studio. Many decades later, he was unable to specifically locate each image. Interspersed were also many religious images, in the form of photographs and little visual keepsakes. "I always had my camera with me then!" *mama* exclaimed. "Always ready to take a photo. Even though I don't take photos now, if I see something interesting on the road, I will tell *thambi* [younger brother], look! Go take a photo of that! It's an instinct." Rajaratnam *mama*'s impulse and instinct to document has left us with about sixty photographs of life in prewar Jaffna and a similar number taken during the war years, sharply divided by the transition from black-and-white to color film. They were photographs of everything and nothing, tracing changes in the landscape. To me these photographs were precious on account of the dearth of photographs from a time before war. Rajaratnam *mama* was bemused by my reaction to the random assortment of photographs. Truth was that these photographs were an exception in a nearly all-encompassing absence induced by war.

Serene portrayals of craftsmen, vendors, bearded mendicants, and fishermen casting their nets into the water evoked the nostalgic idyll of Jaffna *those days*. Looking at a bicycle race captured at an elevated angle, I imagined a younger Rajaratnam *mama* perched on a wall with his camera snapping the action. In a solemn full-length studio portrait of himself in a crisp white *kurta* and *vetti* identical to the clothes he still wore to work many decades later, *mama* stood next to a large antique box camera as tall as he is, appearing to adjust its lens as he gazed confidently into the other lens capturing his image. A portable Rolleiflex had afforded greater mobility, permitting him to seek out temple chariot pullers and the rolling devotees at the Nallur temple festival. In one photo, three unknown women in sari and a little girl in a short dress appeared to walk on water, standing ankle-deep in a shallow lagoon against a copse of coconut trees perhaps while on a family trip. Moments of promise and modernity were mapped in photographs recording the installation of new powerlines and a tall water tank, along with the changing dress of the town's dapper mustached young men who walked past Baby, their sarongs swapped for flared trousers. The bustle of a monochrome bus stand was photographed from above, perhaps from the balcony of an adjacent building.

Rajaratnam *mama*'s photos were not the modernities aspired to and pictured in studios on the subcontinent, but those that demarcated Jaffna's progress through developments unfolding outside Baby's "chamber of dreams."[3] Visitors to *The Jaffna Lens*, an exhibition of photographs featuring the work of local photographers I organized in 2018, marveled at thirty of Rajaratnam *mama*'s early black-and-white photos that were displayed. The subjects of these photographs engaged in occupations such as weaving, metalworking, sweet-making, and rickshaw-pulling. "We have never seen anything like this," a delighted viewer announced. Older visitors mused about the way things used to be, good humoredly challenging one another to recall words for implements and practices that they had not seen since they were children. Younger enthusiasts have since taken on Instagram-centered photographic storytelling projects to document fading livelihoods and other "traditional" curiosities and practices that were fading from the peninsula (chapter 7).

Black-and-white snaps of Rajaratnam *mama*'s encounters with the town transmuted into a color-film landscape that was slowly becoming fractured and reassembled by war in new ways. A bus stand conspicuously flattened to rubble was captured in Kodachrome, emptied of buses and people. It was not difficult to assume the impact of a bomb followed by an overzealous demolition. Though temple festivals surely continued, and devotees congregated, the Jaffna library, maliciously burned down in 1981, was pictured as the charred shell. When the government forces retook the peninsula in the Battle of Jaffna in 1995, new government offices and banks were swiftly rebuilt, as was the Nagavihara Buddhist Temple on Stanley Road, which drew pilgrims and "war tourists" visiting the north. Blocky new compounds embellished with blue-and-white logos announced the arrival of humanitarian aid agencies. Stark white walls were painted with staid, but recognizable emblems that form part of a material global idiom for crisis and intervention. This iconography of aid, by virtue of its deliberate visibility in the landscape, became integrated into the local visual material world in times of conflict. The Thanthai Chelva Monument and the Manthiri Manai were also documented.[4] In the renovated central bus stand a painted billboard sponsored by UNICEF warned against land mines. An army jeep lurked on the side of a bazaar street. Stray dogs wandered out of a bright blue archway that offered a glimpse into a Catholic cemetery. Cadjan huts steeped in floodwater were snapped, the faces of their visibly impoverished residents peeking out at the camera. All that remains of Rajaratnam *mama*'s collection speak to and of war.

The beginning of Baby Photo's second life was also captured with the opening of the new space following *mama*'s return to Jaffna after the 1995 displacement. An assortment of images featured experiments with nature and still life. These were interspersed with photographs and printed images of gods and saints that *mama* had collected. Perhaps most poignant was a photo of the monument to the martyrs killed at the World Tamil Conference held in Jaffna in 1974.[5] The partly visible inscription on the walls that enclose the memorial reads: "The world is my village. All people are my community. Tamil is higher (greater) than our lives. The body belongs to the earth. Life belongs to Tamil." The inscription conjures Ramaswamy's observations on Tamil language devotion, but also a citizenship of devotion that had become normalized by the Tamil liberation struggle (1997) (chapter 3).

What remained of Rajaratnam *mama*'s photography were the only nonpersonal/nonofficial photographs I encountered in the many years I have worked in Jaffna that were situated within the wider documentary-oriented interests of amateur/professional photographic practitioners in Ceylon/Sri Lanka. While an occasional landscape photograph emerged in a surviving family album from a vacation or domestic or garden space, there was little that was intentional in the same way Rajaratnam *mama*'s documents of time were. This is not to say they did not exist, but that they had not survived, were not remembered, or might be found abroad in the personal archives of those who had left Sri Lanka for good. Strassler describes amateur practice in Java as one bound by the "the feel of modern technology and the privilege of leisure," which she distinguishes from the work of studio photographers as well as family "snapshooters" (2010, 35). War and unsafety invariably curtailed leisure and the leisurely practice and collections of photographers. If Jaffna's photographic practices, incidental archives, and memories were defined by war, Colombo where much of the island's documented amateur photographic activity appeared to have been concentrated conformed to Strassler's observations. Early recorded photographic activity was concentrated among Colombo's urban elites who were embedded in the colonial project and who were shaped by English-language education and socialization, carrying through these values and norms into the postcolony. For this purpose, I relied on interviews with photographers in Colombo, the collections of commercial studios and other archival materials, photography books, exhibition catalogs, and photographs published in photography annuals such as the *Times of Ceylon* and *Ceylon Observer* pictorials. Rajaratnam *mama*'s photographs, although unlike those of his Jaffna peers based on what material remained, certainly located his interests as shared with those of "well-known" photographers in Colombo.

CEYLON THROUGH THE LENS

The first existing images of the island were purportedly taken by Frederick Fiebig in the mid-1840s, a German lithographer turned calotypist based in Calcutta, India (Falconer 2008, 286). These photographs framed the imageries and imaginaries associated with the island for a century and a half to come, focusing on architectural views, landscapes, wildlife, plantations, and portraits of "native types," including subsequently centers of economic progress, declaring Sri Lanka's status as a bustling imperial outpost embodying the promise of global commerce (Chowdhry Biswas 2015, 54–55). Amateur and professional photography from and of Sri Lanka even today tends to reflect these themes of nature, culture (as embodied by people and "traditional" performances and practices), and architecture bound invariably to its colonially instituted tourist and plantation economy, glorifying its "Edenic" quality.

During the British colonial period, commercial studios developed in an atmosphere of intense competition largely for the benefit of resident Europeans (Falconer 2008, 287; Stambler 2013). However, little information is available on local Ceylonese photographic practice or patronage from the period. The few scholarly considerations of colonial photography in Sri Lanka examine the work of British photographer Julia Margaret Cameron (1815–79) (see Warnapala 2008, 2012). The island's archaeological heritage, which was for the most part rediscovered during the British colonial period, was also actively photographed.[6] Further documented were various Colombo and Kandy-based colonial studio practitioners such as Joseph Lawton (?–1872), Charles T. Scowen (1852–1948), William Louis Henry Skeen (1847–1903), and A. W. A. Plâté (1862–1931). John Martyn also describes the successful two-decade-old studio practice of a Jaffna-based photographer named James Lawson (Martyn 1923, 342). In addition to this, Adolphus William Andree (1869–1910), a Jaffna-born third-generation Ceylonese studio photographer who founded the Hopetown Studio in Colombo, was noted and awarded for his work internationally at the 1900 Exposition Universelle, Paris, and the 1904 World's Fair in St. Louis (Raheem 2003). The Hopetown Studio was significant for the space and facilities it afforded to young photographers, including the island's most well-known photographer, Lionel Wendt (1900–44), who received his first photography lessons there.

CAMERA CLASS: A PHOTOGRAPHIC SOCIETY

A rich history of amateur photographic practice is evidenced by the formation of dedicated clubs in Colombo from the early twentieth century onward. Budding amateur practice is corroborated by the establishment in 1906 of the Amateur Photographic Association of Ceylon (APAC) to promote photography as a hobby, art, and craft, followed by the island's first photography exhibition in 1907. APAC was started by Henry Lorenz Wendt (1858–1915).

The historical fragments stitched together in this section are largely positioned in Colombo, reflecting the ethnolinguistic and class dynamics along which access to photography and the writing of its social histories operated. Among notable names recorded and remembered, Tamil photographers are barely present despite the city's cosmopolitan history and present. If Ariella Aïsha Azoulay's notion of photographic citizenship is contingent on the democratization of practice, it takes for granted the economics and literacies of photographic production (2008). But perhaps in the sidestepping of historical "other" accounts beyond Colombo as well as the deliberate destruction of photographs in a context of war as seen in Jaffna, what might be signaled is photography's power to be mobilized against sovereign erasures.

THE CAMERA ARTIST

A founding member of the modernist '43 Group who defined Sri Lanka's twentieth-century art, accomplished pianist and critic Lionel Wendt would in his short life go on to posthumously become the island's most famed photographer, having achieved international recognition in his brief career.[7] By 1934, Wendt would also revive the APAC as the Photographic Society of Ceylon. Invited to establish a commercial photography studio at the Lakehouse Press by D. R. Wijewardene, a local press baron, Wendt also founded Chitraphoto as an ancillary to the Associated Newspapers of Ceylon. Between 1938 and 1940, Wendt edited three editions of the *Ceylon Observer Pictorial,* which sought to cultivate an "avant-garde" photographic record of the island (Goonetileke 2000). The pictorials aimed to "fuse" beauty and documentary, highlighting "the spirit of the past, the realities of the present, and something of the promise of the future, as it were, from a Song of Ceylon—things that the people of the country should cherish" (*Ceylon Observer Pictorial* 1938). Wendt's aesthetic aspirations for Chitraphoto were inspired by British modernism, as well as photographers such as Man Ray and Edward Steichen, who viewed their subjects as "a new problem to solve, a fresh stimulus to creation, an individual idea to be expressed" (Pinney 2020, 33; Fonseka 2000, 34). Chitraphoto became extremely popular among Colombo's elites, accounting for some of Wendt's surviving work in the form of portraits of notable patrons, including D. R. Wijewardene. Wendt's experimental sensibility inspired by surrealist artists of Europe intersected with colonial photography's preoccupation with the native bodies and scenery.

Indeed, by the early decades of the twentieth century, those like Wendt who belonged to the capital's anglicized multiethnic upper classes were socialized by travel and education in Europe, several becoming enamored by progressive, anti-imperial left-leaning sensibilities while at university in England. Importantly, these Ceylonese elites easily saw themselves as the visionaries and architects of a nation on the cusp of independence, using their preferred media to project and realize these possibilities. Within contemporaneous artistic pursuits, including those of Wendt's, native subject matter was reclaimed and recomposed with new, more political (albeit largely implicit) ambition. For instance, *Lionel Wendt's Ceylon* (1950), an elaborate composite of documentary-style snapshots of daily life, archaeological sites, and nude studies, interspersed with dream-like photomontages enmeshing bodies and landscapes, was published posthumously in London, signifying the international regard he had secured. Wendt's sense of concern for social issues and his solidarity politics were reflected in his photographs of laboring men; the subjects of which are individually named, rather than relegated to a colonial "type" (Fonseka 2000, 12).

It is this investment in the social and Ceylon as a nation that would link Wendt to Jaffna, as evidenced by a photo salon he participated in, and his contributions to *Kesari* along with various other members of the '43 Group, including the painter George Keyt (Fonseka 2000, 29). The short-lived English-language "people's weekly" that espoused a strongly leftist, anticolonial sensibility was intermittently published in Chunnakam, Jaffna, and in its later stages in Colombo between 1941 and 1944. *Kesari* featured critical commentary on politics, arts, and culture as well as photo essays. A 1943 issue memorably published the manifesto of the newly founded Ceylon Communist Party as its front page, demonstrating nascent left-wing solidarities between north and south, which would soon dissipate in the face of rising ethnonationalism.

Given the dearth of material or recollections in Jaffna, it is difficult to ascertain the frequency and extent of the photographic exchanges between Jaffna and Colombo, except to assume that an energetic relationship *did* exist and that Rajaratnam *mama*'s teachers and predecessors were perhaps imagining together the photographic possibilities for picturing Ceylon. Such vestiges suggest that the relationship was not only vivacious but also one of technical exchange devoted to the development of the medium, which as will be demonstrated later in this chapter, was also highly international. In 1944, after Wendt's untimely passing at the age of forty-four, eerily days before the final edition of *Kesari* was published, his residence, *Alborado* (Spanish for "the dawning of the day"), was converted to a complex to house visual and performing arts in his memory (Fonseka 2000, 41). The Lionel Wendt Memorial Art Center complete with art galleries and theater facilities was opened in 1954. The Photographic Society too was housed on the same premises, which included well-equipped dark rooms and a studio. While the studio spaces were no more, a dynamic photographic community endured with digital photography courses offered to amateur enthusiasts as well as regular exhibitions.

Pinney necessarily expands considerations of the vernacular to frame "ground-up" subaltern photographic practices that are "more than local and less than global" as demotic to adequately "capture dynamics and contours of all 'popular' photographic activity" (Pinney 2023, 30–32; see also Batchen

2000). Ceylonese figures such as Wendt also blurred such distinctions. Wendt's photographic practice fluidly embraced "mundane" studio portraiture with surrealist-inspired pictorialism. Although Wendt's practice as an exception must be no doubt accommodated, the world of amateur and studio photography too was rich with artistic experimentation, even if their makers are viewed as "nonartists." Both socially and practically as seen in Pinney's ethnography of studio photography in central India, the artistry expected of and demonstrated by studio practitioners challenges the parameters of the "ordinary" (Pinney 1997; Pinney and Punjabi 2013). Rajaratnam *mama* himself, studio photographer and itinerant snapshooter, exhibited a desire to practice photography as documentary and art. His portraits of laboring bodies reveal the kind of sophisticated composition and play with light and shadow that would not be out of place among the "avant-garde" work of Wendt and his successors. What must be acknowledged is how talents were typically recognized and fulfilled as much as one's social class and ethno-geographic and linguistic backgrounds permitted amid their increased postcolonial politicization. Rajaratnam *mama*'s Colombo contemporaries such as Joe de Livera (1929–2025), Reg Van Cuylenburg (1926–88), and Nihal Fernando (1927–2015) were not especially different in their photographic pursuits and interests, indicating perhaps an erstwhile possibility of a cohesive photography of the "nation" prior to its ethno-geographic fracture by Sinhalese majoritarianism and war. What separated Rajaratnam *mama* from his Ceylonese predecessors, who made a name for themselves, and his southerly contemporaries were language and the interlinked proximity to the hierarchies of social power instituted by the British Empire.

SALVAGING CEYLON AND THE LANGUAGE OF PHOTOGRAPHY

The Photographic Society of Ceylon revamped by Lionel Wendt as a forum for discussing the work of fellow amateur practitioners was expanded by photography enthusiasts such as P. J. C. Durrant, B. G. Thornley, B. P. Weerawardena, and Joe de Livera. Given its membership of English-speaking elites, it might be ascertained that the society was the purview of wealthy residents of the capital. As has been explored by Yasmine Gooneratne, the cultural life of the cosmopolitan English-educated of the island constituted a world of its own that was intrinsically bound to the empire whereby they also seemed "to distance themselves from the 'chaos' of the larger society of the island" (1992, 5). Despite its century-long history, the society has no archives or documentation to speak of, as its paperwork was destroyed by an infestation of silverfish, reminding also of the vagaries of the tropical climate that makes the preservation of photographic images challenging. Membership in the society is by invitation or application (in English), and its activity centers on photography classes and an annual competition and exhibition of photography that was initiated in 1934 and has run continuously as an international competition and exhibition since 1954.

Born to a wealthy commercial family in Colombo, Joe de Livera, one of the capital's most prominent entrepreneurs, recalled his introduction to photography by way of a Kodak Brownie Box Camera he received from his father as an eighth birthday present. Graduating from the Brownie Box to a Kodak Folding Camera and later a Rolleiflex, he joined the Photographic Society in 1946. Mr. de Livera remembered B. G. Thornley as "an English boy who went on home leave and became fascinated by the Leica"; Thornley brought one back to Colombo. In the following year, during a trip to Europe, Mr. de Livera acquired his own 35mm Leica as a teenager. "Photography was difficult at the time," he recalled; "there were no raw materials, no film, no paper. Nobody knew how to develop." He went on to learn how to develop his own photographs, building a darkroom for himself in his home and using chemicals and other paraphernalia he had bought on trips to London. In 1955, Mr. de Livera began importing Leicas to Ceylon for sale at Titus Stores, his family's business, recalling that British science fiction writer Arthur C. Clarke, who was domiciled in Colombo at the time, was an enthusiastic early customer. Mr. de Livera was the most senior member and patron of what has been renamed The Photographic Society of Sri Lanka (PSSL), and his archive of photographs from the early 1950s reveals the astounding results of his experiments to perfect macro photography before the invention of dedicated lenses. The photographs captured the many-eyed fluorescent heads of insects, the gritty phosphorus tips of safety matches, the speckled petals of orchids, as well as landscapes and ballet dancers. Nearly ninety years old at the time of our meeting, Mr. de Livera had carefully stored away his beautiful Leicas and effortlessly wielded an iPhone 8 Plus instead as he reminisced about the "magic" of the 35mm camera.

Similarly, Reg Van Cuylenburg, who is lesser known within Sri Lanka, found fame in the United States of America. A student of Wendt's, his photography book, *Image of an Island: A Portrait of Ceylon,* published in 1962 in New York, is a rare publication by a Sri Lankan photographer that would punctuate the period between Wendt's and Nihal Fernando's prolific body of work. Van Cuylenburg's photographs marked a break in the preoccupation with the picturesque, as seen in the works of photographers published in the annual pictorials produced in this period. He drew attention to moments of glaring ugliness that lurked on the idyllic island, marking a shift from the halcyon photographic evocations of paradise. A giant sea turtle viscerally gutted on a beach and a man whose leg is swollen with lymphatic filariasis, among other such photographs, were interspersed among the otherwise tranquil imagery. It is also necessary to mention the work of a seldom seen Ceylonese woman photographer, Jeanne Thwaites (1929–2019), who also found success in the United States. Her photographs were published in *Life Magazine*. Born in Kandy, Thwaites established a photography studio in San Luis Obispo, California, in 1965. A contemporary of Van Cuylenburg, Thwaites published two monographs: *Mother and Child* in 1967 following a trip to Sri Lanka and *Horses of the West* in 1968 documenting the horse business in central California. Thwaites adopted a conspicuously racialized visitor's view of the island, presumably for the benefit of an American audience, that expounds the physiological and communal specificities of ethnicity in a manner reminiscent of colonial "types" woven together by themes of maternal love and childhood play. She returned to Sri Lanka in 1993, living on her ancestral family estate until her death. She also found success as a writer, winning the Gratiaen Prize for creative writing in English by a Sri Lankan in 1998 for her collection of short stories, *It Is a Sunny Day on the Moon*.

Meanwhile, Nihal Fernando, perhaps Sri Lanka's best-known postcolonial photographer and a contemporary of de Livera and Van Cuylenburg, founded Studio Times, after acquiring the photography studio established as a part of the *Times* newspaper where he trained as a photographer. Studio Times, which supplied commercial photography services to private companies for advertising purposes, provided financial support for Fernando's passion for conservation. In his outstanding career spanning many decades, Fernando embarked on a vast personal project to document the island's disappearing natural and cultural heritage, in a sense reclaiming through photographs the colonial presentation of the island as one ripe for extraction. Lamenting the losses exacerbated by the European colonial encounter and the rapid socioeconomic changes and modernization that followed marketization, Fernando sought out evidence of the island's precolonial grandeur in his preoccupation with its ancient lithic civilization. This echoed the pursuits of early colonial photographers, including Skeen, Scowen, Plâté, and Cave. Studio Times, which was one of the last facilities in Sri Lanka offering dark room services for photographers to develop film, struggled in recent years with diminishing commercial demand for its service. Fernando's vast collection of photographs, however, remained methodically archived and preserved.

Studio Times is now run by Fernando's daughter, Anu Weerasuriya. She is herself an accomplished photographer, who accompanied her father from a young age in his photographic pursuits. When I first visited in 2017, the studio was in the process of relocating to smaller premises attached to the family home from a neighboring building. Its once impressive but now "useless" photographic paraphernalia were discarded and sold for scrap. The archive formed out of bundles of mostly black-and-white photographs, bound into little books with green filing string, was one of the most comprehensive I encountered. Aside from publications that may occasionally seek out prints, it was rapidly falling into obsolescence with the dominance of the digital. Fernando also published several photography books, including *Serendip to Sri Lanka: Immemorial Isle* (1991, with Luxshman Nadaraja), *Sri Lanka: A Personal Odyssey* (1997), *With the Dawn* (2005, with Herbert Keuneman), and *Eloquence in Stone: The Lithic Saga of Sri Lanka* (2008, with Sinharaja Tammita-Delgoda), during his career, detailing his travels and his lifelong commitment to conservation. Fernando's photography serves as the indisputable mold for contemporary amateur and professional practice across Sri Lanka, in its idealized preoccupation with wildlife, notably leopards and elephants, pristine landscapes, rural life, and tracing the history of the island through stone. These preoccupations conformed to a globalized aesthetic of documentary photography coupled with a desire to salvage fragments of the island that appeared to be under threat by modernity and urbanization as well as war. In its postcolonial guise, the visual language of colonial photography carried through to the island's vision for itself, as a nation-state and economy. However, what might be viewed as self-orientalizing photographic conceptions were assumed as much as unsettled by its resident photographers.

By 1950, the need for a Sinhala-speaking photographers' club was fulfilled in the founding of the Amateur Photographic Association. Renamed The National Photographic Art Society of Sri Lanka, the NPASSL sought to develop the "propagation of photography as an art form, and to disseminate photography as a subject of educational interest" (2022). The society conducted free photography lessons in Sinhalese for aspiring photographers, establishing in 1961 Sri Lanka's first Sinhala-language photography journal: *Camera*. The journal was renamed and published in 1977 as a full-fledged periodical *Lanka Camera* (NPASSL 2022). Wilson Hegoda, the founder, intended the club to cater initially to the Sinhala-speaking photography community. The club as a space for Sinhalese photographers may suggest some features about the membership, likely including the tacit mutual exclusion of Tamils or other Ceylonese who were educated in and predominantly spoke English. This was not an uncommon phenomenon at the time, given how language and ethnicity featured explosively in the political milieu of the period. As observed by Gooneratne, "A Westernized multi-ethnic elite which prided itself on a modern, cultured and civilized outlook that, disregarding outworn race and caste distinctions, regarded its neighbor of whatever origin with tolerant understanding, had been informed by the advocates of 'Sinhala Only'—whether accurately or not, they could not know—that such an outlook, far from being modern, cultured, or civilized, was seen by the Sinhalese majority as merely the contemptible product of a divided inheritance" (1992, 5). A strident rift through language thus also shaped the photography that emerged out of this period and its subsequent circulations and historiographic acknowledgment. In this "history," the efforts of Tamil photographers from northern Sri Lanka scarcely, if ever, appeared.

During this time, the visual and performing arts were increasingly stifled by greater state control and political repression over freedom of expression. This is exemplified by the exile of the political cartoonist and member of the '43 Group, Aubrey Collette. Famous for his caustic wit, Collette, a political cartoonist at the *Times of Ceylon* for nearly two decades, was forced to leave the island "under duress" in 1961 (Cresside Collette quoted in Sadanandan 2010). The "Sinhala Only" political-institutional environment, and subsequent descent to conflict saw to the rapid out-migration of Ceylon's anglicized Eurasian and Burgher communities, who trace their lineage to Dutch, Portuguese, English, and other European ancestors. These communities' links to artistic as well as photographic practices, though unestablished by the existing scholarship, are evident in the apparent access to cameras as well as prolific domestic and social photography, which might be attributed to wealth and social class, as well as a well-traveled lifestyle. An example of this can be seen in the work of Menika van der Poorten, one of Sri Lanka's few established women photographers, who delves into her Eurasian family's archive in her film project *A Lost White Tribe: The Eurasians of Sri Lanka* (2010).

The previously mentioned annuals and pictorials published by the *Ceylon Observer* (1931–72) and *Times* showcased the work of amateur and professional photographers. These spanned documentary, landscape, and portraiture to more experimental attempts, suggesting that Wendt was not alone in his modernist, multicultural "national" inspirations. Yet these also served as advertorials for Ceylon, epitomizing the commercial opportunities of the island, ranging from tea to tourism, albeit still tethering image-making to the economic visions and aspirations of the British crown that are inextricable from the vocations of the upper classes as industrialists and plantation owners. These reveal the kinds of photographic practice that prevailed in elite urban spaces in Ceylon as it transitioned into becoming Sri Lanka, founded on an often nostalgic, salvage paradigm anxious about the effects of colonially instituted loss and industrialization articulated and sometimes subverted through technical experimentation. It is photography that also sought to foster a cosmopolitan way of seeing that was "Ceylonese" and "Sri Lankan," advocated for by those such as Wendt and Fernando, indicating how photography was mobilized in the articulation of post/colonial imaginings of an inclusive nation. Such visual projection found itself at odds with the consolidation of a majoritarian democracy by way of patronage networks and ethnolinguistic and geographic coalition-building through the twentieth century. This photography perhaps evoked merely the visions and desires of the island's multicultural English-speaking elites. The aggressive politicization of identities took place in the hands of the same social class that sought to consolidate democracy by way of patronage networks and ethno-geographic coalition-building.

It is possible to ascertain from Mr. De Livera's account as a photographer and importer that materials were difficult to come by for those who did not have the resources and/or connections to the outside. The closed economy and subsequent economic pressures of the war also entailed that cameras were not especially common outside of urban Sri Lanka. Anecdotally, the compact camera is said to have arrived within households in the early 1980s following Sri Lanka's shift away from the statist economic policies that were in place in the years following independence (1956–77), during which overseas travel and imports were actively restricted. The increased mobility of Sri Lankans after 1977 for foreign employment, especially in the Arab Gulf and Middle East, resulted in an influx of items such as household appliances and consumables. Camera ownership became relatively common in the mid to late 1980s as indicated by the expansion of studios and printers to meet demands for film processing. The products of these cameras remained for the most part within the pages of family albums and focused on documenting special occasions such as birthdays and weddings. Photography was still arguably confined to those who were well-off and able to afford such goods or had overseas links. The sharp urban-rural divide prevalent during the time also suggests that cameras may have remained for the most part a relatively urban phenomenon up until the 2000s. Interlocutors in Jaffna who were themselves not photographers recalled their grandparents' and parents' access to cameras that typically correlated to their higher social class, profession, and/or connections to family members who resided overseas. Capacities for digitization and nostalgic display on the internet, however, also afforded greater visibility of personal photographs otherwise filed away in family albums. Digital archiving efforts such as the Ceylon Memory Project undertaken by one of Sri Lanka's most celebrated contemporary documentary photographers, Dominic Sansoni, offers a partial glimpse into the world of family photographic collections from before 1972.

If Tamil equivalents of the PSSL or NPASSL existed in Colombo, documentation and memories of them have faded. It might be inferred from the linguistic demarcations of these clubs that the politics of ethnolinguistic identity and social class featured prominently in their formations. While I did not happen upon any documented evidence or memories of similar collectives for photographers in Jaffna, anecdotal accounts suggest a relationship between elite arts practitioners in Colombo and Jaffna in the early to mid-twentieth century. These connections between English-speaking local elite photographers and artists in Ceylon reveal tacit class and language demarcations that may have shaped local photographic practices as well as shared postcolonial imaginings of nation. Although mitigated to an extent by increased access to cameras in recent years, language remained an important component of the visual economy of Instagram, for instance, for photographers who were compelled to learn the predominantly English-language social media vernacular of hashtags to enhance the visibility of their work.

Within such a tenuously documented national context, the post/colonial photography of Jaffna was riddled with even greater material and historiographic absences. I hope that the material presented here sheds new light on its overlooked vibrancy and importance.

AN ARCHIVE OF ABSENCES

The effects of war had rendered a parallel survey of photographic practice of Jaffna outside surviving studios and family snap photographers impossible.

However, it is one I believe to be a great necessity, given the pioneering and significant role played by early Jaffna practitioners in the development of photography in Ceylon. For my interlocutors, committing these anecdotes to memory was an unspoken political commitment to community and a means to preserve these histories as they remain unwritten.

The Tamil community's documented history had been subjected to a grievous act of biblioclasm by agents of the state. On 1 June 1981, what was known to be one of Asia's largest and most impressive libraries founded in 1934, which housed 97,000 volumes, including many rare manuscripts and publications, among them the only original copy of the *Yalpana Vaipavamalai* or the *History of the Kingdom of Jaffna*, was burned to ashes in a politically motivated arson by local police and state-sponsored gangs. Sundar Ganesan claims that "the Sinhalese police did not allow even a single sheet of paper to be rescued from the fire" (2014). Although the library was renovated with the support of the local community within the space of a year, a second fire caused by a retaliatory bombing by the Sri Lankan armed forces engulfed the restoration and its revived contents of several thousand books (Ganesan 2014). Over the next two decades, the library was caught in the throes of war. *Ilankai* Tamil history and identity, one which revolves around its remarkable scholarship, was destroyed through this callous burning. During renovation efforts that took place some years later, civil society groups in Jaffna requested that a burned section of the library be maintained as a memorial, but the government rejected these wishes and rebuilt the library in what is viewed as an act of willful erasure.

When I was initially asking about photography in Jaffna, Arumugamsamy, who had gathered with Rajaratnam *mama*'s friends at Baby Studio, inquired what I was doing in Jaffna. "All that you were looking for would have been in our library," he said wistfully, offering me names of books he was certain could no longer be found. "Our culture. Our history. It was all there." There were no local collections to delve into beyond those of various interlocutors whose own possessions were shattered and pared by war. My search for photographers, artists, and other related practitioners or any evidence of societies led to responses which were dispiriting confirmations that persons I would have found most useful to speak to were either dead or had long left for Europe. I heard about late local collectors and archivists anecdotally. The informal honorific Kalaignani (scholar of the arts) positioned A. Selvaratnam, a local historian, as a connoisseur of art and culture. His single-handed effort to save artifacts from Jaffna in a house in Tirunelveli was honored by Prabhakaran in 1991, bestowing him with the highest civilian honor it accorded: *maamanithar* (great man). I was told that Kalaignani's collection, left to the LTTE's custodianship, was destroyed in the war. Similarly, another awardee of the *maamanithar* title, a prominent local dramatist whose theater dealt with subjects of Tamil self-determination, Sivakkolunthu Thirunavukkarasu (S. T. Arasu) was also a well-known photographer, whose work I heard about but was never able to see any examples of. In the pervasive absence of materials, Jaffna's older studio photographers kept safe the oral history of their practice.

"WHEN WAS PHOTOGRAPHY INTRODUCED TO THE EAST?"

At the time of our meeting, Rajaratnam *mama*'s career has spanned over sixty years, since he had picked up a camera as a teenage apprentice.

"When I was studying in school, I developed a deep liking for photography. I was very curious and wanted to see what was happening in the photo studios in town, so I would stand outside and try to see what was going on inside. Because we were little boys then, they wouldn't let us in. One day, I asked a studio what happened inside the dark room, and they let me in to have a look around inside. Here was a room that was in complete darkness, a single red-light bulb and three kinds of chemicals and as if by 'current' (electricity) they would make the pictures appear. I saw this and I was overjoyed! So, I thought to myself that I must find a very good studio and learn photography. In 1958, I joined Sellam's."

Rajaratnam *mama* was invested in passing on his knowledge. This practice held true with the older generation of photographers in Jaffna, who either inherited their studios or trained as photographers under an established studio before they founded their own. The system of apprenticeship has waned with sophisticated digital cameras, which appeared increasingly to be the only test of one's ability to photograph. A black-and-white portrait of his guru, Nicholas, the proprietor of Sellam's, was placed next to one of Nicholas's teachers, Manikkiathambi, the owner of Lilly Studio. Four photographs of a younger Rajaratnam *mama* at his desk in a single frame were placed on the right, and a double exposure of a snake, sacred to the Hindu religion, was hung on the left. Another black-and-white portrait of a younger Rajaratnam *mama* at his desk also fell in line with this spiritual and secular constellation of teaching and learning that he too had actively incorporated into his studio practice (fig. 6).

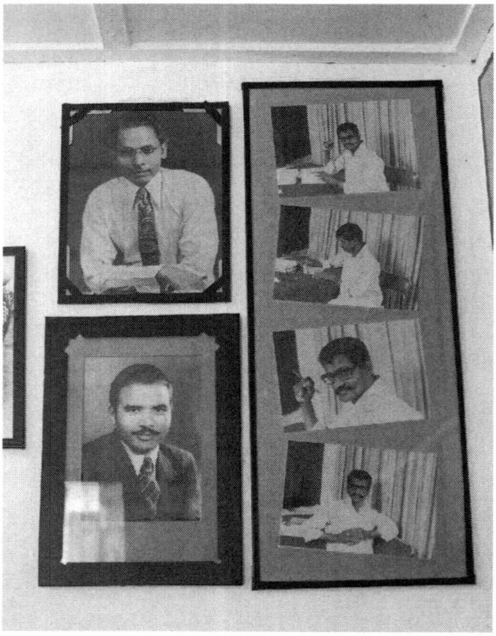

FIGURE 6. Rajaratnam *mama* and teachers (Jaffna, 2018)

My interest in Jaffna arose out of the way in which it has occupied the Sri Lankan Tamil cultural and political imagination. It was a happy accident to discover that Jaffna may be a compelling, but almost entirely neglected, contender to be the birthplace of photography in Ilankai. What was perhaps most remarkable about Jaffna's studio photography was that the older generation of studio photographers such as Rajaratnam *mama* were not only able to effortlessly recall Jaffna's local history of photography but place themselves within the lineage of photographers based on either family or apprenticeship or both. "Martyn, he was the first! First in Jaffna! First in Ilankai! Then there was Lawton. These were the best photographers in Ilankai." Rajaratnam *mama*, declared proudly, swiftly plotting the connections between various studios he would recall. It was *mama* who pointed out to me that Martyn Road, off Main Street, which I walked past regularly was named after the pioneering photographer Henry Martyn (1812–61). Swaminathar Kanagaratnam Lawton (1851–1919) too had a road named after him in Manipay. These were anecdotes echoed in conversations I had with other photographers. *Mama*'s past apprentices, including Sivapragasam and Gajen, had gone on to establish successful studios of their own, as he trained a new cohort at Baby.

The introduction of photography to Jaffna did not come by way of the British colonial administration but by the American Christian Mission (ACM). The ACM was an active proponent of establishing schools based on the tenets and values of Christianity and English-language education for local students. The Jaffna Peninsula is home to several of Sri Lanka's and Asia's oldest surviving schools founded by the ACM, the Wesleyan Methodist Mission, the Church Mission Society of the Anglican Church, and the Roman Catholic Church. Students of mission education were anglicized and Christianized by name and conduct, christened with Christian names for record-keeping purposes. It is possible to speculate that the introduction of photography to the students at these schools entailed that its commercial practice remained limited to those who belonged to wealthy caste and class groups. Jaffna's photography pioneers, Henry Martyn and S. K. Lawton, members of wealthy Jaffna families, were celebrated townsmen and aspiring scientists. Even as both continued to have roads in the peninsula named in their honor, their contributions to photography were mostly undocumented and overlooked outside the peninsula. They were students at the Batticotta Seminary (first and third respective generations of student photographers), which became the prestigious Jaffna College.

In the 1923 publication *Notes on Jaffna: Chronological, Historical, Biographical* compiled by J. H. Martyn, the son of Martyn Senior, writes in his dedication, "To the memory of Henry Martyn Esquire, One of the first Graduates of the far-famed 'Batticotta Seminary,' who rose to the singular distinction of being the first Journalist and first Photographer among the Ceylonese and who was well and widely known as a sound English and Tamil Scholar, Scientist, Poet, Artist and Mathematician, this book is affectionately dedicated" (1923, i). Martyn narrates the introduction of photography to the island in June 1853 by American missionaries to his father (1923, 207). Following various unsuccessful trials, an admirer of Martyn Sr. nudged the missionaries to permit the student at the Batticotta Seminary of "ingenious mind and artistic talents" an "opportunity to try his hand at the new art" (1923, 207). Entrusted by Rev. E. P. Hastings, Martyn Sr. was encouraged to study the process while he met with his visiting colleagues. Upon their return three hours later, Martyn Sr. invited them to sit with him and "took their photo, to their satisfaction the first photo ever taken in Ceylon," underpinning Martyn Jr.'s claim that "Mr Martyn is thus entitled to the rank as the first photographer of the Island" (1923, 207). Pleased with the result, the missionaries presented Martyn Sr. with the photographic apparatus, after which, Martyn turned his house "East of the customs premises" (off present-day Main Street) into a studio along with a partner, Mr. Cyrus Koch, which studio he would use for the rest of his life (1923, 207). Martyn notes that the photographic art was introduced to Colombo only three years later in 1856 by Mr. Parting (1923, 123). Ismeth Raheem suggests that by 1843, four years after its discovery was announced in Paris, daguerreotype processes were being advertised in Colombo, resulting in enthusiastic trade by colonial practitioners even though the coastal weather was unkind to the products of the delicate process, resulting in the need for restoration (2018). The Galle-born Adolphus Wilhelmus Andree (1799–?), A. W. Andree's grandfather, has also been identified as an early pioneer of daguerreotypes.

Jaffna's significance in terms of the photographic history of not simply Ceylon and South Asia, but a broader transnational history of photography and its technological development, repudiates assertions that photography was a purely imperial instrument. This was made apparent in the life and work of S. K. Lawton, the founder of a successful studio practice, S. K. Lawton & Co., in 1876. Martyn recognizes that Lawton was "a self-made man and rose to eminence through indefatigable energy, pluck, and industry. Devoting special attention to photography he acquired great skill and proficiency in it and excelled as a photographer and photo artist. Being a deep thinker, he invented certain photographic processes which were well recommended in British photographic journals. He also invented a recipe for the manufacture of insect proof materials and obtained a British patent for it" (1923, 324).

Lawton interestingly shared a name with a resident English photographer, Joseph Lawton. The latter was noted for photographing the ruins of Anuradhapura, Polonnaruwa, and Sigiriya for the Committee on Ancient Architecture in Ceylon 1870–71 as a part of the colonial project to document the ruins of the island's early kingdoms that had been abandoned for many centuries before their rediscovery and excavation by colonial administrators.[8] S. K. Lawton was recognized for his photographic practice by the British colonial administrators, as evidenced in Arnold Wright's *Twentieth-Century Impressions of Ceylon*, a tome intended to display the industry and economy of Ceylon, alongside its notable individuals and families (1907). Lawton and his son who went on to inherit his practice were also responsible for some of the photography in this volume. Raheem suggests that even Henry Lorenz Wendt (Lionel Wendt's father) sought out Lawton, in his studio in Manipay, Jaffna, in 1903 (2018). Wendt made this grueling 250-mile trek over several days, before the advent of the railway and motorized transport, to observe an obsolete technique still in use in Lawton's studio, and to verify the result, he had his portrait taken by him (Raheem 2018). Raheem also flags Lawton's efforts of going so far as to enlist village craftsmen to manufacture a camera locally, highlighting the extraordinary fascination with photography and its possibilities (2018).[9]

Lawton was also an active contributor to a London-based print and design journal, *Penrose's Pictorial Annual*. He wrote about various technical innovations in photography, including simple experiments for color photography, remedying the challenges of using fish glue due to the effects of oxidation and fading photographs. Lawton was also granted a fourteen-year English patent for preparing paper without damage in the development of photographs (Martyn 1923). Among Lawton's most intriguing contributions to the *Penrose Annual* is an article called "When Was Photography Introduced into the East?" where he suggests that (contrary to Martyn's account) a daguerreotype apparatus "as described in a scientific journal of 1839" may have been in use at the Batticotta Seminary as early as 1840 (1913, 132). While he states that he could not be certain of the date of importation, its technical specifications suggest that it was produced in 1840. Lawton goes on to note, "Certain it is that Daguerreotype process was demonstrated to the students in the early forties, for one of them, a Tamil of great scientific attainments, had opened a studio in Main Street of Jaffna and supplied photographs by the Daguerreotype process. . . . It is, therefore, almost certain that the first photographic Camera to travel to the East was a Daguerreotype, one referred to above, and its first home the Ottley Hall of the Batticotta Seminary" (1913, 133–34).

Some examples of Lawton's studio photography were stored at the archives of Jaffna University. The jumbled collection of early studio photography dating back to 1880 is hidden in a dusty room with little accessible information on provenance. After many weeks of seeking out the good graces of the collection's self-appointed keepers, I was grudgingly shown thirty-seven photographs featuring largely the work of S. K. Lawton and six large, overpainted portraits produced by Subas Studio in the 1950s. Watched over by two undergraduate students, I was not permitted to re-photograph the images, so I wrote down descriptions along with any available details. These included individual and group portraits, Hindu and Christian wedding photographs, and the documentation of a communal Pongal (Tamil harvest festival) ceremony, harvesting activity, and the scene from what appears to be a Christian girls' school play. In what Rajaratnam *mama* described as a "sunlight photo" from the late 1800s and early 1900s, elaborate interiors were set up outdoors for the bejeweled sitters variously dressed in Western and traditional clothing. These featured elements of opulent domestic spaces including colonial Dutch-inspired wooden furniture and Persian carpets. Rattan mats were laid out beneath them or behind them as backdrops, spears of grass and other foliage sometimes peeking through these assembled "interiors." Other examples were captured in studios against painted backdrops that resembled plush interiors with trompe l'oeil curtains and architectural features such as columns reminding one of Walter Benjamin's reflections on European photographic practice ([1931] 2005, 515). Individual portraits also expressed accomplishment as well as social status: An unknown man in a graduate's black gown sat at a desk with a book appearing thoughtful, while an anonymous woman dressed in a fashionable velvet blouse and sari and heavy anklets reclined on a chaise longue playing the accordion. The beginnings of studio photography in Jaffna, catering largely to local elites, evoked elements of the colonial cosmopolitan in their composition. Many of these visual markers and tropes persisted within contemporary Jaffna studio photography.

Unexpectedly, my own "proximity" to Lawton became compressed, expanding the ethnographic arc of this work, following the publication of an article about the beginnings of photography in Jaffna (Buthpitiya 2019). Over the next few months, Lawton's descendants, a few generations removed and now scattered from Washington, DC, to London and Colombo, some of whom were unaware of each other, contacted me to inquire after their ancestor. I conveyed slivers of information that I had acquired during my research, while they enthusiastically offered snippets they had gathered from their parents and grandparents. Their last surviving relative in Jaffna, Mrs. Balakrishna, had passed away a few years ago, leaving the house in Manipay that was once occupied by Lawton abandoned. One correspondent, Lawton's great-great-grandson, remembered the tiles at its entrance being inlaid with photographs when he had visited many years earlier as a child. Another great-grandson related a family fable of how Lawton was believed to have photographed Halley's comet in 1910. Possible visual evidence of this endeavor unassumingly accompanies a *Penrose* article titled "A Simple and Expeditious Method of Making Blocks" (1911, 109). It also compelled them to reach out to relatives they had lost touch with or discover kinships they did not know existed, speaking to a long history of dispersal.

In a subsequent communication with a family member, the wife of one of Lawton's grandchildren recalled the arduous task of attempting to put together a family tree, given that Lawton had two wives and twelve children. The email that connected us across continents was rich with minutiae she had gathered. Lawton's photographs were still hanging on the walls of the family home during her last visit to Sri Lanka in 2015. His Colombo shop was named Prince Studio, and its name was stamped on some of the photographs. She had learned from other family members that the missionaries at Vaddukoddai had presented Lawton with the camera that he had begun his practice with. He had also bought various photographic provisions from Dr. Samuel Green, the founder of the Green Memorial Hospital in Manipay. Beginning from the accounts of studio photographers in Jaffna to these unexpected peeks into family lore, Martyn's and Lawton's legacies as native practitioners warrant far greater attention than the space this book permits. However, I hope it offers a point of departure to rethinking and rewriting histories that claim northern Sri Lanka's insignificance and isolation in the development of an Ilankai Tamil photography (see Falconer 2008, 287). Most important, it accentuates the long and vivid transnational history of photography in the Jaffna Peninsula even though its visual material remains have long vanished if they were not actively destroyed.

Even though the services of Jaffna's older studios were falling out of fashion and may appear to simply subsist and persist out of necessity for their role in the production of identity photographs, they endured as active sites of photographic production, creativity, and social memory. The echoes of photos produced by S. K. Lawton and others reverberated in the photographs that Jaffna studios continued to compose. The most significant conclusion that might be derived from this historical account of Rajaratnam *mama*'s archive is the porosity of Jaffna's photography, in its conceiving, making, and moving, but also how the medium has become defined by its encounter with war. What also became evident is the extraordinary contributions of colonial subjects to the transnational developments of the medium, including those by pioneering photographers such as Lawton, who have been all but forgotten. This pushes against the grain of a simplistic narrative of the camera as an imperial weapon, indicating that its capacities and magic were actively appropriated and uniquely and creatively wielded in ways that are all too often overlooked or forgotten in favor of dominant historical accounts, whether national or international. Such appropriations and their subversions would also inform the photographies of war that follow.

3 PHOTOGRAPHY AS STATECRAFT AND WARCRAFT

"TRUTH IS NOT VISIBLE IN THIS DARKNESS"

Vasanthan abruptly assured me that he had never killed anyone.

I was startled by the earnestness of his sudden confession that sparked out of a recollection about his family, now mostly scattered across Europe. It was as if our long-winded conversations about home and politics had convinced him that it was the right moment to volunteer a detail from his past that we would not discuss again. Vasanthan had become categorically convinced of Tamil liberation and the necessity for Tamil Eelam by the age of thirteen. During this time, in the early 2000s, the LTTE had convincingly established itself as a de facto state actor. His childhood entanglement with the Tigers had been short-lived and difficult but accepted by family members who had become increasingly devoted to the cause, which had already claimed various kin in the name of homeland.

"They [the Tigers] used to come to school in the morning, the tuition class in the afternoon. We wanted to fight the enemy; we wanted to be heroes—that was all we knew. That was our world then." As a Tamil teenager living in northern Sri Lanka, his encounters with the army had been far worse. He told me that he was no longer persuaded that the Tigers, now largely represented by an ardent diasporic support base, had anyone's best interest except their own in mind. But the homeland, Vasanthan insisted, was necessary. "Tamil Eelam is the only future for our people." How this might be realized and what shape this could take in the wake of the brutal quelling of the armed struggle was anyone's guess. Perhaps it was that Tamil Eelam had taken on a new borderless shape in a transnational political community in exile and longing, rooted in a homeland under occupation that many could not return to.

Some months before Vasanthan's admission, Sinnarasa, a Jaffna native who remained a staunch proponent of the militancy, had firmly declared to me that there was no such thing as a child soldier. "No such thing!"

"What do you mean?" I asked him, wondering if I had misunderstood what he had said. The LTTE had, after all, been notorious for their "baby brigades" (HRW 2004).

"Propaganda!" he switched from Tamil to English for the potent length of a single word, as if the Tamil word, *pirachcharam*, more semantically akin to broadcast, could not encompass the measure of deception involved in the untruth of child soldiers. "Children dress up in costumes for school concerts, this, and that. Someone takes a picture and suddenly they are child soldiers!" He conveyed such assurance and incredulousness that anyone could believe that LTTE child soldiers existed. Sinnarasa had lived in northern Sri Lanka through the entirety of the war.

Months later, when Vasanthan confided in me about his involvement with the Tigers, it was impossible not to be reminded of Sinnarasa's words. I wondered about the distinctions between soldier and militant, about choice and socialization, as if discourse on the Sri Lankan conflict does not continue to be mired in arguments of agency and coercion. As if choices to go to war, to fight a war, to remain at war, to flee from war, to die for nation and people were straightforward queries to which there might be ready answers.

Some decades ago, Sivaramani, a young Tamil woman poet in Jaffna wrote,

> To tear off
> the wings of insects
> make guns
> from sticks and logs
> kill friends
> thinking them enemies,
> these are the games
> our children play. In a night
> full of pressure
> during war
> our young have grown up.
>
> (MAUNAGURU 1991, 148)

Sivaramani took her own life on 19 May 1991. She was twenty-three years old. Noting that Sivaramani burned all her poems that she could find prior to her death, Sitralega Maunaguru wrote in an introduction to a translation of the poet's remaining work, "Sivaramani lived and died in a place where the act of suicide is glorified and praised as the ultimate symbol of patriotism. Sivaramani, however, did not die by swallowing a cyanide capsule or leaping at a target with a bomb-fitted bodice, and thus was not praised as a martyr. Instead, her action will go unnoticed and even ridiculed as an act of cowardice" (Maunaguru 1991, 147). Sivaramani's residual words, unveiling her anxieties about the increasingly authoritarian tilt of her world, reveal, foremostly, the deep entanglements of the social world of war, seeping into the home, and the cosseted confines of childhood. Photographs of gun-bearing young men and women and children formed a significant part of the Tamil militancy's photographic chronicle of the liberation struggle. The same images were repurposed by the Sri Lankan government as part of the wartime media regime directed at Sinhalese citizens in the south, casting the north and east of the island as a geography of hazard and dread. The volatility of these photographs heightened their opposing uses as inspiration, caution, and coercion. Tamilness and terror became intertwined through such photographs, as Tamil bodies became embedded with the threat of death: those capable of killing and thus deserving of being killed (Buthpitiya 2023a).

THE VISUAL DEBRIS OF WAR

To understand how the volatile potentials of photographs were deployed as agitants during times of war and postwar is to examine how images and image-making practices were wielded and weaponized by Sri Lanka's competing state actors as a part of their nation-building and citizen-making practices. In this chapter, I chart a visual economy of war through the frame of the Tamil liberation struggle. It is focused on analog image-making technics and practices that were in use from the mid-1970s to the early 2000s to locate the development of recurrent types and genres of "political" images produced by frontline and studio photographers retained by the Tamil militancy, media workers, activists engaged in recording human rights violations, and civilian snapshooters in possession of the rare commodity of a camera. These photographs document death and injury, refugees and the internally displaced and disabled, communal violence, and destruction to property. Other photographs centered on various aspects of militarism such as combat training. There are also heroic depictions of fighters and martyrs' portraits. The photographs encountered in this chapter were largely produced to agitant effect, with a view to disorder the political status quo of the majoritarian Sri Lankan state. These demonstrated the formation of hostile, contradictory imaginaries of nation and state roiled in an armed conflict, showing photography as an uncivil practice. In northern Sri Lanka, the volatility of these images was mobilized toward socializing the eventual citizens of an aspirant Tamil state. Redolent images of war and loss, both devastating and glorious, were utilized to galvanize and cultivate a community expected to value nation above life, pointing to the capacities of such images to engender political violence. Liberation, here, was tied to the desire for state formation, one preemptively demanding devotion and sacrifice from aspirant citizens.

Sri Lanka's conflict seeps through and past orderly calendrical delineations. The period covered in this chapter encapsulates the first three "official" phases of civil war, described by the Sri Lankan government as Eelam War I, II, and III, beginning in 1983 and ending with the 2002 ceasefire agreement signed between the LTTE and the government of Sri Lanka. This timeline is essential for understanding the production and circulation of images and the technologies and local transnational networks in a pre-digital era. It is of further importance to contextualizing the extraordinary transformations enabled by the digital during the final phase of war between 2006 and 2009 (chapter 6). Second, I elaborate how everyday photographic practices were transformed during this period of fighting in response to economic hardship, war deaths, loss and displacement, and expanded militarism and militarization by the state and the LTTE, as well as the latter's efforts to build a nation-state. This is also, principally, an agitant photography of political ambition that envisions the future of nation and state. With an explicit focus on violence and atrocity, that of the perpetrator and one's own, in its capacity to generate political transformation, this photography turns uncivil (Azoulay [2012] 2015). This uncivil photography was deployed to produce violence considered essential to liberation.

Few images from this period survive in Sri Lanka in their material forms of prints and negatives; most were destroyed or proscribed from any visible display or dissemination. A handful, such as those taken by Chandragupta Amarasinghe during the 1983 Black July pogrom, have been copied and reproduced extensively, typically appearing in the form of posters or increasingly shared online on social media platforms such as Twitter (X), Facebook, and Instagram. Overseas, visual-material remains can still be found in private hands, neglected community collections, or more commonly digitized to illustrate or accompany narratives on Tamil websites or shared on social media by diasporic Tamils (chapter 7). These are rarely, if ever, attributed to the original photographers. Such images persist as a visual-political history of violence, underpinning a vocal accusation of genocide. Central to the making and moving of images are also elicitations of death, sacrifice, and terror and their relationship to the extant and aspirant state and the future of ultimately irreconcilable imaginaries of nation.

The visual debris of war considered in this chapter is partial and fragmented, and largely secret and precarious. I encountered photographs by chance and trust in Sri Lanka and the United Kingdom; I piece them together in earnest, along with recollections from those I cannot name and accounts from international and local media coverage, to understand the abiding efficacy and volatility of these insurrectionary images. This situation allows us to grasp how and why certain genres of images materialized in response to the conflict and how their agitant capacities were wielded in a time of war. These photographs remain volatile today, capable of instigating the violence of the state through arrest or worse; they are likewise shared to express belonging to the Tamil homeland. It is also essential to recognize their bearing in relation to various Sri Lankan government prohibitions on Tamil activism, advocacy, and commemoration and their respective image movements, which will be explored in subsequent chapters.

Saidiya Hartman writes, "Every historian of the multitude, the dispossessed, the subaltern, and the enslaved is forced to grapple with the power and authority of the archive and the limits it sets on what can be known, who is endowed with the gravity and authority of historical actor" (2019, xv). What are the limits of the Sri Lankan conflict's intended and unintended photographic "archives" formed out of and pared by war? We confront fragmented, competing records in the service of nation and state, each asserting its political legitimacy toward claims and attempts at retaliation, sovereignty, and justice. How, then, do we engage with the interstitial, the pictured Tamil aspirations for freedom, but also the martial pursuit for authority by a self-appointed representative of cause and consequence? How does this ambition and anticipation of sovereignty by whatever means necessary shape the archives of the oppressed located within a global iconography of revolution? Images of Sri Lanka's war and their uses explain the ouroboros of subjugated nation seeking transition into sovereign state through the politically-generative violence of an armed struggle. Here, the visual and rhetorical language of revolution serves as an expedient mode for mobilization that compels the subjugated to choose what is considered acceptable violence and who was responsible for such violence. Importantly, these archives demonstrate how violence, in its pictured forms and otherwise, was deemed necessary to achieve political liberation, vexing how "conflict photography" has been imbued with a moral, humanitarian lens, giving way to forms of "uncivil spectatorship" (Buthpitiya 2023b). Volatility as a frame expands this transformation where during war any photographic image can be deployed to agitate, just as it can invoke horror, loss, and fear.

THE BOYS PHOTOGRAPHED

The LTTE's awareness and strategic use of photography and its political potentials are apparent from the group's early years. This use of photography was integral not only to how the Tigers established a localized image regime in the service of its political aspiration for an independent Tamil Eelam, but also how it sought to garner support overseas, among the Tamil diaspora and the wider international community. Through such visual and discursive exercises, by the 1980s, the LTTE, largely made up of young Tamil men known locally as "the boys," had positioned itself as "the armed vanguard of the revolutionary struggle," explicitly aligning the group's politics with the "revolutionary theory and practice of Marxism and Leninism" (LTTE, n.d.).

An undated black-and-white photography book produced by the LTTE, which I estimate to be from the mid-1980s, titled *Portrait of a Nation: A Photographic Record of the Tamil Eelam Liberation Struggle,* offers an explicit visual and textual positioning of the group's ethos and aspiration. It borrows from a global political moment and aesthetic of anti-imperialist third world camaraderie and socialist revolution, professing that the LTTE wished "to express support for and solidarity with all revolutionary liberation struggles of the oppressed masses of the world" (LTTE, n.d.). The English-language production makes clear that it was specifically intended for an overseas audience. The chronicle contains an interweaving of text and images of militarism and atrocity in support of the claim for Tamil Eelam and the LTTE as composed of martial-political actors capable of achieving its realization. The cover features LTTE leader Prabhakaran holding an assault rifle in an early iteration of the group's uniform that had not yet settled into its emblematic tiger stripes. Positioned against a felled tree and foliage, legs akimbo, Prabhakaran gazes into the distance. The disembodied legs of a comrade who stands atop a branch are visible in the image, as if he were standing on the shoulders of a future giant. The photograph is flanked by a map of Tamil Eelam delineated out of the island of Sri Lanka, evoking

Benedict Anderson's framing of map as logo of nation ([1983] 1991, 243). The liberation struggle is described here as "an oppressed nation fighting against the oppressor, the Sinhala ruling elite [constituting] an integral part of the international struggle of revolutionary forces against imperialism and neo-colonialism" (LTTE n.d., 1). "The object of this record," the impassioned caption notes, "is to expose the lies and hypocrisy and place before you the reality, the history of immense suffering as well as the heroic struggles of the oppressed Tamil masses who, in facing slavery and slow death, have no choice but to fight for dignity and freedom" (LTTE n.d., 1).

What follows is a brief historical narrative, punctuated by graphic images showing the state-sponsored massacre of Tamils, described as "multidimensional oppression" and "racial pogroms and attempted genocide" (LTTE n.d., 5). Dismembered bodies are placed alongside bloodied children in agony, coupled with images showing deprivation in the hill country affecting Tamil workers of Indian origin and the dire conditions in camps for the internally displaced persons. The failures of Tamil nonviolence represented by post-independence civil disobedience campaigns that were organized by Tamil politicians following various episodes of ethnic violence and/or the introduction of discriminatory legislation are also integrated. The book ends with an account of the Tiger movement and the liberation struggle in which stylized portraits of the leadership are presented alongside successful acts of terror committed by the group, including the bombing of an Air Ceylon plane in 1978. Uniformed combatants are seen in training scenarios and battle formation, triumphantly brandishing guns above their heads. Women fighters, who would become the important subjects of militant photography in the decades that followed, were still absent. What is noteworthy in these representations is that the faces of combatants, except for those of Prabhakaran and his second and third in command, respectively, Charles Anthony alias Seelan and Sathasivam Chelvanayakam alias Sellakili, have been manually obscured. It is reasonable to assume that these photographs were likely taken during the group's clandestine training exercises in South India starting in 1979. Either unevenly scored out by hand in black ink or eyes and mouth colored over in black bars, the identities of the other combatants remain concealed, exalted to anonymous but in an ultimately heroic form through the dress and dramatized poses of fighters. Seelan and Sellakili had been killed at the point of the book's publication, thus also cementing Prabhakaran's trajectory as the face and leader of the LTTE and the Tamil liberation struggle. Such photographic publications were part of the group's international strategy for visibility and fundraising as well as history-writing.

Through this period, the LTTE garnered a reputation for impenitent ruthlessness. By the late 1970s, the group had orchestrated numerous assassinations and executions of key Tamil political actors whom they viewed to be traitors or aligned with government, police officers, and opponents from competing political factions; the group also perpetrated bombings, armed robberies, and attacks on state-owned infrastructure in northern Sri Lanka. In turn, the government deployed greater numbers of military personnel to the north with expanded powers to curb violence, resulting in the greater persecution of politically active young Tamils who were arrested and detained under the newly introduced Prevention of Terrorism Act (PTA), which significantly increased the authority of the police and armed forces with wide powers of search, arrest, and detention.[1] During this period, Tamil militant groups began to take refuge in Tamil Nadu and partake in covert combat preparation activities, aside from forming relationships with Marxist groups such as the Popular Front for the Liberation of Palestine (PFLP).

Internecine violence worsened, even famously escalating to a shootout between Prabhakaran and Uma Maheswaran of the People's Liberation Organization of Tamil Eelam (PLOTE) in 1982. The incident was significant because it yielded to the Sri Lankan state the first photograph of Prabhakaran, who was arrested after the exchange of fire. Though not yet especially notable as a leadership figure, he was wanted for crimes including the murder of the mayor of Jaffna, Alfred Duraiappah. D. B. S. Jeyaraj flags that Prabhakaran destroyed every single photograph of himself in his house in Valvettithurai, Jaffna, so that he could evade apprehension, and police identification had relied on an old postal identity card photograph he had used to sit for public examinations (2014). A Sri Lankan government–issued flyer from this period states, "Handsome rewards will be offered for information regarding the following persons wanted for iterrogation [*sic*] by the C.I.D. [Criminal Investigation Department] in connection with terrorist activities." A boy Prabhakaran's postal ID photograph captioned with his name and home address is first among a group of similar headshots featuring others, including Sabaratnam Sabalingam, who was later assassinated in Paris. He was shot point-blank in the presence of his wife and children for allegedly preparing to publish an anti-LTTE book. Despite the practical fears surrounding photographs as the basis for identification, documents such as *Portrait of a*

Nation indicate how photography was viewed as having wider political and historical import. It also reveals how the volatility of images is managed rather than passively dealt with. An image that can engender apprehension can also become representative of a possible national future. Photography and wider image-making practices became a vital and subversive means to mobilize popular support for the armed struggle.

As conflict escalated through the 1980s, militancy, violence, and atrocity became central to Sri Lanka's photographic repertoire, especially as captured by international photographers. If photographic representations of the island had reliably evoked its Edenic character through the nineteenth and twentieth centuries in the work of visiting and resident photographers, showcasing its remarkable natural beauty and idyllic daily life, by the 1990s it firmly foregrounded the graphic violence of insurgency and war. *Sri Lanka: War Stories*, a 2008 photography book by British photographer Stephen Champion, offers a distressing retrospective on state and militant executions, military parades and checkpoints, gun-toting soldiers and rebels, informants masked with cloth tied across their faces, the internally displaced, returning refugees, bomb attacks and ruins, mourning and destitute families, and amputees, interspersed among photographs of plantation and agricultural labor and landscapes suspended between dream and ruin. As if to validate, with photographic irony, Sinnarasa's assertion about child soldiers, it features a primary school–aged child clad in a striped LTTE uniform posing in front of a paper pandal constructed as part of a Maaveerar Naal (Great Heroes' Day) celebration at Elephant Pass. Against a backdrop of rows of martyrs' portraits housed in tents and red and yellow streamers stretching across the open sky, the boy stands below a composite image of a pair of combat boots placed atop a mound of memorial stones and a cluster of *karthigai* flowers.[2] Designated as the national flower of Eelam Tamils as part of the 2003 Maaveerar Naal celebrations, administrative officials requested residents of the north and east to wear the bloom on all occasions of national significance and grow the vine in homes, business premises, public spaces, and educational institutions, explicitly noting this as significant to the nation-state (TamilNet 2004). A rifle is hoisted between the boots with the downturned barrel pressed into the mound of stones, and an LTTE cap is perched on the butt.

Within such a reorientation, LTTE cadres became the much sought after subjects of international photojournalists. Through the first decade of war, sensational glimpses into northern Sri Lanka were seen in the work of photographers who had been granted cautious access to capture the inner workings of the enigmatic Tamil Tiger "suicide cult" making up the "world's most dedicated guerrilla group" (Fineman 1992). Their liberation war was relayed through dramatic portraits that appeared in international newspapers and magazines, imbuing the group with revolutionary cachet. In the early years, slight, ragtag sarong-clad young men were photographed with customary cyanide capsules strung around their necks as they deftly wielded homemade grenades and T56s, waging war in the jungles. Later, gun-bearing uniformed women and children defiantly presented themselves to the camera, unapologetic in their demand for Tamil Eelam. Women fighters of the LTTE became iconic of the egalitarian and emancipatory possibilities of the militancy (Buthpitiya 2023a).

The Sri Lankan state soon became wary of sympathetic accounts. International media narratives largely romanticized the LTTE as underdog freedom fighters led by the enigmatic yet ruthless Prabhakaran, nimbly decimating the state security forces through guerrilla warfare. Access to the war zone was actively curtailed if not prohibited for security reasons, with reports of war filtered through the capital Colombo rather than the front lines. In response to the LTTE's massacre of 600 surrendered police officers in the Eastern province in 1990, the government had also placed an embargo on food, medicine, and other essential items from entering the Jaffna Peninsula to allay the LTTE. Food, medicine, and other essentials were in grievous short supply, resulting in harsh rationing and hyperinflation, coupled with a strict regime of taxation and "contributions" imposed by the LTTE to support the struggle (Sarvanathan 2003, 1844). Met with a lack of petrol, old British cars, adapted to run on kerosene, ferried the injured and the dead. Shortage in newsprint saw newspapers repurposing cardboard, brown paper, and sheets from school exercise books, running at its lowest point a mere two pages to cover casualties so that relatives might know if a loved one had been killed or wounded. During this period, the north was effectively cut off from the rest of the island even though basic public services including education, health, and social services continued to operate minimally where resources and staff were made available. Censorship had long become institutionalized by the Sri Lankan state to reinforce expanding securitization and state violence.

However, such restrictions and enforcement of a government narrative had not operated without challenge from the international media. In 1987, Shyam Tekwani, an Indian photojournalist, who, after being denied access by the Sri Lankan government at the peak of the IPKF (Indian Peace

Keeping Force) intervention, evaded the media ban to enter the north, spent five days "in the tiger's den" to produce what have been described as the "only authentic pictures from the battlefield" at the time (Tekwani 1987). Tekwani's eyewitness account and photographs that emerged from the thick of the war zone at one of its worst moments were some of the most notable (1987). The photographs document the scale of violence that had pervaded through the Jaffna Peninsula, extending from rows of the civilian casualties of shelling in Chavakachcheri lined up on the red polished floors of unidentifiable outdoor corridors, maimed IPKF soldiers sprawled on dirt roads, and boys with guns rifling through the belongings of dead soldiers: "they pulled out chocolates from the shirt pocket of a bloody corpse and passed them around while idly kicking at the remains of a human brain" (Tekwani 1987). The photographer was also responsible for two portraits of Prabhakaran that would become iconic; they have been said to mirror his idol Che Guevara, one pointing a pistol at the camera and another set against a map of northern Sri Lanka bearing the Tiger insignia. These endure in animated circulation, reappearing periodically on platforms such as Instagram, shared by Tamil youth in the diaspora.

The government's callous policies and its effort to contain news images showing the impact on the northern Tamil community became most visible and controversial in the case of American war correspondent Marie Colvin (1956–2012), who, in 2001, flouted the government ban on journalists' travel to the war zone. In her attempt, Colvin lost an eye in a shooting by the Sri Lankan Army as she tried to cross back into government-controlled territory from the Vanni with the help of local Tamils. Colvin claimed that the Sri Lankan government's prohibition was aimed at blocking journalists from talking to the LTTE leadership but also "prevented any reporting on the plight of the 500,000 Tamil civilians, 340,000 of them refugees, bottled up in the Vanni suffering under an economic embargo that the government denied existed" (Colvin 2001).

THE PENINSULA AT WAR

By the 1990s, the LTTE had established itself as a capable and ruthless military actor demonstrating major success against the Sri Lankan armed forces and the IPKF on land, air, and sea; thus it began to consolidate its presence and authority as a state actor. This extended beyond administrative, policing, and judicial arrangements to a concerted focus on the visual, material, and spatial construction of the Tamil nation-state.

Mira, a teacher, tenderly reminisced about her childhood growing up in Jaffna, even though she and her family had been forced to leave their home in 1992. She had been twelve years old. We were sitting in her Colombo home with her mother Sherine, when Mira dispatched her primary school–aged children to complete various homework tasks, noting that she has not discussed much of "this" with them. "We used to eat under the stars. Though we didn't have electricity, and, in a sense, we had to be in darkness every night . . . We made the best out of the circumstances with the encouragement of my father who worked with the church. We used to play games during the bombing raids. We would sing. My memories of childhood are very positive because of that—even if we lived through the war." For others like Anthony, a fisherman, who suffered multiple displacements and countless interlinked devastations of war at the hands of the Sri Lankan and Indian armies and the rival Tamil militant groups in the 1980s and the 1990s, it was an exercise in adversity and survival. Nearly starving on account of the various privations the town was subjected to, Anthony recalled the harrowing journey of smuggling his two little children out of the Tiger-controlled area after being denied "passes" to leave. For him, the peninsula had felt like, in a sentiment repeated by many, "an open prison," bloodied and sundered by shifting front lines and browbeaten by competing armies as the government engaged in indiscriminate aerial bombing.

As a ten-year-old in 1990, Ganeshan, the son of a doctor, was forced to leave a predominantly Muslim village in Mannar where his father had worked all of Ganeshan's life and return to his parents' hometown of Jaffna with "just three gunny bags" into which the well-off family's worldly possessions had to be whittled down. "We had to leave everything, our house, even my father's car. I still remember it—a Mitsubishi Lancer and one of maybe three cars in the area at the time." When his father eventually returned to check on their property, it had been largely stripped by the army. "Jaffna was terrible. There was no petrol, no soap, no exercise books—I remember going around houses collecting unfinished books and binding the papers together myself. The schools refused to take us because they said we were from Mannar, and they didn't know our standard. My brother and I had to wait more than a year and privately study for exams. In 1995, we were displaced again and lived in Chavakachcheri in a place we shared with thirty-five to forty people. Again, no school for ten months. Though, the thing is that during the LTTE times we were happy." The narratives of Jaffna and the politics of homeland were frequently contradictory even within a single individual's account, much like their sense of allegiance to the cause that had for most of their lives been drilled into them as necessary. Integral to this, of course, was the vast exercise of citizen-making that the LTTE had devised. For those like Mira and Ganeshan, who inhabited the world of Jaffna occupied by the LTTE, the "enemy" took on the shape of the Sinhalese and their army and their capacity for wreaking horror. This held viscerally true for many in their encounters with the armed forces. "We were insulated in a world of LTTE propaganda," Mira reflected. Precious access to the outside was offered by the 9 p.m. BBC news on transistor radios, brought out once a day, given the dearth of batteries, as they had been banned by the government.

As observed by Sharika Thiranagama, examining how the group sought to "reform" the social world of Jaffna, "the LTTE's military regime was also aural and visual" ([2011] 2013, 48). The Tigers' television and radio stations Nitharsanam (Truth or Reality), launched as early as 1986, and Pulikal Kural (Voice of Tigers), coupled with newspapers such as *Eelanatham,* became the dominant sources of news and entertainment in the north. Established as a newspaper in 1988, *Pulikal Kural* had metamorphosed into a radio station by 1990 with an hour-long broadcast between 8 and 9 p.m. It became an outlet for political messaging, news, poetry, and song; it survived tens of airstrikes and multiple dislocations. Nitharsanam, the dedicated film and media unit, specialized in battlefield camerawork and participated in many frontline operations to obtain footage utilized to produce propaganda materials as well as for training purposes. The LTTE also supported publishing, art, photography, and videography to produce posters, handbills, books, pamphlets, photo books, exhibitions, public art installations, and music alongside an early investment in the potential of the internet. The timescape and soundscape of the peninsula and the Vanni were further engineered with the adoption of "international days" such as Women's Day, adapted to mirror aspects of the cause for Tamil Eelam (Roberts 2006). Mira and Ganeshan recalled how patriotic LTTE songs were stridently played on loudspeakers: "They just became the songs we absent-mindedly sang along to—even now sometimes even if I don't support the LTTE." Such martial desires for the making of a Tamil state permeated the world of Jaffna through not only violence but cultural production involving inflammatory depictions of violence deemed essential and generative, especially in the sacrifices and

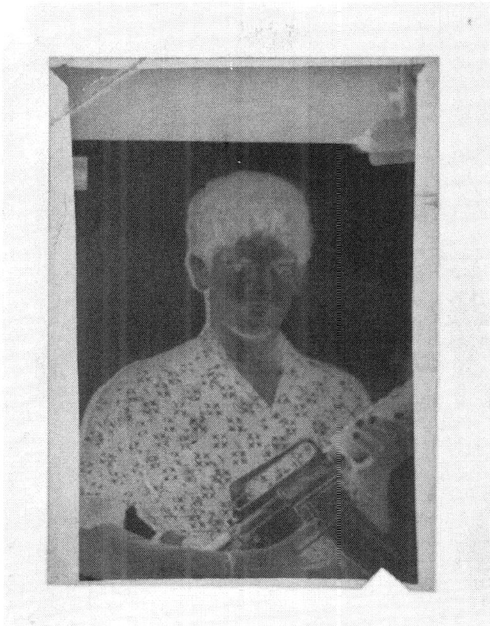

FIGURE 7. Copying negative of combatant portrait (Jaffna, 2018)

acts of devotion that were required of its citizens. Where conflict-induced migration had significantly increased, the consumers of the portable materials were local and overseas. The transnational media operation allied a globally dispersed, temporarily dislocated Tamil audience to the homeland and the ambition of realizing a sovereign Tamil Eelam. Such media coverage was also inextricable from the enumeration, representation, and valorization of death. Images of death and the dead were actively circulated by the LTTE as memorial portraits deifying martyrs, atrocity images showing the horrific cost of Sri Lankan military violence on Tamil bodies dead and injured, and the group's capable reprisal in killing and maiming members of the government forces through guerrilla warfare and its growing arsenal of improvised and imported weaponry. Photographs of the bodies of the war dead became triggers, cautions, and celebrations. As agitants, these photographs were weaponized as propaganda to stimulate further violence and death (fig. 7).

Ganeshan recalled the way in which the bodies of dead army soldiers were put on display in a "nice tent" in Kittu Park in Jaffna as warning and display of might before they were, he guessed, handed over to the International

Committee of the Red Cross (ICRC). "From school we go and at the time we were like ahh very good ahh! We had a very good time as a child and at that time I had never seen a Sinhalese in my life. For us, if we think Sinhalese, we picture a big helmet, big mustache, big boots with the *arm* [gun] who will come and kill your mother and rape your sister. . . . Every cartoon in the *Eelantham* paper was just that." Death for the Tigers went hand in hand with diverse practices of image-making. As Allen Feldman notes, "Political terror is caught between a violence that redresses the past and a violence that addresses the future, and as such it is haunted by a crisis in memory, by its inability to compensate for the past and to fashion a sustainable memory of the future it seeks to create" (2003, 66). This image world of war is also then underpinned by conceptions of a political self and enemy other rooted in ethnicized tropes and caricatures, where acts of terror and mass atrocity were legitimized by their framing through the interest of self as crucial and instrumental to the future of nation and state as well as interlinked civic responsibility. Agitant photographic images served to incite the violence necessary for securing this Tamil political future.

These activities served to rally the Tamil community by attesting to the shared nature of their struggle against a despotic Sinhala state and helped disseminate the symbolism and efforts of the movement in fighting this enemy. The Tigers' acts of cultural production were thus aimed at eliciting the nation as future citizens, while building the state. Through this careful control of representation, the LTTE furthered its ambitions of framing itself as the sole agent and arbiter of the Tamil people and their political prospects. The group's iconography swiftly became conflated with articulations of Eelam Tamil identity and its everyday visual-material evocations, given their prominent use in commemorative activities in Sri Lanka and overseas. This cultural-political enterprise was also essential to cultivating an economy. Local and international fundraising activities relied on voluntary and coerced donations and extortion in the form of money and gold, in addition to taxation. Financial contributions from the Tamil diaspora were a substantial source of income. Constantly engaging its support was central to encouraging continuous donations and international support and visibility for Tamil suffering and the liberation struggle. Much like the "Tamilizing" initiatives in Jaffna, expansive international cultural, educational, business, philanthropic, and political networks and outfits, including Tamilcholai language schools and even temples, were also undertaken (Thiranagama [2011] 2013, 48; 2014; Maunaguru and Spencer 2018).

The iconography of the Tigers—the red, black, yellow of the Tamil Eelam flag depicting a snarling tiger enclosed in a ring of bullets and crossed rifles and the *karthigai* flower—became essential leitmotifs not simply in the LTTE struggle but also the Tamil struggle in the aspiration for nation-state and citizenry that sprawled across and beyond its anticipated borders. The LTTE's symbols and aesthetics, expressed in color and form, have persisted in the north and east of Sri Lanka even after the group's demise. The flag and overt depictions of the Tigers, the use of national colors, calendrical events, and rituals of remembrance, especially in relation to funerary and memorialization practices, continue to call out to a nation-state that could have been despite the organization's effective end in 2009. For the Sri Lankan state, however, LTTE imagery continues to serve as a politically expedient scarecrow that can be wielded when needed, as a basis for apprehending political dissidents, for example, or to remind the Sinhalese public of the military's role in protecting Sri Lanka's sovereignty and territorial integrity by defeating terrorism.

BLACK TIGERS, MARTYRDOM, AND CITIZENSHIP BY DEVOTION

Describing the scale of violence in 1987 Jaffna, the members of University Teachers for Human Rights (Jaffna), or UTHR-J, observed: "LTTE went a step further and confined the people to the role of devotees. Those who sensed danger and wished to offer their counsel were silenced with varying degrees of politeness. The reduction of the people to devotees of the political religion of the LTTE was the culmination of a process begun by the TULF [Tamil United Liberation Front] in the early 1970s. The Federal Party (FP) and later the TULF had demanded allegiance to one party as embodying the destiny of the Tamil nation. All others were branded as traitors of various shades" (1995, 99).

Founded in 1988 at the University of Jaffna, the UTHR-J was significant for its human rights documentation work, calling attention to violations by the military, the LTTE and other Tamil militant groups, and the IPKF. One of its founding members, Dr. Rajani Thiranagama, a fearless Tamil human rights activist who was the head of the Department of Anatomy at the University of Jaffna, was assassinated by the LTTE due to the UTHR-J's critical stance on the LTTE's authoritarian conduct and atrocities. The human rights group, which aimed "to challenge the external and internal terror engulfing the Tamil community as a whole through making the perpetrators accountable, and to create space for humanizing the social and political spheres relating to the life of our community," is still denounced by those sympathetic to the Tigers (UTHR-J 2000). I adapt the UTHR-J's early observation on the makings of Eelam Tamil citizenship to examine the image regime it established in service of its vision for nation and an ideal ethno-state and citizenry.

The LTTE's visual production might be broadly categorized into images of death, injury, violence, displacement and destruction, and those centering on militarism, including combat photographs and portraits of the *thalaivar* and martyrs. The latter crucially demonstrate how photography was mobilized as a part of the LTTE's state and citizen-making project through the medium's associations with death and remembrance. The commemoration of dead cadres featured as a central tenet of the LTTE, reinforcing a sense of political socialization and solidarity among Tamils, thus influencing the formation of a communal memory underpinned by a shared experience of Tamilness (McDowell 2012, 27). From what began as candles and photographs of dead fighters being placed on the backs of trucks and driven through Tamil towns and villages, the LTTE's commemorative practices grew more elaborate (McDowell 2012, 29). Remembering those who had sacrificed themselves in calendrical events were inculcated as a part of the community's *varalaatrukkadamai* (historic duty) to the nation (Jeyaraj 2012). These events relied extensively on photography, film, and the prominent display of Tiger iconography. The LTTE also undertook the construction of sprawling *thuyilam illam* (heroes' cemeteries) and *ninaivu cinnam* (token of commemoration/cenotaphs) as memorials for dead cadres (Schalk 1997). These served as public spaces for mourning, complemented by annual "national" events such as Maaveerar Naal and Karumpuli Naal (Black Tiger Day). Such spaces and events actively encouraged the involvement of bereaved heroes' families and typically featured the lighting of lamps, the raising of the Tamil Eelam flag, numerous religious rituals, parades, and processions, the dissemination of posters and handbills featuring the dead cadres, gatherings at memorials and grave sites, and the veneration of framed photographs and portraits; there was also typically an impassioned speech by Prabhakaran on the necessity of the struggle and the importance of sacrifice, which was broadcast to the wider community in Sri Lanka and abroad (Roberts 2006, 77–80). Maaveerar Naal and Karumpuli Naal continue to be organized annually, at grand scale, by diasporic Tamils overseas and more covertly in the north and east of Sri Lanka.

The LTTE's burial and memorialization of its dead marked a turn away from the funerary practices of cremation prevalent among Tamil Hindus

(Natali 2008, 288). Within the LTTE's state-building project, its superlative citizens were those who valued the importance of the cause of Tamil Eelam more than their own life. The LTTE's iconography projected this ideal, permeated with portraits of valiant men and women who epitomized the virtues of selflessness and loyalty, who were then, in a sense, ideal citizens in their demonstrated willingness to sacrifice themselves. As observed by Sharika Thiranagama, such efforts valorizing militarization and promising "a different route to power, status, and heroism, albeit a dangerous one," were central to the political socialization and recruitment of young Tamils, who became increasingly morally ambivalent toward the group ([2011] 2013, 61). Embellished photographic and painted portraits of cadres drawing on stylistic conventions from South Indian cinema as well as Hindu and Tamil divine images became the focus of national veneration. A 1994 photograph of a painted LTTE pandal by Robert Nickelsberg shows the gun of a dead cadre shot dead by the army picked up by a school child, thus invoking a cycle of necessary death and sacrifice. Martyrs' shrines adorned with honor rolls, portraits, and cinematic cutouts were placed in local neighborhoods, allowing for daily public remembrance and devotions.

The spatial and ritual infrastructure enabling reverence for images of martyrs and the leadership of the LTTE evokes the belief of *darsan* or *darsanam* (Tamil) vital to Hindu worship. Michael Roberts notes the similarities between the act of *darsanam* observed during visits to a Hindu temple and deification realized by the worship of these portraits (2006, 91). *Darsanam* describes a ritual component of "seeing and being seen by a deity, an exchange of vision, an auspicious sight, or a blessing deriving from the gaze of the deity" (Roberts 2006, 91). It speaks also to the efficacy of images and icons. In death, cadres who were previously compelled to remain anonymous to ensure the success of their mission were not only named but visualized in idealized superhuman stature. In their recognition and anointment as *maaverar* (great heroes), they are deified through acts of public devotion. Further, in their death, naming, and imaging, their lives and experiences are distilled into epics turned to film and local legend alike, heroizing individual bravery to mythic proportions. Through the inclusion of martyrs' portraits in the sphere of remembrance and worship, the LTTE succeeded in interweaving the sacrifices of individuals and their families to the grander narrative of its aspirant nation-state; the LTTE embedded personal sentiments and memories into the creation of a shared, public iconography anchored ultimately to photographs of the dead. Children, siblings, spouses, and friends could all, in their service to the nation, become gods. Dying became a central visual and rhetorical invocation essential for the future of the Tamil nation-state. Militant photography, thus in its agitant capacity, invited death.

In 2019, a decade after the end of the war, I went to a Maaveerar Naal commemoration in London with a friend, where hundreds of such photographic portraits were assembled in a rambling convention center along with a reconstructed *thuyilam illam* (fig. 8). The event was attended by a few thousand Tamils during the course of the day. They queued to pay their respects to those who had sacrificed themselves for Tamil Eelam. "I am here because I recognize that all these people laid down their lives for the possibility of a homeland—for the struggle," my companion mused. An elderly attendee ruminated, "I am a mother, and how can I not feel like these are all my own children?" Along with various other LTTE iconographic paraphernalia, large coffee-table books made up of the portraits were also sold as a fundraising effort signaling their reinscription as political commodity, establishing citizenship by economy and consumption. Another interlocutor who refused to attend on principle was critical of such grandiose events being organized at inordinate financial cost, noting that Tamils in the homeland were still suffering on account of poverty, while such displays only benefited those who held onto the illusion of Tamil Eelam for their own personal gain. However, it was impossible not to be amazed by the journey of these photographs, some two or more decades old, from the hands of photographers in northern Sri Lanka to London in an ever-unfolding "event of photography" (Azoulay [2012] 2015, 14). Photography as an agitant continues to mobilize the nation, even as the state has slipped out of grasp.

Examining the aftermath of the Iranian revolution, Roxanne Varzi notes that "martyrdom is meaningless without memorialization, and memorialization is not possible without photography" (2006, 62). Varzi's observation resonates easily within the Sri Lankan context. Hindu and Catholic religious practices were actively syncretized by the LTTE in this process of consolidating Tamil identity with the view of securing a dedicated homeland. This not only permitted the Tigers greater legitimacy in the eyes of their "constituents," but also helped strengthen their "national identity" through immensely personal connection. The "cult of martyrdom" and heroism to honor fallen combatants was fundamental to the LTTE's efforts to rationalize the forced conscription of Tamil youths and the sacrifice of their lives for the cause of Eelam, for the greater good of the Tamil community (Roberts 2005, 2006; Thiranagama [2011] 2013, 42). However, Tamil critics

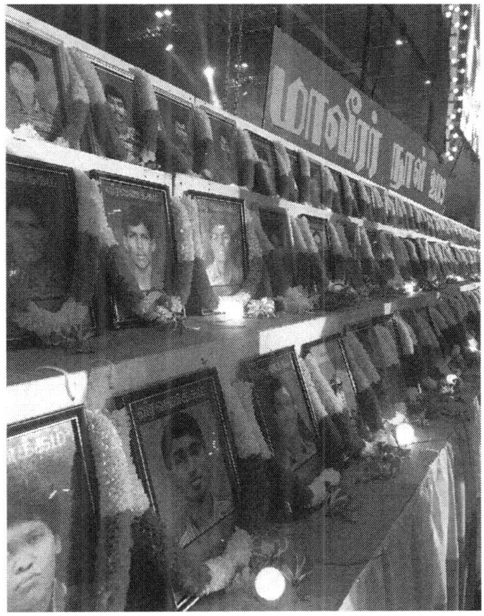

FIGURE 8. Maaveerar Naal commemoration (London, 2019)

and opponents killed by the LTTE due to their alleged treachery to the nation could never become martyrs. The memorialization of fallen cadres draws attention to the LTTE's use of visual (and linguistic) practices to engage the emotions of the Tamil community and garner support for their political cause on the grounds of not only their identity as Eelam Tamils but also common loss. These efforts were fundamental to cultivating a sense of sociality founded on sacrifice, resistance. and ultimately citizenship by devotion, and affirming their legitimacy as custodians of the Tamil people. Every aspirant Tamil citizen, under the Tigers' rule, had the potential to become a hero, and eventual citizenship was made possible by such heroism to secure Tamil Eelam. From the perspective of the Sri Lankan government, every Tamil body could then be transformed by the LTTE into a "terrorist" and a "deadly weapon" to destroy the state and by extension Sinhalese sovereignty. Circulating visuals of identified suspects triggered animosity toward Tamils more generally, flattened into a category of menace through language and racialization. Consequently, Tamils who had to navigate life and travel across Sri Lanka were often held up, searched, and harassed at checkpoints until their identities could be verified, or they were stopped, detained, or even tortured on account of their ethnicity.

MOTHERLAND DREAM

Thayakkanavu (Motherland dream), a 35-minute film produced by the LTTE, is a compelling invocation of death and wartime image-devotions, showing the volatility of photography in its capacity to incite action and the role of the medium in nurturing ideal citizen disciples. It begins with an icon of a Black Tiger whose face has been customarily concealed, for the identities of suicide cadres were only revealed and venerated through acts of public commemoration and devotion after their sacrifice for the nation. The actor-fighters of the cast are introduced as heroes, as they perform combat skills for the camera. A Tiger commander sitting at the head of a table is introduced, instructing his cadres about the necessity of fighting for their land. A map of the northern peninsula was prominently displayed in the background alongside a large portrait of Prabhakaran in uniform. A shrine to Black Tigers adorned with blinking electric lights stands to his right.

The story pivots to its young male protagonist, Seralakan, thumbing through his diary. He affectionately runs his hand over the image of Prabhakaran on the cover, after which he turns to a page dated June 1993, reflecting on his blissful family life by way of a photograph. Each scene of the flashback is triggered by the clicks of a Minolta camera that appears on the screen—a clever audiovisual elicitation of the technology of photography and personal, familial, and political memory and nation making. Seralakan remembers past birthday celebrations when his parents and younger sisters were eating butter cake and posing for photographs in their garden. One day, Seralakan witnesses the brutal and bloody aftermath of an aerial assault by the Sri Lankan Air Force. As planes fly above, giant clouds of smoke emanate from the shelled landscape. These shots rapidly cut back and forth between the face of a Tamil girl who cups her face and looks up at the sky fearfully and a distressed old woman; the images show their vulnerability.

Following impact, the rubble is drenched in "blood" as the old woman's corpse is revealed. A father carrying the body of his dead daughter walks toward Seralakan. The limp bodies are soaked in a saturated, visually powerful vermilion. Seralakan seeks his father's blessing to enlist. Seralakan trains with a cohort of young men, only to be selected in a draw to sacrifice himself as a Karumpuli (Black Tiger). When his superior tells him to go visit his family before he sets out on his mission, the young man declines, saying that he does not need to see his mother and father, and it would suffice for him to see *anna* (older brother, meaning Prabhakaran). Although *anna* is not seen, the film conveys that he was photographed with the leader. After distributing his personal belongings to his comrades, clad in a black uniform (signaling his status as a Karumpuli) Seralakan bids farewell to his dispatcher as he takes the driver's seat of a van. The keychain dangling off the ignition shows a photograph of Prabhakaran. Seralakan drives his explosive-laden van into an unknown target in the dark. His motivation is represented through a tense montage of the mangled bodies of victims of the bombing he witnessed. Death, in other words, necessitates killing and the death of self and potentially enemy others. The explosion is met with a smile from his dispatcher, signaling the success of Seralakan's suicide mission. The film evokes the story of Vallipuram Vasanthan (nom de guerre, Captain Miller) who drove a truck filled with explosives into an army camp in Jaffna, becoming the LTTE's first Black Tiger on 5 July 1987. This is annually commemorated as Karumpuli Naal (Black Tiger Day). His fellow cadres mourn his death, as a musical montage showcases photographs of fallen heroes and the military prowess of the Tigers. His family is informed of his hero's death. The film ends with a poignant scene of his youngest sister in a pink frock weeping, followed by footage of a fluttering Tiger flag and a call to arms in the form of a voiceover.

In many ways, *Thayakkanavu* condenses, through camera clips and the deft weaving together of personal and official images, the blueprint of LTTE image production and dissemination through a hero's journey turned to film. The visual elements of the film echo those that appeared in photo books and even the built landscape, presenting a concerted effort to give ideological and visual-material shape to the spark of the liberation struggle. Such image-based accounts produced by the Tigers, whether in the shape of narrative films or photography books, typically followed a formula of accentuating the violence of the genocidal Sinhalese state, atrocities committed against the Tamil people since independence, the futility of peaceful protest, the necessity for an independent Tamil Eelam, the LTTE as a capable militant-political representative of Tamil political aspirations, and their martial achievements against the state through acts of terror and frontline feats distilled into representations of the killing and destruction of the enemy. Themes of heroism, valor, and sacrifice were unfailingly ingrained in these expressions through interwoven collective and individual storylines. Glorifying death and dying was fundamental to such constructions of the ideal and practice of martyrdom. For it to hold political value, such death also had to be photographable.

The LTTE's extraordinary attention to reconfiguring the visual-material world of the northeast has been largely overlooked in the scholarship in favor of its explicitly militaristic or political preoccupations. The Tigers' calculated co-optation and redesign of the social fabric and interlinked visual-material landscape is how the group would leave its most potent mark in not only strengthening loyalties but also perpetuating its ideology even after its demise. The LTTE's visual economy of death, in particular, fostered and cemented transnational Tamil political socialities into a unique, syncretic form underpinned by existing religious, aesthetic, and popular cultural practices and pursuits. Fragments of visual materials made by the LTTE, now mostly destroyed in Sri Lanka, survived due to their circulation and safeguarding by individuals overseas. Such content was also increasingly being digitized and uploaded onto the internet and social media platforms as a preservation and dissemination effort, where remembrance as a means of resistance contending against erasure became an important political concern.

TRUTH TIGERS

A subsequent conversation with Sinnarasa pivoted to the LTTE's filmmaking efforts following his dismissal of the existence of child soldiers. He whispered a few titles for me to look up. "You can maybe find them on YouTube and see for yourself. The artists—the talent—were also the fighters! That is also why none of them survived and why we don't have many films to speak of." He laughed morosely.

During the ceasefire period, an Australian news channel, delved into the world of Tiger image-making. The LTTE expediently and prolifically produced and disseminated its own photographs, documentaries, and films such as *Thayakkanavu* locally and internationally, by way of Nitharsanam. The Tigers' filmed their training exercises and battles for learning. Footage could be reviewed to improve on strategy and technique. Many of the Truth Tigers died in battle, and their deaths are noted in the credits of the films they produced (fig. 9). It is essential to reiterate that international media access was carefully controlled by the LTTE. The 2002 news documentary *Truth Tigers* is focused on a twenty-one-year-old woman cadre named Nadhi, who had voluntarily enlisted at the age of fourteen. It features footage of and from the LTTE that helps construct a picture of their practice through its narrative and contents of the image world that it peripherally captures. The battlefront camera teams (two for each unit of a hundred fighters) "expected

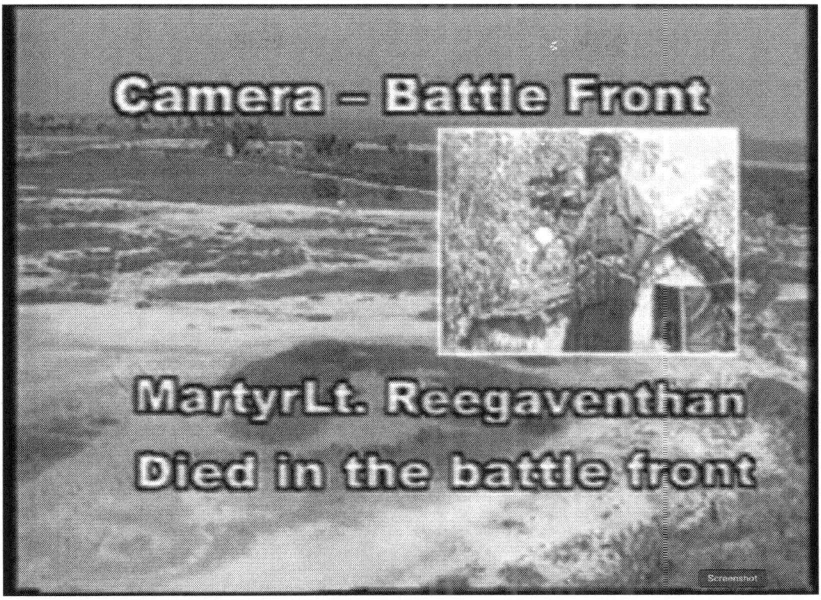

FIGURE 9. Camera martyrs in the credits of an LTTE frontline film

to be in the first wave of any attack recording images of a war fought on a scale few outside Sri Lanka could comprehend" (2002). The filming required special training in exhausting exercises that used live ammunition to remind cadres of the potential costs and refine their skills. "We're looking for two aspects," an LTTE videography coach interviewed in the documentary notes, "One, the person has the potential and the courage to undertake this training. The second, film the fighting beautifully with artistic talent." The latter was necessary for the material that would be transformed into public consumption, featuring not only spectacular battle scenes that emphasized the heroism of the LTTE, but the necessity of bravery and sacrifice to secure Tamil Eelam. These images proved compelling stimuli for cadres as well as the public, upon whom the Tigers relied for compliant recruits, as well as financial and material support.

For Tamils living under LTTE control in the north, images of hostilities became essential to justifications of violence and incentives to engage in further violence to achieve Tamil Eelam. This is to say, the agitant potential of photographs was engaged in war, specifically with a view of justifying and stimulating politically generative violence and normalizing uncivil spectatorship (Azoulay 2008, [2012] 2015). Footage and photographs of Sri Lankan state atrocities were paired with the Tigers' heroic pursuits, involving images of the bodies of Sri Lankan soldiers who had been massacred in battle. Here, the understanding of the civil as it relates to spectatorship subverts Azoulay's expectations, where reprisal violence and/or sacrifice is demanded. Image-making becomes a medium through which political claims are rationalized and "nationalized" rather than "de-territorialized" ([2012] 2015, 25). The civic is cast as martial duty to the nation where the violence of the Sri Lankan state necessitates retaliation. Agitant images were thus wielded to encourage and sustain violence toward realizing acts of nation/state/citizen-making. Here one's civic duty was in fact to engage in acts of violence against others and oneself for the future of the nation-state by whatever means necessary. If a Tamil photography that countered the Tigers' image regime existed, I could not find any evidence of its existence.

War films produced by the Tigers also employed rudimentary CGI (computer-generated imagery) as well as musical numbers to entice the Tamil public, which had, prior to the war, been socialized in a world of South Indian Tamil cinema. Occasionally, spectacular elements of patriotic song-and-dance numbers enhanced the film's entertainment value. Ganeshan recalled how Hollywood war films were shown in co-opted cinema spaces before they mostly closed. The Rambo franchise featuring the exploits of a Vietnam War veteran played by Sylvester Stallone was a popular staple. As early portraits of Prabhakaran have suggested, these films were an important influence in how militants presented themselves to the camera. During the war, cinema spaces in the Tamil-majority northeast of Sri Lanka became places of social and political significance. Prior to the war, cinemas were vibrant spaces for socializing, albeit separated by class, gender, and language, but also implicitly, caste. Demarcated by language, cinemas also transformed into sites of precarity, subject to air raids, but also police roundups, whereby groups of Tamil men were mass arrested. Cinemas became locations of political violence at the hands of other competing militant groups, which took advantage of the space they afforded for use as sites of detention, interrogation, and torture. Jaffna's Sridhar Cinema, which is still unlawfully occupied by the notorious pro-government paramilitary group turned political party—the Eelam People's Democratic Party (EPDP)—is one such example. The closure of larger cinemas made way for "mini theaters" built around makeshift screens. In the absence of electricity, neighbors rallied to put on informal theater productions that were filmed and shown alongside old South Indian Tamil films on rented television sets wired to makeshift generators. Communities gathered in darkness around the light of video screens watching three or four films during a night to make the most of the investment. These provided escape for viewers from the overwhelming realities of war but were also subject to censorship by the Tigers.

OLI KALAI (THE ART OF LIGHT): THE STUDIO AT WAR

Carolyn Nordstrom suggests that during warfare "people at the frontline generate their own solutions" positing a relationship between violence and creativity (1997, xviiii). For the photographers and printers of Jaffna, the demand for their creations thrived, and arguably increased because of the experiences and difficulties of war and the hardships of the embargo. When informal supply routes from and travel to South India were no longer possible, Mr. Krishnarajah, the third-generation owner of a family-run printing press, recalled how he started making letterpress blocks by hand. He used pieces of wood cut from trees in his garden when materials were scarce and imports from India were no longer possible. "The demand was still high. We were working with whatever we could find. Hand-cut and nobody could tell the difference," he affirmed. "That is how good my work was!" Political pressure and demands for such work also escalated. Mr. Krishnarajah recalled how competing parties demanded the production of leaflets, which they were compelled to take on at the risk of getting into trouble with their opponents.

Within this setting, photographic production did not diminish, but by all accounts expanded. A Jaffna-based photographer, Kumaran, who has been running a small studio in town since the early 1990s, said matter of factly, "Just because there were bombs falling doesn't mean people weren't getting married or celebrating their birthdays. If anything, those things became more important to people. I have had customers who would run to the studio with a cake when curfew was lifted to have a family photo taken for their child's birthday." Where life became uncertain and untimely death was all too common, routine and life-cycle events became especially valued. This narrative cannot be separated from the pervasive disruptions to kin relationships in Jaffna that occurred on account of frequent displacement and the fleeing of hundreds of thousands to other parts of the island and overseas. A large Tamil diaspora formed in European, North American, and

Australian cities. Where transnational dispersal has characterized the Tamil community's sociopolitical fabric, such photographic mediations played an important role in connecting de-territorialized kin and nation. Inability to participate in the births, birthdays, puberty ceremonies, weddings, and funerals of their loved ones significantly shaped the output, circulation, and consumption of photographs. These photographs also became central to new kinds of citizenship aspirations during and after the war (chapter 4).

In further conversations with various residents who had experienced the worst of the war in Jaffna through the 1990s, acknowledgments of the endless daily inconveniences and devastations were often sentimental. There were also efforts at creating relief and entertainment amounting to acts of "revitalization," which are often ignored in examinations of war (Nordstrom 1997, 15). "It wasn't that things weren't available," Gajen, a studio photographer who had been taking photographs since the 1980s, said to me. "It was that things became very expensive. If a film roll costs one hundred rupees, we had to pay one thousand. Of course, goods were also smuggled in because of this reason. Film rolls wrapped in paper and hidden in bags of salt!" He grinned, perhaps a little nostalgic for those days, as I would learn many in Jaffna are—even despite the privations of war—because the adversities of the postwar period, its political uncertainty, and its marginalization are frequently perceived as far worse. For many, this melancholy was inseparable from a feeling of lost Tamil autonomy.

The world of Jaffna studio photography was also not exempt from the image-production directives and needs of the LTTE as a state-like patron. I would anecdotally hear about studios and printing presses that had been drafted into the production of identity and memorial photography but no longer existed. The Tigers also invested in photography as a form of public art with an emphasis on producing photo books, hoardings, displays, and exhibitions. Interlocutors recalled how Tamil Eelam was necessitated and envisioned in the LTTE's photographic production, some recalling the specific details of photographs that had inspired them. Among images exhibited were those detailing the hardships of "village life" amid war, the crimes of the Sri Lankan state against the Tamil community showing the maimed and mangled bodies of Tamil civilians, and idealized images of life and landscape in Tamil Eelam where Tiger cadres and their virtues and heroism were afforded special attention. Ganeshan remembered LTTE photography exhibitions organized in tandem with the annual Nallur Temple chariot festival, which would draw thousands of worshippers. Such practices continue during remembrance activities today, where large displays of atrocity photographs are installed at commemoration events.

"There was one photograph from such an exhibition I remember very well," Sivapragasam, a studio photographer who had moonlighted as a documentary photographer for the Tigers, mused. "There was one photograph of a child drinking the *kanji* [porridge] that had spilt from what another child was drinking." To him, the hardships and solidarities forged by war were distilled in that one photograph. It was one of many hundreds that had been printed, turned into pamphlets, or displayed in the northeast to those living amid war, but also shown to Tamils overseas. Sivapragasam, who had apprenticed with Rajaratnam *mama* some decades ago, had set up his first studio in Jaffna before later moving to the Vanni. The Tigers had offered enormous support to local studio photographers, he recalled. This was part of a wider effort to professionalize occupations, notably those bound to marginalized caste identities such as washers and barbers by way of *tholil cangams* (trade unions akin to a professional association). The LTTE was commonly commended for its efforts to eradicate caste hierarchies and stigma in its social reorganization around its political cause. However, it did redistribute emphasis to an ascending three-tiered social structure of *pothu makkal* (public), *poraali kudumbam* (warrior's family), and the esteemed *maaveerar kudumbam* (great hero's family) (Sangarasivam 2000, 63). Benefits were also allocated accordingly, with special privileges including rations, social services, livelihood support, and housing assistance being given to those who belonged to *maaveerar kudumbam* first and *poraali kudumbam* second (Sangarasivam 2000, 63). The professionalization of work associated with oppressed caste identities helped consolidate popular political support for the group, even though its commitment to eliminating caste stigma beyond political expediency has been questioned and disputed. These groupings served as an important *amaippu* (network).

According to Sivapragasam, the Vanni Pranthi Oli Kalai Ondrium (Vanni Province Photographic Arts Union) had at its peak more than three hundred members from the district sub-associations in Kilinochchi, Mannar, Vavuniya, and Mullaitivu. A 50-cent contribution per photograph taken from each photographer would go into a shared account, which permitted the collective to support members with emergency funds, including attending to the costs of family funerals or to mitigate the impact of displacement and the impacts of frequent attacks by the state forces. Sivapragasam recalled how four Mullaitivu district members in Oddusudan had lost all their personal possessions during Operation Riviresa, which was carried out by the Sri Lankan Army, to recapture Jaffna in 1995. The Oli Kalai Ondrium had immediately bought them food and clothes from the central fund. Sivapragasam's recollection highlighted the importance afforded to photography in the aspirant state's incorporation of studio photographers into their image-making practices as a part of their responsibility to the struggle. Malathi, the only professional woman photographer that I encountered in northern Sri Lanka, had similarly worked as a photographer for the *Eelanatham* newspaper through the LTTE years. She did not wish to dwell on the past, largely in fear of the consequences, but in her brief recollection there was a hint of nostalgia for the mobility it afforded her.

Though Sivapragasam too had successfully revived his business under a new name after his displacement in Mullivaikkal, he too was wistful. "Whatever they needed, the association would step in and support. On one occasion, a member got bitten by a snake, and we bought his coffin. The association did very well during the *Iyakkam* time. We were involved in many activities—professional assistance, exhibitions, and learning new technologies—with which the *Iyakkam* was especially encouraging. We do not have any support like that now. Because of these 'technology' skills we were also able to block some people from being taken to fight in the war. We also fulfilled our duty to the *Iyakkam*. For example, we filmed and photographed martyrs' funerals—we had to do that. Now say the Visuvamadu *thuyilam illam* would have fighters from Batticaloa and so on. By the time their parents were able to make it, the body would have been interred, so the parents would come and see the photographs that we took. Videos and photographs. Because of that, filming and photography certainly had to be done. That was part of our occupation. The *Iyakkam* used the photographs in exhibitions that they organized to show the effects of war on village life. These photographs would go 'worldwide'!" Indeed, the "worldwide-ness" of Sivapragasam's photographs would surprisingly find their way back to me in London many months later when I was looking through materials gathered by an advocacy group that focused on victims of enforced disappearances. As I sifted through scans of documents showing photographs or photocopies of images pasted on A4 sheets carefully annotated in pen, I would occasionally encounter a seal belonging to Sivapragasam's old studio. The volatile workings of photography permitted their movement between and among the categorizations of genre.

These losses compound the historiographic deficiencies explored in the preceding chapter. Yet the whittling of the studio and nation by war expanded the transnational ambits of the images produced by Jaffna's photographers, whose practice and technics adapted to keep pace with scarcity, loss, and uncertainty. Much like Rajaratnam *mama,* everyone I met continued to confront loss and absence bound to the war in some way. These were embodied in loved ones killed, disappeared, or migrated across an atlas; the losses also took the shapes of homes and belongings lost or destroyed by war and displacement. Loss could not be separated from the denials and obliterations that marked the community's relationship to the state. Longing and melancholia pervaded the lives of those I encountered. Many had no childhood or family photographs to speak of. The faces of long-gone friends, family, and even their younger selves remained only in their memories, or in unintended photographic keepsakes such as NICs (National Identity Cards), laminated photocopies of photographs, or identity documents printed in black and white. The social history of photography in northern Sri Lanka revealed a social history of loss and how photography helped mediate and make visible those losses in various ways.

When Rajaratnam *mama* reflected on his experience of losing nearly the entirety of his life's work in the 1995 Battle of Jaffna, his tone was not one of resentment, anger, or sadness, but unburdened acceptance—that it was what it was, confirmed by a pensive smile on his face. "In life, there are many little upsets, but there are no major *kavalai* [concerns]. Andavan [god Shiva] has been good to me.[3] If there is enough money to eat and maybe 50–100 rupees here and there for me to give to those in need, what more can I ask for?" Rajaratnam *mama*'s quiet words, at peace about something that to me felt like it would be a devastating loss, puzzled me at first. They were situated, however, in a wider cosmology of life, loss, and attachment: the inevitable, intrinsic interweaving of creation and destruction that underpinned his deep devotion to Hinduism. Rajaratnam *mama* was one of many people I met who had lost virtually everything, along with others who were in a situation that many would find difficult to relate to, in not possessing a single photograph of themselves or their families from when they were younger—lost, destroyed, or sometimes never made.

Mercy, now in her late fifties, did not have any pictures of herself from her younger years. I gave her a print of a portrait I had taken of her at a wedding I had been invited to. "A photograph they can remember me by when I die!" she uttered gleefully to my horror, flipping through the various photographs of her and her family that I had taken.[4] "*Sariyana vadiva iruku enna?* [Don't I look very *vadivu*]."[5] She refused to part with the pictures I had taken for her sisters and nieces. The war had also amplified elicitations of love and death.[6] The latter had become more insistently incorporated into the work of the studio and visual economy of post/war Jaffna. Where the war had distorted the boundaries between intimate and public, the domestic and the institutional, family and state security, the pleasures, loves, and deaths invoked by photography were magnified, in service of the nation as much as the community and the individual. Arumugamsamy kept a photocopy of a stamp-sized headshot taken by Rajaratnam *mama* many years ago taped into his wallet. The original was long lost. "I remember it so well, coming to the studio to take this photo," he directed his memory to Rajaratnam *mama*. "Is that so? Did I take this? That's very good!" They laughed. "It was a very good picture. That is why I have kept this copy," Arumugamsamy confirmed. In the photo, he was wearing a smart "tie coat" borrowed from the studio, as was standard practice. Items of clothing he would never wear in his daily life as a bus driver for the state transport board. Loss was sometimes densely, sometimes delicately, woven over and through the north, through its communities, through their pictures present and absent.

Susan Sontag wrote that the understanding of war among people who have not experienced war is now chiefly a product of the impact of the proliferation of images of conflict enabled by "the ceaseless flow of domestic, small-screen entertainment," alluding to America's video consumption of the Vietnam War (2003, 18–19). However, this "nonstop imagery" was as central to those living in a context of war, being made to receive and understand the war, even as we lived through and in the midst or on the fringes of it, in the way it was mobilized to compel us to pick sides, identify dangers, and inform our wider political socialization as citizens. Everyday photographic practices too were appropriated by the aspirant state in service of the making of the nation, whether in generating funeral photographs, memorial portraiture, or envisioning Tamil Eelam. Importantly, these wartime image regimes persist in the postwar, framing everyday political expression through associated visual practices, extending from protest to commemoration. Such contemporary recursions make up the second portion of this book.

In September 2019, when I returned to Jaffna, the weeklong annual commemoration for the thirty-second anniversary of the death of R. Parthipan, or Lt. Colonel Thileepan, was underway. Thileepan, the LTTE's political leader for the Jaffna Peninsula, fasted unto death as an appeal to the Indian government to honor five demands made on behalf of the Tamil people in 1987. The site of the destroyed memorial, in front of one of Jaffna's most bustling businesses, Rio Ice Cream, frequented by locals, tourists, and the military alike, had been decorated and turned into an elaborate shrine that locals visited to pay their respects. Although explicit Tiger Insignia were perhaps absent, colors associated with the group (red and yellow) evoking the *karthigai* flower were actively used in the form of flags and streamers. Cinematic cutouts of Thileepan were interspersed with photographs of the final days of his fast. The army had visited and attempted to dismantle the site but were asked to overlook the activity by local politicians, given that the elections would be taking place in the next month. As I went to inspect the memorial, a local man who had come bearing flowers and incense encouraged me to take my shoes off and go and pay my respects to Colonel Thileepan. Sinhalese pilgrims, whose tour buses had parked for an ice cream break at Rio's, watched the memorial from across the road in quiet concern and whispered discussion. Patriotic LTTE music blared loudly out from a megaphone attached to an electricity pole. Non-Tamil speakers were impervious to the unapologetic singsong demands for sacrifice and homeland.

Even in the absence of the state actor, aspirant citizenship by devotion and obligation to nation endured, and at its heart was photography.

4 *NAVEENA CAMERA*

POSTCARDS FROM THE POSTWAR

Kugan Photo in Parathathurai, or Point Pedro, was perched at the northernmost tip of the island along a quiet road that curved off at the sliver of ocean separating Sri Lanka from the Indian subcontinent.

The two-story building, in the pastel iced-birthday-cake palette of postwar renovation favored by Jaffna's homeowners, is pale pink. Its name is hand-painted on the side in big letters. At the end of a road, a military-run checkpoint and welfare canteen flanked by a new Buddhist temple and an old Hindu shrine look over a small harbor. The green wire fences that stretch along the coastal road toward Ponnalai demarcate land occupied by the army cutting through and across the area's fishing villages clustered around splendid saint-named Catholic churches. The material effects of war were still scattered through the town. Its municipal buildings, color-washed in a cheerful baby blue nodding lightly to a dated Indo-Saracenic sensibility with a single onion dome, sat alongside a cluster of bright little shops, a bustling central bus stand, and crumbling ruins caved in from bombardment. Oceanside military outposts channeled visitors to a concrete sign embellished with the Sri Lankan flag at the Sakkotei Cape. An English-language caption reads: "Unity in diversity is the strength of Sri Lanka," asserting the state's militarized making of a postwar heritage landscape. Such emblems were scattered across the north and east reminding of the "victory" that had been secured in 2009.

The husks of abandoned homes and thickets of palmyra that occupied the same stretch of road preoccupied photographers of the postwar, featuring in the holiday snaps of tourists and the reportage of international photojournalists alike. Not far off in Kankasanthurai (KKS), the last stop on the Colombo-Jaffna Yaal Devi train, a different set of photographies emerged. In the 1980s and 1990s, the area had been designated a High Security Zone (HSZ) by the military, following which its residents were forcefully evicted without compensation. In large overgrown plots of land zigzagged with barbed wire and military hoardings, houses turned into hollow vessels for eager banyan trees, brick walls cracked open by the tightening grip of roots. The old KKS rest house, built by the British and turned into an officers' mess during the war, had been transformed in its immediate aftermath into a luxury seaside resort for members of the armed forces. Thalsevana was uniquely located, allowing visitors to see the sunrise to the east and sunset to the west over the horizon.[1] Despite vocal public and civil society concerns about expanding militarization in the guise of commercial and tourism ventures, the resort had also unwittingly become a preferred spot for outdoor photography shoots in the peninsula, forming the backdrop for wedding and engagement and girls' puberty ceremony portraits.

Kokulan, a photographer based in Jaffna Town, who traveled with his clients to picturesque locations in the Jaffna Peninsula, including KKS and the new Sangupiddy Bridge, complained that the upkeep of the resort had in fact declined since the Rajapaksas had been defeated in the 2015 election.[2] When I ask him about the Rajapaksa's hardline Sinhala nationalist politics and rampant militarization, he said dismissively, "This is a business matter. . . . It is a picturesque location, and I want my clients to have beautiful pictures." Kokulan was not alone in his "practical" approach to the status quo of the victor's postwar situation; his approach was one of survival. The pristine stretches of seafront land in KKS were also penned for modern holiday bungalows for senior military personnel. They bore signs prohibiting photography, a warning that was once ubiquitous during the war years, but now rarely seen except near military camps. With the change in government in 2015, patches of land and largely destroyed homes were being reluctantly released to their owners. The return of land resulted in a small influx of internally and internationally displaced locals. In 2018, a number of refugees who had been domiciled in Tamil Nadu returned, putting up makeshift fences and concrete block huts. Bold-lettered boards shouted PRIVATE PROPERTY. NO TRESPASSING at passers-by; occasionally, the signs indicated the owner's name and telephone number. In 2024, resettled families in Palaly North still lacked access to water, sanitation, electricity, and basic infrastructure.

At the public ceremony marking the handover, former army commander Mahesh Senanayake reminded recipients, "I request parents to educate their children to not drag this country back into war. You will be the ones who suffer again, not anybody else. If there are people with money, they must have gone abroad or to the south. Only the poor are left here. As the Commander of the Army, I am asking you not to behave in a way or receive ideas that create war in this country again. Just as we give you these lands and facilities, we can also take it back again. . . . I ask of you to not bring back a situation of war in this country again."[3]

STUDIO CITIZENS

This chapter examines how the war still seeps into studios in the Jaffna Peninsula, shaping the making, displaying, sharing, and keeping photography. Volatility here lends itself to personal and communal anticipations tied to mobility, familial relationships, and even romantic love. Shards of war continue to be embedded in their fragmented archives as well as image-making practices expanded and rejuvenated by the digital. These spotlight the improvisations and aspirations emerging out of ongoing impairments to Tamil citizenship in the aftermath of the armed struggle, where expressions in support are violently suppressed, and new configurations of citizenship are in active negotiation. These occur as Jaffna and the northeast of Sri Lanka remain sometimes voluntarily, sometimes involuntarily, framed by a language and aesthetic of war that is entangled with explicitly political demands for justice and accountability and commemoration explored in the second part of this book. This chapter then considers, principally, the production of the kinds of everyday photographs that are reinscribed as agitants, mobilized through acts and sites of postwar political claim-making.

First, the photography studio has been a long-established arbiter of citizenship. It exists as an extension of the state's citizen registration project in its production of national identity card photography, expanding out to the work of border regimes through passport and visa photography. Developments in digital technology have further embedded the state within the space and activity of the studio. By participating in a tedious and cost-intensive process of formal authorization, necessary for the continued production of official images, the studio has been transformed into a portal connected to a centralized system of image data transmission administered by the state. Second, the studio remains vibrantly engaged in documenting life events: birthdays, puberty ceremonies, engagements, and, importantly, weddings. However, these too have become co-opted as evidence and means to authenticate marriages and kin relationships in the borderwork, surveillance, and citizen-making of state actors.

Transnational marriages have become the favored pathway for many aspiring migrants, especially those whose personal and financial circumstances, social class, and networks are conducive for such a match to be made by a marriage broker (see Maunaguru 2019). This preference permits young people to not only secure a marriage and ideally love but also to migrate to Europe, North America, or Australia where a large Tamil diaspora has formed after decades of conflict-induced and economic migration. Without significant wealth or professional expertise, such destinations are often inaccessible to aspiring migrants due to prohibitive visa regimes, especially where the country's passport is ranked among the lowest in the world. Applications for travel are regarded with intense scrutiny and regularly met with frequent arbitrary and unexplained rejections. In Tamil society, weddings have always been an important social occasion often celebrated grandly, with photographers playing a key role in recording the festivities. With new requirements, imposed by immigration regimes, for documentation and determining the authenticity of the marriages, the role of studio photographers has become even more important as mediators of migrant dreams of new citizenship.

Jaffna's photography studios might be categorized by when they were established in relation to the war (prewar, wartime, and postwar) and their un/easy transition from analog to digital. These aspects determined the space, character, output, and clientele of these studios, as well as their role as repositories for the remnant and unclaimed material of broader experiences of war and the trajectories and circulations of the photographs they produced. By 2014, developing film was no longer a possibility. Studios embraced what Rajaratnam *mama* called *naveena camera* (modern or new camera). Digital cameras afforded new options and flexibility to photographers without the requirement of owning or renting studio space and permitted extrication from the demands of the state to produce identity photography. With shop fronts moving to Facebook pages, photographers were able to pursue far more lucrative event photography. The more traditional studios that kept up with these developments and new demands of state actors (and there were many who were unable to manage this transformation to their trade) paired their ambulatory services with standard facilities, including studio portraiture for personal and official purposes. Against a backdrop of war, studios and a network of related practitioners also served as conscious preservers of social histories. Jaffna's image world also cannot be understood without examining a host of subsidiary image-based practices, including most notably picture framing. The owners of framing shops, commonly known as *padamadam* or "picture palaces," play, alongside studios, a crucial role in preparing photographs for display and the preservation of images where the threat of loss or destruction, whether instituted by political violence or digital obsolescence, is ever present.

In this chapter, I consider two broad variants within the range of image-making practices pursued in Jaffna's studios: identity photography, including NIC, passport, and visa photographs, and other forms of everyday portraiture, notably documenting special occasions and memorial images. This chapter sets the groundwork for showing how these volatile pictures rarely stay within the forms and categories they were intended for, especially where their overt political uses were concerned.

THE POSTWAR BACKDROP

Kugan Photo, founded in 1936, was the oldest surviving studio in the Jaffna Peninsula. The large-format wooden box camera from the earliest days of the studio operated by the owner N. Kugan's father stood polished to a shine, displayed in an alcove that is home to three computers that make up an editing suite where photos are now digitally archived. The front room resembled a hall (living room) arranged with a patterned velvet settee and chairs placed around a coffee table. A collection of old cameras, family and other photographs, and other paraphernalia were haphazardly displayed in a large glass cabinet. An old enlarger had been turned into a pedestal for a dusty plastic bouquet. Portraits of Mr. Kugan's parents, photoshopped to look like overpainted photo-portraits, occupied positions of prominence on the wall.

An anteroom housed the cashier's large desk. Underneath the accounting ledgers, a series of sepia portraits of individuals who had passed through the studio have been slid under the glass (fig. 10), along with an informational sheet that shows various headshots modeled by Mr. Kugan in a blazer and red tie, demonstrating the stipulated dimensions of various official photographs (fig. 11). Mr. Kugan's face, framed in squares and rectangles, also set out an atlas of possible mobility that might be mediated by obtaining photographs of one's own, drawing attention to notions of movement and citizenship that necessitate the making of these images. The categories of residence visas also indicated options for permanent movement directed at hopeful citizenship that promised opportunity, mobility, and perhaps reunion with loved ones. Though the studio was registered with the Department for Registration of Persons, an NIC option, it was perhaps revealingly absent aside from a set of government-issued guidelines.

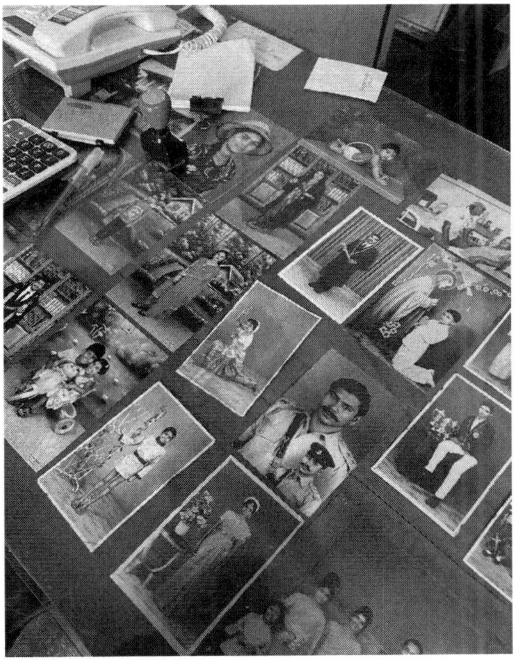

FIGURE 10. Kugan Studio cashier's desk (Jaffna, 2024)

FIGURE 11. Mr. Kugan modeling various official identification photograph types (Jaffna, 2018)

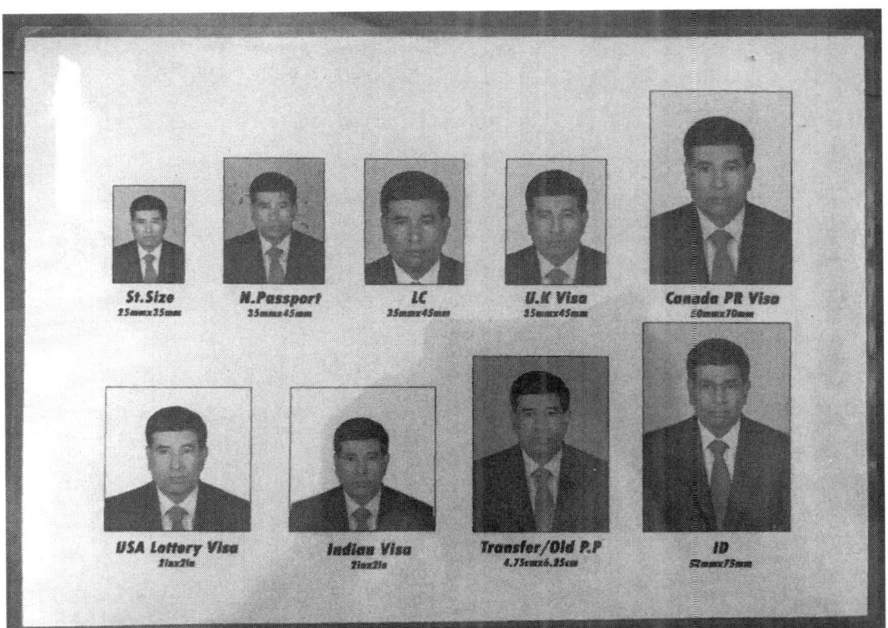

Mr. Kugan and Mr. Gowribala, the resident photographer, had worked alongside Mr. Kugan's father, Nagaratnam, since the early 1980s. Having joined the family business later in the same decade, Mr. Kugan hoped to see the studio through to its centenary. Kugan Studio had suffered five displacements through the war years on account of its inclusion in an HSZ. I sought it out after I had encountered its name in a print advertisement in an old magazine and was amazed to find it was still operational. Many of the older studios were no more: Subhas, Gnanams, Colombo, Prabha, Sithralaya, Ruby, Kalaignani, and Vasana were names that people recalled or I had found stamped on the back of leftover photographs in Colombo and Jaffna.

Up the stairs overlooked by a portrait of Kugan Sr. from the anteroom was a large upstairs space. A brilliant blue *alankaraika madam* (adornment/beautification or dressing room) with a mirror. Scented talcum powder and a hairbrush were on offer. The sun filtered in through the intricate cement grille bathing the foyer in blue-tinged golden light. The large studio, home to various props, studio lights, and backdrops, was Mr. Gowribala's domain. Ties and blazers were hung on hooks for those who wished to *alankaraika* (beautify) themselves. A selection of children's toys, including a bright green plastic tricycle and a wooden rocking horse, were available, along with a tiny wicker saucer chair perfect for propping up unsteady babies and toddlers. Multicolored plastic flower arrangements, with which sitters occasionally posed, were numerous. A selection of backdrops was suspended by a system of pulleys. Staid grey, blue, white, and red cloth were used for identity photographs. A rotation of painted sceneries formed a flipbook of make-believe settings against which clients could choose to be photographed (fig. 12).

Backdrops suited to photographing children were festooned with characters picked out of cartoons, featuring delightful animal characters. The others used predominantly for full-length portraits were no less fantastical. Painted in a style airily suspended between Late Baroque and Impressionist, Jaffna's studio backdrops evoked imaginaries borrowing from and melding together Italian coastal towns such as Capri or Amalfi and the English countryside composed of lush flower gardens, rustic villas, and dainty cottages. French windows opened onto rolling meadows. Empty summertime terraces led to bright blue lakes and oceans. Old-fashioned colonnades, fluted columns, shapely balustrades, and dainty iron gates were prettily painted with flowering vines, reminding one of a scene out of Mary Poppins. Arched bridges located in parks were flanked by autumnal shrubs and spring flowers. Opulent interiors were conjured not to evoke

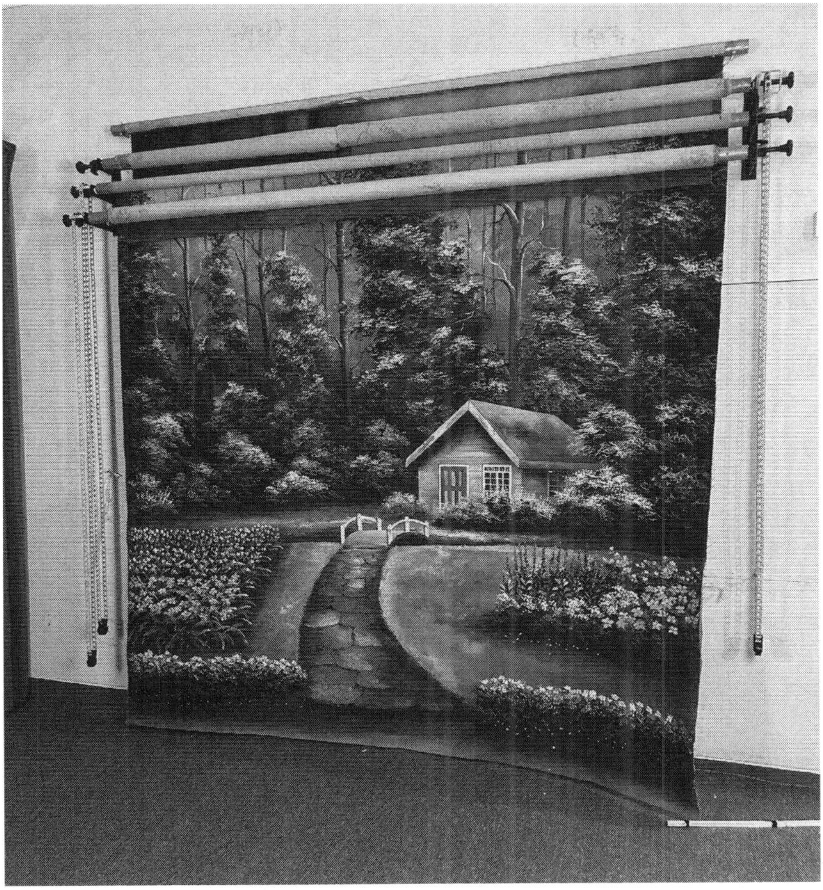

FIGURE 12. Painted backdrops at Kugan Studio (Jaffna, 2024)

recognizable features of identifiable buildings with urban or modern amenities, but fantastical elsewheres.

These backdrops portrayed a perhaps dated sensibility of material wealth, made up of Palladian windows, roman arches, fluted columns, grand staircases, and decorative drapes that hint at a Western colonial grandeur. It was reanimated in built spaces, clothing, and self-fashioning and ceremonial invocations of formality in the postcolony. The aesthetics of these studio backdrops suggest perhaps a lineage of land-me-down borrowings that, according to Mr. Kugan, harked back to those that used to be directly imported from Britain when his father was running the studio. All the studios that still used backdrops like these had a single vendor, a Sinhalese family business based in Kandy, that had been making backdrops for about sixty years. It was not difficult to envisage the pseudo-Italianate aesthetics percolating from historical imaginaries of the grand tour through the British colonial project and lingering still in the interiors of the island's studios, not unlike the ways in which facets of portrait painting seeped into photography. They also caricatured how local elites were photographed during the colonial period. Anoma Pieris notes that the confluence of "eastern" and "western" that marked colonial "bourgeois self-fashioning" in contradictory and hybrid forms of expression carried through to the ensuing decades (2013, 8). Conformity and rejection became embodied in the island's architecture and material culture. This might be examined through the lens of social class. In S. K. Lawton's surviving late nineteenth-century to early twentieth-century portraits, the sitters appeared to pose for inside-outside "sunlight" photos in their brightly lit living rooms and verandas. The "interiors" were craftily staged in the outdoors as visible from the curtains set up behind them and the rattan mats at their feet. Affluence in the form of their dress, often a gendered combination of "Eastern" and "Western," and personal belongings signifying wealth were on casual display. In the studio portraits, the props and backdrops were painted with trompe l'oeil curtains perhaps more "realistically" made than their contemporary incarnations. Those who could afford a visit to the studio had the opportunity to temporarily inhabit these spaces of make-believe luxury. Where colonialism was integral to the cultivation of class hierarchies, studio backdrops take on a greater resonance and complexity in relation to the class dynamics of aspiration. Here, the backdrop made to resemble a "Western" landscape or interior was not one of entrapment, but expressed the possibility for movement, imagined and real. The studio assisted sitters "to exploit the illusionistic potential of photography to bring into material, tangible proximity a fantasy portrayed 'as if' it were real" (Strassler 2010, 77). However, in their social appropriations they helped facilitate aspirations for socioeconomic mobility through make-believe as well as mediations for out-migration. The make-believe—the almost children's book illustration-like character of these backdrops—firmly situated the subject in a fantastical "elsewhere" where they might be momentarily transported within the space of the studio and suspended in the long term in a studio portrait. The fixity of the photograph evokes and catalyzes individual desires for movement. Whether in the literal movement permitted by passport and visa headshots, the mobility fleetingly imagined against an illusory painted landscape, or the aspirational, in the circulation of these portraits in hopes of marriage, maybe love, located ideally in the first worlds of Paris, London, or Toronto; each facet of this anticipated movement had implications for citizenship.

FUTURE PHOTOGRAPHS

Past the studio, there was a small workshop, where frames were cobbled together and mounts were cut to shape and sundry items were discarded. Through there the old darkroom was a rarely entered storage shed littered with equipment: broken picture frames, cardboard boxes, plastic bags, old photographic paraphernalia. The glass of the window was long gone. "This was all *vadiva* (neatly) organized and kept, but nobody has touched this since the army dumped it after our last displacement. We found it like this when we came back in 2013. Nobody has gone near it since." The old darkroom also housed what remained of the studio's history; an accidental archive of several thousand brown little envelopes had until my arrival remained a decaying mound on the floor.

"*Payangaramana dust iruka* [There is a frightening dust]. Who knows what *poochi* [creatures] are in there? I have been too scared to even look through and if I don't do it, no one else will and who has the time. Can you see what a mess it is?" Mr. Kugan complained, pointing to the moldering mountain of photographic waste.

After months of looking for scraps in mostly bare studios, sparse family albums, and among Kugan Studio's partly destroyed vast catalog of negatives, several photographs yielded some of the most valuable material for understanding the social life of photography in Jaffna marked by the losses and absences of war (fig. 13). What I found buried under the envelopes bundled in hemp string were the *payanagaramana* (frightening) bones and feathers of more than one desiccated pigeon. Water damage had turned some of the pile into rotting paper and celluloid dust; each damaged packet unfurled into what resembled a bone-dry paper coral colored with leaching ink and old photo chemicals. Those that could be salvaged yielded marvelous glimpses into the daily life of the studio spanning from the early 1970s to the later 1990s. One wad of envelopes roughly corresponded to a working day in the studio. Some days were made up of multiple lots while a few days or even a week were sometimes compressed into one. The studio would have up to one hundred visits a week. I slowly re-photographed a selection of a few

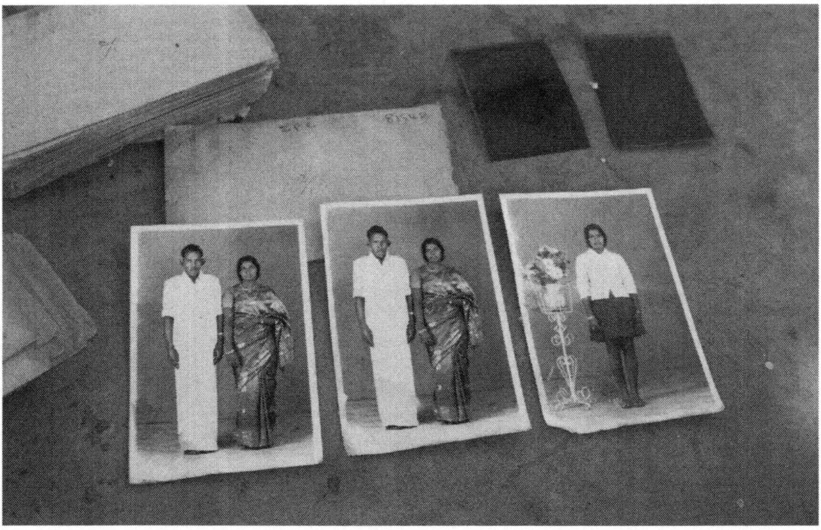

FIGURE 13. Kugan Studio remains (Jaffna, 2018)

thousand negatives, and some leftover, uncollected, or spare photographs. Mr. Gowribala worked alongside me in the adjoining studio space bringing customers up to have their photographs taken. Several passed through each day. Most were young families bringing their babies and children in to be photographed, while others sought out identity photographs. Studio portraits circulated as part of arranged marriage proposals were also popular. Young women, dressed in their finest *salwar kameez*, came to stand before a picturesque painted backdrop as did young men who wore their sharpest shirts and best denim jeans. A few borrowed "tie coats" from the rack. These photos, passed on to marriage brokers, were circulated locally and internationally, with the most sought-after spouses having "status" (meaning legal residence or citizenship) elsewhere.

Each envelope held the material signs of a client's photographic encounter with the studio. This allowed customers to return and request copies when needed, which would be reproduced from the archived negatives. Envelopes were dated, numbered, and sometimes named in pen along with shorthand details of the order in Tamil, English, or sometimes both. They all contained large and medium format negatives initially in black and white and then in color, and ultimately in cut-up 35mm film strips, measuring in celluloid the progress and technical developments of photography. With time and exposure, the negatives had sometimes stuck together forming haunting double or triple portraits bleeding into one another. Some contained instructions and receipts indicating the precise details of the order. Others included notes from customers, especially in the instance of memorial photographs where the deceased's birth and death dates were written down. Occasionally, surplus copies of photographic prints ranging from full-length studio portraits to identity card, driving license, and passport photographs had been left in. Held up to the light these negatives formed inverted impressions of the future photographs they might be developed into, their volatile potentials already fixed through the mechanics of light and chemicals. The negatives, in a sense, summoned the what-could-be of a future photograph through absence. Marks of the photographer's interventions in materializing that possibility could be seen in the red mercurochrome smudged over faces and limbs to lighten complexions or fade backgrounds. Backgrounds of re-photographed images were blurred so that they could become a whole new photograph.

Early large format negatives from the 1970s captured family and friends' outings to the studio. Individual and group portraits. Children who accompanied their parents partook in family photos and individual portraits. Elder aunties sat for the camera, regal in their finest saris, while *vetti* (cloth-wrap)-clad uncles carried themselves solemnly. School children posed in uniform for individual portraits as well as school identity cards. Teenaged girls gathered in saris as well as short dresses prior to attending school socials. Young men posed in sarongs and suits. "Sparks of contingency" lurked in these negatives, offering glimpses of the socioeconomic standing of those who were pictured, most notably by the absence or presence of footwear (Benjamin [1931] 2005, 510). Borrowed suit jackets occasionally belied bare feet or rubber slippers. Short skirts sidetracked from the conservative, gendered social world of Jaffna. Some men with bare torsos posed for requisite NIC photographs, their class and caste identities unexpectedly revealed. The studio afforded a safe space for imagining and performing what was maybe unacceptable beyond the backdrops of its possibility, further affirming Karen Strassler's observation on the "as if" achieved by studio photography (2010, 77). Dark sunglasses were a popular prop, mirroring the stylings of South Indian cinema star MG Ramachandran or MGR. Couples beheld the camera in sari and suit, the wives then changing into Western dress for a second portrait. Little children were pictured with radio sets, as happy graduates posed in cap and gown while clutching their diplomas to their chests. Babies were propped up in a wicker saucer chair that was still used in the studio. The photographer's experiments too would become visible in the props that determined how the shot was exposed or strategically blurred to enhance focus on the subject. However, the largest in number among these negatives were those taken for official purposes, including application for the NIC, reflecting the consolidation of the Sri Lankan state's registration of persons project.

MAKING ශ්‍රී ලංකා (SRI LANKA)

The period of extreme violence that marred the southern portion of the island during the armed revolts led by the Janatha Vimukthi Peramuna (JVP) altered the course of photographic practices on the island with the introduction and expansion of the National Identity Card (NIC) project. In 1971, the stability of the postcolonial Ceylonese government led by Prime Minister Sirimavo Bandaranaike was threatened by an ultimately unsuccessful armed revolt led by the JVP. The date 5 April 1971 coincidentally marked not only the beginning of the insurrection but also the operationalization of the 1968 Registration of Persons Act No. 32 that was gazetted in 1971 to curb illicit immigration from India in the wake of the various citizenship acts passed following independence. Using Malaysia as a model, the Department for the Registration of Persons was established on 1 October 1971. The first NIC was issued on 4 September 1972. That same year the island discarded its dominion status and colonial name of Ceylon to become Sri Lanka.

The NIC, the most ubiquitous photographic object in the island, confirmed individual identity and citizenship; it was essential to availing various state and private sector services, including banking and voting. As noted by James Scott, states secure cooperation by "making clear identity a prerequisite for receiving entitlements; in more coercive systems, harsh penalties are exacted for failure to carry identification documents" (1998, 372). Focusing on the urban poor, Tarangani Sriraman builds on Partha Chatterjee's (2004) conceptualization of governmentality in India to trace how identification projects make up a material infrastructure to determine how "subjects" (as opposed to citizens) are marginalized and compelled to "endure different governmentalities" (2018, xlvii). In Sri Lanka, the NIC determined a citizen's access to state services, movement and safety, but most significantly certified one's ethnicity by way of language and residence. An individual who did not possess an NIC would not only not be able to avail oneself of citizenship entitlements, but within a context of conflict, would become suspect in the eyes of the state security apparatus.

A stamp-sized black-and-white photograph (color as of 2005) was affixed beneath the Sinhalese text ශ්‍රී ලංකා (Sri Lanka) onto a yellow and white plastic-coated card printed with a motif evoking the "Sinhalese" component of the Sri Lankan flag: a sword-bearing lion. Issued to all citizens at the age of sixteen, the personal information written out by hand implicitly confirmed one's ethnolinguistic identity and locality. Initially designed as a paper booklet to include a 2" × 2" Rolleiflex photograph, the NIC was subsequently laminated and made compact by the introduction of 35mm film photographs by Dr. D. B. Nihalsinghe, the erstwhile director of the Government Film Unit (Rathnayake 2016). The German Democratic Republic (East Germany) donated a few thousand Praktica cameras and film for this purpose (Wijekoon 2012). Rajaratnam *mama* and Sivapragasam recalled the government's distribution of cameras to studios to facilitate the issuance of identity cards. Every citizen age sixteen and over was compelled to travel to a studio and have a photograph of themselves taken: 35mm × 45mm, right in semi-profile with the left ear fully visible as per official requirement. While lags in registration continued to exist, especially among marginalized communities including Indian-Origin Tamils and internally displaced persons (IDPs), most Sri Lankans were in possession of an NIC. If studios were previously the purview of those who could afford to have their picture taken, the NIC obliged each adult citizen of Sri Lanka to be photographed. Here "photographic citizenry" takes on a different tone to Azoulay's (2008) suggestion. It was not one conducive to solidarity and resistance, but one where the state sought to enumerate its citizens in line with colonial projects of documentation underscoring photography's indexicality for record-keeping, categorization, and surveillance. Considering the example of colonial Namibia, Lorena Rizzo reflects on how photography was "put at the service of the emergent sciences of the human body—physiognomy, anthropometry and anthropology" (2013, 328). Indeed, the postcolonial Sri Lankan state's NICs incorporated visibility of "unique" physical features such as the ear. French criminologist Albert Bertillon enlisted methods of anthropometric measures in identifying criminals, pioneering various standardizations employed by the police. As noted by Christopher Pinney, "Bertillon advocated for the close scrutiny of ears" (1997, 67). Anthropometric measurements coupled with fingerprinting and photography would be utilized by colonial and postcolonial states in criminological practices. Within a context of ethnopolitical tension, ethnicity hardened as "race" became increasingly politicized in the consolidation of the hierarchy of Sri Lankan citizenship. As Yuvi Thangarajah reminds us, ethnicity is historical, contingent, performative, and a phenomenon that is co-constructed in and through the very acts that give rise to and define interlinked conflicts in the first instance ([1995] 2009, 191). This analysis extends to postcolonial performances of class, as was previously discussed. Variations and fluidities of ethnic or "racial" identities and their everyday lived mitigations and navigations would be expunged by this system of state categorization. For numerically small ethnolinguistic communities, identities were subsumed into one of a dominant group in which they were unrecognized as formal categories based on language or by capricious bureaucratic judgment. Its materialization through photography as a tool of governmentality thus becomes clear.

A number from 1 to 9 stamped in purple ink indicated which province the NIC was issued in. The details of the holder were handwritten and individually signed off by the Registrar of Persons. While Sinhalese citizens' NICs were inscribed in Sinhala, Tamil and Muslim citizens' NICs were written out bilingually in Sinhala and Tamil. The document thus confirmed likeness, name, gender, date and place of birth, occupation, and address. These details embodied a cartography and hierarchy of Sri Lankan citizenship demarcated along ethnolinguistic identity and geographic distribution. These features determined one's mobility and capacity to navigate the island's security apparatus. Sri Lanka's anti-state groups consequently demonstrated a specific fixation on NICs. During the second insurrection, the JVP forcibly collected NICs from households as a measure to reduce the identification and arrest of known JVP activists at police and army checkpoints and threaten the powers of the state in its indexing of citizens. During the war, Tamils who did not have their NIC on their person risked arrest. Those detained sometimes had their NICs taken away, guaranteeing future precarity and hindrances. In addition to household registration lists maintained by the police, the army issued identity cards to those residing in the north in a parallel process of registration. Panchananthan, a retired electrician who lived in Jaffna Town, still carried these multiple identity cards with him. "You never know when you will get stopped and what IC they will want to see."

Harish recalled his desperation for a Number 1 (Western Province) NIC as he commuted between Colombo and Jaffna during the war years as first a student and then an office worker. A Tamil with a Number 4 (Northern

Province) NIC was far more vulnerable in encounters with the state security forces. He recalled being frequently harassed and detained in "roundups" from his bedsit in Wellawatte, Colombo. The predominantly Tamil neighborhood, along with others including Pettah, Kotahena, Dehiwela, were subjected to ceaseless stop-and-search operations and raids. Stints in remand inevitably featured brutality and torture, which had become normalized within practices of incarceration that targeted Tamils even in the postwar. Similarly, Ganeshan remembered the relief he felt when he finally acquired a Number 1 NIC after years of harassment for having lived in Jaffna and Batticaloa in Eastern Sri Lanka and Colombo. Scott asserts that states in their efforts to make citizens "legible" through various measures and tools, seek to not only abstract, simplify, and standardize for the purpose of official observation, but further seek to "create a terrain and a population with precisely those standardized characteristics" (1998, 81–82). Here, existing ethnic distributions were accounted for in provincial numbering, further strengthening the surveillance of sections of the population. As Scott affirms, this was also integral to legal standing, whereby tools, categories, and measures of legibility also institute "an authoritative tune to which most of the population must dance" (1998, 71). Here it was one of suitably performing one's ethnogeographic identity to affirm loyalty to the state and not arouse suspicion, where the rules of suitability were concealed to foster fear and compliance. In January 2007, the Liberation Tigers of Tamil Eelam (LTTE) also began issuing Tamil Eelam National Identity Cards to Tamils resident in areas under their control. The first card was ceremonially received by Prabhakaran. Following his death in 2009, a photograph of this ID found on his person was publicized by the Sri Lankan military in the inter/national media as confirmation of the Tigers' demise and "grand finale." The NIC might thus be read as integral not only to the making of citizens in the eyes of the state but making and asserting the nation-state itself by constructing an ethnicized citizenry, delineating the physiognomic markers, and invoking photographic bodily surveillance and scrutiny.

The NIC project also served as an act of declaring its status as a modern, postcolonial state that actively invested in technological improvements to make the initially used manual process more efficient. By 1978, the handwritten numbers would be typeset. In 2005, the black-and-white photo would be replaced with color. By 2014 all NICs were issued bilingually, typeset in Sinhalese and Tamil, using software-based transliteration. Due to the obsolescence of the 1970s laminating machinery and the state's purported inability to source spare parts or dedicate the necessary human labor, a new e-NIC project was announced "to establish identity of Sri Lankan citizens using modern technology" and "facilitate national security required for the implementation of development programs efficiently, transparently and effectively" (Department for the Registration of Persons 2019). Aimed at enhancing security measures, the computerized database system is anticipated to centrally consolidate personal details, family information, photographs, and "biometric characteristics."

The NIC played a significant role in the state's imagining of ශ්‍රී ලංකා as an independent republic and identity. It became an extension of one's personhood (legal, ethnic, and otherwise). Citizens could not physically separate themselves from their NIC for fear of potentially fatal consequence. Ironically, it is also this state's insistence on the NIC that has resulted in NIC photographs and sometimes NICs themselves persisting in relation to citizen demands for unresolved cases pertaining to the war dead and disappeared.

However, NICs also marked an important shift in the social life of photography in Sri Lanka. After 1972, citizens who were excluded from photography came into possession of a photograph of themselves, which in turn could be endlessly transformed by studios and through their everyday uses and conjugations. NIC photos were, thus, variously appropriated: exchanged between friends, included in family albums, and reframed as memorial images. Strassler notes the complex ways in which "ideologies and practices of documentation tied to bureaucratic knowledge production also reverberate within the intimate realm of personal and familial memory in the photographic documentation of family rituals" (2010, 21). Similarly, in northern Sri Lanka such resonances became compounded by war, notably the pervasive loss of life which would irrevocably shape the Tamil community's photographic practices. NIC photos would also become assumed into war through the photographic remembering of the dead, in a dual evidencing of the necropolitical where the state was a violent intercessor of Tamil life and death (Mbembe 2019). Here, the state's proof of existence was easily transformed to evidence of death.

A VISUAL ECONOMY OF DEATH

In the Kugan archive, identity photographs—postal, NIC, and passport—rapidly expanded in number as the war progressed. These photographs were the most numerously produced, underlining their wartime necessity.

Whole families' studio encounters to have passport photographs taken suggested increasing out-migration, or certainly the need and desire to do so. These requirements also sustained studios despite the increasing access to personal cameras. War potently shaped the studio and its contents and daily rhythms. Death also began to percolate in with a conspicuous increase in the demand for memorial portraits. Abruptly shortened lives were evidenced in the little notes detailing birth and death dates that were placed in the brown paper envelopes. In these negatives and photographs, lives that unfolded in birthday parties, school identity photos, family and friends' portraits, weddings, puberty ceremonies, and identity photographs were cropped and re-photographed, resulting in what were dubbed "copying negatives." These were largely intended to duplicate existing photographs for memorial portraiture.

As Jaffna descended further into war, sweet studio portrait commissions of individuals, families, and friends declined in number, while passport photographs and "copying negatives" to be repurposed into memorial images grew. Occasional "copying negatives" of young Tiger cadres also surfaced. They were mostly pictured bearing guns and sometimes in uniform, smiling into or defiantly posing for the camera and, likely, death. Martyr portraits as well as identity photos produced by the LTTE were also turned into memorial portraits, presumably as mementos for loved ones. Fragments of the NIC as document and details from this process of "copying negatives" remained: the logo of the state, the citizen's unique NIC number that indicated year of birth, and the signature of the Registrar of Persons who hand-signed each card. The metal clips that held the card in place were also intermittently captured. These were most common in the deaths of the elderly, implying that this compulsory photograph may have been the only one available to their family members. The frontality and formality of NIC photographs afforded a sense of clarity, drawing attention to the face in a way that informal images did not.

The photographs printed out of these "copying negatives" were retouched and enlarged to erase any marks of the state or other, in a memorial portrait that would be then further embellished in various ways, including overpainting or framing. In their coloring and embellishment, photo artists variously drew inspiration from divine images as well as cinema posters. Family portraits and identity photographs were thus transformed by war into funerary images. It is impossible to ascertain how memorial portrait making and display among the Tamil community might have looked without war, for if any trace of prior stylings existed, they have largely been forgotten. What is clear, however, is the vastly transformative effects the war years had on the aesthetics of death, especially in the attention afforded to it by the aspiring Tamil nation-state.

Diverse images were often positioned together in displays within households and shops. Photographs of the dead were placed alongside those of gods pictured in posters, prints, and calendars, sometimes garlanded with flowers and anointed with incense daily. Joseph Vaz, whose cycle repair workshop I walked past each day, had one such compelling constellation of photographs, Catholic images, and other "nice pictures" that he had cut out from calendars. Against a peacock green wall, he had assembled a striking display of multiple calendar images of Jesus, the Virgin Mary, the Holy Family, a cartoon assembly of Santa Clauses, an old calendar photo printed by a tire company showing filial devotion in the form a young grandson presenting a basket of fruit to his grandparents, various Bible verses set against Tower Bridge in London and a garden, pictures of the pope, and a sepia photograph of his late father as a young man. "I like these pictures. All these things here are important to me," he said. "I have other photographs, but this is when he was young and most good-looking."

For Panchanathan, the photographs of his parents that flanked his household pantheon symbolized his sentiment, "My *appa* and my *amma* are my *theivangal* [gods]. They are my *bhagavan* [deity]." Panchanathan was wistful in his recollections, "This land on which I have built my house was my father's. We lived in this place for a hundred years! He went to school, and he worked for the British. Look at this photograph of him in tie coat—you can tell he was an important man." He enthusiastically took down the images for me to look at from his household pantheon. His father had passed away when Panchanathan was only three years old. "I was unable to fulfill their dreams." He asks me to photograph him with the portraits of his father, Thiruvengada Suriyanathan, and mother, Pakkyalakshmi, as he did not have any with them by his side. "Maybe you will write their names and put their photo in your book, so that my *theivangal* [gods] can be remembered. So that they can live on." If wartime practices of memorial portraiture contrived the divine for political expedience, its social use was perhaps always suggestive of proximity to the divine as mediated by way of the visual and conceptions of *darsanam*.[4] For Panchanathan, a photograph with the photographs of his late parents permitted them to exist within the same frame (fig. 14).

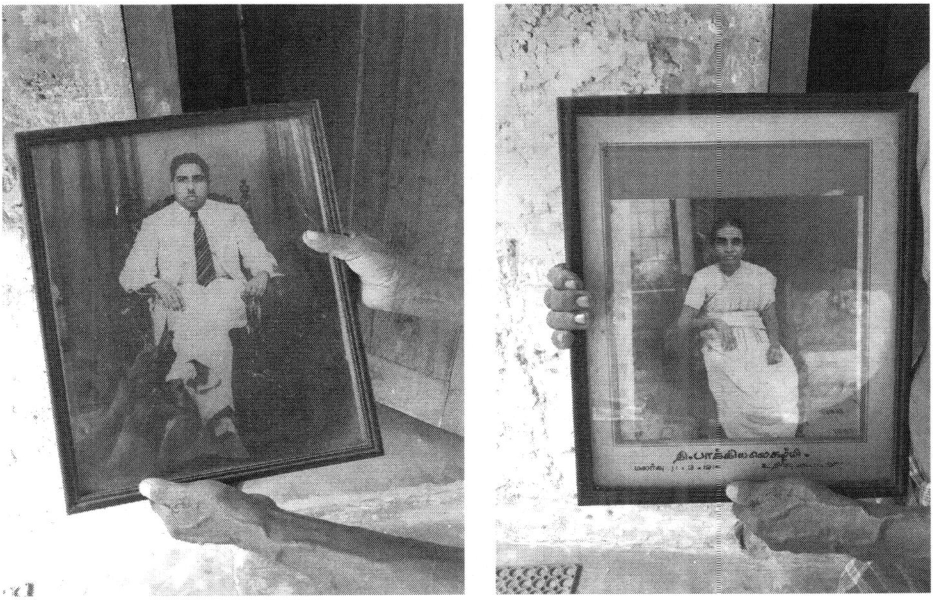

FIGURE 14. Portraits of Panchanathan's father, Thiruvengada Suriyanathan, and Panchanathan's mother, Pakkyalakshmi (Jaffna, 2018)

Memorial portraits, in the form of handbills, posters, flex banners, *anjali malar*, and ornate portraits were omnipresent in Jaffna's image world. *Anjali malar* or *ninaivu malar* (memorial / garland of tributes) are descriptions of a printed memorial booklet distributed at a Hindu or Catholic memorial service that takes place thirty-one days after the death of an individual. Compiled by the family, it typically featured a memorial photograph, a short life history, as well as religious hymns and images, poetry, and messages from friends and well-wishers. *Anjali malar* sometimes featured the deceased's cultural, educational, or even sporting interests and sometimes provided the reader with useful information ranging from health and wellness to computer use. Previously, photographs produced out of "copying negatives" were used to make photo-realistic impressions on zinc printing blocks that allowed the portrait to be printed onto a poster or a handbill. These announced the death and details of the funeral to the neighborhood. The digital allowed for even poor-quality zinc block portraits to be revived with clarity, color, and embellishment. Memorial photography practices grew more elaborate with the possibilities afforded by the digital.

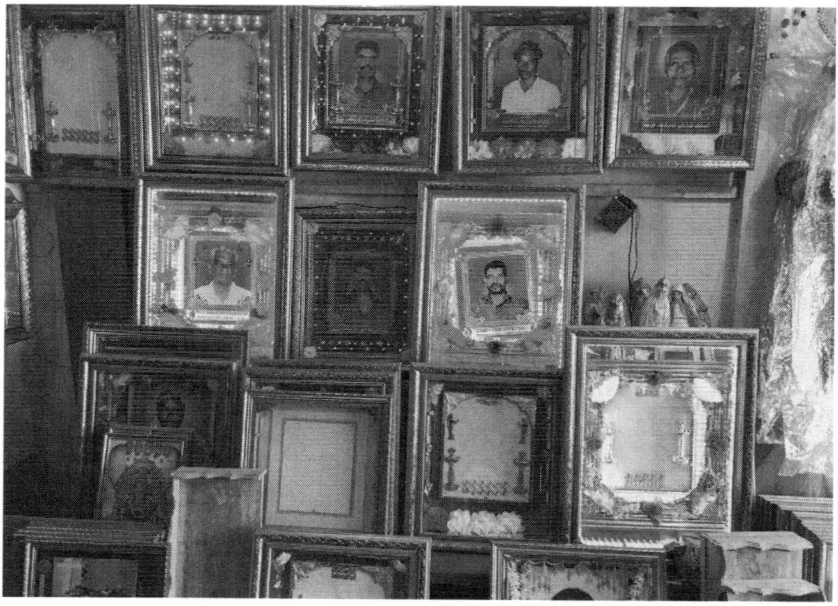

FIGURE 15. Memorial portraits on display at a *padamadam* on KKS Road (Jaffna, 2018)

Photographs were scanned directly and swiftly photoshopped on computers. Dull black-and-white posters were transformed into color or morphed into digitally printed decorative flex banners for public display. Framing shops undertook orders for extravagant memorial frames embellished with electric lights, plastic flowers, and lamps (fig. 15). This economy was also one that was transnational in nature, with diasporic Tamils enlisting the comparably cost-effective services of local practitioners through personal and social media networks. Ganesananthan, the re-touching artist, had clients WhatsApp him photographs from France and Switzerland, which he would patiently transform on Photoshop into a memorial portrait or death notice. The work of the studio was not merely in its photographing, but in its capacity to demonstrate artistry that situated the photograph within the vernacular of local visual-material culture.

PADAMADAM (PICTURE PALACES)

Sivapragasam started manufacturing memorial frames as part of his studio practice after noticing an increase in demand following the 2004 Indian

Ocean Tsunami. Two women assembled each one, using gilded frames, plastic beads and flowers, and electric lights imported from China. Once Sivapragasam printed the digitally enhanced memorial photograph, they were housed in the shrine-like frame flanked by two plastic lamps. For custom orders, a frame could cost well over 10,000 rupees ($33.00), an extravagance that was rarely skimped on. "We get orders for these almost every day," Sivapragasam noted. "Even from those living abroad." It was following my visit to his workshop that I realized that framing shops were an unexpectedly rich repository of photography. "As long as we are here, these will also be here," Sivapragasam observed. "After what we have gone through, we understand that people are not always able to come back for their pictures. It is difficult to make the space and keep cleaning these, but who knows, maybe one day someone will come back looking for their photos, and we must be ready to return them to their owners."

Padamadam or Picture Palaces, as they were known, frame the image world of northern Sri Lanka, whether in the sale of Hindu and Catholic divine images, the stylized portraits of South Indian Tamil stars, or the aesthetics of photographic display. Like Sivapragasam, Nesan, who had been running Padappi Padamadam for over twenty years, considered himself a custodian of the photographs that were left behind in his shop, expressing that war and loss meant that people could not come back for their photos, and that it was his responsibility to keep them. Nesan and his family, who were originally resident in Kurunegala, had fled the North Western Province following the 1978 anti-Tamil riots. "It is my obligation to keep these photos," he said, bringing out an old suitcase tied up with a strip of cloth in which he kept all the photographs that the owners had not returned for.

Most of these were memorial portraits, some (since they were hand-colored) having evidently been there for a very long time. A scattering of graduation pictures and official group portraits were also left behind. There were several wedding photographs, family photographs of children, babies, young couples, elderly parents, and relatives visiting from overseas following dispersals, pictured against unidentifiable foreign backdrops. A composite picture of six children makes it seem as if they were gathered on the lawn of a magnificent East Asian pagoda. It was also possible that they showed the side-by-side growth of siblings or the offspring of a joint-household. The text HAPPY CHILDREN appeared to float in the sky. A young boy, perhaps ordinarily resident in the West as might be inferred from his clothing, was cut and pasted to hover before the Nallur Kandasamy Temple. A little boy dressed as Bala Krishna was photoshopped next to a blue-skinned, crowned *golu* (clay doll) that mimics his hand-on-hip pose against a garden of flowers and an arch that is ethereally obscured by boughs of autumn leaves. Printed Hindu and Catholic divine images were also interspersed, showing various gods, saints, and places of worship. The war had seeped into the suitcase too. A memorial image of a somber boy born on 12 December 1993 and his smiling younger sister born 15 September 1996 announced their premature death on 31 March 2009. Their three-quarter-length portraits were photoshopped against a bright green grassy paddock and two bullock carts. A Sri Lankan soldier in camouflage held up a gun against the purple and red drapes of a studio, a headshot of former President Mahinda Rajapaksa inserted above his right shoulder. It afforded a glimpse into the way in which the presence of the military had threaded into studio photography, along with the number of Sinhalese soldiers stationed in local camps. "I will keep these for as long as I have this shop," Nesan said. "These are important, whether people come back for them or not." Where movement and displacement had become so central to Tamil existence in the north, studios and *padamadam* played a conscious role in preserving its visual-material histories, whether it was the history of the practice or those life histories of individuals unable to collect their images, in anticipation of a possible someday.

This role of studios and frame shops as custodians would be life-changing for some. When I met Chandrakala in Colombo, she had just returned from visiting her son in Toronto. She lived part-time in Toronto and part-time in her daughter's home in Wellawatte. Following the politically motivated murder of her husband in Jaffna, Chandrakala was left to raise her two young children alone on an administrative salary. When the fighting between the government forces and the LTTE escalated, she was compelled to flee after harrowing negotiations to secure passes for her children. "We had to leave suddenly and so left everything, and I lost my wedding photograph. I only returned to Jaffna in 2002 during the ceasefire, more than ten years later. Our house had been occupied by squatters who had taken a liking to the frame my wedding photo was in. They took it to a local studio and asked for one of their own photographs to be put in. The studio owner thought my wedding photograph was very beautifully shot, even if he had not taken it himself. He gave them the frame and kept my photo. When I went back, he happened to see me in the neighborhood and approached me through someone I knew and returned my photograph to me! I was so happy! It meant so much especially since my husband died. Now my son has made copies of this, so I keep one in Toronto, and I keep one here," she said bringing out the framed original to show me. What became evident in the framing practices associated with photography was the significance of embellishment and elevation to popular photographic practice, in terms of making it look *vadivu* for display. Framers also took their role as facilitators of keeping and preserving the image seriously, adapting their work to the uncertainties and losses of war. While embellishment might be viewed as rejection of the real, it is a key mode through which photography is incorporated into a cultural and political register of visibility and multiplication amid absenting and erasure.

COMPUTER MOOLA (COMPUTER BRAIN)

Rajaratnam *mama*'s desire to pass on his skills was also true of other older photographers in Jaffna, who either inherited their studios or trained as photographers under an established studio. This system of apprenticeship has waned with the use of sophisticated digital cameras. Younger photographers in town insisted that clients prioritized what camera was used, casually inquiring into the number of megapixels (the higher the better), while offering opinions on the brand of the camera (Canon was the preferred choice). These studios were accordingly networked into a global vocabulary and market of photographic practice, where brand recognition translated to a quality photograph. Rajaratnam *mama* was as enthralled by the magic of the *naveena camera* as he was by the "current" (electricity) of the darkroom. "There is a simple way to measure the skill of a photographer. No one should be able to tell what time of day a photograph was taken, whether it was in studio light or sunlight. There is a kind of *moola* [brain, meaning skill] for that, now it is a *computer moola* [computer brain]! That is also very good. I have seen some very good pictures," he explained.

Among the most vibrant contemporary photographic practices in Jaffna were those of girls' puberty ceremonies and weddings. Examples from the Kugan archive suggest the sustained popularity of the former, where young girls who attained age were photographed with the same attention as one would a wedding. For young girls, this was an important occasion to dress up in extravagant traditional clothing (sometimes Western and traditional shoots were undertaken) and be pictured either at home or increasingly at an external location. In the past, these photographs would be circulated as a part of marriage proposals when girls were married younger. This has now fallen out of practice, as more recent portraits were commissioned and used.

A popular trope in these albums was photographing the girl along with a camera. Girls looking into the camera lens or screen suggested the glamour of photographic apparatus but also seemed to hint at the possibility of "self-picturing," of these young women taking control of their own images and futures.

Wedding photography was the most lucrative aspect of studio photography, but it was also often the most complex because of clients' demands and standards. Increasingly, Tamil couples from overseas were also choosing to get married locally. Cost played some part, but this was also on account of being able to celebrate their wedding in the "homeland" with their extended family and be photographed against its scenery as backdrop. Brides sought out various material markers of Jaffna and traditional Tamil culture and tradition, including, for example, the addition of palmyra leaves in their bouquets. Those like Kokulan traveled with their clients to scenic locations for shoots, even if it meant the state's postwar recasting of the visual-material landscape leached into the backgrounds of personal photographs. In this way, state power bleeds into the personal and the domestic in a perpetual reminder of postwar unfreedoms. A public who for decades had little access to spaces of recreation or leisure on account of wartime fears and restrictions was enticed with the post-2009 construction and opening of free public parks. These were designed to concretize the ideological symbols and interlinked aesthetics of the regime. In the north, many such locations were built over sites of wartime violence and devastation. These spaces would rapidly become the backdrop for diverse everyday photographies, not only in the casual snapping of friends, family, and lovers on increasingly ubiquitous mobile phone cameras for instant dissemination on platforms such as Instagram and Facebook but also for professional photographers documenting life events. The space of the studio, its quaint painted scenery, in a sense also then permitted sitters to escape this totalizing reinvention of the postwar landscape.

Where marriage was an important migration strategy, proposal portraits pictured against fantastic studio backdrops as well as wedding albums that satiated the demands of immigration regimes were central to studio photography. Marriage made possible new citizenship that afforded more stable or secure futures elsewhere. Identity documents confirming citizenship were a means of navigating precarity while physically moving through the post/war landscape. These documents also supplemented a means of escape through aspirational citizenship. Photographers played a significant role in mediating these possibilities. Realizing personal ambitions cannot be separated from the impairment of current ශ්‍රී ලංකා citizenship, which motivated the desire for citizenship elsewhere.

DREAMING IN CINESTYLE

I attended a Catholic wedding in Point Pedro that was photographed from multiple angles by three camera-bearing men. A fourth man cradled a drone, which I did not see him fly. Having been invited by the bride's aunt, I did not know the couple, but I was told in animated whispers that they had "met" on Facebook. The groom, ordinarily resident in Canada, had seen the girl's photograph and added her as a friend. Across borders, they had begun chatting, and several months later, a marriage had been discussed. Photographs could also engender love despite the divides of distance and borders (see also Maunaguru 2019). If the photographic volatility could yield expectation and community beyond the state, it might be found in the intimacies of family, friendship, community, and romance; the serendipity of images operates most hopefully. However, the state continues to seek to impinge upon such connections. For many of the young women in attendance, dressed in their finest clothes, the wedding was an opportunity to be photographed, to maybe find their own Facebook love stories. Upon seeing my DSLR camera, eager girls requested photographs to be taken and sent to them by WhatsApp. Their camera phones were wielded enthusiastically, as photographs were zipped off to relatives who were unable to attend via Viber. Profile pictures were updated, friends and family tagged, and photographs shared to confirm their presence at the ceremony. Mobile phone editing apps were put to work to *alankaraika* in various ways: skin lightened and smoothened, and multiple adornments of filters and cartoon stickers in the shapes of hearts and flowers added on. The couple's wedding photographs, I learned, would now have to serve an important purpose of validating their relationship to a visa officer, as the bride had to apply to join her spouse in Alberta, Canada. Even the most mundane images of a bridal party could not be disentangled from war and impaired citizenship or the knowledge that states inevitably sought to co-opt even personal documents of life and love. Even so, it suggests hopeful possibility where the volatility of photography is concerned.

Wedding photography was a sizable source of income for studios; a comprehensive package including an album, framed portraits, and a wedding video could cost about 120,000 to 500,000 Sri Lankan rupees ($400–$1,700) or more, depending on the client's requests. Products and services included "pre-shoots" for engagements, video invitations, wedding "trailers," drone videos, and couple photo mugs and cushions. Comparatively, a single studio visit yielded a few prints costing a couple of hundred rupees at most ($1). In response, new photography studios in Jaffna offered photography and videography services that were described as "cinestyle" in their ability to conjure the sparkle of Kollywood. Like a film production, wedding photography was no longer the work of one or two photographers, but that of a crew of photographers, videographers, and assistants, as well as those who offered supplementary services such as invitation printing, album making, and even bridal dressing and salon services. Albums, printed at the local presses located along Kasthuriyar Road, which was also the abode of Jaffna Town's goldsmiths and jewelers, were the most important output and could take months to complete depending on their size. Costs of the albums were charged by the page as well as by paper finish.

Kumaran, a studio photographer in Jaffna Town, has been making wedding albums for over two decades. He showed me various sample books that have transformed from hand-cut and pasted stencils manually decorated with little stickers and ribbons to elaborate Photoshop confections that are now in demand. "Those days we did everything by hand, cutting and pasting with scissors, but now it's all on the computer," Kumaran reminisced. Where clients made various demands about the act of photographing, its subsequent transformations were, in stark contrast, often left to the skill and tastes of the photographer following an initial consultation to select the types of paper to be used. Studios worked with very similar stocks of digital Photoshop templates, which they acquired from a South Indian vendor who sold them various CDs when he visited once a year or so. Much like the studio backdrops, these were fantastical in their presentation, showing fabulous and imaginative renditions of chocolate-box landscapes, and occasionally identifiable Indian landmarks such as the Tanjore temples and the Taj Mahal. The prototypes also incorporated text for inspirational quotes about love and romance (entirely in English) along with other sweet nothings. "I try to 'remix' them a little, cutting and pasting little details and touches so that my clients have something special to keep," Kumaran noted. "They appreciate that." Heavily stylized wedding photographs proved no less indexical in confirming the authenticity of a marital relationship, even though these images were manipulated to extraordinary effect. This ascertained to visa officers its rootedness in Tamil culture, thus proving the legitimacy of

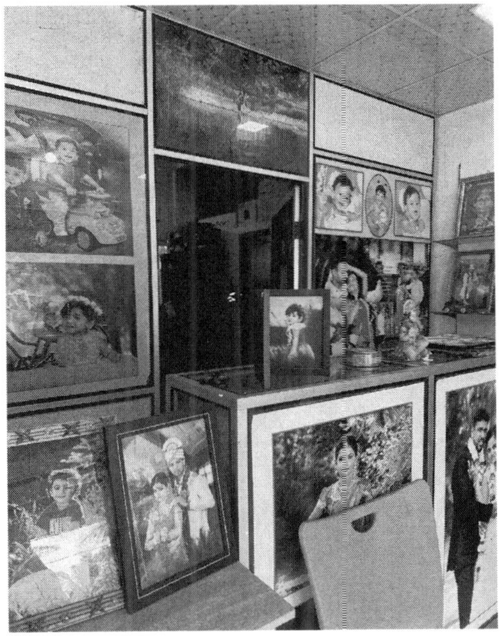

FIGURE 16. Kumaran Photo display photographs, including a couple mirroring Radha and Krishna (Jaffna 2023)

the marriage, even though these occupied a completely different register and aesthetic of "evidence" compared with "official" photographs used for the purpose of identification. Here photography's truth claims were to be found in the meticulous and calculated minimization of their contingency through artifice that located its contents against a backdrop gesturing toward elsewhere. It also shows how even the personal can be transmuted into the official.

As popular knowledge of photography and access to cameras improved, clients had become more demanding of the kinds of photographs they desired, which were often those inspired by South Indian Tamil cinema as well as visual tropes from Hindu iconography. For example, embracing couples were pictured to mirror poses associated with divine lovers Krishna and Radha (fig. 16). Wedding photography was increasingly becoming the purview of young men who spent on "good" cameras (in 2018, a Canon 5D Mark IV at least) and were able to use computer editing tools, much to the annoyance of more established photographers who had spent their youth as apprentices. Photographers actively invested in the most expensive and modern cameras they could acquire. Prices for their services were advertised in line with the make and model of their cameras. This habit was met with scorn by some older photographers who were unable to keep up with the rapid succession of technological advances as well as the increasingly elaborate expectations for "cinestyle" photo shoots.

"We don't undertake wedding photography anymore," Mr. Kugan grumbled. "People want all kinds of pre-shoots and this and that, and we get regular work from the university (graduation and event photography), so we don't do it. It's too much." Clients commonly stipulated wedding photographs that might serve as professional film stills. "You don't need a priest anymore; you just need the photographer," Gajen noted with some contempt, observing that clients frequently prioritized photography over ritual. "I have been to some weddings, and it was the photographer who directed the couple what to do, not the priest." I think of the way in which Rajaratnam *mama* patiently explained to me the practicalities of "bulb photography" which permitted no more than fifteen exposures. "Those days, weddings often happened in the evening, so we would have to be very careful and really prepare for the photographs we wanted to take. Each shot required a bulb and a twist of the film. You had to work quickly. I hand-printed every one of those images myself—all in black and white. Then the fifteen became twenty-four and the twenty-four became thirty-six. Now you can take five hundred, even a thousand photos in one go and choose one that you like. We could not do that." His assistants' computers were filled with hundreds of repetitive bursts of visual-digital detritus.

Sopi, the chief among Baby Studio's apprentice photographers, was thirty years old and oversaw the studio's transition into the digital era. As a part of this, he undertook elaborate open-air shoots, as well as Photoshop and related album-making tasks, and managing a Facebook page for the studio so that prospective clients can view its portfolio online. Sopi was assisted by another young man, Vithu, and two young women, Sajee and Thuvi, who attended to the in-studio photography as well as various administrative tasks. Sajee and Thuvi did not view themselves as "proper photographers," because they did not go out with their cameras to shoot. Photography in this sense appeared to be inseparable from movement. There was an element of a Jaffna photographer as dandy and flaneur that relied on the photographer's masculinity. This was apparent in older photos of Rajaratnam *mama*, where he presented himself with his camera to be photographed as a competent photographer and a stylish subject. Remnants from studios in Jaffna suggest that this was not an uncommon practice. The most fascinating of these photos featured a former assistant at Baby Studio who had himself photographed lying down on a beach embracing his video camera. Sopi and Vithu's self-portraits were influenced also by the latter-day heroes of Tamil cinema, mimicked in Facebook profile pictures and header images. Sopi and Vithu are a new generation of Jaffna photographers, no longer bound to studios in their pursuits, but whose *computer moola* and *naveena camera* permitted for effortless digital photography that dazzled.

Partheepan, a twenty-six-year-old photographer, occupied a small office with only a desktop computer. He was one of tens of new practitioners who were offering their services for location photo shoots. Many of these younger photographers were "unregistered" and uninterested in conventional studio-based practice because identity photography made very little money. Partheepan left Jaffna to live in Mannar for a few years during the war, where he picked up the basics of his trade at a local studio. He returned to Jaffna and set up Amazon Studio manifesting perhaps the potential success of the global retail giant with which it shares its name. "I liked the sound of it. It's a very famous name, I think." He was unaware of Amazon and its business, but there was something of its name that had resonated with Partheepan. "I didn't think too much about it. I bought a good camera and started taking photos." He inquired after my own camera in detail, admiring the choice of lens and was uninterested in a further conversation about the kinds of photographs he took. "Birthdays, weddings, puberty ceremonies, it's all the same," he said after letting me to look through the many folders saved on his computer. When he was not out photographing, he was busy photoshopping. For young men like Sopi, Vithu, and Partheepan, there was also a perceived glamour in what they did. Mobility, not necessarily socioeconomic, but in being out and about and taking photographs of themselves and others and being seen lent itself to offline and online cachet in an age of social photography.

"More people think they understand photography now because everyone has a phone and a camera, so they will also come to tell us what to do sometimes," Arjunan, an established studio photographer griped. "There is no point arguing, so we try to get the latest equipment and look at also what the big wedding photography studios in Colombo are doing based on their Facebook pages because people like it when we can keep up." "Everyone wants to look like their favorite actor," Diluxan, a younger photographer observed, occasionally frustrated by the requests he received from his clients. "For a young person in Jaffna, their life is Vijay. They have posters in their house, they have wallpapers on their phone, if they buy an *auto* (three-wheeler) they also want to cover that with stickers of Vijay. They get their hair cut like Vijay, and they try to dress

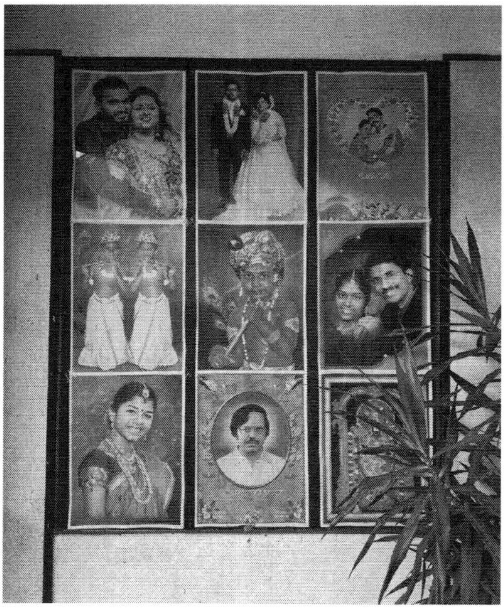

FIGURE 17. Bharath Studio digital photo shop display (Jaffna, 2023)

like Vijay, so of course when it comes to taking a wedding photograph, that also they want to look like Vijay. Women wear so much makeup it is difficult to even identify them outside of their wedding photo because they also want to look like some actress. If you look at the (photoshop) backdrops people request, they are of Indian Temples, the Taj Mahal, or luxury cars like they have been taken from a film scene." Indeed, "cinestyle" packages explicitly sought to cater to these wishes. For Diluxan and several other photographers, this obsession with replicating a South Indian aesthetic was an example of "culture loss" and a diminishing of Eelam Tamil identity. These also contrasted against the wishes of diasporic Tamils who were looking to convey elements of "tradition" and "authenticity," alluding to the conflicting imaginaries of how Jaffna as well as Tamilness might be photographically represented. Criticism aside, cinestyle photography motioned to an important quality about Jaffna's studio photography. It permitted subjects to envision themselves in not merely their best light within fantasies contrived by the photographer, but as whole other personalities, emulating, for example, their favorite stars. The studio was a site of evidencing and establishing identity and citizenship, but its evidentiary quality was determined through its place within an identifiable, socially located aesthetic (fig. 17). Photography as a means for realizing dreams and aspirations involved being pictured in a certain way, enabling imagined and real mobility for those looking to leave Sri Lanka. Here, volatility permits for studio fictions and fantasies to be counted as evidence when these photographs were scrutinized by state actors to authenticate its cultural salience in immigration matters.

KAI RASI

The wedding photographer's business, as I would learn, did not end at photography, but also in his *kai rasi* (auspicious hand) and capacity to assemble a wedding album that might convince the strictest of visa regimes that the marriage was legitimate. Where about a quarter of the Tamil population live outside Sri Lanka, predominantly on account of war, Sidharthan Maunaguru's rich ethnography on transnational marriages analyzes the important role played by photographers in authenticating relationships (2019, 7, 87). A series of visual markers including intimacy between couples, the presence of family members, and the portrayal of Tamil traditions is key to this. Gajen mentioned that he also invariably includes a photograph of the couple's marriage certificate in the albums he designs to not only validate the authenticity of the marriage, but also because it might be of use to the pair because "people lose official documents all the time." Indeed, the authenticity performed for wedding albums, especially where immigration was pending, also resulted in "nontraditional" displays of intimacy for the purpose of appeasing visa officers where public demonstrations of physical affection between men and women, even when married, is rare if not off-limits. The commitment of an embrace or a kiss to the camera was thus considered evidence of a genuine relationship where matters of honor and shame were of social consequence. Such requirements point to the small destructions of the interpersonal set in motion by border regimes. One day, while sitting in Arjunan's studio, I looked through a wedding album and was startled by a photo of the couple kissing on the lips. Such a visible showing of affection would be considered "scandalous" in the context of Jaffna. "The girl needs to apply for a spousal visa to go to the UK," Arjunan chuckled uncomfortably. "You need to do these things whether you want to or not, because this is what embassies are looking for. How many people came to the wedding, are all their family members present, was the priest there, did they do all the rituals, are the couple being loving with one another. . . . It is part of our job now to know what to photograph, so that their journey can happen without any problems." Arjunan's words indicate much more than the role of the photographer within the community, but importantly the photographer's skill lies in his ability to serve as maven intermediary working with the potency of the medium to direct its volatility.

The photographer's *kai rasi* on the subject of visa photographs was one that Arjunan firmly believed in, signaling a kind of destiny, both his own and his clients'. "People come to my studio because they know that I will do a good job with their visa photograph. One time, I had someone who came all the way from Vavuniya to Jaffna because they had tried elsewhere multiple times and had no luck, and I had taken a successful photo for someone in their family. Sure enough, the man got his visa." Such superstitious or ritual mitigations were common among a community that was largely seeking a way out of the island and the trappings of impaired citizenship. In Wellawatte in Colombo, the Visa Pillayar Kovil (temple) was one such example. I was told anecdotally that the small temple had come into existence after the 1983 pogrom. One of its founders dreamed about a Pillayar statue that had washed up from the ocean. When she searched the beach the next day, she located such a statue, for which she built a small temple. It was believed that Ganesh, placed in an orientation facing the ocean, would bestow blessings on those who sought out opportunity overseas. The temple remains a popular stop for those seeking out the benediction of the divine "remover of obstacles." The skill and reputation for auspiciousness is inherently bound up with what is ultimately incontrovertible compliance with the state's specifications. However, by casting this in a language of blessings that elude the precision and rather demands faith and devotion, skillful compliance can also mean trickery or sleight of hand that allows for disobedience, to pull one over the seemingly all-powerful government that suppresses Tamil freedoms, and others which might view potential migrants with suspicion. However, the troubles of visas could not be completely resolved by either Pillayar or Jaffna's canny photographers.

Kirubalini, who worked as an in-studio photographer, was one of several women I met who was waiting for immigration paperwork to be processed. Kirubalini's husband lived in Paris, and she intended to join him as soon as her visa came through. The process had dragged on for months, leaving her in a state of uncertainty after rejection. She had even started taking French lessons in one of the several language schools that had cropped up in Jaffna for the benefit of those seeking to migrate. She was curious about my life in London, anxious about what her own future held for her in a city where she knew no one except her husband, to whom her marriage had been arranged. "I don't know much about Paris. Is it like London? Is it nice?" she regularly asked. She was unsure about her own status as a photographer as she did not "go out" to take photographs like the male colleagues. "Maybe you can take photographs outside there. Paris is beautiful," I reassured her, not knowing what else to say. When I returned nearly a year later, her visa appeal had still not been sorted. "I don't know what next, but we will keep trying," she said.

DIGITAL PRECARITY

Even though the digital afforded photographers and their clients a plethora of possibility and imagining, it was also a site of precarity and hastened obsolescence. Some older studios were unable to keep pace with the requirements of the digital state and the requirements of technologically savvy clients causing their rapid decline. Where securitization and citizen registration had a complex history demarcated by violence, centralization of personal information was a cause for fear for others who were at risk of persecution.

"I was one of the first studios to officially register with the government to provide NIC photographs for the new digital system," Arjunan said proudly. "If you take a good photo that does not exactly match their requirement, the system rejects it immediately. My photos, NIC, passport, visa never get rejected. I can do the job perfectly." Indeed, much of the photographer's prowess here was skillful compliance with specifications provided by state actors pertaining to measurements and background colors that permitted for the efficient digital legibility of the photograph. While such efforts conform to a reading of photography, the afterlives of these "precise" photographs informing state surveillance and citizen-making practices were not quite so straightforward. For Bharath Studio, the oldest working studio in Jaffna Town, founded in 1940 and run by its second-generation owner in 2018, its glory days were behind it. The small two-story studio in 2018 was attended to by its long-term resident photographer, Mr. Mahes, who came into the shop every day and waited patiently from morning until sunset, mostly watching the road from his desk. Times and technologies had proven difficult, with changes to bureaucratic processes. The studio's legal ownership was still the name of its late founder, which meant that it could not be straightforwardly registered with the government as was required for the new biometric photo transmission facilities. It catered instead to a sparse clientele seeking a quick photo for practical needs such as filling an application or commissioning a memorial portrait. When I visited Bharath Studio in December 2024, the studio's activities had been revived with refurbished premises.

The digital also expedited loss in other ways. Ambika, a housewife, showed me the images on her smartphone one day, ranging from multiple selfies to pictures of her husband and children, and her home. "What happens to these photographs after you take them?" I asked. "I keep them on my phone, and I look at them sometimes. I can also show it to my friends and family like I am showing this to you now or share it on WhatsApp or Facebook," she said, swiping the screen with her finger. "What happens when you can't use this phone anymore?" I probed. "See that's a real problem. Two years ago, I lost all the pictures I had on my old phone. I did not know how to save them anywhere else as I do not have a computer. My wedding pictures are on a CD with video, and we play that from time to time. Whatever I post on Facebook might also still be there." It had not occurred to her that she could print her mobile snaps. Ambika's answers were repeated by various interlocutors who had in recent years lost their digital images with device failure or obsolescence. While many unintentionally archived photographs through their sharing practices on social media, they were aware of the relative difficulty of retrieving the original image that had not been subject to compressions and filters. Even active tech-savvy young photographers were not infrequently confronted by botched back-ups or a fried hard drive.

Mira recalled how she had lost a great number of her photographs, including various family photos from a trip to Jaffna, when her computer had crashed some years ago. Even though war and displacement exacerbated material losses of photographs, the digital, for many, was as risky. When I visited Mira, she brought out two cardboard boxes of family albums for me to look through. "These photographs were so important to us. Even as we had to leave Jaffna in a UNHRC ship with only the essentials, we had to bring these with us." Harish, a forty-six-year-old private sector employee in Jaffna, noted how when he was living in Colombo during the war, the only reason his album of photographs had survived was because he had taken them to Colombo. "My *amma* asked why I was taking all these unnecessary things with me, as I packed my bags to go take up a new job, and at the time it was not a priority maybe, but that is how I managed to save these, or we would not have had any photos to speak of." Where the digital in some instances is viewed as a source of expanded state power and surveillance, enhancing a certain kind of precarity, the digital was also subject to another kind of vulnerability that photographs as physical objects were not easily susceptible to. Many recognized the studios' and framers' value in producing lasting materials, especially in marking special occasions and storing or displaying photography as mementos of loved ones in their homes.

Contemporary studio photographers in Jaffna were mediators of fantasies and futures, whether it was helping make a client resemble his favorite Tamil actor or capturing a *vadivana* portrait that would make a prospective spouse take note. Alongside these, they captured photos of another kind, exact, biometric, and machine-readable, as necessitated by the state. Yet these were also composed with a little bit of photographer's *kai rasi*, offering clients the promise and opportunity of passage to a new state and new citizenship, thus fulfilling their own destinies. Such "official" requirements have sustained the continued need for photography studios, in an age of widely accessible mobile phone and compact digital cameras. However, studios and framing shops play a far more significant role in shaping the visual economy of Jaffna's social world as the makers and keepers of pictured life histories and aspirations. The reworking of relatively "mundane" genres of identity and studio portraiture through adaptations by studios permit for mediations that challenge the ideological assumptions of photography (see Tagg 1988). The skill of studio photographers lies in their ability to seamlessly administer the volatility of photography toward a positive outcome, irrespective of the type of image captured. Amid the uncertainties of the postwar period, studio offerings are also entangled with political aspirations and desires for citizenship; they enable a form of future-oriented photographic "worldmaking" entangled with the intimacies of the interpersonal.[5] This practice relies on real and imagined possibilities for movement, understood doubly, as aspirant migrant dreaming for prospects and opportunity elsewhere, and its bearing on the expanding borderless communitas of Tamil Eelam. Moreover, such interventions highlight the possibility for how the language photography might be released from the state even as governments seek to intrude and assume the personal into the official. Photographic worldmaking absorbs long-established visual forms such as the use of painted backdrops and their digital reinventions. Photographers and their subjects must also grapple with bureaucratic framings through the stoic templates of identity photographs that are suspended in the enumerative surveillance gaze of the state, its security apparatus, and border regimes. Here, photographers become arbiters of luck, chance, and fate, wielding their skills of compliance and expertise to help members of their community navigate the choppy waters of current and desired citizenship.

5 PICTURING THE DISAPPEARED

ABSENT PRESENCE / PRESENT ABSENCE

The continuous protests of the Tamil families of the disappeared began in February 2017, some months after I had embarked on this research. Since the end of the war in 2009, I had witnessed protesters gather sporadically to demonstrate against the Sri Lankan government's prevarications on international pressure to investigate war crimes and crimes against humanity as well as decades-long inaction on the subject of enforced disappearances. As I planned the beginnings of this work in London, I watched the unfolding protests captured largely by citizen journalists. Poignant photographs of elderly women and men holding up smiling portraits of their children and grandchildren appeared in various online platforms, photo essays, and social media posts by human rights campaigners and media activists, and as an accompaniment to articles in the international press calling out Sri Lanka's transitional justice failures. The protest photographies were made up of those displayed by the protesters and photographs of the protesters themselves, and insidious state surveillance.

A year later, when I met the families in Maruthankerny, Jaffna, and Kilinochchi, the protests were nearing their one-year mark. Parallel demonstrations were taking place in Vavuniya, Mannar, Mullaitivu, and Trincomalee, forming collectively the Association for Relatives of the Enforced Disappeared (ARED), North and Eastern Province. The protest sites were densely entangled with photography, serving as a microcosm for the kinds of photography that emerged in the previous chapters, collectively inscribed with new political resonance directed at challenging the Sri Lankan state. Photographs of disappeared loved ones initially served a practical purpose of evidence and identification in the submission of formal complaints and the families' navigation of bureaucratic procedures pertaining to missing persons, making one's loss literally visible to the state, often by way of National Identity Cards (NICs), passports, or the photographic images produced for obtaining these documents. The tents at Kilinochchi and Maruthankerny formed ephemeral photographic shrines to several hundred of the thousands of Tamils who disappeared during and after the war. A number of the protesters vehemently believed that their children were still alive. The bodies of protesters formed flesh-and-bone effigies for those whose fate remained unknown, as they weathered the arid heat and erratic monsoons. The color from these portraits' expectant gazes and wide grins had begun to fade with sun and rain. These invoked a different kind of agitation, a challenge and disruption to the state's claim of peace achieved by military victory.

The tents expanded and contracted with impulse and anxiety: fear, anger, frustration, and longing shaped the collective mood on any given day. This was inextricable from a dominant question of visibility that the protesters themselves were conflicted about. Journalists and activists intermittently visited the sites. On certain days, protesters were eager to narrate their stories and rehearse old heartbreaks and trauma for visiting writers and picture-takers. Each iteration was unfailingly underpinned by inconceivable despair and desperation, but also a desire to be seen and acknowledged. Correspondence relating to complaints made to the state and the International Committee of the Red Cross (ICRC) and responses that arrived in languages they did not speak were shown in frustration. Private photographs from tucked-away shopping bags emerged during conversations on quieter afternoons. On some days there were no words, but instead photographs were cupped in their hands and held up as offerings to the camera's eye.

At other times, protesters discouraged photographs and expressed distaste and apprehension around the possible uses and commoditization of images by photojournalists or entrepreneurial immigration brokers. These concerns hinted at the medium's perceived capacity to contract future protections, entitlements, and even citizenships, even though such certainties were virtually impossible to guarantee. Foreign correspondents demanded that their fixers organize assembly lines of hands, photos, and tearful faces for their cameras to add sensation to global news explainers constituting what Arthur Kleinman and Joan Kleinman describe as a "dismay of images" (1996, 9). These situated the protesters within a global visual economy of resistance against state terror. Yet the protesters were anything but passive subjects in the making of these images, constantly thinking through their efficacy and expediency, reiterating the risk and agency involved in the performative politics of "victimhood." It was an understanding that demonstrated fundamentally the global nature of their audience, revealing the failures of civic spectatorship, as well as global governance and rights mechanisms.

This chapter explores the photographies of the protests of the Tamil Families of the Disappeared. This courageous act of civilian resistance was fundamental to the development of this book and its focus on the political mobilizations of photography in northern Sri Lanka.

Despite continuous protests since February 2017, little has changed.[1] No fewer than 280 protesting parents of those disappeared by Sri Lankan state forces have passed away with no answers about the fates of their children.

A SHORT HISTORY OF LONG PROTEST

The first cases of enforced disappearances in Sri Lanka were recorded in the aftermath of the 1971 JVP (Janatha Vimukthi Peramuna, or National Liberation Front) insurrection and have served as a powerful instrument of state terror since (Thomson-Senanayake 2014). The expansion of state powers through greater securitization and militarization was exacerbated by the armed conflict in the north and the second JVP insurrection in the south. The JVP and the Tamil militancy also used abduction and disappearance as a tactic of terror and suppression. An estimated 65,000 enforced disappearances have been reported in Sri Lanka since the early 1980s, making it the second highest case load globally according to the United Nations Working Group on Enforced or Involuntary Disappearances (UNWGEID 2020).

Women-led civilian resistance against such acts of state terror began in northern Sri Lanka in 1984. As has been discussed by Neloufer de Mel, based on a personal communication with Sarvam Kailasapathy, the Jaffna Mothers' Front, also known as the Northern Mothers' Front, was formed in response to the army's rounding up of seven hundred to eight hundred Tamil boys and men between the ages of twelve and thirty and forcibly transporting them to the Palaly and Boossa camps in efforts to suppress the militancy (De Mel 2001, 230). De Mel recounts that "a plea was then issued by the army to the Mothers' Front of Jaffna to bring their children with their identity cards for voluntary checking. The mothers did so and were at the end of the day rewarded with the detention and removal of their male children to army camps" (2001, 230). Similarly, Rohini Hensman recalls how in 1986, the Eastern Mothers' Front "came out with rice pounders to prevent the LTTE [Liberation Tigers of Tamil Eelam] massacre of TELO [Tamil Eelam Liberation Organization], a rival militant group" (Hensman 1992, 503).

Much of the research on enforced disappearances in Sri Lanka has been carried out by civil society and nongovernmental human rights organizations that have recorded the issue over many decades at significant risk. Journalists and activists documenting or drawing attention to enforced disappearances have themselves been disappeared, imprisoned, or abducted and tortured. Protester, activist, and journalist interlocutors continue to be routinely harassed and intimidated at protest sites, in their homes, via telephone calls, and by regular summons and interrogations by the state security forces. Even making submissions to apparatuses established to offer them redress resulted in "friendly" police visits to their homes "advising" families to stop looking for their loved ones. A few have been physically assaulted by anonymous assailants. Others were pressured to accept death certificates to expedite bureaucratic practicalities pertaining to land ownership, banking, and pensions. The absence of a body also entailed that families were unable to carry out funerary rituals which permitted ascent to the afterlife, rendering the practice of enforced disappearance even more malicious.

Malathi de Alwis has extensively analyzed the predominantly Sinhalese Southern Mothers' Front, which comprised 25,000 women who rallied to protest the disappearance of some 60,000 young men during the 1987–89 Bheeshanaya (2008). Given the prominence of mothers, these movements have been primarily analyzed through the lens of gender, which de Alwis describes as a mobilization of "fraught maternalism" against a patriarchal state power (2007, 128). Women's participation within political spaces and discourses in Sri Lanka was especially tense, with strikingly low numbers of women represented in the legislature. Even so, women have been at the forefront of resistance and social movements in various parts of the island. The positioning of motherhood and gender was one that cannot be disentangled from the visual and political representational dynamics of the protest.

Following several years of recurrent marches during the postwar Rajapaksa years, the families of the disappeared in the northeast began their sustained protest based on five demands. These included the release of a list of those who surrendered or were detained by the state forces during and after the war; the release of a list of all secret detention centers; and the release of a list of all the detainees held under the Prevention of Terrorism Act (PTA) and the Emergency Regulations. In addition, the families called for these lists to be given to the families of the disappeared, their lawyers, and other authorized representatives (ARED 2017). The association further requested that all the reports of the state-appointed committees and commissions about disappearances over the previous three decades and the government response to those findings be made public. The state undertook various piecemeal efforts to comply with Sri Lanka's international commitments to reconciliation and transitional justice in the form of establishing several commissions of inquiry, and most notably, the Office on Missing Persons (OMP). Established in 2017, the OMP was intended "to provide appropriate mechanisms for searching and tracing missing persons and to clarify the circumstances in which such persons went missing and their fate" and identify suitable avenues for redress (Parliament of the Democratic Socialist Republic of Sri Lanka 2016). The commission did not possess punitive powers to deal with investigations into testimony identifying perpetrators, with its legal enactment patently stating that its findings shall not give rise to any criminal or civil liability (Parliament of the Democratic Socialist Republic of Sri Lanka 2016).

The OMP's official meetings were boycotted by groups of protesters demanding that minimal conditions, including publishing a list of names of those detained, be met to win their trust. This was underpinned by the fact that many of those who crossed over from LTTE-held territory to government-controlled areas at the end of the war were enumerated, and those who had any "connections" to the LTTE were forced to surrender to the military, whereby they were formally registered. The state forces denied having possession of such a list. Several protesters had personally handed over their children to the army in 2009. This alleged list was the cornerstone to the ongoing strain between the protesters, the government, and the military. The political leadership's hollow promises to release the lists of detainees and surrendees was a significant point of frustration for the protesters (Rajasingham 2018). Support for victims among major political parties as well as the public was also markedly poor. Former President Gotabaya Rajapaksa stated in 2020, "The missing are in fact dead. I cannot bring back the dead" (Abi-Habib and Bastians 2020). Rajapaksa, in his previous capacity as a military officer, is implicated in over 700 cases of enforced disappearances during the second JVP insurrection between 1987 and 1989 (ITJP 2022). The tone of the protests also changed significantly since their inception, becoming "formalized" over time. The Kilinochchi protest tent, for example, morphed into an office. Continuous on-site protest halted at some locations after the five-hundred-day mark with regular demonstrations taking their place. Others persist.

There were also those I met who were not part of the organized protests and others who had various reservations about the "different politics." They claimed the protesters were being manipulated by those with hardline Tamil nationalist interests. Fear of reprisal by the government was also common. Misgivings might also be understood along prevailing class and caste biases. I flag here briefly but necessarily that the protesters themselves were not socially or politically homogenous, and internal tensions and hierarchies bound to class and caste were prevalent. Despite this, there was a concerted effort to present a coordinated front and message, which I will honor in this ethnographic account. This also informed their ambivalent but collective stance toward photography at the protest site. Others had long since given up on their quest for answers and did not wish to participate in these protests, having become resigned to the continued denial of justice. Disappearances had also occurred at the hands of the LTTE, competing paramilitary groups, and the Indian Peace Keeping Force (IPKF) in response to perceived dissidence, threat, or political opposition. These abrupt and unreconciled losses of loved ones threaded through nearly all my interlocutors' lives. Though often aware of who the perpetrators were, they were also resigned to the fact that there would be no justice. What adequate justice might realistically look like was also unresolved where recourse was measured in financial reparations, as was the case with victims of the Bheeshanaya. For the majority of the family members in Maruthankerny and Kilinochchi, the disappearances were firmly linked to the final months of the war in 2008–2009 and its aftermath. Several had witnessed or been forced to surrender their family members to the military at the end of the war in 2009. These cases have been termed "mass disappearances." Questions of ethics and risk in researching and writing an ethnography of an unstable context has required constant rethinking. It treads an anxious line between potentially endangering one's interlocutors by amplifying their demands for visibility or hindering their political agency. This preoccupation strained to unease as I attempted to negotiate the scholarly representation of their political claims. In my engagement with the protesters over many months, it was impossible not to be mindful of the daily devastations they experienced and their expectations for what visibility this work could afford for their struggle. Bearing these considerations in mind, I reiterate that I only recorded what my interlocutors chose to relate to me and allowed me to photograph, noting that this was done with the specific intention (on their part) of accruing greater visibility to their losses and claims. In a context of heavy militarization, swift extrajudicial retribution by the state security apparatus and pervasive impunity for human rights violations, visibility served as an ambivalent source of political cachet and precarity, and sometimes even protection, as protest leaders became recognizable by way of media coverage. I anonymized those featured, assessing ultimately their present and future vulnerability. Their own relationship to the demand to be seen has repeatedly changed in the time that I have known them.

I maintain focus on the political work of photography by considering the "types" of images I encountered as a strategy to mitigate any unintended risk to those who shared their experiences (and images) with me so that their stories might not be easily associated with a single image reproduced in this text. I have also altered secondary contextual details to protect interlocutors' identities, noting also that many of their accounts were in public circulation by way of media interviews. I have used two high profile cases that received wide media coverage on account of the significance of photographs to their narratives to supplement the ethnographic vignettes deriving from fieldwork undertaken in 2018. The illustrations in this chapter were photographs taken on public demonstration days as protesters presented themselves to be photographed. Even with the necessary abstractions that shape this as an academic text, I hope that these words amplify the families' courageous pursuit of justice and, most importantly, their demand to be seen.

PROTESTS IN PICTURES

KILINOCHCHI

For five hundred days, the protest site at Kilinochchi wavered between stillness and activity, each disposition no less saturated by grief oscillating between silence and the deafening wails of its occupants (fig. 18). The spare, makeshift tin-roofed tent on the side of the A9 Kandy-Jaffna highway was cobbled together in the shadow of the golden yellow gopuram of the Kandasamy Kovil. A handwritten paper and plywood board suspended at the front offered a count of the number of days spent in continued vigil for the enforced disappeared. Razed by some of the most intensive fighting between the state forces and LTTE, Kilinochchi had undergone many transformations through the post/war. The town had at one time served as the administrative capital of the aspiring Tamil state. Its postwar reinvention at the hands of the government had been cold and deft. Kilinochchi's recasting as a sprawling showpiece for military triumph sat uneasily with the locals, nearly all of whom were survivors of the darkest devastations of the war. Blocky pastel and chrome government offices, a new *kachcheri* (registry) complex and district court dazzled with fresh white paint. The hospital, at one time per-

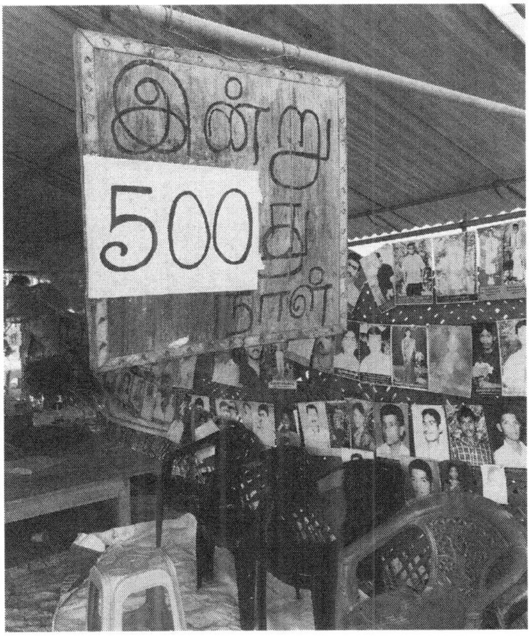

FIGURE 18. 500 Days of protest (Kilinochchi, 2018)

forated by volleys of artillery shelling, had been offered a convincing facelift. A bright orange train station marked a stop in the revived Yal Devi train line connecting Colombo to Jaffna.

Scattered among the Yal Devi's passengers were foreign backpackers and elderly Tamil expatriates laden with suitcases. The new entertainment screens in the coaches were already mostly broken. Its air-conditioned comforts served principally pilgrims and tourists from the south visiting the sacred, ancient capital of Anuradhapura, or traveling onward to Jaffna. The screens that did work played Sri Lanka Tourism videos in French and Korean. The station platform was plastered with a billboard sponsored by the Australian government as part of the "Don't Call Australia Home" campaign. It reminded locals with a picture of a small boat heaving in a stormy sea that they would not be allowed to set foot in the country if they came without a visa. Dangerous, unlawful attempts to flee the country by boat had spiked following the end of the war. These efforts to leave were largely bound to socioeconomic dispossession. However, continued persecution by the state security forces, in what has been described as a "predatory climate against Tamils," targeting former combatants as well as their family members, was also crucial (ITJP 2016, 9). "It doesn't matter that they keep failing; they will give up all they have and try again," I was told by Mannan, an NGO worker who supported unsuccessful returnees. Boat journeys were expensive. Each attempt costs up to a few million rupees. "They will give up everything they have to leave. They can't see a future here." The walls of primary schools in the north had begun to host vivid murals of horror on the instruction of international migration organizations. The occupants of capsized boats were painted as being chewed on by fierce and fantastical monstrous fish. In a place riddled with dreams and desires to leave, as imagined in studio encounters in hope of parity of citizenship and opportunity elsewhere, these murals painted by young children were especially jarring.

Army camps contained within imposing granite walls were made to resemble medieval European fortresses as reinvented in kitsch theme parks. The most conspicuous ruin of war was an enormous water tower bombed by the LTTE before the group abandoned its capital in December 2008. Others, especially those associated with the Tigers, were demolished after the initial surge of "war tourism" from the south had died down. A signboard placed before it declared "Say No to Destruction Never Again" in Sinhala, Tamil, and English. Over time the Tamil and English faded and were stripped off, staying tellingly unrestored. Maintained as a monument in a small park, it was later cleared to make way for a new tower. Busy commuters and lively little shops bustled on the edges of these statement pieces. Ammachi, an international donor-funded initiative to support women's entrepreneurship, where "war-affected women" served "Tamil traditional food," had become a popular stop among locals and tourists en route to Jaffna. The eatery was featured in glossy magazine articles that claimed Sri Lanka was indeed "reawakening." The Vanni, too, had begun to seep into the sketches of travel magazines and the photo stories of Instagram personalities. Staged through stylized photography, their captions delighted in the region's "war-ravaged landscape" and "rustic way of life." A new imaginary of the "unexplored" north was being snapped, filtered, and hashtagged on Instagram to invite holidaymakers. A former war zone could, too, exist as a tourist paradise.

A few hundred feet away, the protesters and the photographs of their disappeared loved ones, inconveniencing this narrative of peace and renewal, remained largely ignored.

The tent was located near the ostentatious headquarters of the 57th Division of the Sri Lankan Army, responsible for several of the most ruthless offensives carried out in the final year of the war. The town's new centerpiece, a prominent victory monument, heralded the country's triumph over terrorism. A bronze lotus bloomed from a titanic concrete block punctured by a large brass bullet. Watchful army soldiers offered visitors, almost entirely Sinhalese tourists from the south, grandiloquent interpretations of its symbolism. The (once) impenetrable block was said to represent the LTTE, while the bullet signified the deathblow dealt to the group by the armed forces. The lotus, imbued with Buddhist iconographic connotations of nirvanic purity, epitomized the "peace" accomplished out of the destruction of the LTTE. A Sri Lankan flag fluttered at its crest. For Kilinochchi's families of the disappeared, the soaring memorial was an unspoken affront to their losses. It stood for loved ones scattered, killed, injured, disabled, missing, and disappeared. It reminded of multiple displacements—homes, belongings, and livelihoods lost and destroyed. Overarchingly, it cemented uncertainty and fear over personal and political futures in a state of foreseeably impaired citizenship.

On demonstration days, marking significant international commemorations such as the Day of the Disappeared or Human Rights Day, or the protest's milestones measured by continuity in the number of days, the families actively presented themselves to be photographed. While the protest site was permanently occupied by a small number of individuals, larger numbers gathered on demonstration days. The "chronic mourners" were extensively snapped, their bodies situated against the photo montages of loss or holding pictures of their disappeared loved ones in their hands (Schirmer 1989, 25). These situated the tent's occupants within a broader aesthetic of resistance against state terror and enforced disappearance, visually linking them to the families of the disappeared in Argentina, Chile, Kashmir, and Nepal, among others, and closer to home in southern Sri Lanka, in a potent formation of Azoulay's photographic citizenship, transcending and challenging the violence of the sovereign (Azoulay 2008). It was a photography that disordered suggestions of a postwar peace.

The defiant presence of the protesters, as proxy for the absent bodies of those who disappeared, reminded also of the absence of justice. Photographs of the protesters were thus transformed into a visual metonym for an unrealized Tamil nation-state, as much as the failures of Sri Lanka's reconciliation and transitional justice processes, recirculated by human rights campaigners and nationalist activists alike. As they faced the cameras, their quiet sadness sometimes gave way to visceral and voluble rage and sorrow as they screamed their pain into the unblinking lenses. Photographs and footage were compressed and linked to social media posts tethered to a series of hashtags #disappearedsl (Disappeared Sri Lanka) #familiesofthedisappeared #releasethelist #nojustice #tamilfod (Tamil Families of the Disappeared) alongside tags denoting ethnicity and location #tamil #eelamtamil #kilinochchi. On Instagram and Twitter (X), these are reposted and retweeted largely by diasporic Tamils and a small number of local activists.

Against the intermittent zips of traffic and the angry quacks of bus horns, life in the tent on non-demonstration days exuded a quiet hum of domesticity, albeit one under the nearly constant watch of military intelligence men from the adjacent army camp. The older men sat on brown plastic chairs chatting occasionally as they watched the road. A few elderly *ammas* (mothers) rested on a wooden dais built on the sun-warmed sand, improvised out of necessity during the last monsoon to stop the rainwater. At lunchtime, the women began to chop onions and rinse red rice and lentils to prepare a modest meal for the occupants. A tea kettle sat over a kerosene stove outside. Washing and drinking water was stored in plastic buckets from which ever-silver tumblers were dipped in and out. On demonstration days, visitors were always offered food and drink—rice and vegetable curry packets wrapped in lunch sheets and white sugar paper and sweet yellow *sharbat* (cordial) in disposable cups scooped out of a roving pail by volunteering *mamas*. "You must eat lunch—come eat something! Have you gotten a rice packet yet? Come!" we were shepherded by various *akkas* who made sure everyone had eaten before they picked up their own meals.[2] It was as if we were guests in their home.

Plainclothes personnel idled in nearby bus stands or neighboring shops, observing the comings and goings of the protest site. They were somehow always discernible by their precise gait and nondescript collared T-shirts and tracksuit bottoms, and they seemed to loiter everywhere. During rallies, they weaved in and out of the huddles of gathered activists, supporters, and journalists. We collectively snapped and recorded on our phones and cameras for irreconcilable purposes—surveillance enmeshed with solidarity. The line between citizen journalists, activists, state intelligence, and even researchers like me became unclear in a perceptible tension between the theoretical positions on photography as instrument of the state and weapon of emancipation. Photographs and footage made up the contents of news reports, personal social media posts, human rights and advocacy reports, documentary films, civil society exhibitions, and state records in equal stride. The event of the demonstration was visually atomized through numerous lenses, framed and redirected into multiple, contrary forms and circuits.

In mutual awareness and occasional acknowledgment, the protesters, supporters, and informers went about their days orbiting one another.

Knotted pink and blue mosquito nets and a flowery crimson and russet bed sheet hung from the aluminum scaffolding that held up a tin roof over the little plot of temple land that had been turned into transient home and shrine. The blue tarpaulin and woven coconut leaf Cadjan "walls" that barely covered the tent's sides were strung with a couple of hundred laminated portraits of the protesters' loved ones printed on A4 paper, each captioned with their name and hometown. Weathered photographic impressions of lost parents, siblings, spouses, children, and grandchildren faced out onto the A9 highway. The photographs displayed showed an assemblage of absence. Children who were forcefully conscripted in last-minute efforts by the LTTE to fill its rapidly depleting ranks or surrendered to the military in its aftermath were nowhere to be found. Grandchildren had been abducted in the harsh months that preceded the end of the armed conflict in 2009. Mothers and fathers had vanished during the long period of postwar internment at squalid and securitized "welfare centers" to which surviving Tamils from the war zone were relegated. Siblings were never seen again following their "rehabilitation" in camps set up for over 12,000 individuals identified by the state as "ex-combatants." Many thousands of dead, disappeared, and missing remained unaccounted for and unacknowledged by the Sri Lankan state. In this Kilinochchi tent, and several others scattered across the island's northeast, their technicolor apparitions endured.

The majority of the photographs were studio portraits; the subjects were poised and smiling in their "Sunday bests" in full and three-quarter lengths set against flamboyant studio backdrops. It was easy to imagine their making in a studio outing with family, a photographer calling out instructions for a photograph intended to be placed in a family album or accompany a proposal. Others were reproductions of NIC and passport pictures. Stamp-sized headshots, perhaps requested to supplement job or visa applications, were enlarged until they became blurred impressions of the identities they once established. The tent was shelter to some, a frequent or occasional stop to others. Each protester, irrespective of the continuity of their presence in the tent, could swiftly locate the photograph of their lost loved one from those fastened to the tarp, narrating a rehearsed and repeated story of loss. In Barthes's poignant terms, "Every photograph (was) a certificate of presence," that in turn evidenced a violent or abrupt absence. Each sweet or solemn portrait indexed an individual life and presence but jarringly signified the insidious violence that necessitated its display ([1981] 2000, 87). They were also importantly objects of resistance confronting the violence of the state which disappeared their loved ones. Their intimate, everyday character afforded them a greater power of visibility against the very state that cast them as subversives and terrorists to be eliminated.

The visuality of the installation drew attention to the plight of the families of the disappeared. This display of photographs had become an allegory of relationships, not simply a "sociogram" sketching extant social roles and relations within family albums, but the tensions between nation, the state, and citizens (Bourdieu 1990, 23). These sociograms steeped in grief and hardship speak to the volatility of photographic images. Family portraits and school identity card photos are transformed through state violence into precious objects of despair, but also evidence and resistance. When turned toward the state in protest, the state only regards their agitant potential to disrupt a narrative of peace. In turn, photographs intended for not much more than the pages of a family album or the plastic insides of a wallet elicit the risk if not likelihood of violence to those who hold them up in desperation and defiance. These photographs then become both demand and sacrifice. In this exchange of gazes, the politics of nations, states, and desired liberation ricochet without resolve. Where the state has actively sought to erase memories and the realities of the war, determine who can and cannot be mourned, and how the war dead and disappeared might be grieved by their loved ones, personal photographs of the war-affected had become objects of inordinate social and political significance. Where these experiences were expressly colored by a history of displacement that saw communities being continuously uprooted, these photographs as carried objects were even more precious. These were also incorporated into visual narratives demanding transitional justice by civil society and media activists through their re-photographing and circulation. Here through photography, the intimate was rendered public and inordinately political, as well as in a sense "national," given their significance to particularly diasporic Tamil nationalist activism.

MARUTHANKERNY

If Kilinochchi was one of the most visible sites of protest, Maruthankerny was the quietest. The Soranpattu-Maruthankerny road turning off from Pudukattu junction on the A9 cuts through a sliver of an impossibly sky-blue lagoon fringed with pale sand dunes wild with lilac-flowered mangroves. Amid this quiet but difficult recovery, it was perhaps the material markers of the state that were most conspicuous. The cream-colored base hospital had been recently refurbished with a new coat of paint. The Vadamaradchi East Divisional Secretariat (DS) Office appeared brand new, washed in brilliant white. A Sri Lankan flag fluttered at its helm. New power lines extended along the rutted path flanked by unkempt thickets of grass and regrowth from shell-shorn palmyra trees, ending at the pristine Thalaiyadi beach fronted by a cobalt fisherman's shrine that housed a bejeweled statue of the Virgin Mary holding a peach-colored baby Jesus. The edges of the village that overlooked the ocean were strewn with rubble, the patchy foundations and brick and concrete detritus of destroyed homes. The housing schemes built along the inner dirt roads were paid for by the Swiss. A large white cross hovered over the shore. Nearby, a bleached concrete pen accommodated a tall indigo cenotaph. Maruthankerny was multiply devastated, by the tsunami and wartime aerial bombardment. "Even the trees here are new," Jude, the driver who accompanied me on one of my regular trips from Jaffna Town observed. Amid this fraught postwar renewal was a meager tent on the side of the road, not far from the DS Office. When I first traveled to Maruthankerny in February 2018, the group had engaged in continuous roadside protest for 343 days, separated by some days in its inception, but firmly standing alongside the groups from other protest sites.

The regular occupants lived within walking distance of the tent, arriving in the morning and leaving at night, laying down rattan mats, and sitting down for their day's work. The cadjan "walls" of the tent were pinned with flex banners printed with enlarged photographs of the disappeared as if to form a morose family album with a collage of birthday portraits and identity headshots; their kinship was formed by absence. Most of those pictured were young men and women, teenagers dressed for birthday parties, puberty ceremonies, or school photo days, or cropped out of celebratory group shots. As in Kilinochchi, each image was captioned with the individual's name and village. The banner is titled in bold red words: "*Kanamel aakkappatta uravukalakku Ilankai arasai patil kuru!*" (The Sri Lankan government must give answers for our enforced disappeared relatives!) There appeared to be a desire to emphasize the nature of the disappearance: they were not merely missing, disappeared, or unaccounted for, but forcefully erased by the state. The front of the tent is patched with salvaged vinyl boards discarded from elsewhere.

One banner showed the Nallur Kandasamy Temple, while the other showed a collection of cartoon characters. Unlike at the Kilinochchi site,

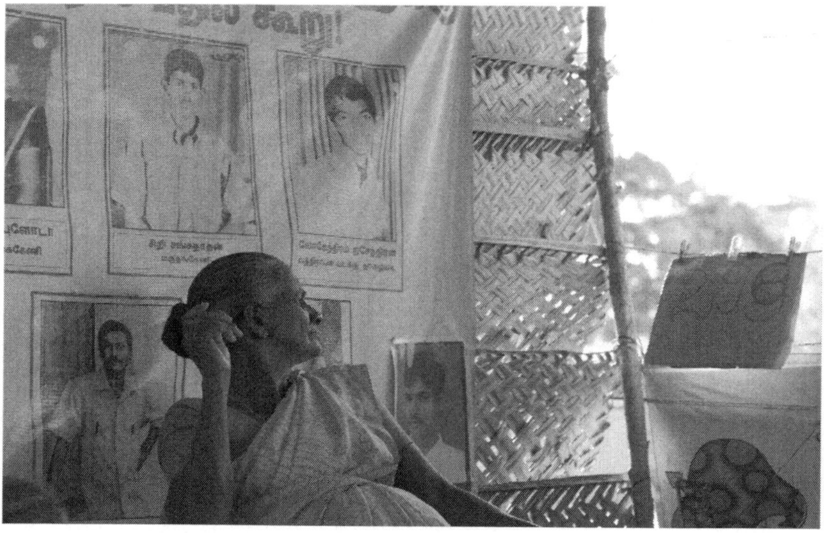

FIGURE 19. Waiting mother (Maruthankerny, 2018)

this interior road was not a location of great visibility or prominence, its only audience being the vehicles that occasionally rumbled past. The Divisional Secretary and other bureaucrats drove past in their pickups each day. In 343 days, only once had a representative of the office that administers registration documents as well as essential citizenship entitlements such as welfare and pension briefly stopped to inquire after the protests. "If the president says there are no disappearances, there are no disappearances," they were told. However, on demonstration days a large number of protesters from the other sites traveled to Maruthankerny in solidarity, along with civil society and media activists. The small tent on a byroad in eastern Jaffna was rarely afforded the same attention; the narrative and sorrows of its protesters merely folded into more prominent locations such as Kilinochchi or Mullaitivu. Yet this group of women came in every single day to sit before the banners printed with their children's faces even in the absence of cameras (fig. 19). "Where else is there left to go?" one mother asked.

THE POLITICS OF VISIBILITY AND "VICTIMHOOD"

To protest in the context of political uncertainty and impaired citizenship was to make oneself visible—as a survivor, as a victim, as a human shrine to

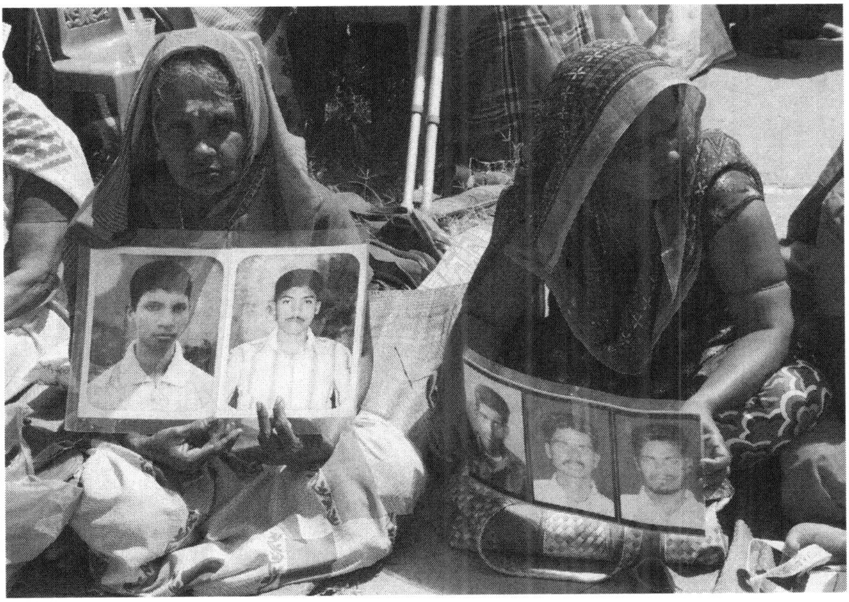

FIGURE 20. Mothers at the Kilinochchi protest (Kilinochchi, 2018)

a disappeared loved one, as a political subject, as a dissident, and as a Tamil, around whom national and transnational solidarities are formed (fig. 20). To be photographed as a protester was to submit to the unpredictable, potentially dangerous or advantageous outcomes of volatility. Yet to make oneself visible was also to render oneself politically precarious. The question of visibility also treads between the national and the global, where accountability mechanisms have continued to fail.

Surenthiran *mama*'s son's headshot, stark against a bright, solid backdrop, offered an unmistakable, frontal view of his face magnified to the size of an A4 sheet. The clarity of the image afforded not only greater visibility but capacity for copying. Reproductions and re-photographing typically rendered photographs less sharp and their sitters less discernible due to pixelation. In *mama*'s possession were various other photographs, a photocopy of his son Darshan's NIC and an elaborately photoshopped studio composite. The young man posed variously for the camera in a hat and sunglasses with cinematic flare. Conscripted by the LTTE, Darshan was injured and taken into army custody in 2008. Surenthiran *mama* has received intermittent updates from various acquaintances who had seen Darshan being taken away from the front line to a hospital and then a government prison in the south. Following that, Darshan had vanished. These sightings were also what assured Surenthiran *mama* that his son was alive. "There is no *kovil* in the island that I have not gone to pray to, and I know with certainty that my son will come back to me." He carried the blessings of those temples in the form of photographs on his camera phone, allowing a different sort of photographic efficacy.

For Kannamma, the only photograph of her daughter, Abhirami, detained by the army at the Omanthai checkpoint never to be seen again, was taken following her puberty ceremony at the age of thirteen. She was dressed in a rose and gold sari and traditional jewelry, her face made up with bright makeup, her lips painted red, and her cheeks smudged in pink. "This is when she looked most beautiful," Kannamma wept. In others, grinning children at birthday parties stood beside extravagant iced cakes. Bright-eyed friends on seaside day-trips squeezed into a single frame. In the absence of usable photographs, there were photocopies—faces stenciled in black-and-white printer ink, and cropped faces and distorted bodies enlarged to the point of pixelation. A disconcerting number of lost children were photographed in school uniform—prize givings, sports meets of years past.

Thavamani's daughter, Kalyani, seemed impossibly young, photographed in her school uniform with a bottle green tie. In 2009, Thavamani had been forced to surrender her only daughter to the army. Kalyani had not been seen since. Individuals snipped from tender and joyful snaps picked out of family albums made up the rest. Coy young brides presented themselves to the camera, as bashful smiling spouses in their wedding-day finery gazed at one another. The protesters' choice of photographs, if there was one, was decided by the degree of visibility it would afford, suspended somewhere between the sentimentality of the cherished and the frontality of the official. Yet in their uses in protest they could agitate to equivalent effect. It was determined as much by clarity as well as how *vadivu* the photograph was. The digital afforded an important avenue for reinventing even damaged images. The possibility for enhancing their prominence was apparent in terms of size, but also commonly the saturation of color, which was seen to improve the appearance of the image (fig. 21). Photographs were also turned into visual-material protest objects in the form of banners and posters. Their re-photographing for the media expanded their circulation even further.

The photographs at the protest sites also served an important purpose of signposting. The fear of being forgotten by those who had disappeared

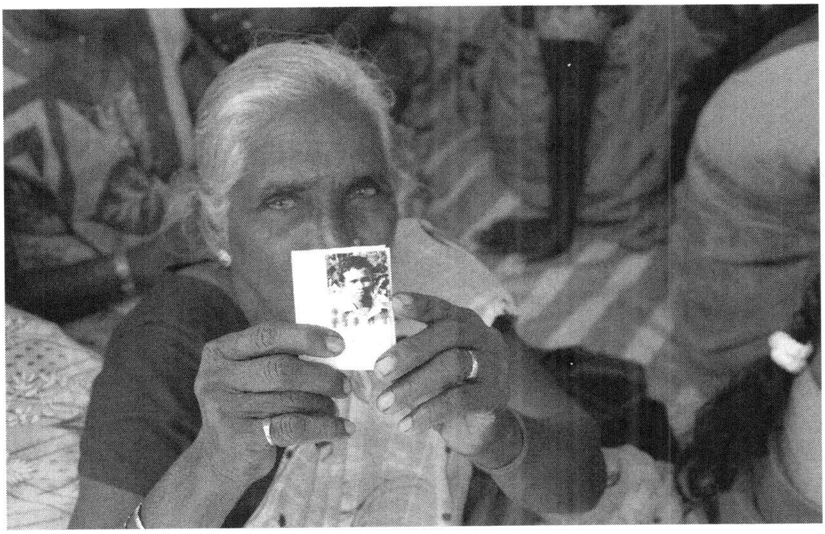

FIGURE 21. A protesting mother holds up a digitally enhanced identity card photo of her son (Maruthankerny, 2018)

was common among the protesters, especially in instances where the victims were young or injured. These photographs were not merely objects of reminiscence and resistance for the living, but a guide for those who may not know how to find their way back. Sivapakkyam, a mother and grandmother, carried with her a board onto which several photographs were pasted. She had personally surrendered her whole family to the military in 2009, her daughter and son-in-law, as well as her three grandchildren all of whom were under the age of ten. "They were little children. They were not terrorists. I can accept the loss of my son-in-law. I can accept the loss of my daughter. But I cannot and will not accept the loss of these children whom I handed over to the army myself. What crimes have they committed? Why can't they let them go? If they are somewhere now and they have forgotten me, maybe by seeing these photographs, they will recognize themselves and know to come find me," she lamented. I would see her at every demonstration I subsequently attended in Kilinochchi, Jaffna Town, and Maruthankerny, holding up a collage of photographs showing her disappeared family. The protesters also traveled in solidarity to rallies held at other sites. These were also occasions for securing greater attention to their individual losses. I had repeatedly seen Sivapakkyam and her photo, illustrating a family tree of loss, in the international news before I had met her in person, and would see it many more times subsequently.

There were also private photographs concealed in this "public" space. I was in conversation with one of the protesters along with a group of visiting activists who were recording testimonies, when a frail elderly woman on the other end of the tent whom I had not met before tried to get my attention. "Call her, won't you? Tell her to come here," she asked after me. Amirthavalli was fifty-seven years old but looked much older. Her diminutive frame was concealed by a too-large housecoat, and she hunched over as she sat on the wooden dais. She wore a pair of spectacles, even though one of the lenses had fallen out. As I sat down next to her, Amirthavalli insisted to everyone present that I resembled her daughter, pointing to the laminated print of a full-length studio portrait on display. Out of her meager belongings stored away in a plastic shopping bag, she took out three photographs to affirm the resemblance. Two were birthday photographs of her daughter Janaki, one where she was pictured alone and the other taken with Amirthavalli. The third is from Janaki's puberty ceremony.

Janaki was twenty-four years old when she was taken away by the army in 2009, a year older than I would have been at the time. I soon realized that many of the missing were around my age, which made such emotional recollections even more painful for some of the protesters. "When I see you, how can I not think of my daughter? See how much you look alike," Amirthavalli started crying. Her husband had passed away some years ago, and she was supported by her sister as the state welfare apparatus did not account for single-person households. As she could not afford the daily bus fare of Rs. 120 (US$0.35) to return home daily, she stayed at the protest site along with a few others.

Like Amirthavalli, many of the protesters kept on hand (if available) copies of their children's identity documents, additional photographs, and various letters from government offices and the ICRC acknowledging the receipt of complaints. "Who haven't I written to?" Surenthiran *mama* asked. "The President, the Prime Minister, the Inspector General of the Police, the Red Cross. Human Rights Commission. There is not a single place I have not sent letters to." He was in tears when he fanned out the letters, which he kept in a small satchel that was always swung over his shoulder. These, mostly in Sinhala and English, neither of which he spoke, were kept in the brown paper envelopes they had been posted in. Darshan's existence was mapped out in these exchanges, suspended somewhere between Surenthiran *mama*'s assertions, his faith in divine reassurance, and the state's polite receipts veiling aloof denial. "The last time I went to a meeting, the police came to my house the next day and told me to stop looking. How can we trust anyone to give us answers?"

DISRUPTIVE SIGNS

Interspersed among the photographs of the disappeared were more patent confirmations of state atrocity in the form of trophy photographs captured by Sri Lankan soldiers coupled with propaganda images produced by the government. Others were produced by LTTE or noncombatant photographers in the war zone as evidence and documentation. In a powerful example of contingency, family members found in the latter inadvertent verification that their loved ones were alive. In Kilinochchi, a few pennants had been fixed to the back of the tent to mark past public demonstrations. An image of a group of men and a young boy in the custody of the army had been printed onto a vinyl banner; one of two examples of photographs displayed at the site showing a group of prisoners of war huddled around a mud pit prior to what was believed to be their summary execution. The still image, one of hundreds of trophy images that emerged out of the final months of the war, was used most famously in Callum Macrae's documentary *No Fire Zone: The Killing Fields of Sri Lanka* (2013), which exposed some of the brutal war crimes committed by the Sri Lankan state forces (chapter 6). One of the men pictured in the banner was known to someone in the group, but they collectively wondered who the anonymous child was and whether he had survived. I later learned that he did not survive. In London, I would see a photograph of the boy's mangled body identifiable by his blue shorts and a bandaged knee, piled into the back of a truck with several other bodies.

Yogeshwarie was in possession of a grainy image of her son photographed, she believed, at an army camp a few years after his detention at a checkpoint. She kept the image of uncertain provenance, given to her she claimed by an "American man," on a dated Chinese cell phone. In the smudged shape of a young man among a few others, including military men in fatigues, seen on a little square screen, there was for her the undeniable possibility that her son might be alive. Held in a government detention center or jail perhaps or still persecuted and tortured at a "secret site." Their loved ones, Yogeshwarie and others were certain, had to be alive. Such visual and aural fragments of "evidence" permeated the world of these protesters. They existed in grapevine "sightings" from prisons and hospitals reported in second- and thirdhand messages from acquaintances. Images such as those on Yogeshwarie's cell phone multiplied and persisted in their private and public circulations, indicating to them the possibility that their child might have survived. They became ubiquitous on the internet and in the global media and disseminated as evidence of state atrocity by way of international and Tamil diasporic advocacy groups demanding justice for victims, and accountability for war crimes. For families of the disappeared and dead, navigating the burdened peace of the postwar, desperate hope and frustration pinned to this visual detritus existed hand in hand.

Like Yogeshwarie, Pushpavalli believed that her son was kept in a secret camp or "black site." "I received a call from this number in 2013," she pointed to a mobile phone number written down in a small notebook. "Four years after he had been detained. I am sure it was my son. There is no doubt in my mind about that. He said that their clothes had been taken away from them, and that they were being kept in complete darkness. He may have gotten the phone from someone who felt sorry for him—I do not know. He cried and cried. I tried the number repeatedly after that but could not get through." These assertions of one-off phone calls from their lost children softly crying into borrowed mobile phones whimpering that they had been "stripped and herded like animals in dark rooms" were not uncommon, reinforcing the fragmentary evidence of their possible survival. Jeyaseeli's son, Senan, had been in a state of shell shock since the age of fourteen. Four years later he too had been taken away by the army and never seen again. "He can't speak. He will not be able to tell them where his home is. After what happened, his education got disrupted. I think maybe if someone gave him a pen and piece of paper, he will be able to write his name, but beyond that, he cannot speak. How will he find his way back? What if they are giving them *oosi* (injections) to forget? We don't know what terrible things are being done to them," she wept. Accounts of detainees being forcibly administered drugs and alcohol prior to rape has also been flagged by advocacy and human rights groups. "We want to know where our children are. If they are dead, then who killed them? All we are asking for is to know what happened to our children." These whispers about the government's cruelty in injecting disappeared children with drugs at secret sites spoke to a broader consciousness and fear of erasure. These erasures were ones that the state's own images unwittingly betrayed.

Evidence also emerged in the form of state-generated photography, where the provenance was not indeterminate, but rather produced by the government to supplement its proclamations of reconciliation or the benevolence of individual politicians. Many late-stage recruits along with other LTTE cadres were executed by the Sri Lankan army upon capture, or subject to cruel processes of years-long "rehabilitation" following surrender. In several cases, surrendees were not seen again, but photographs of children in custody have variously emerged in ambiguous examples such as Yogeshwarie's cell phone photos, but through more formal means. An unexpected photograph emerged from the widely publicized case of Kasipillai Jeyavanitha and her disappeared daughter, Jeromy. Jeyavanitha's account, publicized by various international media outlets, reported that she and Jeromy were picked up and shoved into the back of a truck by men in uniform when they were running to safety during a shell attack. Jeyavanitha recalled being pushed out by the men along with another mother, catching a last glimpse of Jeromy still in the back of the vehicle as it sped away (Haynie 2017). The year 2015 marked a turning point in Jeyavanitha's search for Jeromy and for Sri Lanka, with the defeat of President Mahinda Rajapaksa by his longtime political ally turned opponent Maithripala Sirisena. For the protesters the political shift marked a possibility of hope that the whereabouts of their children might be revealed. It is within such a context of tenuous optimism that Jeyavanitha spotted Jeromy in a photograph used in a campaign leaflet for Maithripala Sirisena.

Standing in the middle of the image, Sirisena gazes away from a gaggle of Tamil children in school uniforms, among whom Jeyavanitha easily and certainly identified Jeromy who stood at the front of the image. In reports offered to the media, Jeyavanitha resolutely stated that the girl had the same face and thick plaits as Jeromy, the only difference being the sadness in her eyes as if she was wondering why her parents were not looking for her (Haynie 2017). She was also sure that the photograph was taken after her daughter's disappearance in 2009, positive that Sirisena had never visited Jeromy's school and that her daughter did not own a red school tie (Haynie 2017). When Jeyavanitha produced the photograph upon meeting Sirisena on his campaign trail he had no answers to offer, except that he would investigate the matter. Four years later, Jeyavanitha and five other mothers who came forward to assert that their missing children were seen in this photograph have not been given any answers by the state.

Another example was seen in the case of Jeyakumary Balendran, who along with her thirteen-year-old daughter, Vipoosika, was maliciously persecuted by state security actors. Jeyakumary was imprisoned under the PTA by the state for her efforts to locate her son who had disappeared.

A photograph of her son, Mahindan, who was forcibly conscripted by the Tigers at the age of fifteen, emerged in a government report on LTTE cadres undergoing "rehabilitation." Mahindan had not been seen since his surrender in 2009. Jeyakumary famously led the families of the disappeared demonstration in 2013 to coincide with the visit of former British Prime Minister David Cameron during his visit to Jaffna, where hundreds of families gathered to draw attention to their search for their missing children. Photographs of the families of the disappeared from this specific protest continue to be widely used in the international media. Following her arrest, Jeyakumary's own image showing her holding her son's picture circulated widely as part of an international campaign demanding her release. The volatility of photographs captured by perpetrators continued to inform important advocacy work pertaining to Sri Lanka's transitional justice concerns, especially as it pertained to the state's atrocities in the final phase of the war. They could even be wielded against those who produced the photograph as a vile memento of violence.

THE SEMANTICS OF SOLIDARITY

The faces of Kilinochchi's and Maruthankerny's enforced disappeared, enlarged, pixelated, yet named, and made momentarily visible in laminated paper and vinyl, were among 23,586 individuals from the northeast of Sri Lanka reported as missing between 10 June 1990 and 19 May 2009. Among the protesters were also those who had lost loved ones to the "shadow state" well before 1990 and after 2009 through various means, including white van abductions and arbitrary arrest. To the families, the hollowness of institutional processes such as the Office on Missing Persons (OMP), supplemented by dismissive political rhetoric by key governmental figures, was seen as confirmation of its disingenuousness and lack of interest in Tamil political grievances.

On some days, the protesters requested that visitors take photographs of them and the site so that they might be seen by the world. These photographs of their activism were printed on demonstration-day banners held up at marches. The photographs also constituted an important act of recordkeeping where the progress of the protests in terms of number of days and visual evidence were preserved as a part of its iconography. The use of photography also permitted the protesters to overcome a barrier of language. The state's frequent relegation of the Tamil language (and citizenship) to second-class status was one of the most significant strains of the postwar. "I have never felt like a citizen of this country!" various interlocutors repeatedly uttered in frustration, with others describing their status as "second-class" or "third-class" citizens. Inequalities instituted within the category of citizenship on account of ethnicity and language were a root cause of the conflict and its postwar impairments. Maheshwarie, one of the protesters, said bluntly, "Maybe if we speak in Sinhala, they will listen to us. We do not know Sinhala, so they have no interest in listening to us. They make statements in a language we do not understand. They send us letters in a language we do not understand. For whose benefit is this?" She showed me a file of correspondence sent by the International Committee of the Red Cross (ICRC), an important mediator in issues of enforced disappearances, and the government, typed in English and Sinhalese, respectively. Like Surenthiran *mama*, Maheshwarie did not speak or read either language.

In their difficult dealings with bureaucracy where they were often cornered by complex legalese even when in Tamil, protesters expressed a sense of frustration with and entrapment by language. Several spoke of being intimidated or compelled into accepting death certificates. "How do we know what we are agreeing to when they send us letters we don't understand? How can I know whether this says if my child is dead or missing?" Selvarani, one *amma* demanded. "It's all the same if we cannot understand what's written." The photographs enabled those who did not have a common language to communicate their losses to the English- and Sinhala-speaking media and activists who documented and disseminated these stories. They offered an arresting visual to an otherwise largely uninterested or hostile mainstream media.

In the shadow of the disappearances associated with the Bheeshanaya, human rights and peace activists from the south have long attempted to forge solidarities between north and south on the issue of enforced disappearances. "The grief is the same, Sinhalese or Tamil," was often repeated by Sinhalese activists, only a small number of whom had traveled north to visit these sites. While appreciative of the support and solidarity, the Tamil protesters remained politely unconvinced, especially given the disproportionate inequalities of citizenship entitlements. While important documentation and advocacy work was carried out by Sinhalese civil society activists from Colombo in assisting and amplifying the demands of the protesters, language remained a challenging barrier. Various tensions between Tamil and Sinhalese activists also lingered. On one occasion, a Sinhalese activist's flippant repeated question, "Why can't you directly go to the commanding officer [army] and ask them?" went unheeded through a loud collective silence. Southern visitors rarely spoke Tamil and did not have interpreters present, having to seek out Sinhala- or English-speakers from among the protesters to help translate. The fact that the protests had not received much attention in the south, the inadequacies of solidarity campaigns, and that the "Tamilness" of the protests were being "erased" were among the gripes expressed by the Tamil protesters. Others from the south remained quietly perturbed or were made uncomfortable by the Tamil nationalist tone or the former LTTE ties of the victims. Some felt privately slighted by criticisms bound to language deficiencies as a lack of acknowledgment for their assistance in truth and justice seeking, foregrounding the perpetual gloss and whataboutery of Sinhalese benevolence toward Tamil victims of state violence. English as a "link" language further underlined class politics and hierarchies aside from how transitional justice and reconciliation discourses had been dominated by anglicized Colombo-based activists and nongovernmental organizations, much to the irritation of local activists in the north.

Although the desire to learn Tamil was regularly expressed, learning Tamil was rarely pursued, stressing the luxury of time and resources necessary, as well as the fact that language differences should not distract from the demonstrated commitment and solidarity of those who worked on human rights issues even though Tamil grievances and justice for war crimes and crimes against humanity were rarely discussed in Colombo's NGO-dominated advocacy spaces. Indeed, "peace building" was a long-established, aid-infused sector in Sri Lanka designed not to meet the needs and demands of those confronting systems of oppression but the neoliberal logics and expectations of "conflict transformation" through imprecise nods to reconciliation and social cohesion. What was often overlooked was that the onus of communication and being understood was then placed on the victims themselves, and the class and ethnolinguistic dynamics and disparities through which accounts and interpretations were filtered. I fell to the intermittent role of mediator and interpreter between activists, image-makers, and protesters extending also to making English-language signs for the protesters, as they wanted to make sure that their placards could be read by an international audience when captured by photojournalists. Of course, the strains were not without exception that to some extent were mitigated by thoughtful photography and video initiatives undertaken by Sinhalese and Tamil civic media organizations in the south. Where language barriers existed, photographs served as a direct and extraordinarily poignant means of communicating their grievances. Affecting visual projects undertaken by Colombo-based citizen journalism websites Maatram (Change) and Vikalpa (Alternative) disseminated online and on social media movingly evoke themes of loss and solidarity (see Rajasegar 2024).

In one of the most heartrending uses of photography, K. Kumanan, a Tamil photographer and media activist from Mullaitivu, organized an evocative and defiant outdoor photography exhibition, *Album of Persecution: Justice-Despair-Tears,* in Jaffna and at the Vadduvakkal Bridge in Mullaitivu in 2019 (2024). The latter was the site of one of the most notorious "mass disappearances" of the final phases of the war: Several hundred surrendees were put on military buses never to be seen again. Distressing photographs of the victims of this mass disappearance taken on board the bus by the army circulated in the hands of victims' families, advocacy groups, and online. I was told that in one instance one of these was the only photograph of a disappeared loved one in the hands of the last surviving family member who had since fled Sri Lanka. Kumanan's exhibition featured poignant portraits of the protesting family members. Photographs of the exhibition circulated widely on Tamil diasporic news and social media channels, including most notably the London-based *Tamil Guardian.* The Tamil nationalist online publication intended for an English-speaking Tamil audience was a key outlet for news linked to local Tamil journalists and civil society activists in the northeast. The mostly anonymous reports rely significantly on captioned photography. Kumanan has continued to document protest and commemoration in northern Sri Lanka despite extraordinary risk and pressures.

Fears of death also lingered among protesters, as they lamented that their only desire was to see their children alive before they die. At the end of my fieldwork in September 2018, seven protesters had passed away. By the 1,000th day of protest in November 2019, at least fifty-three protesters had succumbed to old age and ill-health, with no answers about the fate of their children. Many others have died since. In 2025, the number exceeded 280. Kumanan has also supported the Tamil families of the disappeared with a stirring document listing the stories and photographs of over fifty protesters who had passed away during the course of over one thousand days of protest (2019). On each page, a Tamil and English text providing details of the protester and their disappeared loved one was flanked by their portraits, family members heartbreakingly "reunited" on the page in death and disappearance. Each entry also bore a sketch of Picasso's antiwar painting

Guernica. Such efforts, illustrated with personal and official images, play an important role in the assertion of a counternarrative to that of the Sri Lankan state which resolutely denies its role in these disappearances, as well as any meaningful recourse to the protesters.

The media attention afforded to the protests was not without strain. On a demonstration day in Maruthankerny, an international media organization filmed the protesters' narratives. The site was busy that day with activists and protesters from Kilinochchi and the other districts who had traveled there for the day. Journalists and activists wielded mobile phone cameras, while others directed DSLR cameras. The film crew accompanied by a local fixer, a young Tamil woman photojournalist, Yuvanya, demanded efficiency. Yuvanya, prided herself on her photography-based reporting, which was exceptional for a woman political journalist given the gender norms hindering mobility. In 2018, she survived an assault by unknown attackers.

Photographs of protest were also volatile, where being photographed at a protest could also risk harm as a perceived threat to the state. Protesters were lined up in assembly-line fashion so that the photographs resting on their palms could be filmed. The regulation and performance of grief are demanded by cameras and their wielders just as much as the hollow processes of national and international inquiry into enforced disappearances and human rights violations. Mothers were seated down on a plastic chair in rotation, as the foreign host loudly and jarringly demanded in English, "Do you believe your son is alive? DO YOU BELIEVE YOUR SON IS ALIVE?" Journalists flocked to a grandmother who wailed unconsolably asking to know the whereabouts of her grandchildren surrendered to the military before collapsing onto the ground in a faint. Such sights were also very common at the demonstrations. The sorrow that saturated these events was always overwhelming. Months later when I watched the documentary, there was no mention of Maruthankerny or the narratives of its protesters. The footage was folded in with that from Mullaitivu, describing Sri Lanka as "Abduction Island" (101 East 2018). While international transmissions have elicited solidarity and support, little progress was made in relation to the protesters' demands.

Photographs of the protests, especially on demonstration days, were carefully strategized to enhance their visibility. I recall a particular incident in Kilinochchi where a little girl was moved front and center at the photographers' request, as she sadly held up a placard that asked, "Where is my father?" The "chronic" state of grief and devastation these protesters were suspended in, largely unacknowledged by the state as well as by a majority of their fellow citizens, was elicited in front of a camera where it might be acknowledged and recorded for posterity. This echoes and expands on Rachel Seoighe's theorization that these acts of resistance constituted a form of collective performative politics aimed at challenging the established "state architecture of domination," but also its monumental scripted and sculpted architecture of memory embedded in the violence of the built environment (2016, 1–3).

MOTHERS AND THE NATION

The unintentional aligning of gender as well as "victimhood" permitted for an assertion and appearance that was "counter-political" in character (Spencer 2007, 173). However, this was inextricable from the anti-politics of the ethnonationalist conflict within which their grievances were rooted. The protests were predominantly led by women, and were certainly described as such, where "motherhood" was underscored. While I do not seek to delve into the gendered aspects of the social organization of the protest site, I consider Spencer's differentiation between the "counter-political" and the "anti-political," where the former seeks to defuse the effects of the political, whereas the latter "is rooted in paradox—the exploitation, for political purposes, of popular unease with the moral implications of actually existing politics" (2007, 177). The emphasis on gender, whether in the form of elderly mothers and grandmothers or young girl children, or "victimhood" in their photographic representations in various international uses and circulations afforded a counter-political veneer to anti-political claims. I offer this analysis with the same ambivalence as the protesters. "Victimhood," in camera, was a visual trope that was strategically mobilized to supplement ethnopolitical rhetoric. While the protesters exercised important, if ambivalent, caution and agency in presenting themselves to the camera, the subsequently disruptive circuits within which these images were transmitted varied in their political inscription. However, this troubled how the protests were received or wholly overlooked in Sri Lanka in particular.

Further, referring to the protesters as Tamil *ammas* underpinned articulations of solidarity, especially among Tamil diaspora activists, where the emphasis on Tamilness and motherhood, affirmed nation and kinship in ethnicized terms, further incorporated into transnational Tamil nationalist demands. Here new affinities and intimacies are evoked in the service of nation at once made counter-political and anti-political through the pictures wielded in protest as well as the images of mothers holding up portraits of their children. The politicization of motherhood as anti- and counter-political formation can be seen in the example of Tamil Nadu Chief Minister Jayaram Jayalalithaa (1948–2016), who cast herself as a mother politician. The photographies of the protests thus visually encompassed the tension between the counter-political and the anti-political permitted by the volatility of photography whereby a national kinship is claimed. Kannan Arunasalam's poignant *The Tent* captured this tension in a film installation (2019). Two screens were set up, side by side, with one screen contrasting the quiet days in the protest camp where the camera placed within the tent at the Mullaitivu protest site looks outward onto the road as its residents quietly contemplate the mundane, the war, and their future. The other screen had the camera turned to the 500th-day demonstration at Kilinochchi, where the protesters wail in visceral grief, holding up photos of their loved ones.

In relation to ethnonationalist conflict and the unrealized nation-state, redress and solidarity was complicated by the lingering effects of Tamils "othered" by war, where ethnicity had long been conflated with terror. Affiliations to the LTTE of a number of those who were disappeared was a significant reason as to why the protests were dismissed, overlooked, or condemned by some Sinhalese. Even though southern Sri Lanka was plagued with enforced disappearances during the JVP years, there was little sympathy or solidarity, and overwhelming silence. Perceived sympathy and support for the protests from the nationalist Tamil diaspora were also seen as cause for doubt, criticism, and outright dismissal. Indeed, the protests were supported by various international Tamil groups, which, for example, sponsored the travel of ARED representatives to make submissions at the UN Human Rights Council sessions in Geneva and participate in a demonstration in London in 2019. These connections were ambiguous and inevitable, given the transnational character of the Tamil community, and they were not without political expediency for the concerned parties. However, "the Tamil diaspora," as if it were an easily homogenous political entity wholly uncritical and supportive of the LTTE, had long been demonized by the state alongside civil society activism, nongovernmental organizations, and international governance mechanisms during the war and in relation to international pressure for investigations into war crimes in its aftermath.

The emblem of the protesting mother was not without Tamil nationalist resonance, evoking particularly Annai Poopathy (1932–1988), a mother of ten from Batticaloa who had lost two sons to Sri Lankan state atrocity.

In 1988, she fasted unto death demanding a ceasefire between the IPKF and the LTTE. Her death was soon assimilated into the Tigers' rhetoric on martyrdom, including annual commemoration events whereby she was hailed by Prabhakaran as sacrificing her life for the emancipation of nation "symboliz[ing] the collective upsurgence [*sic*] of the women of *Tamil Eelam*" (1990). Her image circulates in yearly remembrance still today.

Against the militarized, masculinized, material incarnations of the Sri Lankan state, the largely elderly women encompassed a transitory feminized formation, which was striking against a backdrop of ethnonationalist tension. However, this did not spare them from the ire of a state that had repeatedly deployed a narrative of saving Tamil women and children and vilified the LTTE for its victimization and "brainwashing" of women and children to pick up guns (see also De Mel 2001). The feminized nature of the protest was also determined by socioeconomic practicalities, where the elderly who were not employed or did not have care responsibilities were able to spend long periods of time at the protest site. Financial hardship entailed that others like Amirthavalli could not afford to leave or travel to and from the protest site, and they were hence compelled to stay there in harsh surroundings exposed to the elements and numerous privations, which gravely affected their physical and mental well-being. It was these distressing realities of undertaking continuous protest that render the censure and dismissal directed at the protesters and their "politics" deeply unjust and devastating.

Despite the political risk and agency that underlined participation in these protests, the demonstrators consciously stressed their "victimhood," a category that is often viewed as apolitical or marginalized, because of its centrality to the transitional justice discourse. As noted by Laura Jeffery and Matei Candea "victimhood can be a prime way of suspending or attempting to suspend the political through an appeal to something non-agentive and 'beyond' or 'before' politics," although it is one that "establishes a space for a specific kind of politics" (2006, 289). Carolijn Terwindt specifies how "victim mobilization" reliant on an interlinked terminology can serve as an effective driver for processes of criminalization (2020, 56). However, where the state is the perpetrator, the centering of victimhood appealed most directly to international truth and justice mechanisms dominated by legal, criminological, and medical terminologies and protocols that remind of photography's Foucauldian co-option within these fields in its uses to document, evidence, archive, and produce knowledge. This also reflects what Allen Feldman describes as a pathologization of political terror, noting that "this pathogenic stigma serves to ghettoize many countries in democratic transition, which are busy confronting their past, and not surprisingly, absolves many other more supposedly more stable and long-term democratic nations from facing history," asserting the transnational character of this need and process (2002, 235).

After many years of being ignored by the state within a context of complex and impaired citizenship, the protesters' appeal for justice was not directed at the sovereign, but at the global community as mediated by photography and its capacities for amplifying visibility that powerfully conveyed the medium's potential to de-territorialize (Azoulay 2008, 120). Here "victimhood" must be performed for the camera and expectations for justice are latched to its volatility. Photographs that situate the protesters holding images of their loved ones as "victims" position the protesters in a new kind of, globally determined and recognizable, commensurable seriality and transnational affinity and solidarity that overpowers "political" incompatibilities. Within a neoliberal framework of world peace, where Azoulay's call for solidarity and responsibility embolden advocacy and accountability networks, the photographs of these protesters demand, or at least attempt to demand, international governance commitments and action (2008). However, these images also inform the production of a dispersed postwar nation through the foregrounding of kinship, love, and care, where the mothers of the disappeared, in their photographic guise, are reinvented also as mothers of the homeland and its still hopeful citizens.

CITIZENS OF PHOTOGRAPHY/STATES OF EXEMPTION

Applying Azoulay's (2008) notion of photographic citizenry available to the governed as a mode for resistance and emancipation, Christopher Pinney relates how within the setting of colonial India, nationalists and the colonial state enlisted photographs of atrocity as a part of their political project—echoing the trophy photograph turned protest image that was previously referred to (2015, 24). Critiquing John Tagg's theory that photographs are "merely a 'screen' onto which more powerful primary ideologies are projected," Pinney argues for not only photography's "subversive and unpredictable potential," but "new kinds of juxtaposition and seriality" that allow for the world to be seen in new ways (2015, 24–28). The protesters themselves were intimately aware of the volatility of photography, fearing and desiring simultaneously the power and the visibility afforded by the medium. It is an awareness that cannot be separated from expectation and anticipation for a favorable outcome where justice was concerned. The mobilization of photographs is part of this labor of seeking justice. It highlights a departure from the "official" narrative that photography has been theorized (via Foucault) to reflect. Here, its ability to agitate in disrupting and challenging hegemonic narratives through subversive evidencing becomes clear. At the sites of the protests, these theoretical positions jostle in uneasy contention. Photographs of these photographs and their circulation in expanded, globalized circuits of protest and resistance thus offered continuity not only with those moments of life they have captured, but also the hope and struggle of these families of the disappeared in their quest to find answers. Yet the images of the protests also feed into the structured asymmetries of global news-image economies producing distressing "formative fictions" (Gürsel 2016, 113). Instead, their volatility is used by protesters actively to undertake political work for self, community, and nation, and in this context, against the extant, perpetrator state where nation and state are unreconcilable.

The confrontation with the "sovereign" was also enacted through the destabilizing use and political mobilization of identity documents and photography. This is evidenced by the subversive use of the NIC, which asserted an absent presence that tacitly summons an obvious strain of nation, state, and citizenship. NIC photographs and sometimes NICs and passport pages were wielded by protesters on demonstration days, the photographic image and presence of the disappeared as was once authorized by the state (fig. 22). Here, NIC headshots were reverted at the state in a demand for accountability and justice. These served as a means of recalling state terror, especially where the state's vast monuments to the war victory did not acknowledge the losses of the Tamil community. Here, photography's use in governmentality and surveillance, as suggested by Tagg, is defiantly appropriated and undermined (1988). Moreover, the state's narrative of postwar was actively challenged in this transient shrine for lives lost in a war that was precisely intended to weaken the extant state. The recasting of identity photographs was not simply about individual loss, but a collective, tacitly national, politically constituted loss enacted by the state in response to quelling a suspected threat to its sovereignty and territorial integrity.

"They have not given us one reason to trust them, and it is not for the lack of trying because we have done everything they have asked of us—write letters, to go to this commission hearing there, this meeting here. We have been begging them for years. But what have we gotten? Nothing. We are

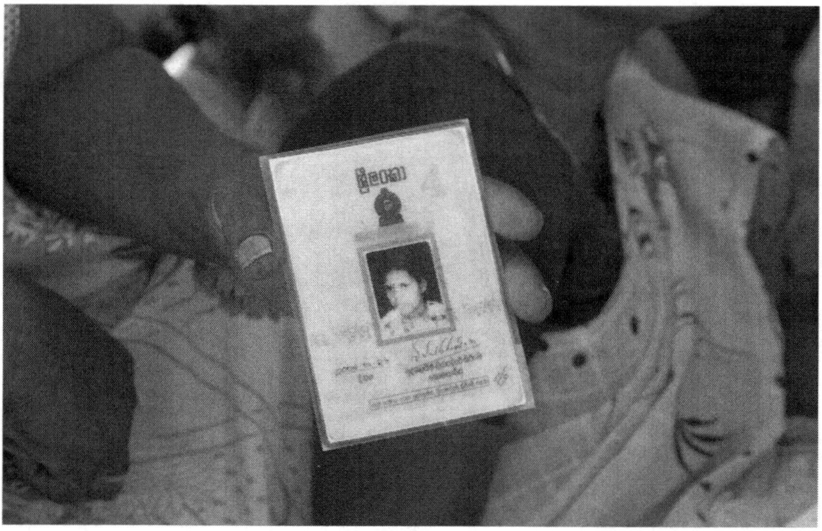

FIGURE 22. A protesting mother holds up a photocopy of the National Identity Card (NIC) of her disappeared daughter (Maruthankerny, 2018)

looking to the UN, the international community to give us answers, and they are our only hope now, but they too continue to disappoint us. Where can we go from here?" Nagammai, one of the mothers whose young son had been disappeared, uttered. The protesters resolutely confirmed their lack of interest in a local mechanism and continue to do so even today, flagging that a perpetrator state asked to hold itself accountable for its own crimes will not yield justice for their loved ones. This was also explicitly articulated in the protest signage which featured English-language demands as well as graphics of flags of the UK, USA, and EU. The audience of the protest was intentionally global. Their mobilization of photographs and presenting themselves to be photographed immediately remind one of the conscious participation in Azoulay's call to enact a new form of civil relations that was not mediated by sovereign power and in a manner that transcended the nation-state (2008, 143). However, that enactment continues to rely on mechanisms for justice and redress that have been founded on global systems of accountability that are made up of and foremostly privilege the concept of a "legitimate" nation-state. If accountability is contingent on states holding other states accountable within partial and unequal geopolitical relations, what justice and redress might civic spectatorship practically yield? Even as this remains unresolved in the Sri Lankan context, the expectations placed on the volatile possibilities of photography cannot be undervalued.

Conceptions of and aspirations for modernity, at the levels of individual/community and nation/state in the global south, have been underpinned by and entangled with economic liberalization and the interlinked modernization project that followed the Second World War and decolonization. Ideological contentions of the Cold War further amplified and shaped global consumer culture—socioeconomic, cultural, and political. However, it was also characterized by the hardening of borders and greater controls on mobility in contrast to that of capital flows, significantly exacerbating global inequalities. The premise of the "modern," postcolonial state in the aftermath of the Second World War would also be framed by a forward-looking global peace language and aesthetic of governance bound to the establishment of an internationalized regime of responsibility. These mechanisms espouse the idealized values of the Universal Declaration of Human Rights, which states that "the recognition of the inherent dignity and of the equal and inalienable rights of all members of the human family is the foundation of freedom, justice and peace in the world" (United Nations 1948). It was also designed in a manner that states would hold one another accountable for violations. Yet these institutions do not speak for the solidarity and community that labor toward justice even when the initiation and outcomes of formal justice-oriented processes cannot be guaranteed.

While these image circulations were intended to supplement promises of peace and dignity bound to international cooperation and governance, the realities of those looking to such institutions for protection, such as the Tamil families of the disappeared, remained tenuous. In truth, those who doggedly pursued accountability comprehended better than anyone else that these institutions could not promise or deliver much beyond necessary acknowledgment and credibility. It was understood that states protected one another and not those who had been subject to the violence and terror of state crimes. They also understood that optics mattered in the work of justice and that photography, because and in spite of its volatility, could achieve the visibility they sought. Although their anger and disillusionment thus signal the failures of responsibility and civic spectatorship at a global level, where the Sri Lankan state remained protected by other states, and accountability was one determined by broader geopolitical strategic interests, they continue to choose, nevertheless, to wield the potentials of volatile photographies in defiance and in expectation of what photography *can do* for their demands for justice.

6 ATROCITY NATION / STATE AMNESIA

"RATA MUDAGENIME VANNI MEHEYUMA" (THE VANNI OPERATION TO SAVE THE COUNTRY)

The final year of the Sri Lankan civil war unfolded through televised atrocity signaling an imminent victory, which would be confirmed on 18 May 2009.

The UN has accused both the Sri Lankan government and the Liberation Tigers of Tamil Eelam (LTTE) of war crimes during the final phase of the war. In September 2008 the United Nations withdrew all its remaining aid agency personnel from northern Sri Lanka following the government's orders ahead of its major military offensive. A 2012 internal review conducted by the UN concluded that various agencies, including the Security Council and Human Rights Council, had failed to meet their responsibilities at every level, stating that "events in Sri Lanka mark a grave failure of the UN" (Petrie 2012; Doucet 2012). After the LTTE's administrative capital, Kilinochchi, was captured by the army, nearly 300,000 Tamil civilians who were fleeing Sri Lanka Air Force shelling were corralled into a series of state-designated Yudha Muktha Kalapa, or No Fire Zones (NFZS) as the offensive against the LTTE intensified. Caught between the aggressively advancing Sri Lankan military and the recoiling Tigers, the Tamils of the Vanni were barraged by severe and sustained state-directed aerial bombing and LTTE gunfire. The Sri Lankan government made little effort to safeguard its Tamil citizens in its pursuit to decimate the LTTE, eschewing its primary responsibility as a state actor. It has continually denied responsibility for the massacre of Tamils, repeating that it did not harm civilians and blamed the LTTE for the high casualties.

The Sri Lankan government bombarded, seemingly deliberately, the NFZS and humanitarian sites, including hospitals and food distribution centers from which it purportedly withheld resources and supplies compounding harm and death and causing mass starvation (Harrison 2012b). A vast majority of the fatalities from the final months of war took place within the NFZS, which were systematically and repeatedly bombed by the Sri Lankan forces. Meanwhile, Tamils who tried to escape to government-controlled areas were ostensibly shot at by the LTTE who were condemned for using the trapped civilian population as a human shield (Amnesty International). Neve Gordon and Nicola Perugini argue that the shielding accusation was deployed to justify the thousands of civilian deaths, but also how legal estimations of proportionality can constitute a form of depoliticization, dehumanization, and legitimizing of war crimes (2020). While the LTTE anticipated that the civilian casualties would compel international intervention, a ceasefire did not materialize. Across cities in Europe, North America, and Australia thousands of members of the Tamil diaspora assembled in demonstrations, marches, and occupations to no avail. As the rebels' command structure collapsed, the able-bodied were drafted in desperation and ordered to fight for a sovereign Tamil homeland that they, like many thousands before them, did not survive to see. On 18 May 2009, the Sri Lankan government declared a military victory over the LTTE. In his address to parliament on 19 May, President Mahinda Rajapaksa declared partly in Tamil, a language he did not speak, "We have liberated the whole country from LTTE terrorism. . . . Our intention was to save the Tamil people from the cruel grip of the LTTE. We all must now live as equals in this free country." The perpetrator's peace of the postwar has proved otherwise.

Through the war years, the media was heavily controlled by the state and the LTTE through heavy and often forceful censorship and suppression. The imposition of hegemonic narratives onto the chaos of war was expertly undertaken by both groups, valorizing a citizenry whose value was determined by its patriotic commitment to sacrifice. The need for public support for the war effort as well as recruitment relied on the increasing normalization of militarism. Newspapers were periodically shut down or banned by the government for violating censorship laws, or they were the subject of anonymous attacks, including arson. For instance, founded in 1985, *Uthayan*, the only Jaffna newspaper that continued publication during the war, was attacked on multiple occasions by the state forces as well as by Tamil paramilitary groups, resulting in a number of deaths, aside from being temporarily shut down by the military for a period of forty-five days for violating censorship laws. Media organizations as well as dissenting journalists and editors critical of the state's conduct became targets of assault, extrajudicial killing, and enforced disappearance, rendering the island one of the least safe places for media workers in the world. Tamil journalists and presses were disproportionately affected. Between 2004 and 2010 alone, at least forty-four journalists and media workers were either killed or disappeared, forty-one of whom were Tamil (JDS 2021). Many fled the country due to threats to their lives. Such attacks continued after the end of the war as allegations of war crimes and crimes against humanity began to heighten. Tamil journalists in the northeast are still at risk.

During this time, the digital marked a notable shift to the technics of photography and the wider media environment. This development transformed how the war was documented and consumed by those in Sri Lanka and abroad, as well as the insistent circulation of narratives and images of conflict even today. Portable digital photographic, videographic, and internet-enabled telecommunications devices coupled with the beginnings and/or consolidation of social media, blogging, and internet-based image-sharing practices and platforms such as Wordpress, Blogger, Twitter (X), Facebook, YouTube, Flickr, and later Instagram gave rise to new photographic repertoires and forms of dissemination and circulation. These simultaneously underpinned and challenged state proclamations of triumphalist obliteration and desperate pleas for a ceasefire from Tamils around the world, amid a climate of heavy censorship. Digital cameras and mobile phones with integrated cameras in the hands of fighters, soldiers, journalists, photographers, aid workers, and civilians trapped in the war zone permitted for visuals and narratives to be rapidly distributed to new audiences around the world. Image dissemination began to rely less on conventional media, with a great volume of images appearing online where swifter dispersal, sharing, reproduction, and remixing into new visual forms and materials such as photographic slideshows, virtual albums, galleries, and images stitched into videos. The digital further enabled new forms of image manipulation as well as accusations of manipulation used to dismiss and discredit evidence. A vibrant visual economy of imitations, hoaxes, and even reenactments surfaced.

This chapter underlines how the photography arising from the final phase of the Sri Lankan civil war disorders and disrupts carefully contrived hegemonic narratives. Here I delve into atrocity photographs and their unstable hereafters within settings of remembrance, resistance, advocacy, and ethnonationalist ambition. The focus here is the capacity of the volatile pictures of war to swiftly move between and among such indices. As discussed in chapter 3, the generative character of violence to achieve political alternatives, contained within photographs, is deployed during times of war. Images are viewed to further such ambitions, possessing the potential to produce violence deemed necessary for political transformation. However, these images are just as easily reappropriated by the victims of this violence. While the possibilities embedded in the medium are actively exercised by those in power and those seeking to challenge that power, the volatility of the medium, to simultaneously evidence, incriminate, and place at risk is also clear. What photography might engender politically is also feared and often actively curtailed. This volatility promises that the theorizing of photography might be more effectively unraveled from state and ideology toward meaningful forms of transnational solidarity.

The intentional and incidental visual remains of the final months of war presented in this chapter have been gathered from a diversity of sources. It is an effort to offer a necessary corrective and honor the work of Tamil photographers, known and unknown, who recorded these horrors as well as the tireless and thankless labor of those engaged in the documentation of human rights violations. First, I consider the diverse productions of frontline images by the state media and military personnel, as well as by Tamil photographers trapped in the Vanni. Where access to international journalists and observers had been obstructed, the final phase of the war has been described as a "war without witness," disregarding the experiences and testimony of thousands of Tamils who did survive—as if amid a war rooted in an ethnonationalist liberation struggle, they could never reliably account for the violence that their loved ones, their communities, and themselves were subjected to (see Harrison 2012a).

Second, I explore how these visual inventories of gross human rights violations, mass death and harm, credibly alleged war crimes, and crimes against humanity continue to be mobilized as a part of public commemoration events, acts of protest, and political claim-making and demands for justice and accountability in the postwar. I consider why such images continue to circulate in Sri Lanka today, notably in their display as a part of public remembrance and protest and what political possibilities they still express. Enabled by the volatile capacities of photography, even trophy and propagandistic images produced by perpetrators are used to confront and challenge hegemonic narratives and denial and support demands for truth and justice. Moreover, within such claims, everyday images, including state-necessitated identity photographs, studio portraits, and family snaps, come to index violence within a context of post/war, speaking to how war fundamentally transforms the reading and circulations of all images, even those that have not been plainly intended to witness or produce political violence. Similarly, explicitly agitant images recording atrocity become then the basis for community and solidarity.

ATROCIOUS IMAGES AND "FUTURE DEAD"

In 1987, during the second Janatha Vimukthi Peramuna (JVP) insurrection, former president J. R. Jayewardene, allegedly spurred the armed forces to "kill, kill, kill and kill the brutes."[1] It echoes an apocalyptic line uttered by the deranged fictional antagonist Kurtz in Joseph Conrad's *Heart of Darkness* ([1899] 2012, 57). Jayewardene's call was followed by the enactment of legislation exonerating the armed forces and police for any criminal offenses they might commit in the course of their duties. Such goading and legal protection sanctioned relentless extrajudicial carnage across Sri Lanka's parallel conflicts. The photographies of this period did not always produce the kind of civic spectatorship that Ariella Aïsha Azoulay called for but instead bolstered racialized othering and ethnicized and territorialized claims of sovereignty in their agitant guise (2008). Images of violation and violence had long been wielded in the making of Sri Lanka's competing ethno-citizenries, underpinning ethnonationalist political claims where atrocities were not necessarily decried, but demanded and celebrated. What emerged is the socialization and interlinked normalization of uncivil spectatorship among Tamil and Sinhalese communities, encompassing death and injury not only of the "enemy" but their own to rationalize reprisal and retribution. Underlying claims of nation endorsed militarism, the martial imperatives and powers of the extant and aspirant state, as well as making visible the consequences to those who did not conform.

As discussed in chapter 3, atrocious images had long played a significant role in the LTTE's exertions in socializing citizens of the aspirant ethno-state, where the violence of the Sri Lankan state was juxtaposed against the necessary violence of armed struggle and self-sacrifice. The Sri Lankan state initially claimed to shy away from officially using atrocity images in its own media campaigns. The civilian casualties of the LTTE's terror attacks had, however, populated the image world of Sri Lankan media for decades. In *Truth Tigers* (2002), an army spokesperson, Major General Seneviratne observed:

> As far as our security forces are concerned, whenever we have successes of this nature, we do not sort of video it and then propagate that because

> seeing lots of dead bodies is not a good sign, so therefore, we don't do it. So, like in the operation at Weli Oya, right, we had lots of dead bodies of the LTTE cadres, but we never use them for propaganda because it is sort of detested by the population. [The] LTTE kills most of the security forces personnel who even surrender, as seen in the Mullaitivu operation, maybe because of administrative problems they may be adopting this system. When you take large number of POWs, you have to administer them, and you have to have places to keep them, and you have to register them and show them to the ICRC and that may be the reason.

By 2006, these comments would prove prescient in relation to the Sri Lankan armed forces' own methods amounting to credibly alleged war crimes.

The strategic shift and intensification of the war between 2006 and 2009 saw the military adopting visual strategies similar to those of the LTTE and making greater investments in crafting a coherent narrative of "liberating the motherland from terrorism" by propagating imagery and language justifying the violence. Consequently, southern Sri Lanka's screens began to fill, more stridently than before, with a visual torrent of violence transmitted by state-owned Sri Lanka Rupavahini Corporation (SLRC) and Independent Television Network (ITN), and other privately run Sinhala-language channels such as Swarnavahini. Scenes from the *Vanni Meyehuma* (Vanni Operation) aired as part of prime-time news on local news channels in Sinhala, Tamil, and English. Recordings watermarked with the Sri Lanka Defense Ministry URL were promptly uploaded onto the web-based video platform YouTube, still in its early years. As Neloufer de Mel assesses in her overview of militarization in Sri Lanka between the mid-1980s and 2005, the state's efforts at direct advertising, cultural production, and acts of commemoration became central to the normalization and celebration of militarization, anchoring war and martial virtue as valor, heroism, and masculine pride not only among soldiers, but among the civilian population (2007, 13). Daily updates from the front lines were provided by well-known media personalities who were embedded with the military. The two- to three-minute situation reports carefully synthesized a storyline of conquest, the bravery of the armed forces, and inevitable victory.

The Vanni was presented as a fertile terra nullius, perforated with sophisticated networks of underground bunkers, training camps, deathtraps, and lethal minefields in "the clutches" of well-resourced, but cruel and cowardly terrorists who were holding hostage rightful Sri Lankan land and bounty. Increased air strikes were shown as essential to dismantling the LTTE's forward defense line, and the LTTE's order for civilians to build bunkers for protection was recast as a part of forced recruitment and training efforts. Tamil civilians scarcely appeared in these broadcasts, and their presence in the north was rarely shown. Their plight, instead, was visually condensed to placid, albeit pitiful, images from internally displaced persons (IDP) camps, and reporters described the Vanni mission as a hostage rescue operation intended to save Tamils from the LTTE. Foreign-funded NGOS were also frequently criticized for their silence. The Tigers' cemeteries in captured territory were shown as confirmation of the hundreds of deaths suffered by the opponent. "The terrorists are directly violating all the human rights of innocent, ordinary Tamil people. The true humanitarians [meaning state and military] are showing that the so-called hundreds of established human rights organizations and their Euro and Dollar agents are in a death-like sleep right now. Their ears are deaf to the sounds of humanity shattering the red earth of the north. However, the moment that Prabhakaran is sent to hell from a bunker like this one is not far off and this sound of gunfire should confirm that to everyone," a correspondent for SLRC (Sri Lanka Rupavahini Corporation) said in an impassioned voiceover to a broadcast in September 2008 that was accompanied by a montage of the Tigers' own (presumably confiscated) training videos, a convoy of IDPs, the bodies of children and adults, LTTE bunkers, and the virulent dispatch of multi-barrel rocket launchers. The visual economy of the final phase of war saw regular reinscriptions of images magnifying their volatility.

The news reported a courageous, forward-moving vanguard making hasty headway through the Mannar, Kilinochchi, and Mullaitivu districts, as Sri Lanka's lion flag was planted in Tamil towns, always shown as abandoned with no indication of where their residents had gone. The intense shelling of villages and the steeply mounting civilian fatalities were never reported. The LTTE's practices of forced recruitment and the imprisonment and torture of those unwilling to fight were showcased to evidence the militants' cruelty against its own community. Commanding officers of the Sri Lankan armed forces regularly pronounced that hundreds if not thousands of LTTE cadres had been killed. Troops described their determination to push forward and keep up the "wondrous fighting" through graphic explanations of the scale of massacre and destruction. They affirmed that "the principal strategy of the Vanni humanitarian operation is to ensure minimum damage to the armed forces and maximum destruction to terrorist lives." Tamils, only rarely presented to the cameras, were always weeping and never spoke for themselves. Sinhalese voiceovers described Tamil experiences of the LTTE's inhumanity and the displaced Tamils' desperation and desire to leave LTTE-controlled areas. The northeast had long been presented as a barely occupied space onto which Sinhalese imaginaries of terror, destitution, and the unknown had been projected. In the final phase of the war, such visuals—underpinned by the Sri Lankan state and military's desire for total conquest—were amplified and dramatized to manufacture support.

Broadcasts of the Eelam War IV, named as if it were a sequel in a film franchise, were given a cinematic character, embellished with elementary digital graphics of moving targets, weapons, and helicopters and a theatrical soundtrack. The government simultaneously launched a prominent, widely televised fundraising campaign named *Api Venuven Api* (Together for All) to support a new parliamentary act to build homes for war heroes. It was accompanied by patriotic songs by popular musicians and moving imagery of members of the armed forces with their own families and communities. This also positively influenced recruitment. By the 1990s, the army was the single largest employer in the island, engineering an economy of citizen livelihoods that was dependent on militarization (Venugopal 2011, 69). The military and in turn militarism had been widely absorbed into rural, impoverished Sinhalese families in the south, just as the LTTE had become integrated into families in the north. However, many of these Sinhalese families not long ago had their family members killed and disappeared for alleged involvements with the JVP by the same armed forces during the Bheeshanaya. For decades, the state-controlled local news had been heavily expurgated, barely reporting on the grave losses suffered by the military. The scale and number of armed forces deaths after three decades of conflict can only be speculated.[2] The period between 2006 and 2009 was no exception. Attention turned to creating a more coherent chronicle of martial success, gallantry, and battlefield benevolence. The military's valor, however, was measured by kills and conquest despite its framing as a "humanitarian rescue operation." Heavy focus was retained on acts of terror perpetrated by the LTTE against civilians in the north and south, fostering a climate of public fear, antagonism, and, importantly, a thirst for achieving a military victory by whatever means necessary.

As the Vanni operation progressed, the Sri Lankan state amplified its proclamations. A filmic narrative of heroism and battlefield benevolence paired with a complacent plot of eradicating terrorism was a public investment in war-as-"entertainment." On camera, soldiers described how the Tigers "became bodies"; kills were discussed as objects.[3] Tamils had long been folded into a category of "terrorist" and within the trajectory of the Vanni Operations as *milechcha thrasthavadeen* (brutal terrorists), "terrorist targets," and "the future dead," as well as other derogatory terms implying foreignness, invasion, and racialized othering. Sinhalese audiences eagerly consumed these narratives, as LTTE parcel and suicide bombings in the south continued. Scores of dead Tiger cadres were lined up on tarpaulins for the inspection of triumphant military men, confirming to the southern audience the bodily vanquishing of a long-standing terrorist enemy of Sri Lanka—an act of annihilation eternalized in film and photography. Theatrical rescues of Tamils were orchestrated for the camera to be televised and printed in newspapers. As the government's aerial attacks escalated, fleeing Tamil civilians who could speak some Sinhalese had cameras turned on them to express gratitude to "the king" Mahinda Rajapaksa and praise the military for saving the long-suffering community. The staging of cameras entailed that some of those surrendering were momentarily treated with greater dignity and sympathy. For the families of the disappeared these visual fragments constituted important but officially overlooked evidence that their loved ones had in fact surrendered to the military. The performative "martial virtues" of Sinhalese soldiers conjured the so-called necessity of war and the armed forces' fearlessness for Sinhalese audiences (De Mel 2007). Decades of state propaganda had already framed Tamils as both victims in need of rescue and perpetrators demanding complete destruction. To be Tamil, then, was to inevitably embody the likelihood of being or becoming a terrorist and thus immanently killable. Tamil death would invariably ensure the sovereignty and territorial integrity of Sri Lanka. These deaths and injuries were deemed to require visual confirmation.

GRAPHIC SPOILS

The proliferation of digital image-making devices enabled soldiers to partake in producing visual narratives of war without the go-between of a color lab as would have been the case with film photography. Vicious celebratory records of annihilation and spoils of war were enthusiastically recorded in trophy photographs and footage shot by soldiers on mobile phones and compact digital cameras. These men captured their frontline experiences: compatriots killed by the terrorist adversary, rows of brutalized Tamil bodies, the stripped and violated Tamil subjects of willful injury, callous execution, and rape, posing triumphant over piles of corpses, makeshift graves, and recovered weapons hauls. Hundreds if not thousands of official and unofficial trophy photographs and fragments of video footage emerged during this time. These visuals endure as a part of a potent transnational visual economy of outrage, evidencing, and celebration. These not only documented past and ongoing violence, but were circulated to necessitate and justify further, future violence by supporters of the state's war effort. Yet the uses of these images were far more variable than their makers could have anticipated, becoming sources of inculpation and Tamil political claim-making.

The death of Velupillai Prabhakaran cemented the demise of the LTTE in Sri Lanka. Photographs of his half-naked and then hastily redressed body, his disfigured face and brain spilling out of a head wound, were captured, and circulated with glee. In news photographs from this final event, we become privy to soldiers hovering over this certification of triumph with personal digital cameras and cell phones. Elsewhere, among the displaced Tamil population, old photographs of the elusive *thalaivar* were reanimated in claims that he was still alive. He was, after all, known to travel with body doubles, tenacious urban legends suggested. Photographs of the corpses of Prabhakaran, his sons, and other known LTTE leaders such as Nadesan and Pulithevan, who had been executed following their surrender in what has been described as "the white flag incident," spread in response with greater dynamism (see ITJP 2014). For many Sinhalese, it expressed rightful vengeance. These visuals were widely mobilized as a part of Mahinda Rajapaksa's successful bid for reelection in 2010 as well as former Secretary of Defense and President Gotabaya Rajapaksa's candidacy in 2019 as a reminder of the victory that had been achieved under their directive. These images continue to be used as political campaign materials, incorporated into music videos, posters, murals, and billboards as reminders of a war victory and the public gratitude owed to the government. Visual edits of atrocity cast as heroism paired with old and new Sinhala-language *ranaviru gee* (war hero songs) became especially popular and shared on platforms such as YouTube, garnering hundreds of thousands of views.

A short-lived informal economy of authentic and counterfeit visuals from the final years of war also emerged to satiate morbid public curiosity as well as political advocacy, locally in Sri Lanka and overseas. In the island's capital, VCDs of bloodshed and success with titles such as *Ape Viruvange*

Veera Kriya: Prabhage Avasanaya (The gallant deeds of our heroes: Prabha's end) sold for no more than a couple of hundred rupees (< $1). An array of CDs sold in markets and neighborhood video shops compiled news footage captured from broadcasts, "handout footage" from the Ministry of Defense, along with film and stills captured on low-grade phones and cameras as well as those shot with professional cameras that were "leaked" for profit. A few months after the end of the war, the Sri Lankan army also hosted a grand commemorative exhibition in Colombo that sought to "bring the heroism witnessed in the Vanni onto the television screen" to Colombo. The event, described as a *sonduru, sajeevi athdakeema* (beautiful, live experience), drew hundreds of thousands of people to partake in the *vismitha vijayagrahanaya* (marvelous triumph) through a display of captured and utilized weapons, armored fighting vehicles, soldiers demonstrating their combat skills, and an expansive exhibition of photographs. The images displayed showed the visceral destruction of the LTTE confirmed by the lined-up corpses of dead cadres that the triumphant military leadership stood over. For Tamils who had been subjected to the horrors of the Vanni Operation, these men were responsible for the deaths and disappearance of their loved ones.

After 2009, visual "evidence" of war crimes was purportedly stashed away in Europe by soldiers in exile for a "rainy day" or secretly proffered for thousands of Euros—even though "purchase" would render them inadmissible in legal proceedings anticipated as a part of truth recovery. Most visibly, trophy footage and photographs became the subject of internationally lauded investigative documentaries, as was the case of Callum Macrae's *No Fire Zone: The Killing Fields of Sri Lanka* (2013) which followed two televised Channel 4 investigatory documentaries, *Sri Lanka's Killing Fields* (2011) and *Sri Lanka's Killing Fields: War Crimes Unpunished* (2012). Through survivor testimony, analyst perspectives, and compilations of images and footage generated by those trapped in the No Fire Zones (NFZs) as well as aid workers, LTTE cadres, soldiers, and nonhuman agents such as satellites, the film substantiates crimes committed by the Sri Lankan military to demand accountability. Trophy photographs and footage in the documentary evidence the sexual violation, torture, and summary execution of prisoners of war; sometimes clothed, sometimes stripped naked and blindfolded with their arms tied behind their backs, they are shot by army men who provide crude commentary to a shaky camera. "It is our government's property, so let us hit it!" a soldier voices in the background as guns are drawn, shots fired, and blood sprays from shattered skulls. Another cadre pleadingly looks to his captors and their camera while tied to a coconut tree. His neck is slit, before his body is dumped into a grave draped with a bloodied Tiger flag. The disembodied hand of a soldier holds up his head from his hair. A soldier's arm is seen extending a mobile phone to film the bodies of those slaughtered. The civilians who surrendered vanished.

Notable among the images discussed in *No Fire Zone* are those of Balachandran Prabhakaran, the twelve-year-old son of Velupillai Prabhakaran, who had surrendered to the military along with his bodyguards. Taken a few hours apart on the same camera, one image shows the boy in a pair of khaki shorts and a checkered blue sarong wrapped around his shoulder snacking on a packet of biscuits on his lap sitting in a bunker and alive and apparently in the custody of the Sri Lankan army. Another image taken a few hours later shows the boy's body lying on the ground shot at close range, his chest riddled with five bullet wounds. Footage shows barefoot soldiers walking amid the slaughtered men. Authorities had held that Balachandran had been killed in crossfire, but the photographs uncovered in 2013 pointed to execution. Photographs and a video of the LTTE's Col. Ramesh shows him inside a military vehicle and then being interrogated on camera by the military in English, who accuse him of lying even as he responded that he understood the question. Another series of photographs shows him dead, face bloodied and swollen with a gunshot wound to the head, dragged outside, and finally cremated in a pyre. In a final image, a soldier stands next to the burning pile of wood. Similarly, twenty-seven-year-old LTTE news presenter Isaipriya was filmed still alive, uninjured but disoriented and in a state of undress in the waters of the lagoon as a prisoner of war and then photographed alongside another young woman since identified as Ushalini Gunalingam. They are wrapped in white sheets, with their arms tied behind their backs. In another horrifying trophy video shot by a Sri Lankan soldier on a mobile phone, Isaipriya and Ushalini are dead. The women are stripped naked and brutalized in a pool of blood, ostensibly sexually violated by the soldiers (Macrae 2015). Videos were turned into photographs by screenshotting to allow for easier and less data-intensive sharing. Such image sequences also foreground that it was not merely death that required substantiation, but the acts of killing, desecration, and annihilation. Moreover, they unwittingly catalog the destruction of evidence with corpses photographed being defiled, pitilessly kicked and stashed onto the backs of trucks. The soldiers filming on their phones call out to their compatriots in Sinhalese "*ko moona pennanna . . . bodies ekka allanna*" (Show your face. . . . Catch [pose] with the bodies). For various Tamil families, such images of alarming and inhumane abuse are the final and sometimes only photographs of their loved ones seen alive or dead where bodies have long disappeared, and deaths denied.

These visuals moved international audiences to outrage and advocacy, resulting in growing pressure on the government to investigate the conduct of the armed forces during the final phase of the war. In Sri Lanka, however, they became the center of state-sponsored agitation aimed to rile up Sinhalese nationalist sentiment. Although the images have been authenticated by specialists, the government claimed that they were forgeries aimed at discrediting its war heroes. I recall a 2012 demonstration, where office workers had mobilized in central Colombo, holding up a confusion of placards in English, a language only a fraction of the population could speak or read: "Channel 4 You Lie Because You Are Paid by LTTE," "No War Crimes in Sri Lanka, Look Elsewhere," "Don't Be Misled by Terrorists, Listen to the People," "All Sri Lankans Hate Violence," "Channel 4 Spreads Violence," "Channel 4 You Have Sold Your Soul to LTTE Diaspora," and "Help Sri Lankans Live as One Nation." Sinhalese patriotic music played loudly. Young women with Sri Lankan flags wrapped around their shoulders fanned themselves in the afternoon heat as men in ties toted corporate-sponsored banners. They linked arms and posed for photographs intended for Facebook. The air was comparable to that of a cricket match or social event. In other protests by those in Sri Lanka and the Sinhalese diaspora, photographs of the LTTE's terror attacks and atrocities inflicted upon Sinhalese bodies were printed onto vinyl banners showing the mangled victims of bomb blasts. *No Fire Zone* was denounced as a threat to hard-won peace, as the government single-mindedly committed to protect its war heroes. Widely publicized efforts were made by the Sri Lankan state to discredit claims of authenticity and witnesses used, as seen in the documentary film *Lies Agreed Upon* (2011) and publications such as *Corrupted Journalism: Channel 4 and Sri Lanka* (2013). Images of atrocity were volatile and thus malleable entities transformed to underpin a range of competing claims. The state used the images within Sri Lanka to suggest it was being persecuted by the West through a language of conspiracy and colonial interference. Despite the "devastating evidence of war crimes and crimes against humanity" and interlinked international pressures, Sri Lanka's transitional justice processes remained stagnant (Macrae 2011). The Sri Lankan state has repeatedly and vehemently rejected visual and other evidence of its atrocities during the final months of the war as lies and fabrications by a foreign conspiracy to smear the country and humiliate its heroes.

The political work of these trophy images of diverse origin and intent far exceeded the island, their potency and relevance shining beyond its shores. Azoulay proposes that photography affords "new means for the photographed, the photographer and the spectator to untether themselves from the bounds of sovereign power or contracts of the nation-state and economy" (2008, 24). She further posits that "the nation-state (re) territorializes citizenship" while photography "de-territorializes citizenship, reaching beyond its conventional boundaries and plotting out a political space in which the plurality of speech and action . . . is actualized permanently by the eventual participation of all the governed" (2008, 25). This premise, Azoulay suggests, permits for "civil skills that are not subject to nationality, but rather to borderless citizenship" that demands an ethical responsibility toward one another (2008, 26). The de-territorialized circuits and proliferation of these images respond to Azoulay's call to arms in civil spectatorship, but they are equally mobilized, on account of their conflict-induced volatility, within the specific context of ethnonationalist struggle and civil war to engender uncivil spectatorship. This uncivil spectatorship is inextricable from the agitant capacity of photography, which demands violence, retaliatory, punitive, and otherwise. The politics of national liberation, understood as deployed by both the Tamil militancy and the Sri Lankan government, to contradictory effect can be grasped through the volatility, and thus mutability of these images, concurrently readable as civil and uncivil practice in their competing political work. Yet these same images are held up in solidarity and commitment by tireless advocates for difficult to achieve justice and accountability in expectation that their shock value might draw them attention. The political work of these images cannot be contained in a single imperative or outcome, but they are wielded in the hope that they might result in one that is favorable.

It is essential then to recognize that the nature of photography and its embedded contingency allows, as has been elucidated by Pinney, for the volatility that permits it to animate and eschew the power of states and aspiring states regardless of the intentions of production and circulation (2012). Images from the final phase of the war underpinned witness accounts, testimony, and international advocacy efforts that underscored violations of International Humanitarian Law, credibly asserted to be war crimes and crimes against humanity. While liberation beyond the constraints of the end goal of the state might yet be believably realized, photography's unruliness deems the medium uncontainable within a singular ideological logic or utility. Instead, photography underscores why this volatility is important for countering hegemonic narratives in a dual sense, as direct evidence for and against, but in how a single image can be read and mobilized multiply as a convenient and an inconvenient agitant.

A RECORD OF SUFFERING

In the midst of shelling and volleys of gunfire exchanged between the state security forces and the LTTE, Amarathaas, a Tamil writer, artist, journalist, and photographer from Jaffna now in exile in Europe, photographed the slow demise of his family. Their home had been obliterated in an explosion, and his kin were among the thousands trapped in the NFZs in the brutal final months of the war. Camera in hand and low on petrol, Amarathaas climbed onto his kerosene-fueled motorbike and painstakingly snapped the many thousand devastations of war. He narrated his losses and his survival with filmic verve, repeatedly making clear that his photography was not intended to service the parties and politics of the ethnic conflict, but the *pathivu* (record). "The world needs to know about our suffering," he said unassumingly. Although he was unwilling to confirm how many photographs he had in his possession on account of fears for his safety, he hoped that their content and volume would serve as evidence of what was done to his people. Through his photographs, shot mostly in black and white and intermittently in color, Amarathaas sought to capture moments of stillness amid chaos. In a vivid Tamil image world, it is the intensity and solemnity of black and white coupled with excess that would demand the viewers' attention.

In Amarathaas's photographs, now circulated and exhibited globally, the minutiae of war was captured vividly. Huddles of young and old fled in incoherent processions, their belongings heaped and strung onto the backs of bicycles and bullock carts. Black clouds of smoke billowed on the horizon verifying indiscriminate salvos the Sri Lankan state continues to deny. A woman embraced a memorial portrait of a loved one wrapped in a cloth, leading a small convoy of exhausted escapees. Dogs and emaciated cattle followed at their heels. Reedy old men and women knee-deep in salt water stacked cooking pots, plastic chairs, tin kettles, and old rice sacks filled with their uprooted material lives into small fishing boats on the lagoon. Young "birds of freedom" (LTTE women cadres), recognizable by their braided hair and the checkered men's shirts belted around their waists, tenderly wrapped up a dead woman's body in polythene sheets. This image evoked the ambivalence of even those who did not support the LTTE's authoritarian methods. The group's contributions to the nation were always recognized, especially in their struggle against the hostile Sri Lankan state. Amarathaas himself expressed concern about his photographs being co-opted to fulfill "political agendas." Kovalan, a Jaffna-based activist, who had been vocally critical about the Tigers and had even been briefly forced into exile as a consequence, said, "In 2009, I felt very sad. Like we had lost something."

Other images recapped seemingly endless catastrophe. Sarong-clad old men dug graves to bury their dead laid out on stretchers fashioned out of rush mats and whittled branches. Families sheltered and caught sleep under the abandoned husks of buses or queued with plastic buckets for water dispensed from a bowser. A young woman carried a rattan mat in the crook of her arm and a tiny pet monkey in a makeshift chicken-wire cage on her back. A stunned young boy in a bright orange shirt sat on the back of a tractor and cradled a baby in his arms: sleeping or dead, it was impossible to say. Two men on a Hero Honda bike gasped in horror at an event unfolding beyond the frame. Sandwiched between them was the half-concealed body of a girl in a blue teddy bear print dress. The jagged bones that jutted out from a bloodied middle made it difficult to gauge whether there was more of her than a pair of legs spilling over the side. A woman carrying a boy in a red bunny cap looked on at the two and a half passengers in resignation. Amid this turmoil, there were also shy smiling toddlers sitting on sari swings tied on tree branches and grandmothers cradling happy babies.

"I wanted to capture the feelings of people through their faces, and so I photographed them directly looking at the camera. No words are required then," Amarathaas mused, nearly a decade after the war had ended. "I don't support any side, but I see this as my responsibility to make sure that the injustices, the war crimes committed against the Tamil people are brought to light. I see these photographs as evidence of genocide. I do not know whether we will get justice, but it is my *nokkam* [purpose]. These photographs must be seen, and these injustices need to be inquired into internationally, but no one is speaking on behalf of us Tamils. This is *neradi sakshi* [direct witness]. There needs to be *neethi* [justice], and no one can deny that it happened. *Varalāraka pathivu ceñci vaikkānōm* [we must record this for history]." Amarathaas's photographs are among many thousands, claimed and unclaimed, mobilized, and concealed, appropriated, and exhibited and disputed, that persist in the aftermath of the armed conflict speaking to a history and loss that has been silenced in a victor's peace. In fact, the Sri Lankan postwar has been densely riddled with visual debris that challenges the silences and absences contrived by the Sri Lankan state.

Since our initial conversation, Amarathaas has self-published an important volume of photography titled *Through the Fire Zones: Photographs of Amarathaas in Sri Lanka's War Zones* (2022). The hundreds of black-and-white photographs are intended to shed light on "the hidden truths about the final war in Sri Lanka and the dimensions of the war time tragic life of Eelam Tamils" (2022, 4). The introduction shows photographs of Amarathaas standing with his camera in conversation with an unknown man amid the chaos unfolding around a Red Cross ambulance, and he continues to remain defiantly located and pictured through the horrors he photographs. The second shows him with a group of six children with whom, he writes, he spent a day in May 2007 playing before the bombing began. They include his nephew who died in May 2009, a month after his father, Amarathaas's brother, was severely injured by shelling in Valayanamadam. Other children in the photo also lost various family members. The photos that follow show what was perhaps one of the final days of stillness the children and Amarathaas knew. They are seen playing with baby goats and climbing trees.

After this tranquil visual pause, a reminder of once idyllic life in the Vanni, viewers are thrust into scenes of displacement with photographs of families piled onto the backs of tractors with their worldly belongings: plastic chairs, bicycles, bed frames, mats, and pots and pans. Children sleep on plastic sheets amid tents constructed of UNHRC tarpaulin. The makeshift domesticity of such a tent is shown where the garlanded portraits of two martyred *veeravengaikal* (heroes) and an assemblage of family photographs flank a clock adjourned at three o'clock. A clothesline hangs on the side with a trail of men's and women's clothes. A sewing machine is covered up with an old sarong. We see the backs of a woman and perhaps a child sitting on plastic chairs, one's head resting on the other's lap—a scene of quiet desolation. A battery radio is slung on the tent pole next to them. In another we see a woman rocking a baby in a cradle fashioned from a sari. ICRC supply boxes are visible at the corner of the image. Women and children queue at the side of a World Vision bowser with pots and buckets. Men move slowly along potholed roads with withered cattle. An elderly woman throws grain out to feed a flock of chickens, later pictured dead and strung onto the back of a bike, presumably as food grew scarce. A young woman tunes a radio connected to a series of wires. A calendar with an image of Durga, the goddess of war, hangs on the side of the tent with no roof. A white aid worker distributes rope and tarp to a long line of people holding files of documents against their faces to shield themselves from the sun. Children bathe in ponds and play carrom outside the tents. An LTTE funeral cortege is guarded by women with guns who sit at the back of the truck carrying a coffin draped in the Tiger flag and flower garlands. Amarathaas's self-portraits reappear throughout the book, amid photos of houses being dismantled by men, and children taking cover in underground bunkers as air force fighter jets fly above. He asserts his own presence, his own witness, as a part of the *pathivu,* alongside those photographed who may or may not have survived.

Through the dated pages, the hardships worsen and queues for relief grow, and the upheaval of recurring displacement worsens against backdrops of the LTTE's photographic billboards showing fighters and children foreshadowing a future that was rapidly disintegrating. As bombing surges, Amarathaas and his community move on foot from LTTE territory to government-controlled areas, to new NFZs, from Kilinochchi to Mullaitivu. Soon, bloodied and bandaged and injured children appear along with women wailing in despair at events that take place beyond the frame, as men look on in silent desolation. A woman holds a small child in one arm and a Jaipur leg detached from its owner and a frayed sack of belongings in the other, as a man in crutches is turned toward her, perhaps in conversation. Men move bodies injured in shell attacks and dig graves into which dismembered limbs folded into gunnysacks are lowered and buried. Crowds of people attempt to cross the lagoon as black smoke from aerial bombardment of the NFZs clouds the background. Even amid such horror, life endures. A man gives a haircut to a child sitting on a plastic chair on the beach. Children play in the shadow of a boat on the sand. Yet so does anguish. Mourners gather around the body of family members killed by the Sri Lankan army. The LTTE's "forced recruitment activity" is gestured to by captions of images showing groups of men and women looking, once more, beyond the frame as if some horrors might never be adequately grasped through one's eyes or lens (Amarathaas 2022, 300–301). The plight of those in camps is exacerbated by heavy rains and flooding. Amarathaas's computer and camera equipment were damaged during shelling in Valayanmadam in April 2009, its detritus too pictured among the amassing misery. The images from Mullivaikkal are the most distressing, strewn with displacement, injury, hopelessness, and death. Rows of bodies are laid out as weeping relatives attempt to identify their loved ones. Parents cry over the maimed corpses of small children. Long lines form to obtain small servings of *kanji* (salt and rice porridge), the only meal available to those trapped in Mullivaikkal. A single photograph exposes a plane dropping two bombs. The adjacent image shows people seeking cover by the side of a truck. The sequence ends in the first week of May. In a week, the Sri Lankan government would declare its military victory. None of these images of absolute carnage made it into the state media broadcasts that showed empty villages ruled by terrorists.

Amarathaas was not alone in his pursuit in photography for the *pathivu*. Yet in its form as aspirant "state" practice echoing that of an archive, the photographic record becomes the screen of ideology legitimating the necessity of Tamil Eelam (Tagg 1988). The significance of the *pathivu* is not merely in its role as a source of historical truth but in what it makes possible in terms of community and solidarity. In its photographic incarnation, it is also politically expedient, to be read for its intentions, contingencies, and disturbances. The photographic *pathivu* is an anxious response to what in the end is unknowable and irresolvable. Sivapragasam recalled the mass confiscation of cameras by the LTTE during the final months. Cornered by the advancing armed forces, the Tigers were actively utilizing photographs from the war zone to document atrocities of the state and strengthen its appeal for an internationally moderated ceasefire. Images, transmitted by way of a single working communications tower, were uploaded onto Tamil news websites such as TamilNet. These spurred the dispersed Tamil diaspora to undertake global protests drawing attention to the plight of civilians trapped in the NFZ. Sivapragasam buried his own cameras in the soil at Mullivaikkal hoping that he might recover them one day. He had not returned to look for them, for he was certain that he would not be able to locate them.

Even for those trapped in a war zone, the rapidly increasing access to image-making devices, whether in the form of mobile phone or compact point-and-shoot digital cameras coupled with internet-based social media and other platforms further facilitated the direct capturing and dissemination of images. For those like Amarathaas, who were caught in the midst of war, photography was not only an exercise in responsibility, but also one that was central to his own ethnopolitical identity not necessarily in terms of nation-state but duty to community. For Tamils in northern Sri Lanka contending against the erasures by the Sri Lankan state, the atrocity image is not one to be shied away from or concealed but mobilized and amplified. The moral-political debates and sensibilities pertaining to photographs of suffering continue to privilege the aesthetics, practices, and networks of circulation that fall within the parameters of documentary and reportage. Their respective "global" ambits and values are defined by the global north embodied by international news agencies and photojournalistic networks. As perhaps inadvertently implied by Arthur Kleinman and Joan Kleinman, the "local population" remains tacitly categorized and homogenized as the subjects of such photographs of the "suffering other," and separate from the "global audience" to which they do not appear to belong as producers, audiences, consumers, or intermediaries in modes of dissemination and circulation (1996, 1). Even within well-meaning analyses, those in distress are rendered as apolitical victims diminished of agency, relegated within tropes of passive, photographed objects of pity and not active subjects, makers, and movers of photography in its evidentiary and agitant forms. It is well to remember the solidarity and community among victims as much as those who seek to advocate for them and the importance of these photographs to evidence their experiences, which have been vehemently denied by perpetrators and overlooked by internationalized mechanisms for justice. Amarathaas and Sivapragasam were very much a part of the production and consumption of these images and were making deliberate choices about what they were or were not capturing, how their images would be shared and used, and the politics of doing so. Here the political work of war photography beyond the grasp of the state becomes visible, where there might be hope yet for community, responsibility, solidarity, and the photographic means that make acknowledgment and remembering possible.

THE ROAD TO MULLIVAIKKAL

On 18 May 2018, the road from Jaffna to Mullivaikkal was punctuated by small towns in mourning. Little roadside shrines were erected around assemblages of photographs turned into makeshift pandals showing the devastations of this final phase of the war. Others housed portraits of the known dead and missing, garlanded with peach hibiscus, white pinwheel flowers, and red ixora—unscented funeral flowers. Oil lamps of sorrow were lit before them. Shuttered shops draped with black flags announced a region-wide hartal. The towns marked by their protest a day of Tamil grief.

It was the ninth anniversary of the last day of the armed conflict between the Sri Lankan military and the LTTE. Nearly a decade had passed since Amarathaas had borne witness in Kilinochchi and Mullivaikkal with his camera.

After the end of the war, communal lamentation and remembrance were deemed a "security threats" and actively prohibited between 2010 and 2014. Following the 2015 regime change, commemoration was permitted for the first time since 2009, albeit under heavy surveillance and continued intimidation. It was in such a context, that in May 2018, a resilient public trickled to Mullaitivu in an act of resistance and solidarity. Mullivaikkal remembrance continues to be fraught today, positioned by Sinhalese nationalists as an attempt to idolize or even revive the LTTE and undermine the victory achieved by the Sri Lankan armed forces. Despite continuing threats, violence, and surveillance, mourners who gather at Mullivaikkal grow in numbers each year.

The arid Mullaitivu landscape was crisscrossed with new power lines and barbed-wire fencing. Houses had begun to slowly multiply in varying stages of completion. Cement-block huts and freshly painted pastel compounds with gabled clay tile roofs peeked out of grassy clearings amid the bombarded ruins of homes and overgrown thickets of palmyra trees charred by artillery shelling. "Peace" had become concretized in the shape of slick, metaled roads built as a part of the Rajapaksa regime's Uthuru Vasanthaya (Northern Spring) initiative bolstered by an estimated two billion dollars of international aid and loans proffered in the name of peace. Sprawling army camps contained within tall fortress-like granite walls were connected by a network of sandbagged boulevards and new Buddhist temples heralding continuing militarization at its most potent. However, Mullaitivu remained a site of tense civilian protest on account of militarization, Sinhalization, and interlinked land grabs. Police officers waved down cars and vans to inquire into the passengers' identities, affiliations, and destination, before writing up drivers for fictional traffic violations. The war years and interlinked escalation of pervasive securitization had polarized the island's communities along ethnic and geographic fault lines. The effects of competing projects of nation/state contriving the ethnic/geographic other into enemies, undesirables, and the perpetually suspect lingered in the postwar. The police were not unaware of the significance of the day, yet idly inconvenienced and penalized on behalf of the state those who chose to attend the Mullivaikkal remembrance event. Drivers had developed an efficient system of warning others by flashing their lights to indicate the presence of hidden police stops. I had enlisted Mr. Fernando to drive me to Mullaitivu, knowing that the public transport links were tenuous, and that security would be of concern. The 2017 remembrance event had sparked controversy following a magistrate court's ban on a church meeting as it "threatened" national security, and there was heightened surveillance and harassment by the state intelligence apparatus. I was accompanied by Kovalan, a Tamil activist from Jaffna; Maanavi, a Tamil NGO worker from Pallai; and Wasana, a Sinhalese filmmaker from Colombo.

Mr. Fernando was tense but hummed along to his Tamil cinema music cassette tape on the radio. In Pallai, black flags tied to sticks and ropes signposted a shared bereavement temporarily sewn into the landscape. Others had spartan memorials set up under temporary tin roof shelters. Some tents were strung with flex banners printed with color-saturated photographs of the dead and injured. In Tharmapuram, the shrine was constructed around photographs, the losses identified and personalized. We too were stopped by the traffic police who claimed we were speeding. We were not. Mr. Fernando left to show them his license, intrepidly letting us know upon his return that he had informed the police that we were a group going to visit a family member in the Mullaitivu hospital. It was an improvisation that all of us in the car were intimately familiar with. They took away his license and issued a fine. He was unblinking in his explanation that there appeared to be a "clear agenda" of stopping, fining, and harassing those traveling to the event. As we drove, Kovalan narrated the events of the final months of war, as we traced its path to Mullivaikkal. Geographic features served as prompts for recollection on how the troops advanced, where people were killed, and which hospitals were bombed. The LTTE was besieged by the army and lost most of its leadership in one fell swoop in the battle of Anandapuram. Kovalan recalled the "public secret" of the "white flag incident" and the series of phone conversations between key political figures who attempted to broker a failed deal for surrender, and the many thousand desolations of its brutal unfolding.

The first event in the proximity to Mullivaikkal was in a school building hollowed out by a shell where people had gathered to light lamps. We were graciously and efficiently ushered by teenaged boys in school uniforms wearing cardboard "Mullivaikkal Commemoration" badges. A large number of attendees of all ages were beginning to find their way to the principal memorial site. The spectral iconographies of the *Iyakkam* were evident upon our entrance into the commemoration strung with red and yellow flags, illustrations of the karthigai flower, and banners displaying technicolor atrocities. "This is just like Maaveerar Naal!" Maanavi exclaimed.

THE TRUTH IS IN THE SOIL

In another life, the sandy turf near the ocean may have played host to a game of cricket or football, but it was now steeped in the detritus of war. The aggressive military "cleanup" that took two years meant there was not a human skull or bone to be found, I was told. "They brought in an incinerator," someone whispered, "to burn all the bodies!" The soil, however, remained tangled and scattered with the material remnants of these devastations: children's shoes, women's saris, the plastic shells of battery-powered radios, men's rubber slippers, woven mats, and blue UN tarpaulins. These remains countered denial as indexes of atrocity denied by the state. Flex banners displayed around the site documented by civilian and LTTE photographers caught up in the last months of the war were strung on tree branches and tents that offered cool *sharbat* to the participants. Hundreds of mourners had gathered before a crop of metal rods which would be transfigured by wicks and matches into torches. Here, they took off their shoes, toes digging into soil consecrated darkly by these relics of nation and violence as if to form an elemental tether to what was lost. Examining the everyday materialities of violence in Sierra Leone, Mariane Ferme considers how local histories are bound up in matter, whereby through objects, language, and social relations "violent historical memory is sedimented and critically appropriated" (2001, 2–6). The visible world as it exists in the form of ritual, political, and domestic appropriations of public space, Ferme argues, is "activated by forces concealed beneath the surface of discourse objects and social relations" (2001, 2). In Mullivaikkal what was buried, though only barely concealed, served as a material reliquary of the nation upon which political continuities and claims are built. Photographs of the soil, tangled with wartime residue reminding of the horrors witnessed by the ground, were posted on Instagram with captions demanding recognition of genocide against the community and justice for the victims.

Where ragged shirts, broken suitcases, and small school bags remained half-chewed by the earth, grievers improvised memorials for their departed loved ones. Among these were protesters from Maruthankerny and Kilinochchi, whose family members had been lost at Mullivaikkal to death and disappearance. Flowers and incense encircled photographs, sometimes elegant studio portraits, an occasional family snap, or staid headshots still laminated into NICs placed on mounds of soil resembling little graves (fig. 23). These everyday photographs of the kind taken in the studios encountered

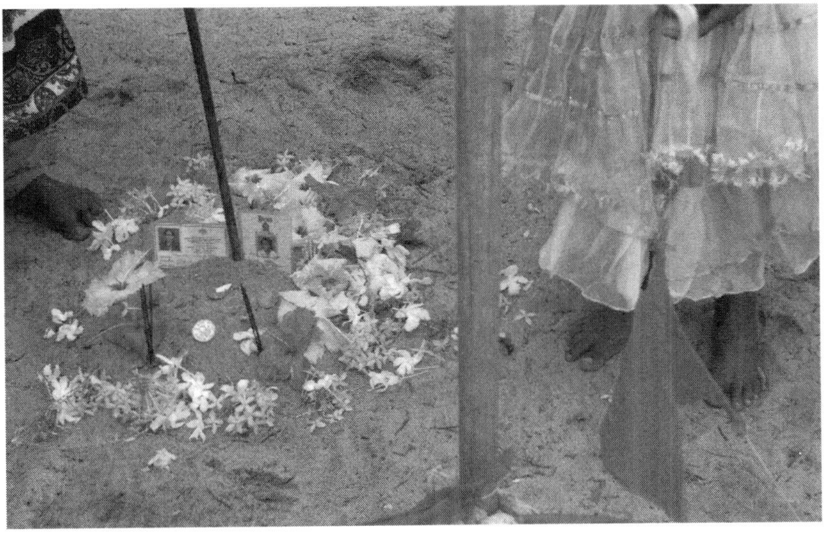

FIGURE 23. Family builds a shrine centered on a National Identity Card (NIC) on the soil of Mullivaikkal (Mullaitivu, 2018)

in the preceding chapters may not immediately corroborate atrocity but nevertheless index state crimes in their volatile capability. Their public display in northern Sri Lanka has become synonymous with individual lives, disappearances, and deaths negated. Where the Sri Lankan state persisted as perpetrator imposing a violent peace, the defiant reorienting of the NIC, in particular, as visual-material anointment of citizenship in an explicitly Tamil space of memory and resistance, asserted its opposite. The NIC photograph here proved precisely the parity of citizenship eluding the Tamil community, resulting in its bodily expendability. Many were elderly women, often alone, weeping with the sort of visceral grief that hung heavy in the air. A stone's throw away, on the strip of beach, where the final days of the war had unfolded, the remains of sun-and-salt-bleached family photograph albums had stayed for some years, though mostly slowly deteriorated, and washed away nearly a decade later.

Community organizers, some of whom were wearing T-shirts emblazoned with karthigai flowers, helped marshal a lamp affixed onto a truck that had been roving the Northern Province as a mobile shrine. The flame actively featured within commemorative activities envisioned by the LTTE, notably Maaveerar Naal, where it represented nation and sacrifice. Activists present discussed in whispers the definite presence of state intelligence men who weaved in and out of the crowd incognito, photographing and documenting much like the activists themselves. The absorption of "rehabilitated" LTTE cadres into informal state surveillance networks was common knowledge. Where social stigma and marginalization stemming from fear were prevalent and opportunities available to them were minimal, many had become absorbed into the Civil Security Force to carry out menial labor and intelligence gathering. It was difficult not to be wary of the men with mobile phones and cameras. As in the protest sites, the line between participants, media and civil society activists, journalists, state intelligence, and researchers like me was blurred once more as we filmed and photographed the commemoration.

"*Intha mannukulla tan unmai irukkirathu* [the truth is in the soil]," an *amma* in a brown sari keened, requiem and curse, as she despairingly grabbed at the earth with her hands. Photographers clustered around her. Two women held her up as she, a postwar Sita, clutches at the soil desperately as if the earth might open up to offer her answers.[4]

Local photographers, press, citizen journalists, and activists congregated around grieving families looking for the most arresting of potential photographic evocations that would in the days that followed the event circulate through the local social-mediascape (fig. 24). Allen Feldman notes that the violent transcription of ethnohistorical codes onto the material surfaces of the body and the urban landscape has the capacity to transform social life, popular memory, and history (2003, 62). Here the living bodies of mourners that made up a bereaved nation transposed onto a soil visibly wounded by violence conjured potent photographs to be captured. The mainstream Sinhalese media were visibly absent. A human rights activist from Colombo, Ruki Fernando, reflecting on the Mullivaikkal commemorations noted that "since 2009, May 18 is the day I feel the strongest disconnect between the north and east and rest of the country, along ethnic lines. Since 2009, the mood of May 18 in the north has been one of mourning," confirming that the event had nothing to do with the LTTE even though it was perceived as such in the south, remaining a point of social unease and contention (2018). The day of 19 May was recognized by the Sri Lankan state not as a day of remembrance and anguish, but "National War Heroes Commemoration Day" to honor the soldiers who had defeated "LTTE terrorism." This amplified the sharp divide in how the end of the war was received by the Sri Lankan public that was also for the most part ethnicized. How families of state military personnel

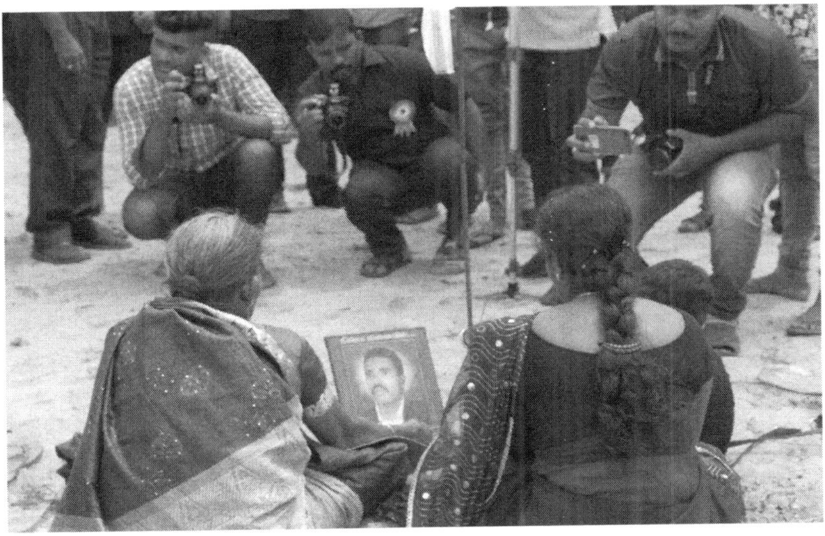

FIGURE 24. Photographers and grieving families at Mullivaikkal (Mullaitivu, 2018)

have accounted for their losses and grief outside state-sponsored celebrations has been remarkably underexplored except for heroic figures such as Hasalaka Gamini.[5]

Where local elections were at stake, the political value of such an event and its audience were also not squandered. "Even in this situation where we are not in a position to deliver any sort of justice to our people who have been affected. Our people are protesting continuously on the streets for justice and their fundamental securities, and our land is becoming colonized by Buddhism by the many thousands of military officers deployed across the northeast," Chief Minister (CM) Wigneswaran read out to the crowd, reminding everyone that it was "the ninth anniversary of Mullivaikkal Genocide Day." It was difficult to say if anyone was listening. Most were preoccupied with their personal rituals of mourning. Kovalan, who was attending the commemoration for the first time, wryly remarked that the CM had been driven right to the grounds in a gas-guzzling military-grade SUV along with guards carrying big guns.

Little children cried over parents they had known only for a few months of their short lives. Greying mothers wept over dead sons and daughters who had not survived past their teenage years, having had guns forcefully thrust into their hands or succumbed to projectiles (fig. 25). A father bore in

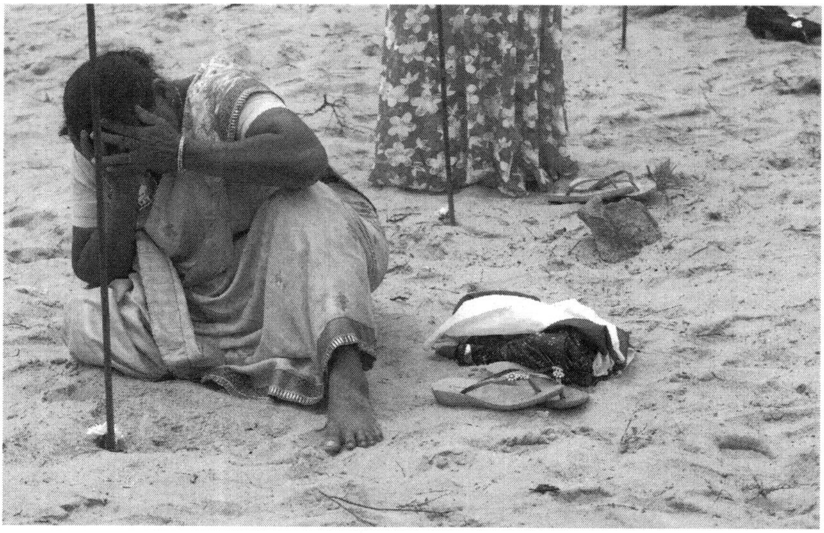

FIGURE 25. Mourning mother at Mullivaikkal (Mullaitivu, 2018)

his hands a large picture frame housing multiple faces, another family tree of death. A mother sobbed over a photoshopped memorial portrait of her son, two images flanking a text that speaks to his memory. A buzzing media drone upset a few elderly mothers who were reminded of the hum of falling shells. Drone photography was also increasingly used to draw attention to scale, particularly of gathered crowds. As has been examined by Zeynep Devrim Gürsel in her discussion of the 2015 post–Charlie Hebdo Unity Rally in Paris, such photographs amounted to a declaration of belonging to a larger, "imaged" community (2017, S138). In its appropriation into a Tamil nationalist register, it also tacitly suggested an appearance of popular sovereignty. The volume of images, as well as images that conjured volume in the form of crowds, was central to articulations of scale and collectivity, as well as defiance. Such images were increasingly used by diasporic Tamil nationalist media to convey cause and cohesiveness, contriving a visual of political homogeneity. Such gatherings also informed an important act of photographed history-making, where violent erasure remained a constant threat. It was inevitably bound to death as much as survival in a regenerative confluence in the service of nation.

Around the site, photographs documenting Sri Lankan state violence inflicted on Tamil bodies adorned banners and paper pandal archways asserting that these crimes would not be forgotten. These images documented by victims and perpetrators underscore the competing image regimes of the Sri Lankan war, but importantly how these cannot be contained by a single ideological script. They took the form of embellished photographic collages interspersed with text and visual motifs that were broadly situated within the same visual formulae as the photoshopped albums or banners encountered in Jaffna's studios. This suggested a cohesiveness of the aesthetic formats within which photographs were located and presented. This heightened their visibility beyond the conventions of "documentary realism" that might authenticate conflict elsewhere. On one banner, an illustration of the Sri Lankan flag's lion with a bloodied sword standing over an anonymous pile of bodies is superimposed over images of Tamil suffering drowned in flaming red and the photograph of a memorial shrine. The iconography of the Sri Lankan state was subverted so that it was shown as inflicting violence on Tamils. The accompanying map of Tamil Eelam was shown to be bleeding. In the absence of bodies, photographs of the dead and injured served as a directory of past violence, signifying in turn the community's present grievances that remain tethered to a desired, alternative political future. The caption read, "*Thyaga kanavudan saavinai taluviyargalin ninaivalayam. May 18, vali sumantha naal* [The martyrs died along with our dreams of a motherland. May 18, the day we carried the pain]."

Echoing practices of cultural production established during the war, there was also the thriving sale of CDs with a grisly cover of a bloody hand and the face of a screaming woman. For 100 LKR each (US$0.30) the disc containing eight songs about the tragedy of Mullivaikkal sold quickly from a makeshift booth swathed in graphic banners of suffering. Mullivaikkal potently evokes what Feldman coins as "trauma-tropism," a form of social-constructed collective memory whereby "single communities and entire societies can reorganize their identities, histories, and projects around the curvature of chosen prior 'historical' wounding" (2002, 236). This notion of a national wounding was central to the image world of Tamil nationalism as defined by the Tigers. It persists in the postwar in the absence of the Tigers as an aspiring state actor in Sri Lanka. The vocabulary and aesthetics around Mullivaikkal were also consciously transnational in the inferences it evoked, linking it to historic brutalities such as most notably the Holocaust, which remains central to much of the discourse on genocide. Moreover, inspired by the Jewish tradition of Passover, the practice of Mullivaikkal *kanji* (rice porridge) was adopted at its tenth anniversary. Through social media campaigns, the local and dispersed Tamil community were encouraged to partake in *kanji*, which was the only sustenance that was available to those trapped in the war zone in 2009. Here photography once more was integral to building a transnational community through its appeal to the (home) land.

ACCOUNTABLE IMAGES

In 2019, I visited a sprawling exhibition hosted in London to mark the tenth anniversary of Mullivaikkal dubbed "Tamils of Lanka: A Timeless Heritage," which sought to imagine a shared history of Ilankai Tamils in Sri Lanka organized by a few Tamil organizations. A "global photo campaign" designed to document Tamil history and resistance informed the wider exhibition as organized by a nonprofit organization run by diasporic Tamil youth. A parallel exhibition, dedicated to the arts and culture of Tamils, included photography, fine art, and traditional crafts. Through a prominent pavilion celebrating the history and prowess of the LTTE and the de facto Tamil state, visitors were led to a large room dedicated to Mullivaikkal, housing a harrowing, exceptionally graphic display photographs, where Tamil injury and death are mobilized to anti-political effect, in service of the still aspiring ethno-state. An installation of a tent, littered with "bloodied" bandages and other debris formed the backdrop for a giant pot of *kanji* being distributed by a few volunteers, a couple of whom I knew to be Mullivaikkal survivors now refugees in London. They eagerly offered *kanji* to visitors explaining the history of the effort. In a corner of the room, an initiative to count deaths requested those who had lost family members in the war to register with them. In northern Sri Lanka, friends messaged to tell me that *kanji* was served on the sides of roads. Such community organization building on extant transnational connectivities was not only forging these ties of nation further but also situating the postwar incarnation of nation within a globalized lexicon of atrocity. The vernacular of the nationalist armed struggle had been transformed into one of international human rights discourses, with the inception of dedicated transnational nongovernmental organizations engaged in translating and enumerating instances of violence. While LTTE iconography is explicitly dangerous to keepers and proscribed in Sri Lanka, visual and sonic codes established by the group endure not merely as an indication of allegiance, but to keep its aspiration of self-determination and a Tamil homeland alive. Abroad, the LTTE's image regime withstands more vibrantly than ever before, with community commemoration events extending from Maaveerar Naal to Mullivaikkal remembrance marked with heightened visibility. It now incorporates the ghastly visual corpus of Mullivaikkal, where the group's downfall in the homeland and Tamil suffering continue to sustain political work. While the LTTE might have expediently capitalized on and reworked the bonds of community, through land, kinship, language, loss, and responsibility, which are not merely statist or ideological political tools, the images imbued with what connects and is felt and valued begin to transcend and achieve more than the desire for state.

Atrocity photographs, often identical in their content, would in divergent, even contradictory, registers accrue new political meaning and mediate new political potentials. For the located and dispersed Tamil community they signaled the hostility of the state that permeated past and present, underpinning a necessary political claim of a separate Tamil nation-state for the future. To a Sinhala Buddhist supremacist, Sri Lankan state photographs confirmed a victory that would be of perpetual value in their Tamil nationalist and human rights–oriented circulations holding political utility. The images confirmed the defeat of the "other" that was a threat to the survival of Sinhalese body and nation, serving as a constant reminder of the Sri Lankan state's role in vanquishing the enemy in securing its own political future where electoral support could be mustered by the incorporation of these images into campaign materials, including songs, posters, and billboards. Their use within international documentaries elicited a different kind of outrage from among predominantly Sinhalese Sri Lankans, where it was deemed a neocolonial "Western conspiracy" bolstered by international LTTE supporters invested in returning Sri Lanka to war. Importantly, these underscore the transnational character of Tamil political claims and community, as well as the movement of these photographs. When framed through Azoulay's notion of civic spectatorship, these images vehemently demand international governance commitments and action, emboldening advocacy and accountability networks (2008). However, this does not diminish their agitant capacity, especially in the eyes of the Sri Lankan state. If anything, the international circulation and visibility of these photographs toward transitional justice demands turned the state more hostile toward their wielders.

What a volatile photography enables is the impossibility of a dominant assumption or singular narrative. Tensions bound to competing powers in cultivating opposing publics through the capacity to disorder are rendered visible by the medium. Photography deployed as an agitant continues to be essential to making political freedoms and radical alternatives conceivable. In a time of nominal peace, photography remains a threat, an easy trigger with the capacity to cause insecurity and destabilize even the most resounding hegemonic assertions. Images, perceived to propel political transformation forward in their capacity to envision but also sustain imaginings of a political future, not only evidence but are actively wielded to interrupt and disrupt in lively transmission and debate.

Where the theoretical language of photography's political possibilities is still anchored to the state and power, or as hopeful democratic action and expression of solidarity to counter the violence of the sovereign, the uncivil reminds us of the inevitabilities and visceralities of violence, which are rarely accounted for, and certainly that photography can generate violence. Photography's volatility and its agitant capacities were exploited by competing state actors to normalize uncivil spectatorship and foster ethnonationalist sentiments, vocabularies, and imaginaries. It helps us better appreciate that those living amid war, whether as its architects, participants, subjects, or victims, are making active political choices that determine how or whether they choose to participate, calculate risk, navigate complexity, hazard chance, envision futures, form allegiances, and back ideological claims and commitments and importantly survive. In the image worlds of war, uncivil spectatorship demonstrates how people demand, compel, and make war, whether for liberation or the supposed eradication of terrorism required for the professed defense of sovereignty. The political work of photography thus illuminates the political work of war.

7 IMAGI(NI)NG EELAM

THE LAND CAN TELL ME SOMETHING ABOUT THE PLACE

At first glance, Sabes Sugunasabesan's 2011 photograph "Home: A View from the Living Room," showing a television set placed in a living room, is an altar to quiet domesticity. Freshly cut pink and red roses in a vase, bookshelves, children's photographs and drawings make up a constellation of the life cast in bright slivers of light and moody shadows reminiscent of the jewel tones of the island on a monsoonal day. However, the sharp blue-green-brown terrestrial image on the screen demands closer inspection and reveals "Home" to be a carefully constructed composite that is repeated in a series through a carousel of maps and black-and-white images superimposed onto the living room screen (fig. 26). Home is a house in London. Home is a man cradling an injured child. Home is the black cloud of smoke arising out of aerial bombing. Home is the bullet-riddled closeup of Balachandran's chest. Home means families fleeing on bicycles. Home is a hungry young girl holding an ever-silver cup. Home is people running away from shelling. Home is a satellite image of Mullivaikkal.

During and after 2009, Sabes found himself repetitively searching the internet asking himself, "I cannot be there. How can I be there?" He became struck by the carnage unfolding through satellite imagery of the Vanni, consuming the war through a sequence of disquieting images interloping into the stillness and safety of his household. He traveled to the homeland by way of the news and Google Earth, scrolling through TamilNet and YouTube where announcements from the Voice of Tigers broadcasts were uploaded. Around him, demonstrations and vigils led by diasporic Tamil groups unfolded, attracting thousands in global protests in India, Singapore, Malaysia, South Africa, France, Belgium, Germany, the Netherlands, Switzerland, Norway, Canada, the USA, Australia, and New Zealand. Sabes regularly went to the marches alone, describing attendees as "sad-looking, worried-looking people." Two young British Tamils, Sivatharsan Sivakumaravel and Parameswarn Subramaniyan, had undertaken a hunger strike to no avail, refusing food or water until a ceasefire was called. Sabes

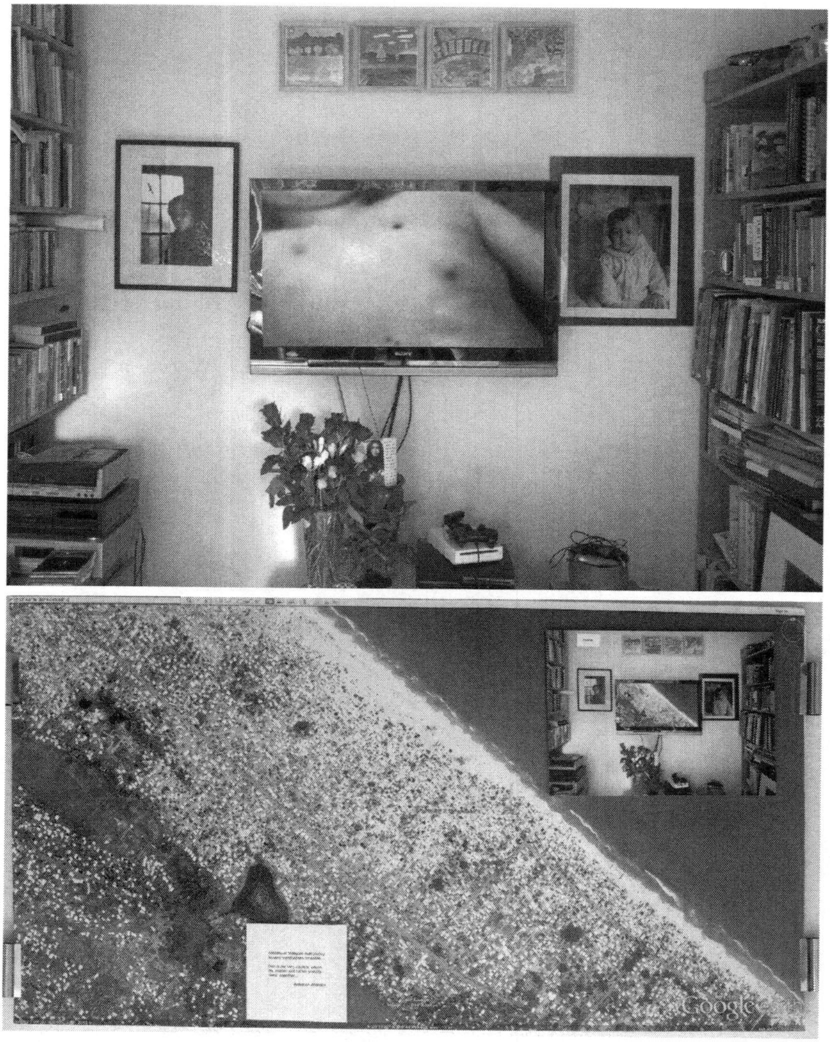

FIGURE 26. "Home: A View from the Living Room," by Sabes Sugunasabesan (London, 2011–16)

joined in discussions with a group of Tamil compatriots in a small room above an Eastham tutory to "talk about what to do." There could be no answers short of an immediate ceasefire.[1] At home, Sabes printed images found on the internet. He cut, reassembled, and drew over in an attempted photocartographic corrective that sought to reckon with his people, their land, and their history and violence that burned its way across northern Sri Lanka and his screens.

In his 2016 series "Last Walk to the Beach," Sabes's interpolation is more direct, confronting the viewer not only with the pictured atrocities of the war but also the vision of a Sri Lanka as imagined by Empire—an island of pristine beaches and verdant tropical jungles. These photographs were shown at various exhibitions and have since appeared in a sequence of Instagram posts shared in 2023. In a subsequent visit to the island, Sabes traced on foot the route followed by those who were fleeing the government's shelling to the designated No Fire Zones leading to the beach at Mullivaikkal. On his journey, Sabes held up in his hand, prints of found images not unlike those captured by Amarathaas documenting the mass violence of the final war. It was "a personal response to witnessing the brutal genocidal war in Sri Lanka from the distance as a diasporic Tamil" where "there were no safe places. Hospitals and food distribution places were bombed. Cluster bombs were used. The people reached a 400-meter strip of shore in Mullivaikkal beach having lost their children, parents, friends, limbs, and belongings." These photographs of photographs are interspersed with his own attentive annotations of the landscape as "insider-outsider." A news image of a weeping woman holding an injured child is photographed against a luxuriant thicket of coconut trees and a woven leaf fence. The shell of a rusted minibus still bears the cheeky stickered words "Don't Kiss Me." Sabes's living room emerges, once more, in a new configuration, now compressed and superimposed onto a large satellite image of Mullivaikkal. Small blue and white dots marking the hundreds of tents that speckled the white sand beach offering temporary shelter to the thousands who were displaced engulfs the docile London still life. Returning to Mullaitivu, a yellow-painted hall, which is hollow with no roof, is striking against a backdrop of spiny palmyra trees. In another, new power lines run parallel to a dirt road flanked by greenery, which runs all the way to the ocean you cannot see, along with the detritus of war and displacement that still litters the sides years later. Through these photographic intermediations, Sabes carries the war, its dislodged violence with him as he always has.

The London-based Tamil photographer and mixed-media artist had seen the entire war begin, unfold, and end from afar. Born in Malaysia, Sabes lived in Jaffna between the ages of seven and twenty-four, leaving for England in September 1974. Among young people in the peninsula, rumblings of ambitions for Tamil self-determination had begun to ferment into armed resistance. That year Pon Sivakumaran, a member of a burgeoning militant group from Valvettithurai, swallowed a cyanide capsule to evade capture and died by suicide, becoming the first martyr of the Tamil armed struggle. Earlier that year, the police had forcefully disrupted the World Tamil Research Conference proceedings in Jaffna by opening fire at the mass gathering, killing nine and injuring over fifty individuals. If a civil war was imminent, it had not yet officially announced itself in full force. The Vaddukoddai resolution and the new Tamil Tigers were a few years away from appearing. Active in leftist political circles in London through this time, Sabes's proximity to the conflict, inescapable as a Tamil migrant from Jaffna, had been tempered by distance and a feeling of dislocation that punctuates his photography. This alienation was mediated by and grappled with through images, in his intake of visuals from the war through the screen and his own image-making extending from protest photography from the 1980s to meditative engagements with the landscape in Sri Lanka, the United Kingdom, and the United States of America. These contemplations mustering the multifaceted sedimentations of people's movements, settler colonialism, and occupation are focused on lens-based readings of multiple terrains interconnected through fine threads of empire and violence.

This final chapter dwells on the unwieldy genre of social photography of the postwar and what it might reveal about the Tamil political imagination. It contains a patchwork of unfolding questions that distill the instability and uncertainty that characterize Sri Lanka's postwar for the island's political minorities. Sabes's "Home" and "Last Walk to the Beach" encapsulate the themes of this chapter. Their many layers of now and then, and emplacement and displacement, mediated through photography, technology, and the capacities of the digital, position us within an amalgam of past, present, and speculation toward the future. As a final chapter, it is also a fitting collage and congregation of the kinds of photography and documentation encountered throughout this book with a focus on how and why this motley assembly of war images broadly conceived continues to circulate. Through the social given shape by the photographic and augmented by the digital, we are able to see a vibrant mosaic of the persistent making and moving, revealing a glimpse into the Tamil political imagination and aspirations in the postwar as one of anticipation and also longing. If the state and the aspirant state's image regimes of ethnonationalism and war coupled with limited access to personal cameras and a reliance on professional media or studio photographers established specific types, registers, and aesthetics of what a photography of war entailed, the digital has expanded our view into the past and present, and the ontology of photography. The digital has multiply magnified what constitutes photography, including the convenience of image-making and sharing through personal devices and social media; the ability to reproduce, remix, edit, and enhance one's own images; and the capacity to build conversation, awareness, and community around these very pictures. Even in the postwar, the volatility of these photographs in their potential to be grasped, used, and wielded has intensified, perceived to trigger new kinds of instability within a victor's narrative of peace. Through this vast flow of everyday image production and circulation, we catch vital glimpses into a more granular, heterogenous view of Tamil political expression than was previously possible. These conform to and challenge the dual hegemonies of Tamil and Sinhalese ethnonationalism and militarism. They articulate diverse political aspirations, instances, and possibilities for belonging. On virtual spaces, such as Instagram, these coexist in a buoyant confab.

BIG HISTORIES, LITTLE PHOTOGRAPHIES

Where political expression is stifled, people summon complex histories in everyday photography to document and confront the harms of the perpetrator's peace. Nathan Jurgenson writes that the "social photo," defined by the "degree to which its existence as a stand-alone media object is subordinate to its existence as a unit of communication," realizes a human impulse to document human experience that keeps pace with technological developments, shaping a "documentary consciousness" (2019, 18–19). As Jurgenson frames it, these everyday photographs are taken to be shared (2019, 7). In the Sri Lankan context, these are not limited to personal snapshots but a broad repertoire of images of diverse origin extending from studio portraits and archival finds to atrocity images and combat photos. What Jurgenson terms "the desire for life in its documented form" highlights how the dichotomies of "amateur vs. professional" and "digital vs. analog" matter less for the social photo than the relations between power, identity, and reality (2019, 2, 8). For Tamils in Sri Lanka, everyday photographic and other documentation have always constituted forms of political speaking rooted in the necessity of surviving normalized state crime, mass human rights violations, censorship, and the active suppression and destruction of records and knowledge countering state and anti-state authority. Photographic practices constitute individual and communal acts of evidencing that have found new visibility and modes of circulation by way of the digital.

For Ilankai Tamils, the war and the injustices within which demands for self-governance were rooted continue amid the state's prevarications and lack of accountability. I consider this amorphous category of social photography emerging from and recirculating through the cameras and phones of amateur and professional Tamil photographers in Sri Lanka and the diaspora. It constitutes a miscellaneous, largely digital or digitalized assemblage extending from mobile phone photography, re-photography, and Instagram to community exhibitions that contain in their numbers the types of photography encountered in the preceding chapters. As effectively encapsulated by Sabes's images, it is necessary to recognize that digital photographs may take physical shape through processes of printing and display, just as analog photographs are regularly re-photographed or scanned and disseminated through digital and physical means. This is made achievable by technologies of reproduction, including phone and computer-based interventions such as saving and screenshotting, as well as editing, enhancement, communication, broadcast, and dissemination that is accessible to individuals through their personal devices in a way and scale that was previously unimaginable.

An examination of contemporary photography would thus not be complete without a consideration of outwardly improved avenues for preservation, dissemination, and visibility afforded by the internet and social media. It is an effort to understand what social media has made possible for photography and those who produce and share photographic images in expanding the social and political ontology of photography (Azoulay [2012] 2015). These modes of circulation transformed how the war and postwar continue to be viewed globally. Importantly, it has significant bearing on how the war is still lived, remembered, discussed, politicized, and reanimated in the present beyond state narratives and the writing of history, where ethnic conflict and the political ruptures of civil war and its causes and consequences are yet to appear in school curricula. These considerations are further relevant given what Jurgenson describes as the increasingly tenuous, if not false, binary of "digital dualism" whereby online and offline are viewed as largely distinct when they are intrinsically and irrevocably entangled, certainly in relation to photographic practice (2019, 68). A photographic record of war and violent peace now accrues on Instagram, Twitter (X), and Facebook, which magnify their volatile potentials.

Here, I extend Jurgenson's framing, not simply of an online and offline interaction, but of temporal and spatial continuity, expansion, and amplified visibility made possible by the digital. This, in turn, strengthens the political work of war and photography. These image-based practices offer vital insight into the vivacity of the Tamil political imagination, simultaneously located in the geography of homeland but cartographically and photographically dispersed and transnational in its social-digital invocations. These uses are not merely recordkeeping of the past or historicizing struggle, but recursion that is marshalled toward the future. It calls attention to what is politically possible in the wake of a demand for a sovereign state being crushed, and that same aspirant state's internecine violence and despotism. Although how that future, in intelligible political terms, might still be realized is unclear, it is visibly unfolding through social photography, speaking politically to the anticipatory in-between of deferred dreams.

The considerations of this chapter necessarily exceed the transformations and expansions to photography made feasible by social media. Although digital and social media have heightened the visibility and reach of such practices, they build on an important lineage of documentation and preservation undertaken by Tamil photographers, activists, journalists, and amateur archivists confronted with state violence. First, I examine practices of incidental and everyday evidencing through amateur photography and documentation made necessary during times of war and how social media has become integrated into these labors, increasing the prominence of such circulations. This is especially apparent in practices associated with digitizing and archiving at the individual level. Second, although Instagram helps visualize the vibrantly transnational character of Tamil political expression and solidarity, it is part of the already established internationalized exchanges that vex how civil wars in the postcolonial global south, and their politics and outcomes, are framed. Tamil political articulation through social photography is not novel or the result of social media, but part of a time-honored practice of socially driven documentation. It was also always transnational in how it was conceived owing to the failings of the nation-state and expectations for international acknowledgment and justice. This also sheds light on intergenerational transmissions of knowledge and the committed ideological and political socialization of the aspirant citizens of Tamil Eelam. A considerable volume of the primary source material that has informed this book has been made possible by the intentional and incidental online and offline accumulations of dedicated individuals. It builds on decades of care, trust, and faith in eventual justice and/or a political alternative, and a political practice compelled by the risk and precarity of war and state violence.

EVERYDAY EVIDENCING

It is an oft-repeated statement of irony among critics of the regime that former President Mahinda Rajapaksa, credibly held responsible by many for overseeing innumerable state crimes, had once been a champion of human rights. The Sri Lanka Freedom Party (SLFP) parliamentarian from Hambantota, in the aftermath of the Bheeshanaya, alongside the late SLFP MP Mangala Samaraweera, had been pivotal in organizing the southern Mothers' Front made up of 25,000 women whose family members had been disappeared. Rajapaksa famously traveled to Geneva to lobby what was the UN Human Rights Commission at the time, carrying with him 533 documents containing information related to enforced disappearances, including nineteen pages of photographs (SCSL 1992, 233). Accused of treason by the United National Party (UNP) government, Rajapaksa responded in parliament stating, "Treachery? We have a right to tell this to the world. Tears of innocent grieving mothers compel us to tell their story of pain and sorrow to the world. We will do it today, tomorrow and always" (Bastians 2016). In the period following 2009, the Rajapaksa regime virulently condemned those who demanded an international inquiry into the conduct of the armed forces during the final phase of the war, insisting that such demands were rooted in a Western conspiracy against the government while dispatching state security personnel to attack holders of images that refuted its perpetrator's peace.

The dissident work of documentation and preservation in Sri Lanka has always been perilous. The country's severe and compounded experiences with political violence since the 1970s resulted in discreet but dedicated and sometimes secretive practices of recording, collection, and safeguarding by steadfast activists, journalists, citizen archivists, errant bureaucrats, and academics despite great risk and danger to their lives and families. Even those who did not view themselves as engaged in human rights or political work diligently gathered and made notes, often furtively, envisaging future use or relevance that rarely if ever came to transpire. Just as Jaffna's studio practitioners and picture framers sought to keep their histories and photographs secure, at least in memory, such responses to a status quo of uncertainty were an acknowledgment of the precarity of knowledge. Its easy loss and fading from social worlds were often contemplated by their keepers where people too were all too easily lost and disappeared. A long durée of armed conflict and state terror coupled with a climate of fear, paranoia, surveillance, displacement, death, and inadequate or inconsistent resources, labor, and skills entailed that such pursuits became increasingly difficult to maintain. In a highly militarized and securitized environment further restrained by the weaponization of anti-terrorism legislation, the collection of information on human rights violations was stymied. Moreover, international observers and journalists, including media personnel, were regularly barred access. This context of state and anti-state terror, reprisal killings, massacre, arbitrary arrest and detention, torture, and enforced disappearance entailed that information too, became, increasingly incendiary. These endeavors, hence, became necessarily transnational, especially due to the threat and hazard of carrying out such work in Sri Lanka.

Sri Lanka's small island war that was largely ignored internationally implanted itself in new cities in Europe, North America, and Australia through conflict-induced migration. As the armed conflict worsened, diaspora activism and advocacy calling attention to the state violence and human rights violations in Sri Lanka demanded new kinds of documentation and visibility. Following Jurgenson (2019), a wartime "documentary consciousness" was cultivated through practices of social evidencing. While judicial and forensic approaches demand specificities that determine legal admissibility, such efforts to document, collect, store, and informally archive even matters of hearsay and rumor were undertaken to counteract perpetrator denials and prepare for future truth-and-justice investigations, if there were any. Photography was sporadic and vulnerable in this regard when personal cameras were rare and visual records of violence were deemed potentially incendiary by the government given that such images were regarded as capable of producing violence that did not serve the state. Photography in public spaces, particularly those deemed sensitive by the government, was largely prohibited during the war as a safeguard against potential LTTE surveillance. Even today, restricted areas, especially in northern Sri Lanka, which have been designated as HSZs, feature signage barring photography. Even so, everyday snapshooters turned their cameras to make note and to communicate the observable facts of violence around them through photographic means. Similarly, as explored in the preceding chapters, unintended, fragmented repositories of leftover photographs gathered in studios, where loss and displacement charged photographic remains with the weight and history of war.

This long history of political violence and human rights violations ensured complex layers and interactions of internationalization and extended to the oversight of international media, global human rights and advocacy organizations, the United Nations and its various organs monitoring human rights and conflict. The Sri Lankan state began to conflate this range of interests as an international scourge against its autonomy. This was exacerbated by the transnational founding and function of Tamil militant groups. For instance, the LTTE's global network and economy was renowned, feared, and regularly maligned in Sri Lanka, in no small part due to illicit activities of fraud, extortion, money laundering, cyberattacks, arms smuggling, and human and drug trafficking. Amid this, the Tamil struggle became simultaneously geographically located in the aspiration of Tamil Eelam, but deterritorialized through its aspiring globally dispersed ethno-citizenry through movement of people and the interlinked migrant economies, polities, and camaraderie. As observed in the memoir of Adele Balasingham recounting the early years of the liberation struggle led by the Tigers, "It was an age of revolutions: Britain was wracked by the extreme left politics of trade union power and militancy; many Third World countries in Africa, central and South America waged national liberation struggles for freedom from the archaic institutions of colonialism and the economic rape of imperialism" (2001, 30). London, notably, became a base for Tamil political activism and advocacy with the formation of Marxist-inspired political and student groups committed to ideas of decolonization, transnational solidarity, and third world friendship.

The Tamil Information Center (TIC) was established during this time, in 1983, as a focal point for the collection and documentation of information and resources related to human rights, as well as the social, cultural, and political life of the Tamil-speaking people of Sri Lanka. The TIC countered disinformation where there was a serious threat to freedom of expression and association in Sri Lanka. The TIC declined affiliation with political or militant organizations to work across ideologies, stating that a "mission is to empower people, particularly those suffering persecution and subjected to human rights abuses, valuing the distinct identities and differences among them and to improve the quality of life through access to knowledge" (TIC 2024). As a part of this commitment, the TIC collected, processed, and filed thousands of documents and visual materials, including newspapers, journals, magazines, reports, affidavits, habeas corpus applications, letters from detainees, political prisoners, and war victims, eyewitness statements and testimony, photographs, audio and video recordings, and even drawings dispatched from the war zone. Driven by its inimitable executive director, the late Mr. V. Varadakumar, an equivalent repository likely does not exist elsewhere in the world and certainly not in Sri Lanka itself. Following Mr. Varadakumar's sudden death in 2019, the TIC became embroiled in substantial operational challenges, which led to the dismantling of its substantial archive and library, now placed in storage.

The TIC was, however, not entirely isolated in this regard, with internet-based counterparts such as Sangam, Tamilnation, TamilNet, and Noolaham becoming established in the 1990s and 2000s. Sangam, the web archive of the Ilankai Tamil Sangam of the United States of America, an association of Tamils from the island of Sri Lanka residing in the United States of America formed in 1977, has engaged in archiving English-language news items and articles published online since 1996. In line with its aim to "publicize facts about the condition and welfare of the Tamil-speaking people of Sri Lanka" and "foster the growth and development of art, culture, economy, human rights and general welfare of Tamils and Tamil-speaking people resident in the Island known now as Sri Lanka," the extensive archive is an invaluable resource (Ilankai Tamil Sangam, USA, 2024). News and scholarly articles focused on the Tamil issues are swiftly reproduced and archived on the website for posterity alongside decades' worth of commentary, op-eds, and out of print books. Tamilnation (1998–2009), founded by Nadesan Satyendra, is an extensive virtual storehouse of materials spanning 6,000 webpages pertaining to Tamil politics and culture, where the website's philosophy affirms, "Tamils are today a trans state nation. They are a nation without a state" ([1998] 2009).

Similarly, the Noolaham Digital Library and the Noolaham Multimedia Archive founded by Rathina Iyer Pathmanaba Iyer, a pioneer of digitalizing Tamil archival materials, and maintained by the Noolaham Foundation founded in 2005, is an invaluable virtual repository. It was "created with a view to documenting, preserving and disseminating texts and sources that speak about the social, economic, cultural and political discourses related to the Sri Lankan Tamil-speaking communities," in acknowledgment of the reality that "sites of knowledge production and knowledge preservation of the Tamil-speaking communities such as the Jaffna Public Library have been lost" and that these materials were at continued endangerment and risk (Noolaham 2024). Noolaham is importantly a digital library and a digital archive that emphasizes community leadership, stewardship, and ownership and is based out of Jaffna with international chapters. It is in the process of implementing a vast undertaking of archiving and digitization of printed materials extending from newspapers to periodicals and books. These transnational community-driven virtual projects also mark the early adoption of the digital and the internet as a site for preservation and dissemination, though the future of these online repositories, especially those managed by dedicated, but elderly, individuals are also inexorably uncertain. This is clear from the fate of Tamilnation, which while still accessible online, ceased its archiving in 2009 due to the founder's changed personal circumstances.

More explicitly cartographically conceived repositories of information also took shape through internet cemeteries. As a part of its postwar reconfiguration of the landscape of the northeast of Sri Lanka, the Sri Lankan state razed all signs of the LTTE. This included the destruction of the sprawling and numerous *thuyilum illams* where Tiger cadres were interred, in what constitutes a war crime. While the physical sites are no more, these graveyards have found a home(land) on the internet. Spanning hundreds of pages, *Veeravengaikal* (Heroes) hosts a visual archive of the names, photographs, hometowns, and "date(s) of martyrdom" of the many thousands of LTTE cadres who died between 1982 and 2009. The virtual *thuyilum illam* refers to the specific geographic locations in which the physical spaces now destroyed once were. Analog-digital reproduction and embellished hybrid portraits flanked by downturned, capped guns identify each fighter. Where photographs, personal or official, are not available, martyrs are represented by the image of headstone bearing a *karthigai* flower or the LTTE's growling tiger icon. These simulated graveyards are linked to a Facebook page for mourners, thus continuing to shape new forms of sociality in a virtual Tamil Eelam.

Digital archival endeavors have principally focused on the written word. Photographs were only afforded incidental attention, explained in part by their wider scarcity. In their early activities, the quality of digitized analog images could not be retained due to limitations in the technologies of capture and reproduction. Similarly, high-resolution visual material takes up more storage space and was harder to process, upload, and download in a time of dial-up internet. Securing adequate storage for visual digital material is also costly. While associated technologies and internet speeds have substantially improved alongside an increased interest and focus, the visual, early digitized images, gradually stripped through digital reproduction, are sometimes only barely viewable on high-definition screens or when re-materialized through printing. Even such reduced images continue to be shared. Hito Steyerl writes, "Poor images . . . testify to the violent dislocation, transferals, and displacement of images—their acceleration and circulation within the bitter cycles of audiovisual capitalism. Poor images are dragged around the globe as commodities or their effigies, as gifts or as bounty. They spread pleasure or death threats, conspiracy theories or bootlegs, resistance or stultification" (2009). The poor images of Sri Lanka's war continue to circulate precisely on account of the violent dislocations necessitated by war, but also the imperatives of a desire to preserve lest acknowledgment and justice for the aggrieved might require evidence. This is where volatility further lends itself to community, solidarity, and responsibility untethered from the state. Just as iconic images such as Amarasinghe's photographs of Black July or Shyam Tekwani's portraits of Prabhakaran endure in constant digital reproduction and online recursion, the continual reproduction of poor images also perseveres. These photographs persist as atemporal stencils that account for abiding violence.

What is remarkable about the ad hoc collection of photographic materials gathered by the TIC is its ordinariness. In their lack of professional or photojournalistic polish or precision, they convey, significantly, the banality of violence experienced by Tamils in Sri Lanka. The jumble of professional and amateur photographs that belonged to the TIC were kept in brown manilla envelopes and faux leather-bound albums of the kind that might typically hold memories of beloveds—except that they contained inventories of death, injury, and destruction, bearing handwritten labels such as "Killings," "Air Raid Killings," "Persons killed/Injured in [year]," "Destruction of Property," and "Refugees." I encountered continuations of these blunt classifications in computer folders of recent digital photographs collected by those engaged in advocacy work related to the final phase of the war. A click of a "war photos" folder yielded graphic offerings of "Body Parts," "Corpses Lying Around," "Executions," and "Hospital Dead or Injured" compiled in anticipation of future justice. The types of images encountered in these paper and plastic containers represent the breadth of photographic genres encountered in the preceding chapters, direct and indirect records and categorizations of violence directed against Tamils in Sri Lanka. It validates, once more, how diverse everyday photographies were taken up into war but also imagined as evidencing and countering state narratives beyond the local.

The producers and senders of these images are unknown. However, it is a photography of the concerned.[2] There is no visible desire to claim these images or assert authorship or ownership because asserting witness or proximity to violence was dangerous. These are the outputs of those who had access to the convenience and power of a camera and were willing to risk the task of photographing. They are largely rushed, occasionally blurry or underexposed, haphazardly composed, and lacking the photojournalistic polish and framing of media images. Death is itemized by eerie photographs taken in hospital beds, morgues, coffins, and visceral images of violent massacre, dismemberment, scorch and rot, as well as identity headshots and commonplace snapshots. Charred, bombed-out buildings are shown in sometimes hazy records. Shattered and bloodied household interiors of homes hollowed out by shells are pictured alongside burning shops. Displacement and the dire situation of IDP and refugee camps in Sri Lanka and South India are documented. The backs of the images are sometimes annotated by hand in Tamil or English, presumably by their takers, collectors, and dispatchers, and stamped as received and sorted by TIC. Tamil protests against state violence in Sri Lanka and the UK make up their own bundles. Intermittent images of the landscape also emerge to locate this violence. The movement of these photographs from Sri Lanka to the UK bear material signs in airmail envelopes, stamps, and postal redirection via activist, human rights, and relief organizations in Sri Lanka, Madras (Chennai), and the UK. It is a physical assemblage of photographs that would not be out of place on an algorithmically produced grid, sanitized of atrocity images by the demands of internet safety guidelines, clustered under #tamilgenocide. In fact, similar images, scanned, re-photographed, and reposted, can easily be found on various social media platforms.

SRI LANKA ONLINE

Through the first decade of the 2000s, current affairs and personal blogging and photography-focused websites, such as Flickr, were in their heyday with virtual communities forming around now defunct aggregate websites, as well as citizen media and news blogs maintained by journalists and independent commentators. Additionally, digital photography and more affordable and accessible cameras paired with access to internet-based sharing had also led to a revival in amateur photography. This allowed enthusiasts to showcase their work online. These collectives soon transitioned to social media platforms still in their early years with relatively limited reach and audience. Yet eventually, notably Twitter (X), Flickr, Facebook, and subsequently Instagram unlocked new avenues for dissemination, allowing amateur photographers, photojournalists, citizen journalists, and activists in Sri Lanka to reach a new, global audience. They permitted lively real-time discussions to happen not just locally but internationally among Sri Lankans at home and abroad, and for images to be shared without the interventions of mainstream media and publication restrictions. The internet also afforded the option of anonymity.

The kinds of photographic and other documentation such as those preserved by the TIC moved to new circuits of cataloging and visibility in pseudonymous blogs, Flickr galleries, and tweets, which amplified their volatility. On Flickr, photographs of displacement and war, uploaded by accounts managed by activists, nongovernmental organizations, and advocacy groups posted on long abandoned accounts, remain in internet graveyards to this day. Trophy images taken by soldiers were acquired and published online, providing evidence on war crimes. Galleries and albums with titles such as "Sri Lanka Soldier War Crimes" and "Sri Lanka War Crime Photos—Crimes Committed by Soldier" can be easily located by an internet search. Where freedom of expression was curtailed and mainstream media was heavily censored, the war was also written and discussed in these Sri Lanka–centered internet spaces, largely the purview of English-speakers though local language content was not wholly absent. While there was little visible public remonstration in Sri Lanka against the Sri Lankan government's Vanni operation and the vast civilian casualties, everyday tensions and ardent disagreements spilled over onto the internet. What was most significant here is that such online spaces eliminated any appearance of political cohesion or homogeneity, permitting a range of supportive, concerned, critical, and dissenting views from Tamil, Sinhalese, and Muslim communities in Sri Lanka and abroad to emerge. Such representation and texture had been largely absent in government- and LTTE-dominant media narratives, where there was little offline space for denunciation or disagreement.

Today, more than sixteen years after the war ended, images and visual invocations of war still frequently resurface on Instagram, Twitter (X), and Facebook shared by a generation of young Tamils who had been young children in Sri Lanka or in the diaspora during the final years of war. Similarly, Tamil social photographers and activists in northern Sri Lanka look to these platforms to directly share their visual evidence of violence with a global audience, where they become unintentionally archived.

#FIELDNOTESFROMJAFFNA

When I began fieldwork in northern Sri Lanka, I started documenting various, often humdrum, daily happenstances largely for the benefit of family and friends filed under the hashtag #fieldnotesfromjaffna (field notes from Jaffna) on Instagram. However, this effort in personal documentation intended for friends, through photographs accompanied by a few stray written observations, garnered me a new following of interlocutors in an unforeseen way. These included those in Jaffna and abroad who were curious about what my work in the north entailed based on the photographs I posted. My ethnicity as perceived by last name, its seeming incongruence with my current location, political views, and language skills were repeatedly observed and queried by strangers on the internet in a way that mirrored offline social interactions. It was not long before these strangers also began sending me personal and sometimes despondent recollections of homes and towns they had been compelled to leave behind. Messages such as "I keep looking at your page, because you put so many pics from Jaffna right. I always had that feeling of finding memories back from your pics," collected in my inbox. Some even shared family photographs and their memories of their hometowns, while others who had been born abroad were delighted by these Instagram dispatches about their parents' and grandparents' home. Many found political resonance and solidarity in the things that I had posted as I attended protests and commemorations. What I could not have anticipated is the unintended and powerful role social photography played in forging the exchanges and solidarities that became formative in helping me imagine the possibilities of and for this work and identifying a community that sought and connected itself to the homeland by social photography.

Established in 2010, Instagram was intended originally for photography emulating analog film and particularly polaroid-inspired practices through an invocation of instantaneity coupled with grainy, nostalgic filters. Instagram's image-sharing now extends to a broad repertoire of still and moving digital images that, at present, take the form of single image or multiple image posts, video reels, and time-limited stories. Without specialist knowledge or skills, users can capture, upload visual and audiovisual media in the form of single or multiple image posts, videos, and music-augmented reels. These can be enhanced through various editing tools and filters and categorized and connected to a wider collection of posts by way of user-generated hashtags and geotags that permit for posts to be positioned on a map. While the blogging platforms Flickr and Facebook had already established image-sharing through photography uploads and virtual galleries and albums, Instagram users were able to take, alter, and share personal photographs directly from their smartphones. This led to the formation of new social photographic genres and popular photographic aesthetics, alongside new modes of interaction, audiences, socialities, and communities tethered to photography and image-making and sharing.

The ability to edit images and use filters on a smartphone enabled amateur photographers to elevate their photography in step with professional photographers, while aspiring and professional photographers, artists, and other creative practitioners were able to readily share their work with a global audience without formal representation through a gallery or the resource commitment of organizing a public exhibition. By creating a profile on the platform, a user can upload their own content, browse others' contents by hashtags and geotags, view posts that are popular or trending, as well as "for you" content tailored to individual users by way of the application's algorithm. A user can interact with other users through public forms of interaction and communication such as following their accounts, liking and commenting on their posts, re-posting, tagging users in stories, posts, or comments, and posting shared content. I draw specific attention to the political utility of hashtags and geotags as a means of organizing the photocartographic through this chapter. Hashtags have played a significant role in internet community formation and the development of social movements and political organizing on platforms such as Twitter (X), as seen during #BlackLivesMatter and #MeToo. The app also permits for technologically mediated co-presence whereby users can "go live" and be joined by other users. Live streaming by way of an internet-enabled device such as a smartphone allows users to create, watch, and transmit videos in real time without needing to record and store the contents first, enhancing the app's capacity for immediacy, also influencing how news is produced and disseminated.

The platform allows for private, direct communication through audio, visual, and text messaging, view-once photo-sharing, voice, and video calling. Users are also able to post Stories, which can be viewed on their accounts for a period of twenty-four hours, or beyond, if saved as a highlight. When a user logs on to the app, they see a feed composed of photos and videos shared by users they follow as well as advertisements and "suggested" posts as determined by Instagram's algorithm. New features are regularly rolled out to maintain its competitiveness in relation to other popular image-sharing apps such as TikTok and Snapchat. The app's capacities and uses change regularly. Instagram users can control who sees their content, by choosing to keep their accounts private and only visible to those whom they allow to follow, or they can make the accounts public, for all viewers. Users are also able to control what they see on the app by muting, restricting, or blocking other users by modulating or preventing contact. Instagram also upholds "community guidelines," which in short state, "We want Instagram to continue to be an authentic and safe place for inspiration and expression. Help us foster this community. Only post your own photos and videos and always follow the law. Respect everyone on Instagram, don't spam people or post nudity" (Meta 2024). This extends to only sharing images users have taken or have the right to share, images deemed "appropriate" to diverse audiences, abiding by the law, preventing content glorifying self-injury, graphic violence, spam, and maintaining respectful interactions (2024).

Community guidelines must be grasped in relation to Meta's Facebook platform coming under repeated scrutiny for its role in electoral manipulation, inciting violence, propagating hate speech, and disinformation and misinformation, especially where investments in local language content moderation is limited. Accordingly, users can report offending posts that are then reviewed and potentially removed. Repeated offenses can lead to accounts being restricted or deleted. Instagram states, "In some cases, we allow content for public awareness that would otherwise go against our Community Guidelines—if it is newsworthy and in the public interest. We do this only after weighing the public interest value against the risk of harm, and we look to international human rights standards to make these judgments" (Meta 2024). In 2018, Facebook was accused of and compelled to apologize for its role in exacerbating anti-Muslim violence in Sri Lanka in 2016 due to the spread of hate speech and detrimental rumors. Facebook also instituted an independent human rights impact assessment. The Sri Lankan government has repeatedly blocked access to Facebook, as well as other Meta platforms including Instagram and WhatsApp, during episodes of postwar communal violence, including the 2018 Digana riots and in the aftermath of the 2019 Easter Sunday attacks to curb incitement and the spread of rumors.

INSTAGRAMMING EELAM

On Instagram, Tamil Eelam, as imagined and visualized by eponymous use-generated geotags, makes up an atlas of photographs tethering the globally dispersed Tamil community (fig. 27).

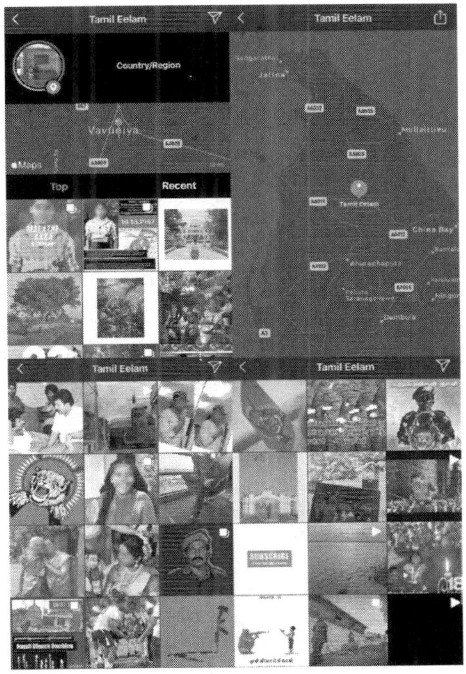

FIGURE 27. Screen capture of the public images tethered to the Tamil Eelam geotag on Instagram, 2020

Tidy photographic squares reveal a dynamic mosaic of life and death. These are pinned not only to a handful of mapped locations in the northeast of Sri Lanka, but the streets of France, Switzerland, Germany, and Denmark. The borderless Tamil Eelam was lived and possible everywhere. It is as if the nation and its desire for an independent state, for cartographic acknowledgment, had been carried outward in visual form in the hands of the many thousands who had been compelled to leave their country behind. Snapshots of the beauty of the landscape, sweet family photographs, opulent wedding pictures, joyous selfies locating photographers within or as belonging to the homeland, and diasporic successes in film, music, and media as well as sport and dance are interspersed with images of protest and commemoration, digitized recirculations of memorial portraits and thematic illustrations, artwork, memes, and historical images. Atrocity is euphemized and minimized through the limitations of "community guidelines," either visualized by other means through a focus on the material debris of war, the injured landscape, the suffering of those still alive but harmed at the time of being photographed or recast into other visual forms such as drawing and illustration.

In this internet republic, bite-sized political histories and ambitions mingle with personal recollection, remembrance, and mourning visualized by young Tamils in Sri Lanka and abroad. The red and yellow colors, iconography, and the heroic portraiture and combat photographs of Tamil Tiger *veeravengaikkal* (heroes) and *maaveeravengaikkal* (great heroes or martyrs), as well as images of distress, artistic rearticulations and those associated with accounts dedicated to sharing archival materials, histories, and counter-histories of Tamil resistance ripple through this congregation. New kinds of social evidencing emerge from this panoply, underscoring the enduring violence of the postwar. They echo afflictions to the landscape of the Tamil homeland through militarization, land grabs, surveillance, threats and intimidation by the armed forces, the Sinhalization of the landscape through the construction of Buddhist temples, military infrastructure, and the imposition of Sinhalese place names. The distributed hashtags and geotags of Tamil Eelam form a fluid photographic constellation that is regularly rearranged and recirculated "for you" by the invisible hand of Instagram's algorithm. The "trans state nation" on Instagram is visibly built on collective loss, dislocation, relocation, and longing, but also lasting aspirations for belonging and sovereignty still tethered to the landscape of Sri Lanka's northeast despite its largely diasporic incidence.

This virtual nation is always embellished with the persistent iconography of the Tigers, though such posts are regularly removed due to the group's international proscription. Although the Tamil community's relationship to the authoritarian Tigers is fraught at best, the group's effort at contriving a Tamil nation/state and ideal citizenry over the decades left an impression on the vocabulary and aesthetics of Tamil political articulation and in the use and mobilization of photographic images. This iconography of Tamil nationalism is hypervisible on Instagram even though images associated with the LTTE are banned from the platform due to associations with terrorism. Indeed, these images are predominantly if not entirely shared by diasporic Tamils removed from the restrictions of survival within Sri Lanka's repressive environment. As Thiranagama perceptively notes, "The younger generations who grew up with the LTTE as a repressive quasi-state rather than a liberation group saw the LTTE not as a vehicle for meaningful utopianism but only as a pragmatic necessity. This means that they may not rush to resuscitate it now, unlike diasporic youth for whom it is utopian still" ([2011] 2013, 40–41). For those in Sri Lanka who were sympathetic to the *Iyakkam*, fear of repercussion was also ever present, where their views had to be guarded rather than shared. However, social media and the internet also afforded the option of anonymity, which was sometimes preferred. Strains between those resident in Sri Lanka, for whom the stakes of political expression and negotiations of impaired citizenship are immediate, and those elsewhere, idealizing the political possibility of Tamil Eelam, also played out in these competing social photographies. The aspiration for a nation-state as delineated by the LTTE endures in the aesthetics of the de facto state.

At first glance, it might be argued that the global Tamil public's continuance of de facto state-centered image-based practices instituted by an aspiring state actor, the LTTE, merely affirms Tagg's emphasis on photography's role in processes of ideological regulation (1988). By contrast, I would stress the unlikely ways in which the volatile social photography of the postwar, in everyday improvisations and mitigations, permits insight into political divergences within the Tamil community that were difficult to express during the war on account of self-censorship, fear, or the resolve to project political unanimity. Ideological disagreements often led to claims of treachery and betrayal, as well as potentially deadly reprisal (see Thiranagama 2010). What becomes clear in the social photography of the postwar is greater freedom and space for discussing the complexities of war and choosing armed resistance, the entanglements of the personal and the political, and what those futures might look like in the face of ongoing uncertainty. This extends to the critique of the martial imperatives of the LTTE, especially by Tamils in Sri Lanka, who actively reflect on the group's suppression of dissenting voices, enactments of violence within and outside the Tamil community that hampered a diversity of political expression and aspiration as well as current impairments to their Sri Lankan citizenship. Where Tamil citizenship during the war has been described as "complex," postwar imaginings of belonging are equally stretched and complicated between home and elsewhere, of ideological allegiance and the freedom to challenge and critique (Brun 2008, 401).

For Tamils in Sri Lanka, citizenship, loosely defined as the relationship between the individual and the state premised through franchise and fundamental rights, remains unequal in the postwar, yet a separate state as defined by the LTTE is not necessarily or uniformly viewed as the automatic solution. In the mobilization of social photography, this tension of postwar citizenship, not only between state and citizen, but those Tamils who make up the "trans state nation," as termed by Satyendra, becomes immanently visible ([1998] 2009). It affords insight into everyday negotiations of the political and assertions of belonging that transcend the limits of an ethno-state. The

Tamil political future, in terms of nation, state, homeland, and citizenship, cannot be separated from the LTTE or conflict-induced transnational dispersal. But long-silenced disparate views on what that future might look like in practice and how these are actively discussed and navigated by those in Sri Lanka and abroad take visual shape through postwar social photography.

Despite the vivacious virtual impression made by Instagram, when I arrived in Jaffna in 2017, its use, locally, was still limited. This was partly on account of language, as English literacy was necessary to set up and navigate the platform. Instagram also required possessing a smartphone with a "good" camera. However, this changed rapidly in a matter of months, in no small part due to an incidental revival of photographic activity within the peninsula extending from storytelling initiatives to the eventual establishment of a photographic society in 2019. Although Facebook remains the social media platform of choice for many of my Tamil interlocutors in Sri Lanka, including aspiring and established photographers, Instagram facilitated an unexpected frame of interactions and connections with important methodological and theoretical bearing. When I began researching Tamil photographic practices, I did not explicitly set out to examine social media, but rather focused on the attendant ways in which these informed how photography was produced and shared. Yet online connections permitted a spatial and temporal extension of the "field" of study beyond the place and time frame of fieldwork as defined activity. My interlocutors were able to "follow" my work, just as I was able to keep in touch with them. I continue to open my Instagram, Twitter (X), or Facebook feeds to see what they are up to and/or to post and interact with them in various ways—just as they would with me. Some became invested in the progress of my writing, enthusiastically engaging with brief pieces of work or photographs from my time in the field that I posted online—even making the effort to translate these into Tamil for a wider audience. It is a potent reminder that both photography and writing ethnography can be the ongoing work of community and solidarity.

THE RESISTANCE WILL BE HASHTAGGED

In April 2018, in an unprecedented act of bravery, a women-led group of Iranaitheevu residents reclaimed their homes following twenty-six years of forced displacement. In 1992, following intense fighting between the Sri Lankan Navy and the Sea Tigers (the naval wing of the LTTE), 650 islanders were compelled to flee to Iranaimathanagar. Although the island itself was not touched by the fighting, the Sri Lankan Navy continued their occupation of the island by building and settling in a camp. On 23 April 2018, 350 community members, including men, women, children, civil society activists, and a group of Catholic priests and nuns led by the Women's Development Society, organized in secret, piled into forty-four motorboats fastened with white flags and set sail to the island following a series of protests that were ignored by the government. The navy chose not to intervene, and the community finally relocated to their long-abandoned homes despite various hardships. Mariyaseeli, one of the women who led the charge, said to me, "We have waited twenty-six years for this, and even though rebuilding is difficult, and we have nothing, we will not be discouraged. We are here to stay, and Iranaimatha [Mother of Iranai, the island's patron saint, the Virgin Mary] has kept our home safe for us." This chance encounter with this warm, welcoming, and defiant community remains, to me, one of the most hopeful and inspiring of my research to date.

I visited the island for the first time with two activists from Jaffna and Colombo, who wanted to see how the residents were settling in. The community was very interested in how news of their protest had been covered. After an hour on a small fishing boat belonging to one of the fishermen from the community, we arrived at the picturesque island dotted with five little churches and various community buildings dating back to the late 1800s. Beneath these was a sophisticated water storage system for rainwater, which permitted the community self-sufficiency. The decision to defiantly return had been motivated by the fact that life on the mainland had hampered these Iranaitheevu women's economic independence, as they had previously made a lucrative living out of diving for sea cucumbers and mussels. No one in the community had a camera in hand. Since I had my DSLR with me, they were eager to show us around and have their efforts to rebuild documented. Upon my return a couple of months later, I distributed the photographs that I had printed, which they received and discussed enthusiastically. One of the activists had printed out international and local news coverage of the community's return so that the community might keep them. "Was it also on Facebook?" one of the community members asked. "Bring us those too if you can, please." The possibilities for dissemination were not merely recognized by young users, but by those who had heard of its powers for transmission. Difficulties and restrictions to access due to military controls mean that Iranaitheevu is very rarely visited by outsiders, with informal injunctions in place preventing those without a Sri Lankan

NIC from traveling to the island. Even so, on Instagram, #Iranaitheevu and its spelling variants yield a handful of images from citizen journalists and the few visitors, including myself, in an entanglement of faith, landscape, and resistance through pictured churches, icons, and protest.

Only a day prior, during the 2018 Mullivaikkal commemoration, mourners, civil society activists, and citizen journalists actively engaged in social photography. They reflected on and decried the devastation of the day. Meanwhile, others took selfies against the brightly colored banners covered with images of dead children and maimed adults to document their participation in this new ritual of nation, resilience, and survival. While immediately jarring, the photos suggested solidarity and remembrance as an act of resistance and an assertion of nation and identity that had become so inherently bound to the violences inflicted upon it. Tamil Eelam, a dispersed nation and desired homeland, was thus sustained in hashtags and geotags that stake denied political claims. The hashtags #mullivaikkal, #tamileelam, #eelam, #tamil, #freetamileelam, #tamilgenocideday, #may18tamilgenocide, #remembranceisresistance, #remember2009, #weremember #weresist suture the local images to a global constellation of hundreds of images posted on Instagram, Facebook, and Twitter (X). This homeland accommodated diverse expressions of belonging rooted in the landscape as well as the desire for a sovereign state. It comprised a parallel digital public bound to an imagined nation that existed virtually in the form of a geotag and various hashtags. The hashtags and geotags constituted, in virtual iconographies and photocartographies at least, a home and aspiring nation-state containing more wide-ranging political possibility than before, as imagined by thousands of Tamils from Sri Lanka. The homeland, for many, exceeds the machinations of governance. In its soil, its language, its community, and importantly its volatile photographies, it exists, transcends, and is felt and claimed. The demand for an authoritative bordering of the ethno-state as an exertion of power rather than freedom is only one facet of how this homeland exists. The nation-state is merely what is desired institutionally. As Michael Warner suggests, this was not merely a pre-defined public bound by the media that it consumed, and one constituted through this very circulation, but made up in the space of Instagram by users' media itself (2002, 69). The digital, in the re-photographing of these acts of resistance centered on photography, and through its disseminatory platforms, allowed greater amplification, extending and consolidating the nation beyond the territorial limits of the state through a network of hashtags.

In an early example of internet community formation as well as digital anthropological inquiry into Tamil internet socialities, Pradeep Jeganathan considers the "stretching, fragmenting form of the contemporary nation" through an examination of Tamil Eelam's relationship to "webspace" (1998, 515). Flagging the "rootlessness" of the LTTE, Jeganathan notes its "placelessness" that is "equidistant from everywhere, not quite anywhere" despite the imperative of its hyper-located claim (1998, 525). Three decades later, Jeganathan's words are prescient in how we might view the dispersed, virtual photocartography of Tamil Eelam. "It cannot simply become an organization that intersects with 'Tamils' all over the world," Jeganathan emphasizes, "for then it would lose that one idea, that so many of its supporters have died for and paid for: that small piece of land in northeastern Sri Lank—the nation as bounded territory" (1998, 525). With social media as well as user-generated capacities to enhance and construct online maps, Tamil Eelam has found a more defined, photocartographic form. It is made tangible by accounts of "lived place" by expectant citizens who give social and political texture to its simultaneously located and transnational manifestation. It coexists with a virtual cartographic layer that also imagines the northeast as part of Sri Lanka, concurrent Tamil photographies entangled and in conversation and debate through images, captions, hashtags, and geotags echoing the complexities and contradictions of the Tamil political imagination.

However, such political expression was not without tension or censorship, as nationalist squabbles and even threats of violence regularly played out in comment sections and direct messages. Instagram's community guidelines which allow users to report images they believed to be offensive or harmful resulted in images hashtagged or geotagged under #TamilEelam or #LTTE being reported and taken down as the group remains proscribed in the EU, UK, and North America, among others. Improvisations such as the use of Tiger emoji (🐅, 🐯) or the use of Tamil text were also likely to encourage the policing of the spaces in which they occurred. A Jaffna-based interlocutor whose account was suspended for posting personal photographs, including one showing a Tiger cadre, said, "I'll try my best to do it in my capacity. Somehow, I feel we have a duty to pass this history with all the ups and downs to the next generation." Indeed, where this history, particularly within Sri Lanka, was absented from textbooks and is regarded as inconsequential within more global framings, social media provided an avenue for recordkeeping, learning, transmission, discussion and continued social evidencing of past and present state crimes and violence.

This largely diaspora-dominated narrative was not without steadily increasing nascent photographic contributions from Tamils across Sri Lanka that interrogated Tamil home, identity, and citizenship as "Sri Lankan." In Jaffna, for amateur photographers, all in their twenties when we first met in 2018, using photography and social media was a means to get to grips with their own histories and experiences of war while forming online and offline communities. The harsh realities of the postwar and threats of state violence have also meant that there is little desire to romanticize resistance where the violence of war continues to be lived and felt intimately. Many Tamils in northern Sri Lanka actively look beyond Sri Lanka to secure their futures. A consequence of war and the unsafety of the postwar is that young Tamil men, in particular, are still regarded as threats and suspects. In addition, a lack of opportunity pervades the wider global south in a time of economic crisis. This condition is also essentially a failure of citizenship, where an accrual of ethnicized impairments has resonance for what is feasible through democratic process. Tamil citizens' involvement in any activity deemed explicitly political by the state security forces is constantly inspected and becomes the basis for routine arrest and torture as warning. Even within such an oppressive climate and a general lack of supportive infrastructure and resources, creative expression in various forms has also begun to blossom, with young Tamil artists from the northeast achieving local and international success through their work responding to and critiquing a history and present of violence. The artists signal renewed articulations of veiled resistance, endurance, and critique of the status quo that might not be immediately perceptible but are present and potent in their artwork.

Within such a context coupled with easier access to phones and cameras, social photography emerged as a space where social evidencing of the postwar is most visible. A photo-stories initiative, founded in Jaffna by Dhanushan, was invested in using photography as a tool for empowerment and bringing together a photographic community to document and interrogate lived histories, presents, and possibilities for the future together. Dhanushan, a remarkable and charismatic university student and native of Jaffna who worked in Colombo, commuted to his hometown each weekend to voluntarily run the free program for those interested in learning more about photography. The program was based at a foreign aid–funded community space. This involvement also conveyed the range of bilateral and multilateral international interventions extended to foster "capacity-building" for peace and reconciliation where Sri Lanka was positioned as a post-conflict success story. These initiatives took shape in the form of arts and culture-based initiatives as had become common in the postwar. Using Instagram as well as various online photo-story tools such as Adobe Spark, over the course of about three months, each group discussed social photography initiatives from around the world, their shared history, and learned not only the basics of photography but how to use the medium to tell stories. The program culminated in an individual photo story that each participant researched and presented to the group. The war pervaded the photographs from this diverse group of mostly young people from Jaffna and others who commuted from as far as Kilinochchi.

Alumni of the group have gone on to set up their own photography projects, with topics ranging from documenting the fading traditional livelihoods in Jaffna and reflections on war to celebrations of the local life and landscape. Dhanushan is an active Instagram user. He posts photographs of Jaffna's social life, portraits of persons, and landscapes from his travels around the island and abroad. These images offer glimpses of a past and present whittled by war, dwelling on the necessary conversations that were being sidestepped in favor of nationalist demands or political avoidance. The photographs imagined the possibility for a Tamil political future within the parameters of "Sri Lanka," with sharp, but thoughtful, critique of the impairments and inequalities that shaped Tamil citizenship and the necessity for a political solution through representative politics. Dhanushan's own politics, in my understanding at the time, were critical of the state and Sinhalese majoritarianism but hopeful, focused on reconciliation and peacebuilding, whereby common ground might be found. His photography focused on those surviving, despite these tensions, who demand equality and recognition within Sri Lanka.

Haran, a young professional, set up his Instagram account as a means of using photography to supplement his long-time blog. Haran noted he was "seeking the faces of the day workers and registering their stories" through portraiture and narratives. His other social media–driven efforts, carried out alongside fellow bloggers, were more explicitly political, and sought to assert the uncomfortable truths and realities of the postwar pertaining to demands for justice as well as preserving accounts of the war as a part of the Tamil community's history on Instagram and Facebook. For example, "the war dictionary" by Oorukai (lime pickle), a civic media initiative that reports on local events as well as historical narratives, dubbed itself a "side dish of democracy." One of its Instagram projects documented the colloquial vocabulary associated with the war, using text and images. These included Tamil or adopted English words for fighter aircrafts, bunker, checkpoint, Army IC (photo identity card issued by the army), *vandu sooththu* (turning beetle, meaning surveillance aircrafts), as well as demands made on Tamil bodies such as "hands-up" (army orders to raise hands in order to carry out a full body search) and *thalayadi* (head-shaker or person in the military vehicle brought around to betray supporters during roundups).

The photographs of others were more ethnonationalist in their intonation but restrained by state surveillance. Collectively, these social photographers documented state violence to the landscape and people, as well as ongoing #Sinhalization and #Militarization, where images were sometimes meaningfully hashtagged and geotagged as Tamil Eelam. It is essential to mention that the period following former President Gotabaya Rajapaksa's election occasionally permanently scuppered such critique, with accounts focused on social evidencing becoming abandoned in fear and self-censorship. Notable among these was an account on Instagram and Twitter (X) of a Tamil citizen journalist named Garikaalan whose ground reports of past and ongoing state violence in the postwar shed important light on what was unreported in the mainstream Sri Lankan media. A mere three days after the 2019 election, in a great loss to critical local documentation and reporting from northern Sri Lanka, the account owner signed off with a final note that stated: "Decided to leave this platform for a while due to security concerns coupled with systematic racist-hatred-threatening campaign leveled against me soon after alleged war criminal @GotabayaR took office; deeply grateful for those who supported me in past. #Journalism_Is_Not_A_Crime."

Although social photography afforded a plethora of possibility and imagining, it was also, for reasons alluded to above, a site of danger. The internet and social sharing also led to direct encounters with state violence. A litany of social photography-related arrests targeting dissent has accumulated in recent years. In 2018, two young Tamil men were arrested for posting a Facebook photograph showing a government building. The same year, images of a leopard killed by a group of villagers in Kilinochchi sparked a days-long social media furor, indicating the "ethnic conflict" had not quite diminished. In 2020 and 2021, a Batticaloa-based journalist and a young Tamil man from Trincomalee were arrested under the provisions of the PTA for sharing photos of Prabhakaran on Facebook. Another young man was arrested in 2021 for sharing a photo relating to Maaveerar Naal. Tamil citizen journalists and media photographers documenting state threats and intimidation at protests are routinely harassed and threatened with arrest if not detained. New regulations such as the controversial 2024 Online Safety Bill alongside numerous arrests of critics of the state have further fueled fears about what can be shared on social media.

Postwar social photography also makes women photographers visible in a way that was not previously noticeable. While women assistants employed in Jaffna's male-dominated studios shied away from identifying themselves as photographers, among Jaffna's Instagrammers, young women were keen to document their lives and interests. "It is difficult to get around, and sometimes men will tease and laugh when they see me with a camera, but I am a feminist, and I will continue to take photographs," Kaushila a university student stated boldly. Many of her photographs captured women's labor in Jaffna, dwelling particularly on elderly women vendors at its bustling markets. She focused on the beauty of their coarsened hands against woven palmyra and glossy fruits and vegetables to evoke a theme of femininity as well as resilience. For Komathy, a twenty-three-year-old who mostly grew up in Kilinochchi, aside from various periods of displacement, photography, notably Instagram, was a means to draw attention to the challenges of navigating the postwar as a young Tamil woman and dwell on the "forgotten" beauty of her home that has for so long been associated with the horrors of conflict. "I want people to see that my village is beautiful and that it has a history that is not just defined by the war. I want to tell the stories of its residents and how proud they are of their homes, their fields, and their heritage." Those like Komathy were subject to criticism and even occasional threats by their Tamil peers abroad who believed that such idealizations were "misrepresentations" and "distractions" from the plight of Tamils and counterproductive to avowing the political necessity of Tamil Eelam. This foregrounds once more how photography is perceived to be politically generative, and how images of direct and indirect violence were still necessitated to underpin ethnonationalist claims.

In contrast to Jaffna's studios, this social photography was inspired by documentary realism, where easier access to the internet and information permitted amateur photographers to hone their techniques in line with international photojournalistic and documentary aesthetics. In Varun's computer, along with his many photographs, were internet tutorials that he had saved so that he could learn how to use his camera better. Having started off with a borrowed camera, he has since acquired his own to pursue documentary photography. Language remained a barrier where the world of

Instagram existed predominantly in English, but many of my interlocutors who started using the platform deftly studied and adopted the hashtags that existed almost entirely in English to afford their images greater visibility. Little technological shortcuts such as the ability to copy and paste text as well as translate using online tools were actively used to share their photographs and their lives pinned onto Jaffna's virtual map.

Social media also afforded a vibrant space for a local photographic community to form and interact in a manner that was perhaps not possible before. This was made evident in the founding of the Jaffna Photographic Society in 2019 by Tilaxan Tharmapalan, a young, dynamic, and talented Jaffna-based documentary photographer. The group quickly accumulated a Facebook membership of 3,500 individuals in less than a year and stands at 8,500 members in 2024. Members were encouraged to share their photographs, share skills, and participate in photography outings. The society has since held various exhibitions, including multiple iterations of a Jaffna Photography Festival and a Jaffna Vintage Photography Festival (2020). Much of this was on account of Tilaxan's tireless efforts and dedication to foster a community and encourage those who wished to learn. He regularly hosted workshops at his home and organized photo walks for anyone interested, even persevering through the Covid-19 lockdowns marked by island-wide curfews.

Tilaxan's own photographs delved into the war in immensely personal ways: He retraced his personal history to his birth village in the Vanni, which his family was forced to leave behind, contemplating through photography the shared scarring on the landscape as well as Tamil bodies. The homeland and its bodies wounded by war may no longer bleed, but the ugliness of mutilation, the deep, visceral pain felt by those who bear the marks of the wounds, cannot and must not be concealed. They are laid bare to the camera, echoing Allen Feldman's suggestion that the body serves "as the material and visual bearer of history" (2003, 65). Like Amarathaas, Tilaxan preferred black-and-white photographs to underscore the solemnity of the subjects he captured because the vividness of color distracted from the severity of their plight. In a cultural milieu where photographs, especially those produced by studios, were characterized by vibrancy and vividness, this choice, he stated, was latently political. In his haunting black-and-white portraits of Jaffna's senior citizens, he spoke to and photographed, among others, the destitute elderly who congregated at Jaffna's Hindu Temples; they had nowhere to go largely as a result of war. Tilaxan said that many of them had never had their photograph taken and were puzzled by why anyone would want to. When shown the photographs on the camera's display, they marveled at how *vadivu* they looked.

If Instagram offered a glimpse into the photocartographic representation of Tamil aspirations, it also encompassed the diversity, tensions, contradictions, and complexities of those personal and political desires and ambitions. Re-photographed old family photographs and studio portraits become conversation pieces for reflecting on displacement and dispossession. Street scenes offer prompts to critique militarization and "Sinhalization" through which the land of the northeast is transformed by state-sponsored development and heritage regimes. War crimes and crimes against humanity as debated over photographs of detritus of war and displacement still embedded in the Mullaitivu soil. Photographs of martyrs and LTTE cemeteries destroyed by the state are turned to anchors for #remembranceisresistance. Ongoing protests in response to enforced disappearance, land grabs, and expanding military presence and infrastructure in the northeast become anchors for continuities in Tamil resistance, sustaining political claims for the future. Though the photographs might be located in Jaffna, Batticaloa, Zurich, or Toronto, through the dispersed community, the geographically situated claim of nation is de-territorialized through its aspiring citizenry or in the least those who assert their roots and belonging to the Tamil homeland. This entanglement with conflict speaks to the dispersal of nation in a manner that vitalizes its territorial claims, complicating Ariella Aïsha Azoulay's (2008) analysis of photography's de-territorializing potentials. Counter to Azoulay, however, the civic skill in this instance was very much driven by the desire of a borderless nation for a located state or at least free homeland. State and homeland, however, as read through photography might not at present be synonymous.

The speed at which images are transmitted, made visible, and boosted through internet-based platforms distills transformations to Tamil sociality and polity. These circulations emphasize how the transnational character of the Tamil political imagination has fortified and dispersed a bordered claim of homeland. It is here that photography might show signs of being freed of its tether to the state, through connections to land and landscape as means to articulate inheritance, belonging, and even longing and dislocation that is perhaps deeper rooted than that of the nation-state and citizenship. It becomes then, importantly, also a critique of coloniality through its imperial, neoliberal, and postcolonial statist forms and goals. While the medium was integral to the consolidation of competing nation-state imaginaries, militarism, and securitization, it underscores the disruptive formation of de-territorialized communities and narratives that seek to eschew hegemonic representations and discourses. The social and political become increasingly interwoven with the digital as a decidedly transnational means of and site for possibility and precarity. Here, the transmission and continuity of images exhibit and enable new formations of nation and belonging to take place. It is a volatile photography of evidencing, but it is also a volatile photography of dreaming and imagining.

CONCLUSION

A PHOTOGRAPH OF A PHOTOGRAPH

In May 2019, I attended a discussion on the failures of Sri Lanka's transitional justice process in London hosted by the International Truth and Justice Project, alongside an exhibition of photography at the School of Oriental and African Studies. *War on Civilians* traced the final months of the war through a sequence of testimony collected from survivors of Mullivaikkal, maps, and photographs, including those captured by Amarathaas, paired with quotations from key United Nations reports (ITJP 2019). The images showed mass displacement and the horrors taking place amid the dark cloud of bombardment, as people sought shelter in bunkers, tents, and hospitals that would be eventually shelled. The event marked the tenth anniversary of the conclusion of the war. Demands for justice had been vocalized globally for a decade, but the demands were ineffectual, and justice was slow to be delivered by the reluctant but performative Sri Lankan state.

In the foyer, I was approached by a smiling young man in a baseball cap, who came up to me and asked forthrightly, "Are you Vindhya?" I was surprised and taken aback by this unexpected greeting, until he reminded me that about a year ago, we had a startling interaction on Instagram. "Your photograph confirmed to me that my *ammamma* [grandmother] had made it to heaven," he said. On 17 May 2018, the day before the Mullivaikkal commemoration, I visited a framing shop in Jaffna Town that I periodically frequented. Indran had been a frame-maker for nearly twenty-five years. That day, a memorial portrait of an elderly woman in a pale pink sari, which had not been collected, was placed in the vivid display among Hindu and Catholic divine images. Its composition and pale blue background suggested it was likely a re-purposed identity photograph. With Indran's permission, I took a picture of this evocative arrangement that potently summed up the way the dead and the divine coexisted in Jaffna's image world (fig. 28). Later that day, I posted the photograph on my Instagram page, hashtagged under #fieldnotesfromjaffna. Minutes later, I received a direct message from a stranger inquiring where the photograph had been taken. "That is my

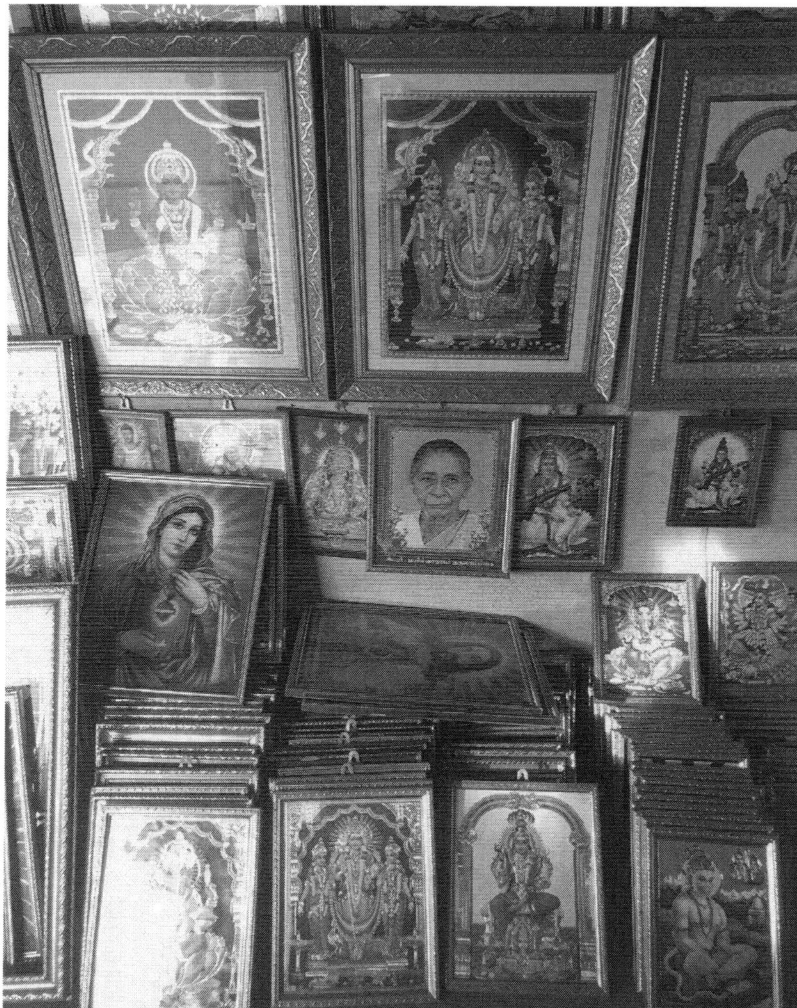

FIGURE 28. Janahan's grandmother's portrait among the gods (Jaffna, 2018)

ammamma in the middle," he wrote. Mortified, I responded, saying that I hope he was not offended and that I would take down the photograph immediately. "No, no. That's okay. When did you take this?" he pressed. "Just two hours ago," I replied. In return he responded with a photograph of an identical memorial portrait taken on 2 April, a month and half prior, set on a coffee table as part of a family's remembrance proceedings.

"This was from the thirty-first day thing." We gathered that Janahan's *ammamma*'s portrait may have been accidentally left behind at the framing shop, slipping the mind of a family member tasked with picking it up. "I was so surprised to be honest. Her picture was in the middle of all the gods. It made my month. It is so amazing. People have suggested my *ammamma* has reached heaven, and that is why she is in the middle of the gods. Thank you for letting me know that," he responded. Our conversation concluded after I emailed him the original photograph as a keepsake. Following this encounter in London, I learned that Janahan, who had grown up in Jaffna, had fled to the UK at the age of seventeen. His parents still lived there, but Janahan was unable to go back to Sri Lanka to lay his *ammamma* to rest. "I was only able to watch the funeral while I was at work as I was not allowed a day off," he later observed. Janahan had tuned in to the proceedings remotely on a WhatsApp video call during his shift at an Off License in Doncaster.

He had followed my Instagram account after encountering photographs from the hometown he was unable to return to. In a completely surreal turn of events, a photograph of a memorial portrait of his late *ammamma* would surprisingly wind up on his Instagram feed by way of a stranger from Colombo whom he had never met or interacted with. A year later, he unexpectedly crossed paths with that same stranger at a lecture in London examining the tribulations of Sri Lanka's postwar. A photograph of a photograph left in a framing shop on KKS Road in Jaffna was the beginning of our friendship. This spark of chance bound to the unruliness of photography underscored the extraordinary ways in which the local entangled with the transnational, the public with the private, the personal with the political, and death with the divine, as a result of the violent and intimate dispersals and connections of war. We remain friends to this day, our acquaintance formed out of the photograph of a photograph left behind in Indran's Picture Palace on KKS Road.

A Volatile Picture is a determined gathering of what cannot be easily contained and what has been or will be easily lost, threaded together with the potency of photography and what it makes politically possible for those who look to the camera to capture what they see and experience. In that spirit, I end on this fortuitous event of photography as the distillation of the essence of this book that hope in the political work of photography endures. Here, the political, the epistemic, and personal are inextricable and magnified through conflict. However, even when fear or despair threatens to overwhelm, confidence in the volatility, and thus possibility, of photography rarely wavers. It is an acknowledgment of how even if volatile pictures can and do precipitate state power and violence, their unruliness and mutability also permit for the repair and remedy that do not rely on the state and the institutional. Photography also makes community and friendship conceivable through its singular powers. Perhaps this is where the medium's potency can be conceived of beyond the state—in the liberatory possibilities of friendship, community, care, solidarity, and responsibility, which form outside and often in spite of it. Where truth and justice may feel out of reach amid ongoing terror or the outcomes of their labor may sometimes feel futile, it is community that sustains the political work of anticipation, trust, and courage. As Sabes one day observed, "People are gaining confidence from the journey of these photographs." If photography permits such expectations to be buoyed through dark times, its volatility may yet engender accountability and redress. In fact, it is yearned for deeply.

WHAT PICTURES CAN DO

Where the postwar has been defined by continued tension between the Sri Lankan state and the Tamil community, photography directly supplements a variety of personal and political improvisations to address citizenship impairments. Conflict continues to define and underpin the transnational economies of photographic production, echoing Tamil claims and experiences that the war in fact was not over. Spaces and communities of postwar civilian resistance and activism still form around photographs, both in the entangled offline and online. Image-making is wielded to make visible histories, counternarratives, political claims, injustices, and the state's violences and erasures. Where international processes for truth and accountability remain unmoved by the victims' appeals, mobilizations evidencing state violence flag the failures and disappointments of civic spectatorship and visibility in advancing claims to justice, often where global apparatuses designed to encourage accountability privileged the state as sovereign, even as the citizens of photography demanded action. Nevertheless, these acts of rendering visible were integral to the formation of transnational solidarities and political socialities, just as they are to still contending hegemonic discourses. Further, the volatile potentials of these photographs enabled critique and conversation around troubled politics, histories, and power. The ways that diverse individual efforts and shared efforts to navigate Tamil political histories, identities, claims, and futures in the postwar are expressed and imagined have become more visible through photography. The political work of photography thus also necessarily continues, for the work of accountability has never been easy or straightforward.

It is essential to note that at present, pursuits of justice for the Tamil community and holding the Sri Lankan state and its perpetrators accountable cannot be disentangled from the broader geopolitical conditions and machinations authorizing impunity, and the bolstering of globalized systems of securitization and oppression that actively seek to dismantle avenues and instruments for accountability. In Palestine, the Democratic Republic of Congo, Sudan, Kashmir, and elsewhere, communities are confronted by the inordinate harms and violence of militarization, state crime, genocide, and extractive capitalism. The demands on photography's volatile and agitant potentials have never been greater as cameras and images are simultaneously wielded as weapons of war and essential, expectant modes of confronting, witnessing, and documenting in the hands of those challenging manipulation, disinformation, and erasure. Even against the repression of state security apparatuses, photographies continue to be mobilized in expectation, in solidarity, in calls to community and responsibility. Everyday photography, generated by studio practitioners like those encountered through this book, make up a significant part of these economies and expectations.

A Volatile Picture was an attempt to examine the Sri Lankan civil war, and its aftermath through everyday photographic practices. Where the devastations of decades of armed conflict and aspirations for national liberation continue to shape the Tamil political imagination, the Tamil community resolutely looks to the camera to evidence, articulate, and visualize what is politically possible. Across various contexts ranging from studios, protests, commemoration events, and virtual maps on Instagram, photography is used, directly and indirectly, to amplify the visibility of political claims and grievances, or in everyday mitigations of the limitations and effects of these grievances. It has permitted divergence, refusal, and critique, which offer a granular view of the quotidian politics of the postwar. The medium's volatile and agitant capacities for inducing transformation and mediating possibilities were not only observed, but recognized, wielded, and sometimes even minimized by their makers and consumers to imagine and intercede in individual futures and political ambitions. Here photographers were important intermediaries whose skills of direction helped facilitate positive outcomes.

The photographies encountered in this book are extremely diverse, expeditiously traversing between and along official and intimate circuits and registers defined, blurred, and conflated by war. Collectively, whether intended as explicit political document and record or incidentally made during and impelled by conflict, these volatile images can expand our understanding of nation, state, war, and postwar in a way that conventional inquiries cannot. Photography, even in its democratized guise, becomes a medium through which political claims and politically generative violence toward realizing acts of nation, state, and citizen-making were stirred and sustained, drawing into question the notions of the civil. Agitant images hold the capacity to produce and justify violence, especially where ethnonationalist claims bound to concerted ideological processes of racialized othering were at play. However, the same images can become the basis for community and demands for justice and accountability. Paying attention to the volatility of images allows us to conceive of photography's contradictory capacities for producing both agitation and solidarity.

The unruliness of these photographies propelled by their social and political contingencies sheds indispensable light on the jostling, interstitial Tamil imaginaries and aspirations. Gruesome images of atrocity circulate in equal step with studio portraits, family photographs, and identity card headshots, their political work diverse but no less central to interceding for the individual and collective possibility of what comes next—whether personal or political, where the lack of freedom and equality were so inherently tied to one's ethnic identity. Even analog and digital social photographs that were mundane and unremarkable in their making became *of war* in their production and circulations. Such images revealed banal political realities and violence as well as the astonishing potentials in their mobilization within spaces and narratives of resistance. More directly, photographs also plainly mediated social and bureaucratic processes that paved the way for new citizenships, where the nation continues to disperse across states. Photography as a form of self-representation serves as a lens through which to examine what being Tamil in postwar Sri Lanka might entail, as not only ethnic identity, but as a category of impaired and othered citizenship, national belonging in Sri Lanka and abroad, and everyday political self-making and world-making in Sri Lanka and abroad. Photography was integral not only to the consolidation of competing nation/state imaginaries and securitization, but the disruptive formation of deterritorialized, trans/national political socialities, solidarities, and friendships that make multiple and sometimes discrepant desires and aspirations for belonging and community possible.

CAN A STATE EVER BE HOME? CAN HOME EVER BE A STATE?

When I asked this question of Sabes, as I wrote these concluding words, he responded with characteristic wisdom. "Home begins with emotion. State begins with power."

Photography's volatility is a kaleidoscopic mirror to the individual and collective pasts, presents, and anticipated futures. Essentially, war as a political phenomenon might be grasped through its diverse attendant photographies. But the volatile photographies of this book while of war are also of home. Our home.

Where the medium has been ambivalently posited as a means to sustain power, or conversely claim citizenship, we see through the complex interweaving of post/war image-making what photography can achieve and is believed to achieve in practice toward the personal and political aspirations of those surviving in between nation and state. Photography is a volatile, agitant, and generative intermediary holding the perceived promise for achieving personal, communal, and political transformation amid the post/war. Inextricable from its volatility and agitant capacities is, however, its power to underpin expectation and imagine what is possible and what a photograph can do.

Even as photography conforms to the hegemonies of state propaganda, securitization, and militarization, the medium's volatility renders difficult subjects visible, resists erasure, preserves history, permits debate and disagreement, mediates personal and political futures, and fosters borderless solidarities and intimacies. Ultimately, it is the volatility of the photograph that permits the expectation of what photography can do in the multiplicity of concurrent interpretations that are eternally unfolding through space and time, much like political transformation in the making. Across these everyday photographs, sweet, formal, and abhorrent, it was apparent that local photographic practices have been shaped by, interpreted, contradicted, and contributed to located claims of a Tamil nation, tethered to a homeland that exceeds the aspiration of state in its dispersal around the globe in a true invocation of the demotic.

While photography's violent outcomes might signal cynicism, the photographies of this book also highlight how and why the medium, in its grotesque and hopeful forms, are mobilized by the community as a means of evidencing, political expression, imagining, and dreaming. These manifold conjugations enhance our understanding of how those living amid uncertainty and in anticipation of radical political alternatives picture and articulate truths, histories, identities, grief, and pain to exploit the volatility of the medium. Its extraordinary potential to locate, de-territorialize, and re-territorialize political imaginaries and commonalities discloses how not only the language of photography but also home and community might be liberated from the state on account of the contingency engendering its inherent instability. Photography speaks horizontally and powerfully to the immense connection, solidarity, and expectations of justice and even political alternatives that their makers and sharers hope for. This visibility heightened by rapidly advancing technologies of image-making permits us a glimpse into the dynamic transnational consolidation of a postwar Tamil political imagination, but importantly the scale and vivacity of its political reimagining pinned to belonging and desires for homeland. It makes a case for the political work of photography beyond its ideologically defined agitant capacities, to one of exchange and confidence in articulating refusal, ambitions, personal and political experiences, and aspirations that do not passively follow hegemonic scripts and demands, but reaffirm care, community, and responsibility.

NOTES

INTRODUCTION

1. *Tamil Eelam* refers to the aspirant Tamil state spanning the Northern, North-Western, and Eastern Provinces of Sri Lanka. References to the "northeast" encompass the predominantly Tamil areas that were under the LTTE's de facto control during the war.
2. For detailed contemporary accounts of the events of July 1983, see Dissanayaka (1983); Thornton and Nithyanandan (1984); Piyadasa (1984); and Tambiah (1986).
3. The Official Language Act (No. 33 of 1956), referred to as the "Sinhala Only Act," replaced English with Sinhala as the official language of Ceylon, and excluded Tamil. The act was partially reversed in 1958, giving official status to Tamil as a medium of instruction in schools and universities, admission to public service employment, as well as administration in the North and Eastern Provinces. Tamil was afforded official language status on par with Sinhalese in 1987, though its implementation is irregular.
4. Sri Lanka's Tamil population is broadly distinguished as Sri Lankan Tamil or Indian-origin Tamil. The latter largely comprises those brought to Ceylon by the British colonial administration as indentured labor to build roads and railways and work on the island's tea plantations in the hill country (known as Malaiyaha or Up Country Tamils), as well as migrant merchants and professional communities residing in Colombo. The Indian-origin Tamil community was gravely affected by the events of Black July, as has been examined by Daniel (1996).
5. There is no consensus on the number of casualties or damage caused by the Black July pogrom.
6. Manohari Velamati notes that according to UNHCR data, around 917,000 Sri Lankans left the country, a vast majority of whom were Tamil (2009, 271).
7. In 2004, President Chandrika Bandaranaike Kumaratunga extended a formal apology following the appointment of the Presidential Truth Commission on Ethnic Violence 1981–84 to inquire into the events of Black July, when nearly 1,000 died and 18,000 properties were destroyed. Nominal compensation for 937 individuals was recommended.
8. Amarasinghe retraces his steps and visits the site of the photograph in the documentary *Demons in Paradise* directed by Jude Ratnam (2017).
9. Amarasinghe's photographs became the focus of a landmark court case in intellectual property, which recognized the "economic rights" of the photographer after the publication of these images in the *Daily News* and *Dinamina* newspapers on 24 July 1999 without acknowledgment or consent (Weerasooria 2012).

10. *Mama* is the Tamil word for uncle. A term of respect and endearment used to address an older man to whom one may not necessarily be related.
11. *Iyakkam* or movement refers to the Tamil militancy in everyday usage.
12. Excerpt from President Mahinda Rajapaksa's address to the parliament on 20 May 2009 following the Sri Lankan armed forces' victory over the LTTE.
13. *Ilankai* is the Tamil name for (Sri) Lanka. I use the terms *Ilankai Tamil* or *Lankan Tamils/Tamils of Lanka* to encompass the multifaceted character of Tamil identity on the island.
14. The Vanni is the mainland area of the Northern Province spanning the Mannar, Mullaitivu, and Vavuniya Districts and a portion of the Kilinochchi District. Forming the backdrop for the final phases of the war between 2006 and 2009, the Vanni was among the hardest hit in terms of war-related casualties.
15. Following Bronislaw Malinowski's "imponderabilia of everyday life" comprising "a series of phenomena of great importance that cannot possibly be recorded by questioning or computing documents" (or in this case merely the visual analysis of photographic images) (1922, vii).
16. The use of the term *photographies* follows from John Tagg's terminology to indicate its use as a set of discursive practices as informed by Michel Foucault's examinations of power (Tagg 1988, 119) and Geoffrey Batchen's consideration of vernacular photographies made up of a multiplicity of everyday photographic practices (2001, 57).
17. Deborah Poole uses the term *image world* to capture the complexity and multiplicity of material and social exchange, where "seeing" is not merely a matter of the image, but how it is presented (1997, 7).

1. HOME(LAND)

1. Deborah Poole defines "visual economy" as where images form part of "a comprehensive organization of people, ideas, and objects" determined by "social relationships, inequality, power relationships" as much as "shared meanings and community" (1997, 8).
2. *Multilingual* denotes Tamil, Sinhalese, and English, Sri Lanka's three official languages.
3. *Deferred dream* invokes Langston Hughes's 1951 poem "Harlem," which begins with the question "What happens to a dream deferred?"
4. In 2023, the Jaffna district was home to 630,119 persons, out of which 624,756 were Tamil, alongside 5,002 Muslims, and 343 Sinhalese. Religious backgrounds include 529,604 Hindus, 95,194 Christians, 5,002 Muslims, and 319 Buddhists (Northern Provincial Council 2024).
5. Locally produced sweet cordial made with Indian gooseberries. A savoury fried snack made of spiced black gram named after Paruthithurai or Point Pedro in Jaffna.
6. Following Trautmann (1997), Lynch examines the relevance of skin color to "racial" identification in Sri Lanka, where orientalist linguistic and racial constructions were absorbed into popular discourses (2004, 179, 191). The Sinhalese considered themselves "Aryan" and fair-skinned, while Tamils were thought to be dark-skinned

Dravidians. Dark or "black skin" evoking "racial impurity" is used as racial slur against Tamils (Lynch 2004, 179, 191). The racialized undertones of casteism in relation to skin color is also relevant. *Pottu* is the colored dot worn on one's forehead, and is of Hindu religious or culturally determined decorative purpose. *Vibhuti* is the sacred ash from Hindu ritual applied on one's forehead.

7. For example, in 2007, following various explosions that took place in the capital, 376 Tamils from the north and east who were deemed "temporary occupants" were evicted from Colombo on police-escorted buses and temporarily placed in a detention camp in Vavuniya.
8. The island's first republican constitution since independence from Britain in 1948 saw the country's name change to Sri Lanka from Ceylon in 1972. The inclusion of a Sanskritized "Sri" to its vernacular name "Lanka" (Sinhala) and "Ilankai" (Tamil) was negatively received by the Tamil community; it was seen as an attempt to consolidate Sinhala Buddhist hegemony within the state/political structure. The 1972 constitution has been regarded as a turning point in exacerbating the ethnic tensions that eventually led to war on account of the removal of section 29(2) of the 1947 Soulbury Constitution formulated to safeguard the rights and freedoms of the country's minority communities, including those distinguished by religion and language.
9. See Thiranagama's critique of Trawick (2013, 21).

2. THE JAFFNA STUDIO

1. A smiling baby also evokes that of *bala* Krishna or child Krishna, a staple in the Hindu image world. See Pinney 1997, 190–91.
2. Given examples of mob violence directed at Tamil businesses in 1983 and subsequently, these harmonious pantheons also in a sense plead for a different sort of protection from the physical destruction of properties, as it was perhaps unlikely that perpetrators of violence would destroy the abodes of their own gods.
3. Pinney poetically describes studios in Central India as chambers of dreams where aspirations for coming out better are envisioned through photography (1997, 108).
4. The Thanthai Chelva Monument is a memorial to S. J. V. Chelvanayakam, the founder and leader of the Ilankai Tamil Arasu Kachchi (ITAK) and Tamil United Liberation Front (TULF). He is known as Thanthai Chelva or Father Chelva and has been described as a father figure to the island's Tamils. Manthiri Manai is a historic building believed to have been a residence of the King of Jaffna, before the fall of the Jaffna kingdom to the Portuguese in 1619.
5. A police-led attack on the participants of the International Tamil Conference focused on academic and cultural attainments of the Tamil civilization held in Jaffna in 1974 led to nine "accidental" deaths and over fifty individuals injured. The Sinhalese police officer leading the charge was promoted by the Sirimavo Bandaranaike-led Sri Lankan state as reward for his "patriotic act" (Tambiah 1986, 17).
6. See Raheem and Thome 2000; Raheem 2009; National Museum of New Delhi and the Alkazi Foundation for the Arts 2015.

7. In 1938, camera manufacturer Leica invited Wendt to show his photographs in a solo exhibition at the Camera Club in London in an honor they had afforded to only one other living photographer. Wendt also participated in several exhibitions in Ceylon and internationally in North America, Europe, South Africa, and Asia. See Fonseka 2000.
8. The documentation of these archaeological sites in shaping the narratives and aesthetics of state-sponsored Sinhala Buddhist nationalism in the aftermath of the war is of significance See also Jeganathan ([1995] 2009).
9. Raheem does not include a source for this claim.

3. PHOTOGRAPHY AS STATECRAFT AND WARCRAFT

1. The Commander of the Security Forces dispatched to the Northern Province in 1979 was granted unprecedented powers, which allowed him to supersede all civilian officials including the government agent (Dissanayaka 1983, 36).
2. The poisonous *Gloriosa superba* or *karthigai* flower also has an association with suicide due to the plant's toxic root. The flower's resemblance to a flame served as a potent symbol of the "flame of sacrifice" that featured in Maaveerar Naal ceremony.
3. Andavan is the Tamil name for Lord Shiva, one of the principal deities of Hinduism and the supreme being of the Shaivite tradition for which Jaffna is known. Shiva (the Destroyer) along with Brahma (the Creator) and Vishnu (the preserver) form the triad of cosmic functions that they each personifies.
4. Hindu iconography and the centering of the visual in worship as well as memorial practices in the context of India have been explored by Pinney (1997, 138–49) and Eck (1998).
5. The Tamil word *vadivu*, which eludes adequate direct translation, is suspended somewhere between beauty (*alakha*) and properly done or well-presented. *Vadivu* was used to describe the photograph and how a sitter might be represented in a photograph. It evokes in some sense Christopher Pinney's observation of the desire to "come out better" as encountered in Indian studio photography (1997, 180).
6. In *Camera Lucida*, a deeply personal contemplation of the photographic image that followed the death of his mother, Roland Barthes muses, "I had understood that henceforth I must interrogate the evidence of Photography, not merely from the viewpoint of pleasure, but in relation to what we romantically call love and death" ([1981] 2000, 73).

4. *NAVEENA CAMERA*

1. *Thalsevana* is the Sinhalese word for palmyra shade.
2. This bridge opened in 2011; it is one of two bridges linking Jaffna Peninsula with the mainland.
3. Excerpt from Mahesh Senanayake's speech at an event launching the second phase of the Nallinakkapuram Housing Complex in Thellipalai, Jaffna, on 30 March 2018 (translation my own). See also *Tamil Guardian* 2018.
4. Darsanam describes a ritual component of "seeing and being seen by a deity, an

exchange of vision, an auspicious sight, or a blessing deriving from the gaze of the deity" (Roberts 2006, 91).

5. Gürsel's describes media images as "formative fictions" (2016, 11–13). These visuals are selected, mediated, and consumed within the space of a marketplace, contributing to a form of "worldmaking" (adapted from Goodman 1978) that underwrite the understanding and building of the realities in which we live (Gürsel 2016, 11–13).

5. PICTURING THE DISAPPEARED

1. As of July 2025, the Tamil families of the disappeared have engaged in over 3,000 days of continuous protest.
2. Kinship terms such as *amma* (mother), *mama* (uncle), *akka* (elder sister), among others, are used as a mode of informal address.

6. ATROCITY NATION / STATE AMNESIA

1. Quoted by Lord Avebury in a 1991 House of Lords debate on Sri Lanka Human Rights [HC Deb 23 (23 January 1991, vol. 525)].
2. In 2018 former president Maithripala Sirisena announced that, according to the security forces, 28,708 soldiers were killed and 40,107 disabled. The basis of these numbers is unknown.
3. News interview with unnamed soldier 1 August 2008.
4. Sita is a principal character in the Hindu epic *The Ramayana*, attributed to Valmiki. Sita is believed to be the daughter of the earth goddess Bhoomi. During her marriage to Rama, the prince of Ayodhya, they are exiled to a forest when she is abducted and imprisoned by the king of Lanka, Ravana. Following her rescue by Rama, Sita is asked to prove her chastity by way of a test of fire, which she does. In the *Luv Kush Kand*, the final book of *The Ramayana*, which has not been attributed to the original writers, Sita, plagued with continued questions about her purity, finds refuge in an ashram, where she gives birth to two children, Luv and Kush. In a final challenge by a detractor, overcome with emotion, Sita prays to Mother Earth. The earth opens up beneath her and she disappears. The legend of Ravana pervades the Sinhalese and Tamil nation (Sanmugeswaran et al. 2019; Witharana 2019).
5. Corporal Gamini Kularatne (1966–91), known as Hasalaka Gamini, was a Sri Lankan soldier who was the first awardee of the Parama Weera Vibhushanaya, the highest award for military gallantry in Sri Lanka for his bravery during the Elephant Pass Siege, during which he was killed.

7. IMAGI(NI)NG EELAM

1. A tutory is a place where tuition classes are conducted.
2. Cornell Capa (1918–2008) chose the phrase "concerned photographer" to describe those photographers who demonstrated in their work a humanitarian impulse to use pictures to educate and change the world, not just to record it (1968).

REFERENCES

Abi-Habib, Maria, and Dharisha Bastians. 2020. "'I Can't Bring Back the Dead': Sri Lanka Leader Ends Search for War Missing." *New York Times*, 21 January. https://www.nytimes.com/2020/01/21/world/asia/sri-lanka-civil-war.html.

Amarathaas. 2022. *Through the Fire Zones: Photographs of Amarathaas in Sri Lanka's War Zones*. Switzerland: Wide Vision Studio.

Amnesty International. 2010. "Amnesty International Public Statement Submitted to Human Rights Council Session 14 (Ref:SL A/HRC/14/NGO/53)." Geneva. https://www.amnesty.org/en/wp-content/uploads/2021/07/asa370102010en.pdf.

Anderson, Benedict. (1983) 1991. *Imagined Communities: Reflections on the Origin and Spread of Nationalism*. Rev. ed. London: Verso.

ARED. Association for Relatives of the Enforced Disappeared. 2017. "Release of Lists of Surrendees/Detainees."

Arunasalam, Kannan, dir. 2019. *The Tent*.

Azoulay, Ariella Aïsha. 2008. *The Civil Contract of Photography*. Translated by Rela Mazali and Ruvik Danieli. New York: Zone Books.

Azoulay, Ariella Aïsha. (2012) 2015. *Civil Imagination: A Political Ontology of Photography*. Translated by Louise Bethlehem. London: Verso.

Balasingham, Adele. 2001. *The Will to Freedom: An Inside View of Tamil Resistance*. Mitcham: Fairmax.

Bandaranayake, J., J. Amarasinghe, and J. Dheeraratne. 1992. *Mahinda Rajapaksa vs. Kudahetti and Others*. Supreme Court of Sri Lanka (SCSL).

Barthes, Roland. (1981) 2000. *Camera Lucida: Reflections on Photography*. Translated by Richard Howard. London: Vintage.

Bastians, Dharisha. 2016. "The Politics of the 'Missing.'" *Daily FT*, 11 August. https://www.ft.lk/columns/the-politics-of-the-missing/4-560777.

Batchen, Geoffrey. 2000. *Each Wild Idea: Writing, Photography, History*. Cambridge, MA: MIT Press.

Benjamin, Walter. (1931) 2005. "Little History of Photography." In *Walter Benjamin: Selected Writings, 2: 1931–34*, edited by Michael W. Jennings, Howard Eiland, and Gary Smith, translated by Rodney Livingstone. Cambridge, MA: Belknap Press of Harvard University Press.

Bourdieu, Pierre. 1990. *Photography: A Middle-Brow Art*. Oxford: Polity Press.

Brothers, Caroline. 1997. *War and Photography: A Cultural History*. London: Routledge.

Brun, Cathrine. 2008. "Birds of Freedom: Young People, the LTTE, and Representations of Gender, Nationalism, and Governance in Northern Sri Lanka." *Critical Asian Studies* 40 (3): 399–422. https://doi.org/10.1080/14672710802274128.

Buthpitiya, Vindhya. 2019. "'Paradise' in Missing Pictures: A Brief and Incomplete History of Sri Lankan Photography." *History Workshop*, 15 July 2019. https://www.historyworkshop.org.uk/empire-decolonisation/paradise-in-missing-pictures-a-brief-and-incomplete-history-of-sri-lankan-photography/.

Buthpitiya, Vindhya. 2022a. "Absence in Technicolour: Protesting Enforced Disappearances in Northern Sri Lanka." *Journal of the Royal Anthropological Institute* 28 (S1): 118–34. https://doi.org/10.1111/1467-9655.13758.

Buthpitiya, Vindhya. 2022b. "In Sri Lanka, A Perpetrator State Demands Non-Violence." *Urban Violence Research Network*, 2 May. https://urbanviolence.org/perpetrator-state/.

Buthpitiya, Vindhya. 2022c. "Naveena Camera." *Dastavezi | The Audio-Visual South Asia*, October, vol. 4 (2022). https://doi.org/10.11588/DASTA.2022.1.19131.

Buthpitiya, Vindhya. 2022d. "'The Heavy Footed State, Which Made a Mess.'" *Urban Violence Research Network*, 31 August. https://urbanviolence.org/the-heavy-footed-state-which-made-a-mess/.

Buthpitiya, Vindhya. 2023a. "How to Capture Birds of Freedom: Picturing Tamil Women at War." *Trans Asia Photography* 13 (1). https://doi.org/10.1215/21582025-10365016.

Buthpitiya, Vindhya. 2023b. "'The Truth Is in the Soil': The Political Work of Photography in Northern Sri Lanka." In *Citizens of Photography*, edited by Christopher Pinney, The PhotoDemos Collective, Naluwembe Binaisa, Vindhya Buthpitiya, Konstantinos Kalantzis, Ileana L. Selejan, and Sokphea Young, 63–110. Durham, NC: Duke University Press. https://doi.org/10.1215/9781478024590-002.

Buthpitiya, Vindhya. 2024. "Fables of Recovery and Revolution." *Urban Violence Research Network*, 29 November. https://urbanviolence.org/fables-of-recovery-and-revolution/.

Capa, Cornell. 1968. *The Concerned Photographer*. New York: Grossman.

Champion, Stephen. 2008. *Sri Lanka: War Stories*. London: Hotshoe Books.

Chatterjee, Partha. 1999. "Anderson's Utopia." *Diacritics* 29 (4): 128–34. https://doi.org/10.1353/dia.1999.0025.

Chatterjee, Partha. 2004. *The Politics of the Governed*. New Delhi: Permanent Black.

Chelvanayakam, S. J. V., and Tamil United Liberation Front (TULF). 1976. "Vaddukoddai Resolution." *Sangam*, 14 May. https://www.sangam.org/FB_HIST_DOCS/vaddukod.htm.

Cheran, R. 2009. "Pathways of Dissent: An Introduction to Tamil Nationalism in Sri Lanka." In *Pathways of Dissent: Tamil Nationalism in Sri Lanka*, edited by R. Cheran. New Delhi: Sage India.

Chowdhry Biswas, Jennifer. 2015. "A Landscape of Desire." In *Imaging the Isle across Vintage Photography from Ceylon*, edited by Alkazi Collection of Photography, 52–69. New Delhi: National Museum.

Colvin, Marie. 2001. "Blasted in the Eye in Sri Lanka, I Was Taking a Long Time to Die." *The Times*, 22 April. https://www.thetimes.com/article/blasted-in-the-eye-in-sri-lanka-i-was-taking-a-long-time-to-die-dgkcnzp2z8m.

Conrad, Joseph. (1899) 2012. *Heart of Darkness*. New York: Penguin.

Daily FT. 2014. "Beauty Fused with Documentary Value." *Daily FT*, 14 June. https://www.ft.lk/article/306926/Beauty-fused-with-documentary-value.

Daniel, E. Valentine. 1984. *Fluid Signs: Being a Person the Tamil Way*. Berkeley: University of California Press.

Daniel, E. Valentine. 1996. *Charred Lullabies: Chapters in an Anthropography of Violence*. Princeton, NJ: Princeton University Press.

Darusman, Marzuki, Yasmin Sooka, and Stephen R. Ratner. 2011. *Report of the Secretary General's Panel of Experts on Accountability in Sri Lanka*. New York: United Nations Secretariat. https://reliefweb.int/report/sri-lanka/report-secretary-generals-panel-experts-accountability-sri-lanka.

De Alwis, Malathi. 2007. "Feminism." In *Companion to the Anthropology of Politics*, edited by David Nugent and Joan Vincent, 121–34. Malden, MA: Blackwell.

De Alwis, Malathi. 2008. "Motherhood as a Space of Protest: Women's Political Participation in Contemporary Sri Lanka." In *Women in Peace Politics*, edited by Paula Banerjee, 154–74. New Delhi: SAGE Publications India.

De Mel, Neloufer. 2001. *Women and the Nation's Narrative: Gender and Nationalism in Twentieth-Century Sri Lanka*. Lanham, MD: Rowman & Littlefield.

De Mel, Neloufer. 2007. *Militarizing Sri Lanka: Popular Culture, Memory and Narrative in the Armed Conflict*. New Delhi: SAGE India. https://doi.org/10.4135/9788132100072.

Department for the Registration of Persons. 2019. "Identity Card, The Trusted Personal Identity." Government of Sri Lanka. https://drp.gov.lk/Templates/aboutus.english.Department-for-Registration-of-Persons.html.

Dissanayaka, T. D. S. A. 1983. *The Agony of Sri Lanka: An In-Depth Account of the Racial Riots of 1983*. Colombo: Swastika.

Doucet, Lyrse. 2012. "UN 'Failed Sri Lanka Civilians,' Says Internal Probe." *BBC News*. 13 November. https://www.bbc.co.uk/news/world-asia-20308610.

Eck, Diana. 1998. *Darsan: Seeing the Divine Image in India*. New York: Columbia University Press.

Engage Sri Lanka. 2013. *Corrupted Journalism: Channel 4 and Sri Lanka*. Engage Sri Lanka.

Falconer, John. 2008. "Ceylon." In *Encyclopaedia of Nineteenth-Century Photography*, edited by John Hannavy, 286–87. London: Routledge.

Fanon, Frantz. 1963. *The Wretched of the Earth*. Translated by Constance Farrington. New York: Grove Press.

Fatima, Iffat. 2022. "Lanka—The Other Side of War and Peace." *Dastavezi | The Audio-Visual South Asia*, October, vol. 4. https://doi.org/10.11588/DASTA.2022.1.19130.

Feldman, Allen. 2002. "Strange Fruit: The South African Truth Commission and the Demonic Economies of Violence." *Social Analysis: The International Journal of Social and Cultural Practice* 46 (3): 234–65. https://www.jstor.org/stable/23170175.

Feldman, Allen. 2003. "Political Terror and the Technologies of Memory: Excuse, Sacrifice, Commodification, and Actuarial Moralities." *Radical History Review* 85 (1): 58–73. https://muse.jhu.edu/pub/4/article/37724.

Ferme, Mariane C. 2001. *The Underneath of Things: Violence, History, and the Everyday in Sierra Leone*. Berkeley: University of California Press.

Fernando, Nihal. 1997. *Sri Lanka: A Personal Odyssey*. Colombo: Studio Times.

Fernando, Nihal, and Herbert Keuneman. 2005. *With the Dawn*. Colombo: Studio Times.

Fernando, Nihal, and Luxshman Nadaraja. 1991. *Serendip to Sri Lanka: Immemorial Isle*. Colombo: Studio Times.

Fernando, Nihal, and Sinharaja Tammita-Delgoda. 2008. *Eloquence in Stone: The Lithic Saga of Sri Lanka*. Colombo: Studio Times.

Fernando, Ruki. 2018. "Mullivaikkal and the May 18 Disconnect." *Sri Lanka Brief*. https://srilankabrief.org/2018/05/mullivaikkal-and-the-may-18-disconnect-ruki-fernando/.

Fineman, Mark. 1992. "Rebels' Weapon: Cyanide: With a Cult of Suicide, the Tamil Tigers Rank among the World's Most Dedicated Guerrilla Groups. Their Liberation War in Sri Lanka Has Entered the Realm of Fanaticism." *Los Angeles Times*, 20 January. https://www.latimes.com/archives/la-xpm-1992-01-20-mn-481-story.html.

Fonseka, Manel. 2000. "Rediscovering Lionel Wendt." In *Lionel Wendt: A Centennial Tribute*, 17–44. Colombo: Lionel Wendt Memorial Fund.

Ganesan, Sundar. 2014. "A Requiem for the Jaffna Library." *Himal Southasian*, 14 January. https://www.himalmag.com/comment/requiem-jaffna-library.

Geismar, Haidy. 2015. "Anthropology and Heritage Regimes." *Annual Review of Anthropology* 44 (1): 71–85. https://doi.org/10.1146/annurev-anthro-102214-014217.

Gooneratne, Yasmine. 1992. "The English-Educated in Sri Lanka: An Assessment of Their Cultural Role." *Comparative Studies of South Asia, Africa and the Middle East* 12 (1): 2–33. https://doi.org/10.1215/07323867-12-1-2.

Goonetileke, Ian. 2000. "Lionel Wendt and George Keyt—A Close-Up." *The Island*, 26 November. http://www.island.lk/2000/11/26/featur08.html.

Gordon, Neve, and Nicola Perugini. 2020. *Human Shields: A History of People in the Line of Fire*. Oakland: University of California Press.

Gürsel, Zeynep Devrim. 2016. *Image Brokers: Visualizing World News in the Age of Digital Circulation*. Oakland: University of California Press.

Gürsel, Zeynep Devrim. 2017. "Visualizing Publics: Digital Crowd Shots and the 2015 Unity Rally in Paris." *Current Anthropology* 58 (S15): S135–48. https://doi.org/10.1086/689742.

Hallinan, Bridget. 2017. "Sri Lanka Inspiration Anthony Bourdain Finds the 'Holy Grail' of Sri Lankan Food in 'Parts Unknown.'" *Condé Nast Traveler*, 30 October. https://www.cntraveler.com/story/anthony-bourdain-finds-the-holy-grail-of-sri-lankan-food-in-parts-unknown.

Harrison, Frances. 2012a. "Journalists Failed to Tell the Story of War Crimes in Sri Lanka." *Journalism.co.uk*, 17 May. https://www.journalism.co.uk/news-commentary/frances-harrison-sri-lanka-journalists-failed-to-tell-the-story-of-war-crimes/s6/a549285/.

Harrison, Frances. 2012b. *Still Counting the Dead: Survivors of Sri Lanka's Hidden War*. London: Portobello Books.

Hartman, Saidiya. 2019. *Wayward Lives, Beautiful Experiments: Intimate Histories of Riotous Black Girls, Troublesome Women, and Queer Radicals*. London: Serpent's Tail.

Haynie, Devon. 2017. "Facing Sri Lanka's Ghosts." *US News*, 18 May. https://www.usnews.com/news/best-countries/articles/2017-05-18/on-the-8-year-anniversary-of-civil-wars-end-sri-lankas-political-fate-looks-grim.

Hensman, Rohini. 1992. "Feminism and Ethnic Nationalism in Sri Lanka." *Journal of Gender Studies* 1 (4): 500–509. https://doi.org/10.1080/09589236.1992.9960516.

Hoole, Rajan, Daya Somasundaram, Kopalasingham Sritharan, and Rajani Thiranagama. University Teachers for Human Rights. 1992. *The Broken Palmyra: The*

Tamil Crisis in Sri Lanka—An Inside Account. 2nd ed. Claremont, CA: The Sri Lanka Studies Institute.

HRW. Human Rights Watch. 2004. *Child Soldiers and the Tamil Tigers in Sri Lanka*. New York: Human Rights Watch. https://www.hrw.org/report/2004/11/10/living-fear/child-soldiers-and-tamil-tigers-sri-lanka.

HRW. Human Rights Watch. 2011. "Sri Lanka: Military Conference to Whitewash War Crimes: Invited Countries Should Stay Home, Press for Accountability." https://www.hrw.org/news/2011/05/23/sri-lanka-military-conference-whitewash-war-crimes.

Hughes, Langston. 1951. "Harlem." The Poetry Foundation. https://www.poetryfoundation.org/poems/46548/harlem.

Hyndman, Jennifer, and Amarnath Amarasingham. 2014. "Touring "Terrorism": Landscapes of Memory in Post-War Sri Lanka." *Geography Compass* 8 (8): 560–75. https://doi.org/10.1111/gec3.12149.

Ilankai Tamil Sangam, USA. 2024. "About Us." The Ilankai Tamil Sangam, USA. https://sangam.org/about/.

ITJP. International Truth and Justice Project. 2014. "White Flags." London: International Truth and Justice Project. https://itjpsl.com/reports/white-flags.

ITJP. International Truth and Justice Project. 2016. "Silenced: Survivors of Torture and Sexual Violence in 2015." London: International Truth and Justice Project. https://itjpsl.com/reports/silenced-survivors-of-torture-and-sexual-violence-2016.

ITJP. International Truth and Justice Project. 2019. "War on Civilians Exhibition." London: International Truth and Justice Project. https://itjpsl.com/reports/war-on-civilians-exhibition.

ITJP. International Truth and Justice Project. 2021. "Death Toll in Sri Lanka's 2009 War." London: International Truth and Justice Project. https://sangam.org/wp-content/uploads/2021/03/ITJP-Death-Toll-in-Sri-Lanka.pdf.

ITJP. International Truth and Justice Project. 2022. "Gotabaya Rajapaksa: The Sri Lankan President's Role in 1989 Mass Atrocities." London: The International Truth and Justice Project. https://itjpsl.com/reports/gotabaya-rajapaksa-the-sri-lankan-presidents-role-in-1989-mass-atrocities.

ITJP. International Truth and Justice Project. 2023. "Mass Graves and Failed Exhumations in Sri Lanka." London: The International Truth and Justice Project. https://itjpsl.com/reports/mass-graves.

ITJP. International Truth and Justice Project. 2025. "VVT: Testimonies of a Massacre." London: The International Truth and Justice Project. https://itjpsl.com/reports/vvt-testimonies-of-a-massacre.

Jathika Jana Balawegaya (NPP Sri Lanka). 2024. "A Thriving Nation, a Beautiful Life." Battaramulla, Sri Lanka, August. https://www.npp.lk/up/policies/en/nppolicystatement.pdf.

JDS. Journalists for Democracy in Sri Lanka. 2021. "Introduction: Media Workers Killed in Sri Lanka (2004–2010)." Journalists for Democracy in Sri Lanka. http://www.jdslanka.org/index.php/killed-media-workers.

Jeffery, Laura, and Matei Candea. 2006. "The Politics of Victimhood." *History and Anthropology* 17 (4): 287–96. https://doi.org/10.1080/02757200600914037.

Jeganathan, Pradeep. 1998. "Eelam.Com: Place, Nation, and Imagi-Nation in Cyberspace." *Public Culture* 10 (3): 515–28. https://doi.org/10.1215/08992363-10-3-515.

Jeganathan, Pradeep. 2000. "On the Anticipation of Violence Modernity and Identity in Southern Sri Lanka." In *Anthropology, Development and Modernities Exploring Discourse, Counter-Tendencies, and Violence*, edited by Alberto Arce and Norman Long, 111–25. London: Routledge.

Jeganathan, Pradeep. (1995) 2009. "Authorizing History, Ordering Land: The Conquest of Anuradhapura." In *Unmaking the Nation: The Politics of Identity and History in Modern Sri Lanka*, edited by Pradeep Jeganathan and Qadri Ismail, 2nd ed., 157–73. Colombo: Social Scientists' Association and South Focus Press.

Jeganathan, Pradeep. 2010. "In the Ruins of Truth: The Work of Melancholia and Acts of Memory." *Inter-Asia Cultural Studies* 11 (1): 6–20. https://doi.org/10.1080/14649370903403496.

Jegathesan, Mythri. 2019. *Tea and Solidarity: Tamil Women and Work in Postwar Sri Lanka*. Seattle: University of Washington Press.

Jeyaraj, D. B. S. 2012. "The Enduring Mystique of 'Maaveerar Naal': What Makes the 'Great Heroes Day' Tick?" DBSJeyaraj.com. 28 November. https://dbsjeyaraj.com/dbsj/?p=12790.

Jeyaraj, D. B. S. 2014. "Life and Times of Tiger Supremo Veluppillai Prabhakaran." *Daily Mirror Online*, 21 November. https://www.dailymirror.lk/dbs-jeyaraj-column/life-and-times-of-tiger-supremo-veluppillai-prabhakaran/192-57129.

Jeyaratnam Wilson, Alfred. 1988. *The Break-Up of Sri Lanka: The Sinhalese-Tamil Conflict*. London: C. Hurst.

Jeyaratnam Wilson, Alfred. 2000. *Sri Lankan Tamil Nationalism: Its Origins and Development in the Nineteenth and Twentieth Centuries*. London: C. Hurst.

Jurgenson, Nathan. 2019. *The Social Photo: On Photography and Social Media*. London: Verso.

Kleinman, Arthur, and Joan Kleinman. 1996. "The Appeal of Experience; The Dismay of Images: Cultural Appropriations of Suffering in Our Times." *Daedalus* 125 (1): 1–23. https://www.jstor.org/stable/20027351.

Kumanan, Kanapathippillai. 2019. "The Departed: While Searching for Their Enforced Disappeared Loved Ones." Pamphlet. Sri Lanka.

Kumanan, Kanapathippillai. 2024. "Exhibitions." Kumanan Images. https://kumananimages.com/exhibitions/.

Lawton, S. K. 1907. "Deterioration of Fish Glue and Its Remedies." *Penrose's Pictorial Annual* 12:96.

Lawton, S. K. 1909. "Simplified Colour Photography." *Penrose's Pictorial Annual* 14:64.

Lawton, S. K. 1911. "A Simple and Expeditious Method of Making Blocks." *Penrose's Pictorial Annual* 16:109.

Lawton, S. K. 1913. "When Was Photography Introduced into the East?" *Penrose's Pictorial Annual* 18:132–34.

Lawton, S. K. 1914. "On Faded Photographs." *Penrose's Pictorial Annual* 19:47–48.

Lies Agreed Upon. 2011. Sri Lanka Ministry of Defence.

LLRC. Commission of Inquiry on Lessons Learnt and Reconciliation. 2011. *The Report of the Commission of Inquiry on Lessons Learnt and Reconciliation*. Colombo: Government of Sri Lanka. https://reliefweb.int/report/sri-lanka/report-commission-inquiry-lessons-learnt-and-reconciliation.

LTTE. Liberation Tigers of Tamil Eelam. n.d. *Portrait of a Nation: A Photographic Record of the Tamil Eelam Liberation Struggle*. London.

Lubkemann, Stephen C. 1997. *Culture in Chaos: An Anthropology of the Social Condition in War*. Chicago: University of Chicago Press.

Lynch, Caitrin. 2004. "Economic Liberalization, Nationalism, and Women's Morality in Sri Lanka." In *Economy, Culture, and Civil War in Sri Lanka*, edited by Deborah Winslow and Michael D. Woost. Bloomington: Indiana University Press.

Macrae, Callum, dir. 2011. *Sri Lanka's Killing Fields*. Channel 4. https://www.channel4.com/programmes/sri-lankas-killing-fields/on-demand/51949-001.

Macrae, Callum, dir. 2012. *Sri Lanka's Killing Fields: War Crimes Unpunished*. Channel 4. https://www.channel4.com/programmes/sri-lankas-killing-fields/on-demand/52949-001.

Macrae, Callum, dir. 2013. *No Fire Zone: The Killing Fields of Sri Lanka*. https://nofirezone.org/.

Macrae, Callum. 2015. "Sri Lanka Massacred Tens of Thousands of Tamils while the World Looked Away." Pulitzer Center. 11 August. https://pulitzercenter.org/stories/sri-lanka-massacred-tens-thousands-tamils-while-world-looked-away.

Malinowski, Bronislaw. 1922. *Argonauts of the Western Pacific: An Account of Native Enterprise and Adventure in the Archipelagoes of Melanesian New Guinea*. New York: Dutton.

Mampilly, Zachariah Cherian. 2015. *Rebel Rulers: Insurgent Governance and Civilian Life during War*. Ithaca, NY: Cornell University Press.

Martyn, John H. 1923. *Notes on Jaffna: Chronological, Historical, Biographical*. Tellippalai, Jaffna: American Ceylon Mission Press.

Maunaguru, Sitralega. 1991. "Two Poems of Sivaramani Translated from Tamil." *Comparative Studies of South Asia, Africa and the Middle East* 11 (1& 2): 147–50. https://doi.org/10.1215/07323867-11-1_and_2-147.

Maunaguru, Sidharthan. 2009. "Brides as Bridges? Movements, Actors, Documents and Anticipation in Constructing Tamilness." In *Pathways of Dissent: Tamil Nationalism in Sri Lanka*, edited by R. Cheran, 55-80. New Delhi: SAGE Publications India Pvt Ltd. https://doi.org/10.4135/9788132104322.n3.

Maunaguru, Sidharthan. 2019. *Marrying for a Future: Transnational Sri Lankan Tamil Marriages in the Shadow of War*. Seattle: University of Washington Press.

Maunaguru, Sidharthan, and Jonathan Spencer. 2018. "'You Can Do Anything with a Temple': Religion, Philanthropy, and Politics in South London and Sri Lanka." *Modern Asian Studies* 52 (1): 186–213. https://www.jstor.org/stable/26599586.

Mbembe, Achille. 2019. *Necropolitics*. Durham, NC: Duke University Press.

McDowell, Sara. 2012. "Symbolic Warfare in the Ethnocratic State: Conceptualising Memorialisation and Territoriality in Sri Lanka." *Terrorism and Political Violence* 24 (1): 22–37. https://doi.org/10.1080/09546553.2011.598196.

Meta. 2024. "Community Guidelines." Instagram. 2024. https://help.instagram.com/477434105621119/?helpref=uf_share.

Mookherjee, Nayanika. 2015. *The Spectral Wound: Sexual Violence, Public Memories, and the Bangladesh War of 1971*. Durham, NC: Duke University Press.

Narayan, Kirin. 1993. "How Native Is a 'Native' Anthropologist?" *American Anthropologist* 95 (3): 671–86. https://doi.org/10.1525/aa.1993.95.3.02a00070.

Natali, Cristiana. 2008. "Building Cemeteries, Constructing Identities: Funerary Practices and Nationalist Discourse among the Tamil Tigers of Sri Lanka." *Contemporary South Asia* 16 (3): 287–301. https://doi.org/10.1080/09584930802271323.

National Museum New Delhi and the Alkazi Foundation for the Arts. 2015. *Imaging the Isle Across: Vintage Photography from Ceylon*. National Museum New Delhi and The Alkazi Foundation for the Arts.

Nithiyanandam, V. 1987. "An Analysis of Economic Factors behind the Origin and Development of Tamil Nationalism in Sri Lanka." In *Facets of Ethnicity*, edited by Charles Abeysekera and Newton Gunasinghe. Colombo: Social Scientists Association.

Noolaham. 2024. Home Page. https://noolaham.org/wiki/index.php.

Nordstrom, Carolyn. 1997. *A Different Kind of War Story*. Philadelphia: University of Pennsylvania Press.

Northern Provincial Council. 2024. "Provincial Statistical Information—2024." Jaffna. https://np.gov.lk/statistical-information/.

NPASSL (National Photographic Art Society of Sri Lanka). 2022."About Us." https://npassrilanka.org/about-us/.

101 East. 2018. "Sri Lanka: Abduction Island." Al Jazeera. https://www.aljazeera.com/video/101-east/2018/5/10/sri-lanka-abduction-island.

Parliament of the Democratic Socialist Republic of Sri Lanka. 2016. "Office on Missing Persons (Establishment, Administration and Discharge of Functions) Act, No. 14 of 2016." Colombo: Department of Government Printing.

Pavey, Eleanor. 2008. "The Massacres in Sri Lanka during the Black July Riots of 1983." *SciencesPo: Mass Violence and Resistance—Research Network*. 13 May. https://www.sciencespo.fr/mass-violence-war-massacre-resistance/en/document/massacres-sri-lanka-during-black-july-riots-1983.html.

Peirce, Charles Sanders. 1955. *Philosophical Writings of Peirce*. New York: Dover.

Petrie, Charles. 2012. "Report of the Secretary-General's Internal Review Panel on United Nations Action in Sri Lanka." Geneva: United Nations. https://digitallibrary.un.org/record/737299?ln=en.

Photographic Society of Sri Lanka. 2019. "About Us." Photographic Society of Sri Lanka. 2019. https://www.pssl.lk/about-us/.

Phu, Thy. 2022. *Warring Visions: Photography and Vietnam*. Durham, NC: Duke University Press.

PIAC (Public Interest Advocacy Centre). 2019. "Tides of Violence: Mapping the Sri Lankan Conflict from 1983 to 2009." Sydney: Public Interest Advocacy Centre. https://piac.asn.au/wp-content/uploads/2019/05/TIDES-OF-VIOLENCE-FINAL-3-PIAC.pdf.

Pieris, Anoma. 2013. *Architecture and Nationalism in Sri Lanka: The Trouser Under the Cloth*. London: Routledge.

Pieris, Anoma. 2014. "Southern Invasions: Post-War Tourism in Sri Lanka." *Postcolonial Studies* 17 (3): 266–85. https://doi.org/10.1080/13688790.2014.987899.

Pillen, Alex. 2002. *Masking Terror: How Women Contain Violence in Southern Sri Lanka*. Philadelphia: University of Pennsylvania Press.

Pinney, Christopher. 1997. *Camera Indica: The Social Life of Indian Photographs*. London: Reaktion Books.

Pinney, Christopher. 2003. "Introduction: 'How the Other Half . . .'" In *Photography's Other Histories*, edited by Christopher Pinney and Nicolas Peterson, 1–14. Durham, NC: Duke University Press.

Pinney, Christopher. 2012. "Seven Theses on Photography." *Thesis Eleven* 113 (1): 141–56. https://doi.org/10.1177/0725513612457864.

Pinney, Christopher. 2015. "Civil Contract of Photography in India." *Comparative Studies of South Asia, Africa and the Middle East* 35 (1): 21–34. https://doi.org/10.1215/1089201X-2876068.

Pinney, Christopher. 2020. "Locating Photography." In *A Companion to Photography*, edited by Stephen Bull. Hoboken, NJ: John Wiley.

Pinney, Christopher. 2023. "Introduction: Photographing; or, The Future of the Image." In *Citizens of Photography: The Camera and the Political Imagination*, edited by Christopher Pinney, The PhotoDemos Collective, Naluwembe Binaisa, et al. Durham, NC: Duke University Press. https://doi.org/10.1215/9781478024590-001.

Pinney, Christopher, and Suresh Punjabi. 2013. *Artisan Camera: Studio Photography from Central India*. Chennai: Tara Books.

Pinney, Christopher, The PhotoDemos Collective, Naluwembe Binaisa, Vindhya Buthpitiya, Konstantinos Kalantzis, Ileana L. Selejan, and Sokphea Young, eds. 2023. *Citizens of Photography: The Camera and the Political Imagination*. Durham, NC: Duke University Press. https://doi.org/10.1215/9781478024590.

Piyadasa, Lionel. 1984. *Sri Lanka: The Holocaust and After*. London: Marram Books.

Poole, Deborah. 1997. *Vision, Race, and Modernity: A Visual Economy of the Andean Image World*. Princeton, NJ: Princeton University Press.

Presidential Truth Commission on Ethnic Violence (1981–84). 2005. *Report of the Presidential Truth Commission on Ethnic Violence (1981–84)*. Colombo: Government of Sri Lanka.

Prabhakaran, Velupillai. 1990. "Annai Poopathy's Fast for Freedom Second Anniversary Message." *Tamilnation*. 19 April. https://tamilnation.org/ltte/vp/messages_speeches/900419annai_poopathy.htm.

Ragavan. 2024. "The Truth about the LTTE and the Palestinian Struggle." *Himal Southasian*, 8 October. https://www.himalmag.com/politics/ltte-plo-gaza-tamil-tiger-eelam-sri-lanka-palestine-liberation.

Raheem, Ismeth. 2003. "Andree, A(dolphus) W(illiam)." In *Oxford Art Online*. Oxford University Press. https://doi.org/10.1093/gao/9781884446054.article.T002787.

Raheem, Ismeth. 2009. *Archaeology and Photography: The Early Years 1868–80*. Colombo: National Trust Sri Lanka.

Raheem, Ismeth. 2018. "Looking Back Through the "Lens" of Time." *Sunday Times*, 2 September. https://www.sundaytimes.lk/180902/plus/looking-back-through-the-lens-of-time-309243.html.

Raheem, Ismeth, and Percy Colin Thome. 2000. *Images of British Ceylon: Nineteenth-Century Photography of Sri Lanka*. Singapore: Times Editions.

Rajasegar, Selvaraja. 2024. "Virtual Memorial." *Maatram*. 1 April. https://maatram.org/articles/11548.

Rajasingham, K. 2018. "Can OMP Deliver Justice When Sri Lanka's President Won't?" Journalists for Democracy in Sri Lanka. 12 June. http://www.jdslanka.org/index.php/news-features/human-rights/782-can-omp-deliver-justice-when-sri-lankas-president-wont.

Ramaswamy, Sumathi. 1997. *Passions of the Tongue: Language Devotion in Tamil India, 1891–1970*. Berkeley: University of California Press.

Rathnayake, P., ed. 2016. *Sala Roo Sihanada: Maha Eduru D. B. Nihalsinhage Mathaka Semaruma* [D. B. Nihalsinghe memorial]. Colombo: Faculty of Fine Arts, University of Kelaniya and The National Film Corporation.

Ratnam, Jude, dir. 2017. *Demons in Paradise*.

Richards, Joanne. 2014. *An Institutional History of the Liberation Tigers of Tamil Eelam (ltte)*. Geneva: Graduate Institute of International and Development Studies-CCDP. https://www.graduateinstitute.ch/library/publications-institute/institutional-history-liberation-tigers-tamil-eelam-ltte.

Richards, Paul, ed. 2005. *No Peace, No War: An Anthropology of Contemporary Armed Conflicts*. Athens: Ohio University Press.

Rizzo, Lorena. 2013. "Shades of Empire: Police Photography in German South-West Africa." *Visual Anthropology* 26 (4): 328–54. https://doi.org/10.1080/08949468.2013.804701.

Roberts, Michael. 2005. "Tamil Tiger 'Martyrs': Regenerating Divine Potency?" *Studies in Conflict & Terrorism* 28 (6): 493–514. https://doi.org/10.1080/10576100590950129.

Roberts, Michael. 2006. "Pragmatic Action and Enchanted Worlds: A Black Tiger Rite of Commemoration." *Social Analysis: The International Journal of Social and Cultural Practice* 50 (1): 73–102. https://www.jstor.org/stable/23181943.

Sadanandan, Renuka. 2010. "Weaving Memories." *Sunday Times*, 3 October. https://www.sundaytimes.lk/101003/Plus/plus_01.html.

Sangarasivam, Yamuna. 2000. "Liberation Tigers of Tamil Eelam and the Cultural Production of Nationalism and Violence: Representing the Integrity of Nation and the Choice for Armed Struggle." PhD thesis, Syracuse University.

Sanmugeswaran, Pathmanesan, Krishantha Fedricks, and Justin W. Henry. 2019. "Reclaiming Ravana in Sri Lanka: Ravana's Sinhala Buddhist Apotheosis and Tamil Responses." *South Asia: Journal of South Asian Studies* 42 (4): 796–812. https://doi.org/10.1080/00856401.2019.1631900.

Sarvananthan, Muttukrishna. 2003. "Economic Revival in North and East Sri Lanka: What Are the Impediments?" *Economic and Political Weekly* 38 (19): 1844–50. https://www.jstor.org/stable/4413543.

Satyendra, Nadesan. (1998) 2009. "Tamils: A Nation Without a State." *Tamilnation*, 10 May. https://tamilnation.org/diaspora/.

Schalk, Peter. 1997. "The Revival of Martyr Cults Among Ilavar." *Temenos* 33: 151–90. https://tamilnation.org/ideology/schalk01.htm.

Schirmer, Jennifer G. 1989. "'Those Who Die for Life Cannot Be Called Dead': Women and Human Rights Protest in Latin America." *Feminist Review*, no. 32, 3–29. https://doi.org/10.2307/1395361.

Scott, James. 1998. *Seeing Like a State: How Certain Schemes to Improve the Human Condition Have Failed.* New Haven, CT: Yale University Press.

Seoighe, Rachel. 2016. "Nationalistic Authorship and Resistance in Northeastern Sri Lanka." *Society and Culture in South Asia* 2 (1): 1–30. https://doi.org/10.1177/2393861715608971.

Sharpe, Christina. 2023. *Ordinary Notes.* London: Daunt Books Publishing.

Silva, P. L. D. (1995) 2002. "The Efficacy of 'Combat Mode': Organisation, Political Violence, Affect, and Cognition in the Case of the Liberation Tigers of Tamil Eelam." In *Unmaking the Nation: The Politics of Identity and History in Modern Sri Lanka*, edited by Pradeep Jeganathan and Qadri Ismail, 2nd ed., 174–87. Colombo: Social Scientists Association and South Focus Press.

Sluka, Jeffrey A. 2000. "Introduction: State Terror and Anthropology." In *Death Squad: The Anthropology of State Terror*, edited by Jeffrey A. Sluka, 1–45. Philadelphia: University of Pennsylvania Press.

Solomon, Andrew. 2016. "Sri Lanka Is Ready for Its Close-Up." *Condé Nast Traveller*, 7 December. https://www.cntraveler.com/story/sri-lanka-is-ready-for-its-close-up.

Sontag, Susan. 2003. *Regarding the Pain of Others.* New York: Farrar, Straus and Giroux.

Sooka, Yasmin. 2014. "An Unfinished War: Torture and Sexual Violence in Sri Lanka 2009–14." United Kingdom: The Bar Human Rights Committee of England and Wales and The International Truth & Justice Project, Sri Lanka. https://barhumanrights.org.uk/wp-content/uploads/2014/03/an_unfinihsed_war._torture_and_sexual_violence_in_sri_lanka_2009-2014_0-compressed.pdf.

Spencer, Jonathan. 1990. "Introduction: The Power of the Past." In *Sri Lanka: History and the Roots of Conflict*, edited by Jonathan Spencer, 1–16. London: Routledge.

Spencer, Jonathan. 2007. *Anthropology, Politics, and the State: Democracy and Violence in South Asia.* Cambridge: Cambridge University Press.

Sriraman, Tarangani. 2018. *In Pursuit of Proof: A History of Identification Documents in India.* New Delhi: Oxford University Press.

Stambler, Benita. 2013. "Maintaining the Photographic Legacy of Ceylon." *Trans-Asia Photography Review* 4 (1). http://hdl.handle.net/2027/sp0.7977573.0004.105.

Steyerl, Hito. 2009. "In Defense of the Poor Image." *E-Flux*, no. 10. https://www.e-flux.com/journal/10/61362/in-defense-of-the-poor-image/.

Stokke, Kristian. 2006. "Building the Tamil Eelam State: Emerging State Institutions and Forms of Governance in LTTE-Controlled Areas in Sri Lanka." *Third World Quarterly* 27 (6): 1021–40. https://www.jstor.org/stable/4017738.

Strassler, Karen. 2010. *Refracted Visions: Popular Photography and National Modernity in Java.* Durham, NC: Duke University Press.

Strassler, Karen. 2020. *Demanding Images: Democracy, Mediation, and the Image-Event in Indonesia.* Durham, NC: Duke University Press.

Sugunasabesan, Sabes. 2016. *Last Walk to the Beach.* Photography series.

Tagg, John. 1988. *The Burden of Representation: Essays on Photographies and Histories.* Minneapolis: University of Minnesota Press.

Tambiah, Stanley Jeyaraja. 1986. *Sri Lanka—Ethnic Fratricide and the Dismantling of Democracy.* Chicago: University of Chicago Press.

Tamil Guardian. 2018. "Sri Lankan Army Commander Tells Tamils: As We Give to You, We Can Take Back." 4 April. https://www.youtube.com/watch?v=oaHOnyg-Ab4.

TamilNet. 2004. "Karthigaipoo Declared as National Flower of Eelam Tamils." *TamilNet*, 14 April. https://www.tamilnet.com/art.html?artid=11322&catid=79.

Tamil Times. 1982. "Kuttimani and Jegan to Hang." August.

Tekwani, Shyam. 1987. "In the Tiger's Den." *India Today*, 15 November. https://www.indiatoday.in/magazine/cover-story/story/19871115-any-one-of-our-tiger-cubs-can-take-on-the-ipkf-in-man-to-man-combat-and-defeat-them-799504-1987-11-14.

Terwindt, Carolijn. 2020. *When Protest Becomes Crime*. London: Pluto Press.

Thangarajah, Yuvi. (1995) 2009. "Narratives of Victimhood as Ethnic Identity Among Veddas of the East Coast." In *Unmaking the Nation: The Politics of Identity and History in Modern Sri Lanka*, edited by Pradeep Jeganathan and Qadri Ismail, 188–213. Colombo: Social Scientists' Association and South Focus Press.

Thiranagama, Sharika. 2010. "In Praise of Traitors: Intimacy, Betrayal, and the Sri Lankan Tamil Community." In *Traitors: Suspicion, Intimacy, and the Ethics of State-Building*, edited by Sharika Thiranagama and Tobias Kelly, 127–49. Philadelphia: University of Pennsylvania Press.

Thiranagama, Sharika. (2011) 2013. *In My Mother's House: Civil War in Sri Lanka*. New Delhi: Zubaan.

Thiranagama, Sharika. 2013. "The Self at a Time of War in Northern Sri Lanka." *Journal of Historical Sociology* 26 (1): 19–40. https://onlinelibrary.wiley.com/doi/10.1111/johs.12013.

Thiranagama, Sharika. 2014. "Making Tigers from Tamils: Long-Distance Nationalism and Sri Lankan Tamils in Toronto." *American Anthropologist* 116 (2): 265–78. https://doi.org/10.1111/aman.12099.

Thomson-Senanayake, Jane. 2014. *A Sociological Exploration of Disappearances in Sri Lanka*. Hong Kong: Asian Human Rights Commission.

Thornton, E. M., and R. Niththyananthan. 1984. *Sri Lanka: Island of Terror and Indictment*. Middlesex: Eelam Research Organization, Great Britan.

Thwaites, Jeanne. 1967. *Mother and Child*. South Brunswick, NJ: A. S. Barnes.

TIC. Tamil Information Centre. 2024. "About Us." Tamil Information Centre. https://ticonline.org/aboutus.php.

Trautmann, Thomas R. 1997. *Aryans and British India*. Berkeley: University of California Press.

Trawick, Margaret. 2007. *Enemy Lines: Warfare, Childhood, and Play in Batticaloa*. Berkeley: University of California Press.

Truth Tigers. 2002. Australia: ABC.

UK Parliament. 1991. "Sri Lanka: Human Rights Volume 525 (Hansard, Lords Chamber)." UK Parliament. 23 January. https://hansard.parliament.uk/Lords/1991-01-23/debates/8ff98ab7-2823-41a6-999a-45671b969060/SriLankaHumanRights.

United Nations. 1948. "Universal Declaration of Human Rights." https://www.un.org/en/about-us/universal-declaration-of-human-rights.

UNWGEID (United Nations Working Group on Enforced or Involuntary Disappearances). 2020. "Enforced or Involuntary Disappearances: Report of the Working Group on Enforced or Involuntary Disappearances." https://docs.un.org/en/A/HRC/33/51/Add.2.

UTHR-J (University Teachers for Human Rights Jaffna, Sri Lanka). 1989. "Report No 1." Jaffna. January. https://www.uthr.org/Reports/Report1/Report1.htm.

UTHR-J (University Teachers for Human Rights Jaffna, Sri Lanka). 1995. "The Exodus from Jaffna." Special Report No. 6. Jaffna. https://uthr.org/SpecialReports/spreport6.htm.

UTHR-J (University Teachers for Human Rights Jaffna, Sri Lanka). 2000. "History of the Organisation." https://uthr.org/history.htm.

Uyangoda, Jayadeva. 1994. "Ethnicity, 'Nation,' and State Formation In Sri Lanka: Antinomies of "Nation-Building." *Pravada* 3 (4): 10–17. https://polity.lk/pravada-vol-3-no-4/.

Van Cuylenburg, Reg. 1962. *Image of an Island: A Portrait of Ceylon*. New York: Orion Press.

Van der Poorten, Menika, dir. 2011. *A Lost White Tribe: The Eurasians of Sri Lanka*.

Varzi, Roxanne. 2006. *Warring Souls: Youth, Media, and Martyrdom in Post-Revolution Iran*. Durham, NC: Duke University Press.

Velamati, Manohari. 2009. "Sri Lankan Tamil Migration and Settlement: Time for Reconsideration." *India Quarterly* 65 (3): 271–94. https://www.jstor.org/stable/45072946.

Venugopal, Rajesh. 2011. "The Politics of Market Reform at a Time of Civil War: Military Fiscalism in Sri Lanka." *Economic and Political Weekly* 46 (49): 67–75.

Virilio, Paul. 1986. *War and Cinema: The Logistics of Perception*. Translated by Patrick Camiller. London: Verso.

Vitale, Tom, dir. 2019. "Sri Lanka." *Anthony Bourdain: Parts Unknown*. United States: CNN.

Warnapala, Kanchanakesi Channa. 2008. "Dismantling the Gaze: Julia Margaret Cameron's Sri Lankan Photographs." *Postcolonial Text* 4 (1). https://www.postcolonial.org/index.php/pct/article/view/753.

Warnapala, Kanchanakesi. 2012. "The Portrait of the Colonial Artist in Sri Lanka: Encounters, Negotiations and Contestations." *Interventions* 14 (2): 169–84. https://doi.org/10.1080/1369801X.2012.687895.

Warner, Michael. 2002. *Publics and Counterpublics*. New York: Zone Books.

Weerasooria, Wickrema. 2012. "Landmark Supreme Court Judgment Upholds Journalist's Ownership of His Photographs." *Sunday Island*, 21 October. http://www.island.lk/index.php?page_cat=article-details&page=articledetails& code_title=64211.

Weereratne, Neville. 1993. *43 Group: A Chronicle of Fifty Years in the Art of Sri Lanka*. Melbourne: Lantana.

Wendt, Lionel. 1950. *Lionel Wendt's Ceylon*. London: Lincolns-Prager.

Wijekoon, Channa Bandara. 2012. "Magic Hour." *Daily News*, 30 May. http://archives.dailynews.lk/2012/05/30/fea20.asp.

Witharana, Dileepa. 2019. "Ravana's Sri Lanka: Redefining the Sinhala Nation?" *South Asia: Journal of South Asian Studies* 42 (4): 781–95. https://doi.org/10.1080/00856401.2019.1632560.

Wright, Arnold. 1907. *Twentieth-Century Impressions of Ceylon: Its History, People, Commerce, Industries, and Resources*. London: Lloyd's Greater Britain Publishing Company.

INDEX

Page numbers in italics denotes figures

GLOBAL
SOUTH
ASIA

Padma Kaimal, K. Sivaramakrishnan, and Anand A. Yang, SERIES EDITORS

Global South Asia takes an interdisciplinary approach to the humanities and social sciences in its exploration of how South Asia, through its global influence, is and has been shaping the world.

A Volatile Picture: War and the Political Work of Photography in Sri Lanka, by Vindhya Buthpitiya

India's Mithila Painting, edited by Paula Richman and David L. Szanton

Mumbai on Two Wheels: Cycling, Urban Space, and Sustainable Mobility, by Jonathan Shapiro Anjaria

Lahore Cinema: Between Realism and Fable, by Iftikhar Dadi

Adivasi Art and Activism: Curation in a Nationalist Age, by Alice Tilche

New Lives in Anand: Building a Muslim Hub in Western India, by Sanderien Verstappen

Mumbai Taximen: Autobiographies and Automobilities in India, by Tarini Bedi

Outcaste Bombay: City Making and the Politics of the Poor, by Juned Shaikh

The Ends of Kinship: Connecting Himalayan Lives between Nepal and New York, by Sienna Craig

Making Kantha, Making Home: Women at Work in Colonial Bengal, by Pika Ghosh

A Secular Need: Islamic Law and State Governance in Contemporary India, by Jeffery A. Redding

Making the Modern Slum: The Power of Capital in Colonial Bombay, by Sheetal Chhabria

History and Collective Memory in South Asia, 1200–2000, by Sumit Guha

Climate Change and the Art of Devotion: Geoaesthetics in the Land of Krishna, 1550–1850, by Sugata Ray

Bhakti and Power: Debating India's Religion of the Heart, edited by John Stratton Hawley, Christian Lee Novetzke, and Swapna Sharma

Marrying for a Future: Transnational Sri Lankan Tamil Marriages in the Shadow of War, by Sidharthan Maunaguru

Gandhi's Search for the Perfect Diet: Eating with the World in Mind, by Nico Slate

Mountain Temples and Temple Mountains: Architecture, Religion, and Nature in the Central Himalayas, by Nachiket Chanchani

Creating the Universe: Depictions of the Cosmos in Himalayan Buddhism, by Eric Huntington

Privileged Minorities: Syrian Christianity, Gender, and Minority Rights in Postcolonial India, by Sonja Thomas

High-Tech Housewives: Indian IT Workers, Gendered Labor, and Transmigration, by Amy Bhatt

Making New Nepal: From Student Activism to Mainstream Politics, by Amanda Thérèse Snellinger

The Rebirth of Bodh Gaya: Buddhism and the Making of a World Heritage Site, by David Geary

Mobilizing Krishna's World: The Writings of Prince Sāvant Singh of Kishangarh, by Heidi Rika Maria Pauwels

Banaras Reconstructed: Architecture and Sacred Space in a Hindu Holy City, by Madhuri Desai

Displaying Time: The Many Temporalities of the Festival of India, by Rebecca M. Brown

The Gender of Caste: Representing Dalits in Print, by Charu Gupta

Sensitive Space: Fragmented Territory at the India-Bangladesh Border, by Jason Cons

The Afterlife of Sai Baba: Competing Visions of a Global Saint, by Karline McLain

A Place for Utopia: Urban Designs from South Asia, by Smriti Srinivas